Matt Zandstra

SAMS
Teach Yourself
PHP
in 24 Hours

SECOND EDITION

SAMS

201 West 103rd St., Indianapolis, Indiana, 46290 USA

Sams Teach Yourself PHP in 24 Hours, Second Edition

Copyright © 2002 by Sams Publishing

International Standard Book Number: 0-672-32311-7

Library of Congress Catalog Card Number: 2001096665

Printed in the United States of America

First Printing: December 2001

04   03   02   01   4   3   2   1

Trademarks

Warning and Disclaimer

ACQUISITIONS EDITOR
Scott D. Meyers

DEVELOPMENT EDITORS
Scott D. Meyers
Jill Hayden

MANAGING EDITOR
Charlotte Clapp

INDEXER
D&G Limited, LLC

PROOFREADER
D&G Limited, LLC

TECHNICAL EDITOR
Andrei Zmievski

TEAM COORDINATOR
Amy Patton

INTERIOR DESIGNER
Gary Adair

COVER DESIGNER
Aren Howell

PRODUCTION
D&G Limited, LLC

Contents at a Glance

Contents

About the Author

Matt Zandstra (matt@corrosive.co.uk) is a technical consultant. With his business partner, Max Guglielmino, he runs Corrosive Web Design (http://www.corrosive.co.uk), a company specializing in information design, usablity, and the creation of dynamic environments. Before this book took over his life once again, Matt was writing an XML/Java-based scripting language and interpreter for extracting content from Web pages. He is currently keen on design patterns, unit tests, extreme programming, and space operas. Matt is fatter than he was, but is still an urban cyclist. He says he is working on a novel, but he has been saying that for a long time. He lives by the sea in Brighton, Great Britain, with his partner, Louise McDougall, and their daughter, Holly.

Dedication

For my father. Who would have approved.

Acknowledgments

Thanks to Louise for moving us from London to Brighton while I was writing this book. I looked up, and my desk just seemed to be in a prettier room. Thanks to Louise for glazing over conspicuously when I begin to babble nonsense, for drinking beer and reading books with me, and for holding Holly's other hand when we one-two-three-swing her at the beach. Thanks to Holly for the way she says "OH NO! Dropped it!" All these things and more made the second edition fun.

From Sams, thanks once again to Scott Meyers. Thanks are also due to Jill Hayden and Andrei Zmievski.

Thanks, as always, to Max Guglielmino, who dealt with horrors above and beyond the call of duty during the last month or so of my disappearance to produce this edition. Here's to our next project. Do we know what it is, yet?

Thanks to all at CitiPages (http://www.citipages.net) for putting up with my abrupt departure to work on this book. Particularly Charlie, James, Jim, Tolan, and Rares.

Tell Us What You Think!

As the reader of this book, *you* are our most important critic and commentator. We value your opinion and want to know what we're doing right, what we could do better, what areas you'd like to see us publish in, and any other words of wisdom you're willing to pass our way.

You can e-mail or write me directly to let me know what you did or didn't like about this book—as well as what we can do to make our books stronger.

Please note that I cannot help you with technical problems related to the topic of this book, and that due to the high volume of mail I receive, I might not be able to reply to every message.

When you write, please be sure to include this book's title and author as well as your name and phone or fax number. I will carefully review your comments and share them with the author and editors who worked on the book.

Email: webdev@samspublishing.com

Mail: Mark Taber
       Associate Publisher
       Sams Publishing
       201 West 103rd Street
       Indianapolis, IN 46290 USA

Introduction

This is a book about PHP, the open source Web scripting language that has joined Perl, ASP, and Java on the select list of languages that can be used to create dynamic online environments. It is also a book about programming. In the space available, it is neither possible to create a complete guide to programming in PHP nor to cover every function and technique that PHP offers. Nevertheless, whether you are an experienced programmer considering a move to PHP or a newcomer to scripting, the steps in this book should provide enough information to get your journey off to a good start.

Who Should Read This Book?

This book will take you from the first principles through to a good working knowledge of the PHP 4 programming language. No prior experience of programming is assumed, though if you have worked with a language such as C or Perl in the past, you will find the going much easier.

PHP 4 is a Web programming language. To get the most from this book, you should have some understanding of the World Wide Web and of HTML in particular. If you are just starting out, you will still be able to use this book, though you should consider acquiring an HTML tutorial. If you are comfortable creating basic documents and can build a basic HTML table, you will be fine.

PHP 4 is designed to integrate well with databases. Some of the examples in this book are written to work with MySQL, a SQL database that is free for personal use on some platforms. We include a short introduction to SQL, but if you intend to use PHP to work with databases, you might want to spend some time reading up on the subject. Numerous introductory SQL tutorials are available online. If you intend to work with a database other than MySQL, many of the examples in this book will be relatively easy to reproduce with the equivalent PHP functions designed to query your database.

How This Book Is Organized

This book is divided into four parts:

- Part 1 is an introduction to PHP 4.
- Part 2 covers the basic features of the language. Pay particular attention to this section if you are new to programming.

- Part 3 covers PHP 4 in more detail, looking at the functions and techniques you will need to become a proficient PHP programmer.
- Part 4 examines library code, both code that you can create yourself and an extensive third party library.

Part 1 contains Hours 1 through 3 and handles the information you will need to get your first script up and running:

- Hour 1, "PHP: From Homepage to Portal," describes the history and capabilities of PHP and looks at some of the compelling reasons for deciding to learn this scripting language.
- Hour 2, "Installing PHP," explains how to install PHP on a UNIX system and discusses some of the configuration options you might want to choose when compiling PHP. In this hour, we also look at ways of configuring PHP once it is installed.
- Hour 3, "A First Script," looks at the different ways in which you can embed a PHP script in a document and create a script that writes text to the user's browser.

Part 2 comprises Hours 4 through 8. In this part, you will learn the basic components of the PHP language:

- Hour 4, "The Building Blocks," covers the basics of PHP. You will learn about variables, data types, operators, and expressions.
- Hour 5, "Going with the Flow," covers the syntax for controlling program flow in your scripts. In addition to `if` and `switch` constructs, you will learn about loops using `for` and `while` statements.
- Hour 6, "Functions," explores the use of functions to organize your code.
- Hour 7, "Arrays," discusses the array data type that can be used to hold list information. We will also look at some of the functions that PHP 4 provides to manipulate arrays.
- Hour 8, "Objects," introduces PHP's support for classes and objects. Throughout the course of the hour, we will develop a working example.

Part 3 consists of Hours 9 through 22. In this part, you will come to grips with the features and techniques of the language:

- Hour 9, "Working with Forms," introduces the dimension of user input through the mechanism of the HTML form. You will learn how to gather data submitted via a form.
- Hour 10, "Working with Files," shows you how to work with files and directories on the local machine.

- Hour 11, "Working with the DBA Functions," demonstrates PHP's support for DBM-style database systems, versions of which are available on most systems.
- Hour 12, "Database Integration—mySQL," provides a brief introduction to SQL syntax and introduces the PHP 4 functions that can be used to work with the MySQL database.
- Hour 13, "Beyond the Box," covers some of the details of HTTP requests and looks at PHP network functions.
- Hour 14, "Images On-the-Fly" explores PHP's image functions. With these, you can create GIF or PNG files dynamically.
- Hour 15, "Working with Dates and Times," covers the functions and techniques you can use for date arithmetic. We create a calendar example.
- Hour 16, "Working with Data," revisits data types and explores some more of the functions you can use to work with data in your scripts. More array functions are also covered.
- Hour 17, "Working with Strings," covers the functions that you can use to manipulate strings.
- Hour 18, "Working with Regular Expressions," introduces regular expression functions. You can use these to find and replace complex patterns in strings.
- Hour 19, "Saving State with Cookies and Query Strings," shows you some techniques for passing information across scripts and requests.
- Hour 20, "Saving State with Session Functions," extends the techniques explored in Hour 19, using PHP's built-in session functions.
- Hour 21, "Working with the Server Environment," shows you how to call external programs from your scripts and incorporate their output into your own.
- Hour 22, "PHP 4 and XML," looks at PHP's support for XML (Extensible Markup Language). We examine the XML Parser functions as well as taking in some features for
  navigating XML documents and converting XML to other formats.

Part 4 consists of Hours 23 and 24. In these, we move beyond the core language to examine the ways that libraries can be used to extend PHP's functionality.

- Hour 23, "Smarty: A Template Engine," introduces a sophisticated third party library that allows coders to separate application logic from presentation logic.
- Hour 24, "An Example: Page.inc.php," builds up a code library of our own. The library is designed to help with some of the common tasks encountered in the creation of dynamic sites. We extend the core library to support password protection and access control.

PART I
Getting Started

Hour

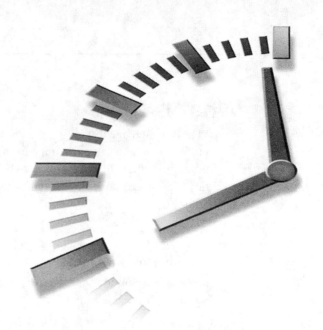

Hour 1

PHP: From Homepage to Portal

Welcome to PHP! Throughout this book you will look at almost every element of the PHP language. But first you will explore PHP as a product—its history, features, and future.

In this hour, you will learn:

- What PHP is
- About PHP's history
- What improvements can be found in PHP 4
- Some options that add features to your PHP binary
- Some reasons you should choose to work with PHP

What Is PHP?

PHP is a language that has outgrown its name. It was originally conceived as a set of macros to help coders maintain personal home pages, and its name grew from its purpose. Since then, PHP's capabilities have been extended, taking it beyond a set of utilities to a full-featured programming language, capable of managing huge database-driven online environments.

As PHP's capabilities have grown, so too has its popularity. According to NetCraft (http://www.netcraft.com), PHP was running on more than 1 million hosts in November 1999. As of September 2001, that figure had already risen to over 6 million hosts. According to SecuritySpace.com, PHP is the most popular Apache module available, beating even mod_ssl.

PHP is now officially known as PHP: HyperText Preprocessor. It is a server-side scripting language usually written in an HTML context. Unlike an ordinary HTML page, a PHP script is not sent directly to a client by the server; instead, it is parsed by the PHP engine. HTML elements in the script are left alone, but PHP code is interpreted and executed. PHP code in a script can query databases, create images, read and write files, talk to remote servers—the possibilities are endless. The output from PHP code is combined with the HTML in the script and the result sent to the user.

What Need Does PHP Fulfill?

There have been scripting solutions for as long as there has been a World Wide Web. As the need to create sites with dynamic content has grown in recent years, so has the pressure to create robust environments quickly and efficiently. Although C can be a great solution for creating fast server tools, it is also hard to work with, and can easily produce security holes if not carefully deployed. Perl, a language originally developed for text processing, naturally filled the gap created by the demand for dynamic Web environments. Much easier to deploy safely than C, its slower performance has always been more than balanced by the comparatively fast development cycle it offers. Even more useful has been the increasing availability of a large number of stable code libraries for Perl.

So where does PHP fit in? PHP has been written specifically for the Web. The issues and problems faced by Web programmers are addressed within the language itself. While a Perl programmer will need to use an external library, or to write code to acquire data submitted by the user of a Web page, PHP will make this data automatically available. While a Perl programmer will have to install modules to enable him or her to write database-driven environments, PHP provides built-in support for a whole range of databases (though you may need to supply some information at installation time). In short, because PHP has been created for Web programmers, it will have a set of functions for almost any typical problem you might encounter from managing user sessions to handling XML documents.

So, do we have to pay for this ease of use with even slower performance? Not at all. PHP, when run as a server module, is lightning fast, much more so than Perl running as a CGI.

When the first edition of this book was written, PHP 4 was still in the final stages of development. It is now a mature and stable coding environment, and its popularity continues to grow.

What's New in PHP 4

PHP 4 introduces numerous new features that will make the programmer's life more interesting. Let's take a quick look at some of them.

- A new foreach statement, similar to that found in Perl, makes it much easier to loop through arrays. We will be using this for most of the array examples in this book. Additionally, a raft of new array functions have been added, making arrays easier to manipulate.
- The language now includes the boolean data type.
- A particularly useful feature of PHP3 was the capability to name form elements as if they were elements in an array. The elements' names and values are then made available to the code in array form. This feature has been extended to support multi-dimensional arrays.
- Support for object-oriented programming was somewhat rudimentary in PHP. This is significantly extended in PHP 4; for example, it is now possible to call an over-ridden method from a child class.
- PHP 4 now provides native support for user sessions, using both cookies and the query string. You can now "register" a variable with a session, and then access the same variable name and value in subsequent user requests.
- A new comparison operator (===) has been introduced that tests for equivalence of type as well as equivalence of value.
- New associative arrays containing server and environmental variables have been made available, as well as a variable that holds information about uploaded files.
- PHP 4 now provides built-in support for both Java and XML.

Although these and other features significantly improve the language, perhaps the most significant change has taken place under the hood.

The Zend Engine

When PHP3 was written, an entirely new parser was created from the ground up. PHP 4 represents a similar change to the scripting engine. This rewrite, though, is more significant by orders of magnitude.

Zend is a scripting engine that sits below the PHP-specific modules. It is optimized to significantly improve performance.

These changes in efficiency will ensure PHP's continued success. Most code written for PHP 3 will continue to run with no changes; however, these scripts may run up to 200 times faster!

A commercial addition to the Zend engine will be the facility for compiling PHP scripts. This will provide a further gain in performance that should leave most, if not all, competitors far behind.

Zend is built to improve performance but is also designed for increased flexibility. Communication with servers has been improved, so it will be possible to create PHP modules that work with a wider range of servers. Unlike a CGI interpreter, which sits outside a server and is initialized every time a script is run, a server module runs in conjunction with the server. This improves performance because the scripting engine does not need to be started for a PHP page to be executed.

Why Choose PHP?

There are some compelling reasons to work with PHP 4. For many projects you will find that the production process is significantly faster than you might expect if you are used to working with other scripting languages. As an open source product, PHP 4 is well supported by a talented production team and a committed user community. Furthermore, PHP can be run on all the major operating systems with most servers.

Speed of Development

Because PHP allows you to separate HTML code from scripted elements, you will notice a significant decrease in development time on many projects. In many instances, you will be able to separate the coding stage of a project from the design and build stages. Not only can this make life easier for you as a programmer, it also can remove obstacles that stand in the way of effective and flexible design.

PHP Is Open Source

To many people, "open source" simply means free, which is, of course, a benefit in itself.

Well-maintained open source projects offer users additional benefits, though. You benefit from an accessible and committed community who offer a wealth of experience in the subject. Chances are that any problem you encounter in your coding can be answered swiftly and easily with a little research. If that fails, a question sent to a mailing list can yield an intelligent, authoritative response.

You also can be sure that bugs will be addressed as they are found, and that new features will be made available as the need is defined. You will not have to wait for the next commercial release before taking advantage of improvements.

There is no vested interest in a particular server product or operating system. You are free to make choices that suit your needs or those of your clients, secure that your code will run whatever you decide.

Performance

Because of the powerful Zend engine, PHP 4 compares well with other server scripting languages including ASP, Perl, and Java Servlets in benchmark tests, consistently beating the rest of the pack in simple "hello world" tests. You can see the results of such a benchmark test at `http://www.perlmonth.com/features/benchmarks/benchmarks.html?issue=4&id=9351`. PHP used in large projects is unlikely to show such a hugely marked lead over other solutions, though it is possible to acquire a caching tool (Zend Accelerator) from `http://www.zend.com/` which is designed to provide even greater performance than that shown by PHP alone.

Portability

PHP is designed to run on many operating systems and to cooperate with many servers and databases. You can build for a Unix environment and shift your work to NT without a problem. You can test a project with Personal Web Server and install it on a UNIX system running on PHP as an Apache module.

What's New in This Edition

Since the first edition of this book, PHP has consolidated its position as one of the best options for Web development. PHP, in common with any popular open source project, is a fast moving target. In this edition we have extensively checked and updated the examples and tutorials. Where new features have appeared we have extended our coverage.

Significant new sections have been added covering functions, arrays, objects, databases, and dates.

After the publication of the first edition we received many requests for source code. We have now made all listings available online at [source url].

In addition to reviewing and extending existing material, we have added coverage for XML, and a chapter on the Smarty template engine, a powerful library for organizing large projects.

Summary

In this hour, we introduced PHP. You learned the history of PHP from a simple set of macros to the powerful scripting environment it has become. You found out about PHP 4 and the Zend scripting engine, and how they incorporate new features and more efficiency. Finally, you discovered some of the features that make PHP a compelling choice as a Web programming language.

I hope that you've been convinced by this chapter that PHP is the language for you. In the next hour we dive straight in and install the PHP engine.

Q&A

Q Is PHP an easy language to learn?

A In short, yes! You really can learn the basics of PHP in 24 hours. PHP provides an enormous wealth of functions that allow you to do things for which you would have to write custom code in other languages. PHP also handles data types and memory issues for you (much like Perl).

Understanding the syntax and structures of a programming language is only the beginning of the journey, however. Ultimately, you will only really learn by building your own projects and by making mistakes. You should see this book as a starting point.

Workshop

Quiz

1. True or false: PHP was originally developed for use in the banking industry.
2. How much does PHP cost?

3. What is the name of the new scripting engine that powers PHP?

4. Name a new feature introduced with PHP 4?

Quiz Answers

1. False. PHP was originally developed for Web publishing.

2. PHP costs nothing at all.

3. Sitting below PHP 4 is an entirely new scripting engine called Zend.

4. PHP 4 introduces (among other things) new array functions, a new statement to loop through arrays called `foreach`, a `boolean` data type, enhanced support for objects, session functions, new built-in variables, and Java and XML support.

Activities

1. Jot down the reasons you have for deciding to learn PHP. How will the features covered in this chapter help you with your projects? Define two or three projects that you would like to be able to complete once you have finished this book. As you read the book, keep a note of language features and techniques that will help you in the development of these projects.

Hour **2**

Installing PHP

Before getting started with the PHP language, you must first acquire, install, and configure the PHP engine. PHP is available for a wide range of platforms and works in conjunction with many servers.

In this hour, you will learn

- Which platforms, servers, and databases are supported by PHP 4
- Where to find PHP and other useful open source software
- One way of installing PHP on Linux
- Some options that add features to your PHP binary
- Some configuration directives
- How to find help when things go wrong

Platforms, Servers, Databases, and PHP

PHP is truly cross-platform. It runs on the Windows operating system, most versions of UNIX including Linux, and even the Macintosh. Support is provided for a range of Web servers including Apache (itself open source and cross-platform), Microsoft Internet Information Server, WebSite Pro, the iPlanet Web Server, and Microsoft's Personal Web Server. The latter is useful if you want to test your scripts offline on a Windows machine, although Apache can also be run on Windows.

You can also compile PHP as a standalone application. You can then call it from the command line. In this book, we will concentrate on building Web applications, but do not underestimate the power of PHP 4 as a general scripting tool comparable to Perl. The fact that PHP runs as a CGI application means that any server that supports CGI scripts should be able to work with it. Configuration, though, will vary from server to server.

PHP is designed to integrate easily with databases. This feature is one of the factors that make the language such a good choice for building sophisticated Web applications. PHP supports almost every database currently available, either directly or via ODBC (Open DataBase Connectivity).

Throughout this book, we will be using a combination of Linux, Apache, and MySQL. All these are free to download and use, and can be installed relatively easily on a PC.

Where to Find PHP and More

You can find PHP 4 at <http://www.php.net/>. PHP 4 is open source software, which means that you won't need your credit card handy when you download it.

The PHP WebSite is an excellent resource for PHP coders. The entire manual can be read online at <http://www.php.net/manual/>, complete with helpful annotations from other PHP coders. You can also download the manual in several formats.

You can find out more about getting Linux for your computer at <http://www.linux.org/help/beginner/distributions.html>. If you want to run Linux on a Power PC, you can find information about LinuxPPC at <http://www.linuxppc.org>. Alternatively, Mac OS X, Apple's latest operating system, is based on Unix, and can run PHP with no problems. If you are running OS X you can find installation information at <http://www.php.net/manual/en/install.macosx.php>.

MySQL, the database we will use in this book, can be downloaded from <http://www.mysql.com>. There are versions for many operating systems including UNIX, Windows, and OS/2.

Installing PHP 4 for Linux and Apache

In this section, we will look at one way of installing PHP 4 with Apache on Linux. The process is more or less the same for any UNIX operating system. You might be able to find prebuilt versions of PHP for your system, which are simple to install. Compiling PHP, though, gives you greater control over the features built into your binary.

Before you install you should make sure that you are logged into your system as the root user. If you are not allowed access to your system's root account, you may need to ask your system administrator to install PHP for you.

There are two ways of compiling an Apache PHP module. You can either recompile Apache, statically linking PHP into it, or you can compile PHP as a Dynamic Shared Object (DSO). If your version of Apache was compiled with DSO support, it will be capable of supporting new modules without the need for recompiling the server. This method is the easiest way to get PHP up and running, and it is the one we will look at in this section.

In order to test that Apache supports DSOs you should launch the Apache binary (httpd) with the -l argument.

```
/www/bin/httpd -l
```

You should see a list of modules. If you see

```
mod_so.c
```

among them, you should be able to proceed; otherwise, you may need to recompile Apache. The Apache distribution contains full instructions for this.

If you have not already done so, you will need to download the latest distribution of PHP 4 (PHP 4.0.6 at the time of writing). Your distribution will be archived as a tar file and compressed with gzip, so you will need to unpack it:

```
tar -xvzf php-4.0.6.tar.gz
```

After your distribution is unpacked, you should move to the PHP 4 distribution directory:

```
cd ../php-4.0.6
```

Within your distribution directory you will find a script called configure. This accepts additional information that should be provided when the configure script is run from the command line. These 'command line arguments' will control the features that PHP will support. For this example, we will include some useful command line arguments, although you might want to specify arguments of your own. We will discuss some of the configure options available to you later in the hour.

```
./configure   --with-gdbm=/usr \
              --with-apxs \
              --with-mysql \
              --with-xml \
              --with-sablot=/usr \
              --with-expat-dir=/usr/local \
              --with-xslt-sablot \
              --with-gd=/usr \
              --enable-gd-native-ttf \
              --with-ttf=/usr \
              --with-dom=/usr \
              --with-zlib=/usr
```

The directives chosen in this example are designed to support the features discussed in this book. Most of them require that your system has certain libraries installed before you can compile PHP. The configure script will complain if the relevant libraries cannot be located.

After the configure script has run, you can run the make program. You will need a C compiler on your system to run this command successfully.

```
make
make install
```

These commands should end the process of PHP 4 compilation and installation. You should now be able to configure and run Apache.

Some configure Options

When we ran the configure script, we included some command-line arguments that determined the features that the PHP engine will include. The configure script itself gives you a list of available options. From the PHP distribution directory type the following:

```
./configure  --help
```

The list produced is long, so you may want to add it to a file for reading at leisure:

```
./configure  --help > configoptions.txt
```

Although the output from this command is very descriptive, we will look at a few useful options—especially those that might be needed to follow this book.

--with-gdbm

This option includes support for the Gnu Database Manager. This or another DBM type library will need to be supported in order for you to work with the DBA functions discussed in Hour 11. If you are running Linux it is likely that this library will be present, but see Hour 11, "Working with the DBA Functions," for alternatives. If your DBM library is in a non-standard location you may need to specify a path.

```
--with-gdbm=/path/to/dir
```

--with-gd

`--with-gd` enables support for the GD library, which, if installed on your system, allows you to create dynamic GIF or PNG images from your scripts. You can read more about creating dynamic images in Hour 14, "Images On-the-Fly." You can optionally specify a path to your GD library's install directory:

```
--with-gd=/path/to/dir
```

If your compile fails you should try explicitly setting the path when using this option.

--with-ttf

`--with-ttf` provides support for the FreeType 1 library that will allow you to include fonts in any dynamic image you create. To enable this option you must have the FreeType 1 library installed. You can find out more about FreeType at <http://www.freetype.org>. As with many other directives, if you run into problems you should try specifying a path.

```
--with-ttf=/path/to/dir
```

--with-mysql

`--with-mysql` enables support for the MySQL database.

```
--with-mysql=/path/to/dir
```

As you know, PHP provides support for other databases. Table 2.1 lists some of them and the configure options you will need to use them.

TABLE 2.1 Some Database configure Options

Database	configure Option
DBA	--with-dba
DBM	--with-dbm
GDBM	--with-gdbm
Adabas D	--with-adabas
FilePro	--with-filepro
msql	--with-msql

TABLE 2.1 continued

Database	configure *Option*
informix	--with-informix
iODBC	--with-iodbc
OpenLink ODBC	--with-openlink
Oracle	--with-oracle
PostgreSQL	--with-pgsql
Solid	--with-solid
Sybase	--with-sybase
Sybase-CT	--with-sybase-ct
Velocis	--with-velocis
LDAP	--with-ldap

XML configure options

This book explores a number of XML features. In particular the --with-sablot option enables support for XSLT and requires that you have installed the Sablotron engine. You can find Sablotron at <http://www.gingerall.com/>.

To explicitly include Expat support you should use the --with-xml option.

In order to run the DOM XML functions you will require the libxml library (version 2.2.7 or better) which is available from <http://www.xmlsoft.org>. The required configure option is --with-dom=/path/to/lib.

Configuring Apache

After you have compiled PHP and Apache, you should check Apache's configuration file, httpd.conf, which you will find in a directory called conf in the Apache install directory. Add the following lines to this file:

```
AddType application/x-httpd-php .php
AddType application/x-httpd-php-source .phps
```

This ensures that the PHP engine will parse files that end with the .php extension. Any files with the .phps extension will be output as PHP source. That is, the source code will be converted to HTML and color-coded. This can be useful for debugging your scripts.

If you want to offer to your users PHP pages with extensions more familiar to them, you can choose any extension you want. You can even ensure that files with the .html extension are treated as PHP files with the following:

```
AddType application/x-httpd-php .html
```

Note that treating files with the .html extension as PHP scripts could slow down your site, because every page with this extension will be parsed by the PHP engine before it is served to the user.

If PHP has been preinstalled and you have no access to the Apache configuration files, you may be able to change the extensions that will determine which files will be treated as PHP executables by including an AddType directive in a file called .htaccess. After you have created this file, the directive will affect the enclosing directory, as well as any subdirectories. This technique will only work if the AllowOverride directive for the enclosing directory is set to either FileInfo or All.

Although the filename .htaccess is the default for an access control file, it may have been changed. Check the AccessFileName directive in httpd.conf to find out. Even if you don't have root access, you may be able to read the Apache configuration files.

An .htaccess file can be an excellent way of customizing your server space if you do not have access to the root account. The principal way of configuring the behavior of PHP, however, is the php.ini file.

php.ini

After you have compiled or installed PHP, you can still change its behavior with a file called php.ini. On UNIX systems, the default location for this file is /usr/local/lib; on a Windows system, the default location is the Windows directory. You should find a sample php.ini file in your distribution directory, which contains factory settings. Factory settings will be used if no php.ini file is used. Directives in the php.ini file come in two forms: values and flags. Value directives take the form of a directive name and a value separated by an equals sign. Possible values vary from directive to directive. Flag directives take the form of directive name and a positive or negative term separated by an equals sign. Positive terms can be '1,' 'On,' 'Yes,' or 'True.' Negative terms can be '0,' 'Off,' 'No,' or 'False.' Whitespace is ignored.

If PHP has been preinstalled on your system, you might want to check some of the settings in php.ini.

You can change your php.ini settings at any time, though if you are running PHP as an Apache module, you should restart the server for the changes to take effect.

short_open_tag

The `short_open_tag` directive determines whether you can begin a block of PHP code with the symbols <? and close it with ?>. If this has been disabled, you will see one of the following:

```
short_open_tag = Off
short_open_tag = False
short_open_tag = No
```

To enable the directive you can use one of the following:

```
short_open_tag = On
short_open_tag = True
short_open_tag = Yes
```

You can read more about PHP open and close tags in Hour 3, "A First Script."

Error Reporting Directives

To diagnose bugs in your code, you should enable the directive that allows error messages to be written to the browser. This is on by default.

```
display_errors = On
```

You can also set the level of error reporting. For working through this book, you should set this to the following:

```
error_reporting = E_ALL & ~ E_NOTICE
```

This will report all errors but not notices that warn about potential problems with your code. Notices can interfere with some PHP techniques. This setting is the default.

Variable Directives

PHP makes certain variables available to you as a result of a GET request, a POST request, or a cookie. You can influence this in the `php.ini` file.

Prior to version 4.0.3 the `track_vars` directive instructed PHP to create associative arrays containing elements generated as a result of an HTTP request. This feature is now enabled by default. If you are using an older version of PHP, and are not in a position to upgrade, you should set this directive to 'On.'

The `register_globals` directive determines whether values resulting from an HTTP request should be made available as global variables. Many scripts in this book will require the following setting to be enabled.

```
register_globals = On
```

Changing `php.ini` Directives Locally

If you are running Apache with the module version of PHP and your configuration allows the use of the `.htaccess` file, you can enable and disable `php.ini` directives on a per-directory basis.

Within the `.htaccess` file you can use the `php_flag` directive to set a `php.ini` flag (a directive that requires `'On'` or `'Off'`) and the `php_value` directive to set a `php.ini` value (a directive that requires a string or number).

```
php_flag   short_open_tag  On
php_value include_path ".:/home/corrdev"
```

If you are not running Apache, all is not lost. As of PHP 4.0.5 the function `ini_set()` was introduced. It allows you to set some `php.ini` directives from within your code. `ini_set()` requires two strings; the directive name, and the value to set.

```
ini_set( "include_path", ".:/home/corrdev" );
```

You can read more about functions in Hour 6 "Functions."

Help!

Help is always at hand on the Internet, particularly for problems concerning open source software. Wait a moment before you hit the send button, however. No matter how intractable your installation, configuration, or programming problem might seem, chances are you are not alone. Someone will have already answered your question.

When you hit a brick wall, your first recourse should be to the official PHP site at `<http://www.php.net/>`, particularly the annotated manual at `<http://www.php.net/manual>`.

If you still can't find your answer, don't forget that the PHP site is searchable. The advice you are seeking may be lurking in a press release or a Frequently Asked Questions file. Another excellent and searchable resource is the PHP Builder site at `<http://www.phpbuilder.com>`.

Still no luck? You can search the mailing list archives at `<http://www.php.net/search.php>`. These archives represent a huge information resource with contributions from many of the great and the good in the PHP community. Spend some time trying out a few keyword combinations.

If you are still convinced that your problem has not been addressed, you may well be doing the PHP community a service by exposing it.

You can join the PHP mailing lists at <http://www.php.net/support.php>. Although these lists are often high volume, you can learn a lot from them. If you are serious about PHP scripting, you should certainly subscribe at least to a digest list. Once subscribed to the list that matches your concerns, you might consider posting your problem.

When you post a question it is often a good idea to include as much information as possible (without writing a novel). The following items often are pertinent:

- Your operating system
- The version of PHP you are running or installing
- The configure options you chose
- Any output from the configure or make commands that preceded an installation failure
- A reasonably complete example of the code that is causing you problems

Why all these cautions about posting a question to a mailing list? First, developing research skills will stand you in good stead. A good researcher can generally solve a problem quickly and efficiently. Asking a naive question of a technical list often involves a wait rewarded only by a message or two referring you to the archives where you should have begun your search for answers.

Second, remember that a mailing list is not analogous to a technical support call center. No one is paid to answer your questions. Despite this, you have access to an impressive resource of talent and knowledge, including that of some of the creators of PHP itself. A good question and its answer will be archived to help other coders. Asking a question that has been answered several times just adds more noise.

Having said this, don't be afraid to post a problem to the list. PHP developers are a civilized and helpful breed, and by bringing a problem to the attention of the community, you might be helping others to solve the same problem.

Summary

PHP 4 is open source software. It is also open in the sense that it does not demand that you use a particular server, operating system, or database.

In this hour, you learned where to locate PHP and other open source software that can help you host and serve Web sites. You learned how to compile PHP as an Apache module on Linux. If you download a PHP binary for another platform, your distribution will contain step-by-step instructions. You learned some of the configure options that can change the features that your binary will support. You learned about php.ini and some of the directive it contains. Finally, you learned about sources of support. You should now be ready to come to grips with the language itself.

In the next hour we will write and run our first script. We will encounter some of the special syntax you will need to use to distinguish HTML from PHP code.

Q&A

Q You have covered an installation for Linux and Apache. Does that mean that this book will not apply to my server and operating system?

A No, one of PHP's great strengths is that it runs on multiple platforms. If you are having trouble installing PHP to work on your operating system or with your server, don't forget to read the files that come with your PHP distribution. You should find comprehensive step-by-step instructions for installation. If you are still having problems, review the "Help!" section earlier in this hour. The online resources mentioned there will almost certainly contain the answers you need.

Workshop

Quiz

1. Where can you find the PHP online manual?

2. From a UNIX operating system, how would you get help on configuration options (the options that you pass to the `configure` script in your PHP distribution)?

3. What is Apache's configuration file typically called?

4. What line should you add to the Apache configuration file to ensure that the `.php` extension is recognized?

5. What is PHP's configuration file called?

Quiz Answers

1. The manual for PHP 4 is available at `<http://www.php.net>`.

2. You can get help on configuration options by calling the `configure` script in the PHP distribution folder and passing it the `--help` argument:

   ```
   ./configure --help
   ```

3. The Apache configuration file is called `httpd.conf`.

4. The line

```
AddType application/x-httpd-php .php
```

ensures that Apache will treat files ending with the .php extension as PHP 4 scripts.

5. PHP's configuration file is called php.ini.

Activities

1. Install PHP on your system. If it is already in place, review your php.ini file and check your configuration.

Hour **3**

A First Script

Having installed and configured PHP, it is now time to put it to the test. In this hour, you will create your first script and spend a little time analyzing its syntax. By the end of the hour, you should be ready to create documents that include both HTML and PHP.

In this hour, you will learn:

- How to create, upload, and run a PHP script
- How to incorporate HTML and PHP in the same document
- How to make your code clearer with comments

Our First Script

Let's jump straight in with a PHP script. To begin, open your favorite text editor. Like HTML documents, PHP files are made up of plain text. You can create them with any text editor, such as Notepad on Windows, Simple Text and BBEdit on MacOS, or VI and Emacs on UNIX operating systems. Most popular HTML editors provide at least some support for PHP.

Keith Edmunds maintains a handy list of PHP-friendly editors at
http://www.itworks.demon.co.uk/phpeditors.htm.

Type in the example in Listing 3.1 and save the file, calling it something like `first.php`.

LISTING 3.1   A First PHP Script

```
1: <?php
2:     print "Hello Web!";
3: ?>
```

The extension to the PHP document is important because it tells the server to treat the file as PHP code and invoke the PHP engine. The default PHP extension for a PHP 4 document is `.php`. This can be changed, however, by altering the server's configuration. You saw how to do this in Hour 2, "Installing PHP." System administrators occasionally configure servers to work with non-default extensions, so some server set-ups may expect extensions such as `.phtml` or `.php4`.

If you are not working directly on the machine that will be serving your PHP script, you will probably need to use an FTP client, such as WS-FTP for Windows or Fetch for MacOS to upload your saved document to the server.

For historical reasons, different operating systems use different character combinations to denote the end of a line of text. It is a good idea to save your PHP documents with the correct linebreaks for the operating system which runs your server. A document with the wrong linebreaks for the operating system may be read as a single very long line of text by the PHP engine. This usually causes no problems, but the occasional bug can result. Most good text editors will allow you to nominate your target operating system.

After the document is in place, you should be able to access it via your browser. If all has gone well, you should see the script's output. Figure 3.1 shows the output from the `first.php` script.

If PHP is not installed on your server or your file's extension is not recognized, you may not see the output shown in Figure 3.1. In these cases, you probably will see the source code created in Listing 3.1. Figure 3.2 shows what happens when an unknown extension is encountered.

FIGURE **3.1**
Success: The output from Listing 3.1.

FIGURE **3.2**
Failure: The extension is not recognized.

If this happens, first check the extension with which you saved your PHP script. In Figure 3.2, the document was accidentally called `first.nphp`. If the file extension is as it should be, you may need to check that PHP has been installed properly and that your server is configured to work with the extension that you have used for your script. You can read more about installing and configuring PHP in Hour 2.

Now that you have uploaded and tested your script, you can take a look at the code in a little more detail.

Beginning and Ending a Block of PHP Statements

When writing PHP, you need to inform the PHP engine that you want it to execute your commands. If you don't do this, the code you write will be mistaken for HTML and will be output to the browser. You can do this with special tags that mark the beginning and end of PHP code blocks. Table 3.1 shows four such PHP delimiter tags.

TABLE 3.1 PHP Start and End Tags

Tag Style	Start Tag	End Tag
Standard tags	`<?php`	`?>`
Short tags	`<?`	`?>`
ASP tags	`<%`	`%>`
Script tags	`<SCRIPT LANGUAGE="php">`	`</SCRIPT>`

Of the tags in Table 3.1, only the standard and the script tags can be guaranteed to work on any configuration. The short and ASP style tags must be explicitly enabled in your php.ini. You examined the php.ini file in Hour 2.

To activate recognition for short tags, you must make sure that the short_open_tag switch is set to "On" in php.ini:

```
short_open_tag = On;
```

Short tags are enabled by default, so you would only need to edit php.ini if you want to disable these.

To activate recognition for the ASP style tags, you must enable the asp_tags setting:

```
asp_tags = On;
```

After you have edited php.ini, you should be able to choose from any of the four styles for use in your scripts. This is largely a matter of preference, although if you intend to include XML in your script, you should disable the short tags (`<? ?>`) and work with the standard tags (`<?php ?>`).

> The character sequence '<?' tells an XML parser to expect a processing instruction and is therefore frequently included in XML documents. If you include XML in your script and have short tags enabled, the PHP engine is likely to confuse XML processing instructions and PHP start tags. Disable short tags if you intend to incorporate XML in your document

Let's run through some of the ways in which you can legally write the code in Listing 3.1. You could use any of the four PHP start and end tags that you have seen:

```
<?
print("Hello Web!");
?>
```

```
<?php
print("Hello Web!");
?>

<%
print("Hello Web!");
%>

<SCRIPT LANGUAGE="php">
print("Hello Web!");
</SCRIPT>
```

Single lines of code in PHP also can be presented on the same line as the PHP start and end tags:

```
<? print("Hello Web!"); ?>
```

Now that you know how to define a block of PHP code, take a closer look at the code in Listing 3.1 itself.

The `print()` Function

`print()` is a function that outputs data. In most cases, anything output by `print()` ends up in the browser window. A *function* is a command that performs an action, usually modified in some way by data provided for it. Data sent to a function is almost always placed in parentheses after the function name. In this case, you sent the `print()` function a collection of characters, or *string*. Strings must always be enclosed by quotation marks, either single or double.

> Function calls generally require parentheses after their name whether or not they demand that data be passed to them. `print()` is an exception, and enclosing the data you want to print to the browser in parentheses is optional. This is the more common syntax, so we will usually omit the brackets in our examples.

You ended your only line of code in Listing 3.1 with a semicolon. The semicolon informs the PHP engine that you have completed a statement.

NEW TERM A *statement* represents an instruction to the PHP engine. Broadly, it is to PHP what a sentence is to written or spoken English. A sentence should end with a period; a statement should usually end with a semicolon. Exceptions to this include statements that enclose other statements, and statements that end a block of code. In most cases, however, failure to end a statement with a semicolon will confuse the PHP engine and result in an error.

Because the statement in Listing 3.1 is the final one in that block of code, the semicolon is optional.

Combining HTML and PHP

The script in Listing 3.1 is pure PHP. You can incorporate this into an HTML document simply by adding HTML outside the PHP start and end tags, as shown in Listing 3.2.

LISTING 3.2   A PHP Script Including HTML

```
 1: <html>
 2: <head>
 3:     <title>Listing 3.2 A PHP script including HTML</title>
 4: </head>
 5: <body>
 6: <b>
 7: <?php
 8:     print "hello world";
 9: ?>
10: </b>
11: </body>
12: </html>
```

As you can see, incorporating HTML into a PHP document is simply a matter of typing in the code. The PHP engine ignores everything outside PHP open and close tags. If you were to view Listing 3.2 with a browser, as shown in Figure 3.3, you would see the string "hello world" in bold. If you were to view the document source, as shown in Figure 3.4, the listing would look exactly like a normal HTML document.

FIGURE 3.3

The output of Listing 3.2 as viewed in a browser.

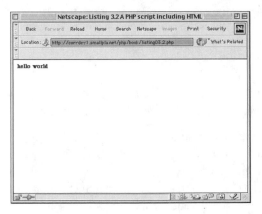

FIGURE 3.4

*The output of Listing
3.2 as HTML source
code.*

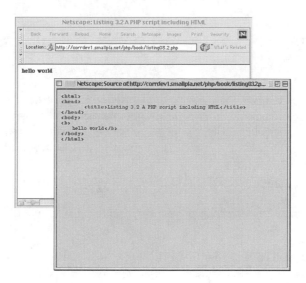

You can include as many blocks of PHP code as you need in a single document, inter-
spersing them with HTML as required. Although you can have multiple blocks of code
in a single document, they combine to form a single script. Any variables defined in the
first block usually will be available to subsequent blocks.

Adding Comments to PHP Code

Code that seems clear at the time of writing can seem like a hopeless tangle when you
come to amend it six months later. Adding comments to your code as you write can save
you time later on and make it easier for other programmers to work with your code.

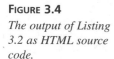 A *comment* is text in a script that is ignored by the PHP engine. Comments can
be used to make code more readable, or to annotate a script.

Single line comments begin with two forward slashes (//) or a single hash sign (#). All
text from either of these marks until either the end of the line or the PHP close tag is
ignored.

```
// this is a comment
#  this is another comment
```

Multiline comments begin with a forward slash followed by an asterisk (/*) and end with
an asterisk followed by a forward slash (*/).

```
/*
this is a comment
none of this will
```

```
be parsed by the
PHP engine
*/
```

 With a third party tool called PHPDoc it is possible to convert your comments into hyperlinked documentation. This is extremely useful for maintaining large projects. You can find PHPDoc at http://www.phpdoc.de.

Summary

You should now have the tools at your disposal to run a simple PHP script on a properly configured server.

In this hour, you created your first PHP script. You learned how to use a text editor to create and name a PHP document. You examined four sets of tags that you can use to begin and end blocks of PHP code. You learned how to use the print() function to send data to the browser, and you brought HTML and PHP together into the same script. Finally, you learned about comments and how to add them to PHP documents.

In the next hour you will be able to use these skills to test some of the fundamental building blocks of the PHP language, including variables, data types and operators.

Q&A

Q Which are the best start and end tags to use?

A It is largely a matter of preference. For the sake of portability the standard tags (<?php ?>) are probably the safest bet. Short tags are enabled by default and have the virtue of brevity, but with the increasing popularity of XML it may be safest to avoid them.

Q What editors should I avoid when creating PHP code?

A Do not use word processors that format text for printing (such as Word, for example). Even if you save files created using this type of editor in plain text format, hidden characters are likely to creep into your code.

Q When should I comment my code?

A This is a matter of preference once again. Some short scripts will be self-explanatory to you, even after a long interval. For scripts of any length or complexity, you should comment your code. This often saves you time and frustration in the long run.

Workshop

Quiz

1. Can a user read the source code of PHP script you have successfully installed?

2. What do the standard PHP delimiter tags look like?

3. What do the ASP PHP delimiter tags look like?

4. What do the script PHP delimiter tags look like?

5. What function would you use to output a string to the browser?

Quiz Answers

1. No, the user will only see the output of your script.

2.
```
<?php
// your code here
?>.
```

3.
```
<%
// your code here
%>.
```

4.
```
<script language="php">
// your code here
</script>.
```

5. `print()`

Activities

1. Familiarize yourself with the process of creating, uploading, and running PHP scripts. In particular, create your own 'hello world' script. Add HTML code to it, and additional blocks of PHP. Experiment with the different PHP delimiter tags. Which ones are enabled in your configuration? Take a look at your `php.ini` file to confirm your findings. Don't forget to add some comments to your code.

PART II
The Language

Hour

Hour 4

The Building Blocks

In this hour, you are going to get your hands dirty with some of the nuts and bolts of the language.

There's a lot of ground to cover, and if you are new to programming, you might feel bombarded with information. Don't worry—you can always refer back here later on. Concentrate on understanding rather than memorizing the features covered.

If you're already an experienced programmer, you should at least skim this hour's lesson. It covers a few PHP-specific features.

In this hour, you will learn:

- About variables—what they are, why you need to use them and how to use them
- How to define and access variables
- About data types
- About some of the more commonly used operators
- How to use operators to create expressions
- How to define and use constants

Variables

A variable is a special container that you can define to "hold" a value. Variables are fundamental to programming. Without them we would be forced to 'hard-code' all the values in our scripts. In adding two numbers together and printing the result, I have achieved something useful.

```
print (2 + 4);
```

This script will only be useful for people who want to know the sum of 2 and 4, however. To get round this, I could write a script for finding the sum of another set of numbers, say 3 and 5. This approach to programming is clearly absurd. Variables allow us to create templates for operations (adding two numbers, for example), without worrying about what values the variables contain. The variables will be given values when the script is run, possibly through user input, or through a database query.

You will want to use a variable whenever the data that is being subjected to an operation in your script is liable to change from one script execution to another, or even within the lifetime of the script itself.

A variable consists of a name that you can choose, preceded by a dollar ($) sign. The variable name can include letters, numbers, and the underscore character (_). Variable names cannot include spaces or characters that are not alphanumeric. They should also begin with a letter or an underscore. The following code defines some legal variables:

```
$a;
$a_longish_variable_name;
$2453;
$sleepyZZZZ;
```

Remember that a semicolon (;) is used to end a PHP statement. The semicolons in the previous fragment of code are not part of the variable names.

New Term   A *variable* is a holder for a type of data. It can hold numbers, strings of characters, objects, arrays, or booleans. The contents of a variable can be changed at any time.

As you can see, you have plenty of choices about naming. To declare a variable, you need only to include it in your script. You usually declare a variable and assign a value to it in the same statement.

```
$num1 = 8;
$num2 = 23;
```

The preceding lines declare two variables, using the assignment operator (=) to give them values. You will learn about assignment in more detail in the Operators and Expressions section later in the hour. After you give your variables values, you can treat them exactly as if they were the values themselves. In other words:

```
print $num1;
```

is equivalent to

```
print 8;
```

as long as $num1 contains 8.

Data Types

Different types of data take up different amounts of memory and may be treated differently when they are manipulated in a script. Some programming languages therefore demand that the programmer declare in advance which type of data a variable will contain. By contrast, PHP 4 is loosely typed, which means that it will calculate data types as data is assigned to each variable. This is a mixed blessing. On the one hand, it means that variables can be used flexibly, holding a string at one point and an integer at another. On the other hand, this can lead to problems in larger scripts if you expect a variable to hold one data type when in fact it holds something completely different. You may have created code that is designed to work with an array variable, for example. If the variable in question contains a number value instead, then errors might occur when the code attempts to perform array specific operations on the variable.

Table 4.1 shows the six standard data types available in PHP 4.

TABLE 4.1 Standard Data Types

Type	Example	Description
Integer	5	A whole number
Double	3.234	A floating-point number
String	"hello"	A collection of characters
Boolean	true	One of the special values true or false
Object		See Hour 8, "Objects"
Array		See Hour 7, "Arrays"

Of PHP's six standard data types, we will leave arrays and objects for Hours 7 and 8.

PHP 4 also provides two special data types. These are listed in Table 4.2.

TABLE 4.2   Special Data Types

Type	Description
Resource	Reference to a third party resource (a database for example)
NULL	An uninitialized variable

Resource types are often returned by functions that deal with external applications or files. You will see examples of resource types throughout the book in Hour 10, Hour 11 and Hour 12. The type NULL is reserved for variables that have not been initialized (that is, have not yet had a value assigned to them).

You can use PHP's built-in function gettype() to test the type of any variable. If you place a variable between the parentheses of the function call, gettype() returns a string representing the relevant type. Listing 4.1 assigns five different data types to a single variable, testing it with gettype() each time.

You can read more about calling functions in Hour 6, "Functions."

LISTING 4.1   Testing the Type of a Variable

```
 1: <html>
 2: <head>
 3: <title>Listing 4.1 Testing the type of a variable</title>
 4: </head>
 5: <body>
 6: <?php
 7: $testing; // declare without assigning
 8: print gettype( $testing ); // null
 9: print "<br>";
10: $testing = 5;
11: print gettype( $testing ); // integer
12: print "<br>";
13: $testing = "five";
14: print gettype( $testing ); // string
15: print("<br>");
16: $testing = 5.0;
17: print gettype( $testing ); // double
18: print("<br>");
19: $testing = true;
20: print gettype( $testing ); // boolean
21: print "<br>";
```

LISTING 4.1 continued

```
22: ?>
23: </body>
24: </html>
```

This script produces the following:

```
NULL
integer
string
double
boolean
```

When we declare our $testing variable in line 7 we do not assign a value to it. So when we first use the gettype() function to test the variable in line 8, we get the string "NULL". After this we assign values to $testing by using the = sign before passing it to gettype(). An *integer,* assigned to the $testing variable in line 10, is a whole or real number. In simple terms, it can be said to be a number without a decimal point. A *string*, assigned to the $testing variable in line 13, is a collection of characters. When you work with strings in your scripts, they should always be surrounded by double (") or single (') quotation marks. A *double*, assigned to the $testing variable in line 16, is a floating-point number. That is, a number that includes a decimal point. A *boolean*, assigned to the $testing variable in line 19, can be one of two special values, true or false.

Prior to PHP 4, there was no boolean type. Although true was used, it was actually a contstant (a special kind of variable that we will cover later in this chapter) with the integer value of 1.

Both NULL and Resource types were also added with PHP 4.

Changing Type with settype()

PHP provides the function settype() to change the type of a variable. To use settype(), you must place the variable to change (and the type to change it to) between the parentheses and separated by commas. Listing 4.2 converts the value 3.14 (a double) to the four types that we are covering in this hour.

LISTING 4.2 Changing the Type of a Variable with settype()

```
1: <html>
2: <head>
3: <title>Listing 4.2 Changing the type of a variable with settype()</title>
```

LISTING 4.2   continued

```
 4: </head>
 5: <body>
 6: <?php
 7: $undecided = 3.14;
 8: print gettype( $undecided ); // double
 9: print " is $undecided<br>";  // 3.14
10: settype( $undecided, 'string' );
11: print gettype( $undecided ); // string
12: print " is $undecided<br>";  // 3.14
13: settype( $undecided, 'integer' );
14: print gettype( $undecided ); // integer
15: print " is $undecided<br>";  // 3
16: settype( $undecided, 'double' );
17: print gettype( $undecided ); // double
18: print " is $undecided<br>";  // 3.0
19: settype( $undecided, 'boolean' );
20: print gettype( $undecided ); // boolean
21: print " is $undecided<br>";  // 1
22: ?>
23: </body>
24: </html>
```

In each case, we use gettype() to confirm that the type change worked and then print
the value of the variable $undecided to the browser. When we convert the string "3.14"
to an integer in line 13, any information beyond the decimal point is lost forever. That's
why $undecided still contains 3 after we have changed it back to a double in line 16.
Finally, in line 19, we convert $undecided to a boolean. Any number other than 0
becomes true when converted to a boolean. When printing a boolean in PHP, true is
represented as 1 and false as an empty string, so in line 21, $undecided is printed as 1.

Changing Type by Casting

By placing the name of a data type in parentheses in front of a variable, you create a
copy of that variable's value converted to the data type specified.

The principle difference between settype() and a cast is the fact that casting produces a
copy, leaving the original variable untouched. Listing 4.3 illustrates this.

LISTING 4.3   Casting a Variable

```
1: <html>
2: <head>
3: <title>Listing 4.3 Casting a variable</title>
4: </head>
```

LISTING 4.3   continued

```
 5: <body>
 6: <?php
 7: $undecided = 3.14;
 8: $holder = ( double ) $undecided;
 9: print gettype( $holder ) ; // double
10: print " is $holder<br>";    // 3.14
11: $holder = ( string ) $undecided;
12: print gettype( $holder );  // string
13: print " is $holder<br>";    // 3.14
14: $holder = ( integer ) $undecided;
15: print gettype( $holder );  // integer
16: print " is $holder<br>";    // 3
17: $holder = ( double ) $undecided;
18: print gettype( $holder );  // double
19: print " is $holder<br>";    // 3.14
20: $holder = ( boolean ) $undecided;
21: print gettype( $holder );  // boolean
22: print " is $holder<br>";    // 1
23: print "<hr>";
24: print "original variable type: ";
25: print gettype( $undecided ); // double
26: ?>
27: </body>
28: </html>
```

We never actually change the type of $undecided, which remains a double throughout. We illustrate this on line 25 by using the gettype() function to output the type of $undecided.

In fact, by casting $undecided, we create a copy that is then converted to the type we specify. This new value is then stored in the variable $holder, first in Line 8, and then also in Lines 11, 14, 17 and 20. Because we are working with a copy of $undecided, we never discard any information from it as we did in lines 13 and 19 of Listing 4.2.

So now that we can change the contents of a variable from one type to another, either using settype() or a cast, we should consider why this might be useful. It is certainly not a procedure you will use often because PHP will automatically cast for you when the context requires. However, an automatic cast is temporary, and you might wish to make a variable persistently hold a particular data type.

Numbers typed into an HTML form by a user will be made available to your script as a string. If you try to add two strings containing numbers, PHP will helpfully convert the strings into numbers while the addition is taking place. So

```
"30cm" + "40cm"
```

will give the integer 70. In casting the strings PHP will ignore the non-numeric characters. However, you may wish to clean up your user input yourself. Imagine that our user has been asked to submit a number. We can simulate this by declaring a variable and assigning to it.

```
$test = "30cm";
```

As you can see, our user has mistakenly added units to the number. We can make sure that our user input is clean by casting it to an integer.

```
$test = (integer)$test;
print "Your imaginary box has a width of $test centimeters";
```

You can read more about automatic casts in Hour 16, "Working With Data."

Why Test Type?

So why might it be useful to know the type of a variable? There are often circumstances in programming in which data is passed to you from another source. In Hour 6, for example, you will learn how to create functions in your scripts. Functions can accept information from calling code in the form of arguments. For the function to work with the data it is given, it is often a good idea to first check that it has been given values of the correct data type. A function that is expecting a resource, for example, will not work well when passed a string.

Operators and Expressions

You can now assign data to variables. You can even investigate and change the data type of a variable. A programming language isn't very useful, though, unless you can manipulate the data you can store. Operators are symbols that make it possible to use one or more values to produce a new value. A value that is operated on by an operator is referred to as an operand.

 An *operator* is a symbol or series of symbols that, when used in conjunction with values, performs an action and usually produces a new value.

 An *operand* is a value used in conjunction with an operator. There are usually two operands to one operator.

Let's combine two operands with an operator to produce a new value:

```
4 + 5
```

4 and 5 are operands. They are operated on by the addition operator (+) to produce 9. Operators almost always sit between two operands, though you will see a few exceptions later in this hour.

The combination of operands with an operator to manufacture a result is called an expression. Although most operators form the basis of expressions, an expression need not contain an operator. In fact in PHP, an expression is defined as anything that can be used as a value. This includes integer constants such as 654, variables such as $user, and function calls such as gettype(). The expression (4 + 5), therefore is an expression that consists of two further expressions and an operator. When an expression produces a value, it is often said to 'resolve to' that value. That is, when all sub-expressions are taken into account the expression can be treated as if it were a code for the value itself.

NEW TERM An *expression* is any combination of functions, values, and operators that resolve to a value. As a rule of thumb, if you can use it as if it were a value, it is an expression.

Now that we have the principles out of the way, it's time to take a tour of PHP's more common operators.

The Assignment Operator

You have met the assignment operator each time we have initialized a variable. It consists of the single character =. The assignment operator takes the value of its right-hand operand and assigns it to its left-hand operand:

```
$name = "matt";
```

The variable $name now contains the string "matt". Interestingly, this construct is an expression. It might look at first glance that the assignment operator simply changes the variable $name without producing a value, but in fact, a statement that uses the assignment operator always resolves to a copy of the value of the right operand. Thus

```
print ( $name = "matt" );
```

prints the string "matt" to the browser in addition to assigning "matt" to $name.

Arithmetic Operators

The arithmetic operators do exactly what you would expect. Table 4.3 lists these operators. The addition operator adds the right operand to the left operand. The subtraction operator subtracts the right-hand operand from the left. The division operator divides the left-hand operand by the right. The multiplication operator multiplies the left-hand operand by the right. The modulus operator returns the remainder of the left operand divided by the right.

TABLE 4.3 Arithmetic Operators

Operator	Name	Example	Example Result
+	Addition	10+3	13
–	Subtraction	10–3	7
/	Division	10/3	3.3333333333333
	Multiplication	10*3	30
%	Modulus	10%3	1

The Concatenation Operator

The concatenation operator is a single dot. Treating both operands as strings, it appends the right-hand operand to the left. So

```
"hello"." world"
```

returns

```
"hello world"
```

Regardless of the data types of the operands, they are treated as strings, and the result always is a string. We will encounter concatenation frequently throughout this book when we need to combine the results of an expression of some kind to with string.

```
$centimeters = 212;
print "the width is ".($centimeters/100)." meters";
```

Combined Assignment Operators

Although there is really only one assignment operator, PHP 4 provides a number of combination operators that transform the left-hand operand as well as return a result. As a rule, operators use their operands without changing their values. Assignment operators break this rule. A combined assignment operator consists of a standard operator symbol followed by an equals sign. Combination assignment operators save you the trouble of using two operators yourself. For example,

```
$x = 4;
$x = $x + 4; // $x now equals 8
```

may instead by written as

```
$x = 4;
$x += 4; // $x now equals 8
```

There is an assignment operator for each of the arithmetic operators and one for the concatenation operator. Table 4.4 lists some of the most common.

TABLE 4.4 Some Combined Assignment Operators

Operator	Example	Equivalent to
+=	$x += 5	$x = $x + 5
-=	$x -= 5	$x = $x - 5
/=	$x /= 5	$x = $x / 5
*=	$x *= 5	$x = $x * 5
%=	$x %= 5	$x = $x % 5
.=	$x .= " test"	$x = $x." test"

Each of the examples in Table 4.4 transforms the value of $x using the value of the right-hand operand.

Comparison Operators

Comparison operators perform tests on their operands. They return the boolean value `true` if the test is successful, or `false` otherwise. This type of expression is useful in control structures, such as `if` and `while` statements. You will meet these in Hour 5.

To test whether the value contained in $x is smaller than 5, for example, you would use the `less than` operator:

$x < 5

If $x contained 3, this expression would be equivalent to the value `true`. If $x contained 7, the expression would resolve to `false`.

Table 4.5 lists the comparison operators.

TABLE 4.5 Comparison Operators

Operator	Name	Returns True if	Example ($x is 4)	Result
==	Equivalence	Left is equivalent to right	$x == 5	false
!=	Non-equivalence	Left is not equivalent to right	$x != 5	true

4

TABLE 4.5   continued

Operator	Name	Returns True if	Example ($x is 4)	Result
===	Identical	Left is equivalent to right and they are the same type	$x === 5	false
>	Greater than	Left is greater than right	$x > 4	false
>=	Greater than or equal to	Left is greater than or equal to right	$x >= 4	true
<	Less than	Left is less than right	$x < 4	false
<=	Less than or equal to	Left is less than or equal to right	$x <= 4	true

These operators are most commonly used with integers or doubles, although the equivalence operator is also used to compare strings.

Creating More Complex Test Expressions with the Logical Operators

The logical operators test combinations of booleans. The or operator, which is indicated by two pipe characters ('||') or simply the characters or, for example, returns true if either the left or the right operand is true.

```
true || false
```

would return true.

The and operator, which is indicated by two ampersand characters ('&&') or simply the characters and, only returns true if both the left and right operands are true.

```
true && false
```

would return false. It's unlikely that you would use a logical operator to test boolean constants, however. It would make more sense to test two or more expressions that resolve to a boolean. For example,

```
( $x > 2 ) && ( $x < 15 )
```

would return true if $x contained a value that is greater than 2 and smaller than 15. We include the parentheses to make the code easier to read. Table 4.6 lists the logical operators.

TABLE 4.6 Logical Operators

Operator	Name	Returns True If...	Example	Result
`||`	Or	Left or right is true	`true ||` `false`	`true`
`or`	Or	Left or right is true	`true ||` `false`	`true`
`xor`	Xor	Left or right is true but not both	`true xor` `true`	`false`
`&&`	And	Left and right are true	`true &&` `false`	`false`
`and`	And	Left and right are true	`true &&` `false`	`false`
`!`	Not	The single operand is not true	`! true`	`false`

Why are there two versions of both the or and the and operators? The answer lies in operator precedence, which you will look at later in this section.

Automatically Incrementing and Decrementing an Integer Variable

When coding in PHP, you will often find it necessary to increment or decrement an integer variable. You will usually need to do this when you are counting the iterations of a loop. You have already learned two ways of doing this. I could increment the integer contained by $x with the addition operator

```
$x = $x + 1; // $x is incremented
```

or with a combined assignment operator

```
$x += 1; // $x is incremented
```

In both cases, the resultant integer is assigned to $x. Because expressions of this kind are so common, PHP provides some special operators that allow you to add or subtract the integer constant 1 from an integer variable, assigning the result to the variable itself. These are known as the post-increment and post-decrement operators. The post-increment operator consists of two plus symbols appended to a variable name.

```
$x++; // $x is incremented
```

increments the variable $x by one. Using two minus symbols in the same way decrements the variable:

```
$x--; // $x is decremented
```

If you use the post-increment or post-decrement operators in conjunction with a conditional operator, the operand will only be modified after the test has been completed:

```
$x = 3;
$x++ < 4; // true
```

In the previous example, $x contains 3 when it is tested against 4 with the less than operator, so the test expression returns true. After this test is complete, $x is incremented.

In some circumstances, you might want to increment or decrement a variable in a test expression before the test is carried out. PHP provides the pre-increment and pre-decrement operators for this purpose. On their own, these operators behave in exactly the same way as the post-increment and post-decrement operators. They are written with the plus or minus symbols preceding the variable:

```
++$x; // $x is incremented
--$x; // $x is decremented
```

If these operators are used as part of a test expression, the incrementation occurs before the test is carried out.

```
$x = 3;
++$x < 4; // false
```

In the previous fragment, $x is incremented before it is tested against 4. The test expression returns false because 4 is not smaller than 4.

Operator Precedence

When you use an operator, the PHP engine usually reads your expression from left to right. For complex expressions that use more than one operator, though, the waters can become a little murky. First, consider a simple case:

```
4 + 5
```

There's no room for confusion, here. PHP simply adds 4 to 5. What about the next fragment?

```
4 + 5 * 2
```

This presents a problem. Does it mean the sum of 4 and 5, which should then be multiplied by 2, giving the result 18? Does it mean 4 plus the result of 5 multiplied by 2, resolving to 14? If you were to read simply from left to right, the former would be true. In fact, PHP attaches different precedence to operators. Because the multiplication operator has higher precedence than the addition operator does, the second solution to the problem is the correct one.

You can force PHP to execute the addition expression before the multiplication expression with parentheses:

```
( 4 + 5 ) * 2
```

Whatever the precedence of the operators in a complex expression, it is a good idea to use parentheses to make your code clearer and to save you from obscure bugs. Table 4.7 lists the operators covered in this hour in precedence order (highest first).

TABLE 4.7 Order of Precedence for Selected Operators

Operators
++ -- (cast)
/ * %
+ -
< <= => >
== === !=
&&
||
= += -= /= *= %= .=
and
xor
or

As you can see, or has a lower precedence than || and and has a lower precedence than
&&, so you could use the lower-precedence logical operators to change the way a complex
test expression is read. This is not necessarily a good idea. The following two expressions are equivalent, but the second is much easier to read:

```
$x and $y || $z
$x && ( $y || $z ) )
```

The order of precedence is the only reason that both && and and are present in PHP. The
same is true of || and or. In most, if not all circumstances, however, use of parentheses
will make for clearer code and fewer bugs than code that takes advantage of the difference in precedence of these operators. Throughout this book, we will tend to use the
more common || and && operators.

Constants

Variables offer a flexible way of storing data. You can change their values and the type of
data they store at any time. If, however, you want to work with a value that you do not
want to alter throughout your script's execution, you can define a constant. You must use
PHP's built-in function define() to create a constant. After you have done this, the constant cannot be changed. To use the define() function, you must place the name of the
constant and the value you want to give it within the call's parentheses. These values
must be separated by a comma:

```
define( "CONSTANT_NAME", 42 );
```

The value you want to set can only be a number or a string. By convention, the name of
the constant should be in capitals. Constants are accessed with the constant name only;
no dollar symbol is required. Listing 4.4 defines and accesses a constant.

LISTING 4.4   Defining a Constant

```
 1: <html>
 2: <head>
 3: <title>Listing 4.4 Defining a constant</title>
 4: </head>
 5: <body>
 6: <?php
 7: define( "USER", "Gerald" );
 8: print "Welcome ".USER;
 9: ?>
10: </body>
11: </html>
```

Notice that in line 8 we used the concatenation operator to append the value held by our constant to the string `"Welcome"`. This is because the PHP engine has no way of distinguishing between a constant and a string within quotation marks.

`define()` optionally accepts a third `boolean` argument which determines whether or not the constant name should be case-independent. By default constants are case-dependent, but by passing `true` to the `define()` function you can change this behavior. So if we were to set up our USER constant in this way

```
Define( "USER", "Gerald", true );
```

we could access its value without worrying about case:

```
print User;
print usEr;
print USER;
```

would all be equivalent. This feature can make scripts a little friendlier for programmers who work with your code, in that they will not need to consider case when accessing a constant that you have defined. On the other hand, the fact that other constants are case-sensitive could make for more rather than less confusion as programmers forget which constants to treat in which way. Unless you have a compelling reason to act otherwise, the safest course is probably to keep your constants case sensitive and define them using upper-case characters, which is an easy-to-remember convention.

Predefined Constants

PHP automatically provides some built-in constants for you. `__FILE__`, for example, returns the name of the file currently being read by the PHP engine. `__LINE__` returns the line number of the file. These constants are useful for generating error messages. You can also find out which version of PHP is interpreting the script with `PHP_VERSION`. This can be useful if you want to limit a script to run on a particular PHP release.

Summary

In this hour, you covered some of the basic features of the PHP language. You learned about variables and how to assign to them using the assignment operator. You were introduced to operators and learned how to combine some of the most common of these into expressions. Finally, you learned how to define and access constants.

Now that you have mastered some of the fundamentals of PHP, the next hour will really put you in the driver's seat. You will learn how to make scripts that can make decisions and repeat tasks, with help—of course—from variables, expressions and operators.

4

Q&A

Q Why can it be useful to know the type of data a variable holds?

A Often the data type of a variable constrains what you can do with it. You may want to make sure that a variable contains an integer or a double before using it in a mathematical calculation, for example.

You explore situations of this kind a little further in Hour 16, "Working with Data."

Q Should I obey any conventions when naming variables?

A Your goal should always be to make your code both easy to read and understand. A variable such as $ab123245 tells you nothing about its role in your script and invites typos. Keep your variable names short and descriptive.

A variable named $f is unlikely to mean much to you when you return to your code after a month or so. A variable named $filename, on the other hand, should make more sense.

Q Should I learn the operator precedence table?

A There is no reason why you shouldn't, but I would save the effort for more useful tasks. By using parentheses in your expressions, you can make your code easy to read at the same time as defining your own order of precedence.

Workshop

Quiz

1. Which of the following variable names is not valid?

   ```
   $a_value_submitted_by_a_user
   $666666xyz
   $xyz666666
   $____counter____
   $the first
   $file-name
   ```

2. What will the following code fragment output?

   ```
   $num = 33;
   (boolean) $num;
   print $num;
   ```

3. What will the following statement output?

   ```
   print gettype("4");
   ```

4. What will be the output from the following code fragment?

```
$test_val = 5.4566;
settype( $test_val, "integer" );
print $test_val;
```

5. Which of the following statements does not contain an expression?

```
4;
gettype(44);
5/12;
```

6. Which of the statements in question 5 contains an operator?

7. What value will the following expression return?

```
5 < 2
```

What data type will the returned value be?

Quiz Answers

1. The variable name $666666xyz is not valid because it does not begin with a letter or an underscore character. The variable name $the first is not valid because it contains a space. $file-name is also invalid because it contains a nonalphanumeric character.

2. The fragment will print the integer 33. The cast to boolean produced a converted copy of the value stored in $num. It did not alter the value actually stored there.

3. The statement will output the string "string".

4. The code will output the value 5. When a double is converted to an integer, any information beyond the decimal point is lost.

5. They are all expressions because they all resolve to values.

6. The statement 5/12; contains a division operator.

7. The expression will resolve to false, which is a boolean value.

4

Activities

1. Create a script that contains at least five different variables. Populate them with values of different data types and use the `gettype()` function to print each type to the browser.

2. Assign values to two variables. Use comparison operators to test whether the first value is

   - the same as the second
   - less than the second
   - greater than the second
   - less than or equal to the second

   Print the result of each test to the browser.

   Change the values assigned to your test variables and run the script again.

Hour 5

Going with the Flow

The scripts created in the last hour flow only in a single direction. The same statements are executed in the same order every time a script is run. This does not leave much room for flexibility.

You now will look at some structures that enable your scripts to adapt to circumstances. In this hour, you will learn:

- How to use the `if` statement to execute code only if a test expression evaluates to `true`
- How to execute alternative blocks of code when the test expression of an `if` statement evaluates to `false`
- How to use the `switch` statement to execute code based on the value returned by a test expression
- How to repeat execution of code using a `while` statement
- How to use `for` statements to make neater loops
- How to break out of loops
- How to nest one loop within another
- How to use PHP start and end tags within control structures

Switching Flow

Most scripts evaluate conditions and change their behavior accordingly. The facility to make decisions makes your PHP pages dynamic, capable of changing their output according to circumstances. Like most programming languages, PHP 4 allows you to do this with an if statement.

The if Statement

An if statement is a way of controlling the execution of a statement that follows it (that is, a single statement or a block of code inside braces). The if statement evaluates an expression between parentheses. If this expression results in a true value, the statement is executed. Otherwise, the statement is skipped entirely. This enables scripts to make decisions based on any number of factors.

```
if ( expression ) {
    // code to execute if the expression evaluates to true
    }
```

Listing 5.1 executes a block of code only if a variable contains the string "happy".

LISTING 5.1   An if Statement

```
 1: <html>
 2: <head>
 3: <title>Listing 5.1</title>
 4: </head>
 5: <body>
 6: <?php
 7: $mood = "happy";
 8: if ( $mood == "happy" ) {
 9:     print "Hooray, I'm in a good mood";
10: }
11: ?>
12: </body>
13: </html>
```

You use the comparison operator == to compare the variable $mood with the string "happy". If they match, the expression evaluates to true, and the code block below the if statement is executed. Although the code block is wrapped in braces in the example, this is only necessary if the block contains more than one line. The following fragment, therefore, would be acceptable:

```
if ( $mood == "happy" )
    print "Hooray, I'm in a good mood";
```

If you change the value of $mood to "sad" and run the script, the expression in the if statement evaluates to false, and the code block is skipped. The script remains sulkily silent.

Using the else Clause with the if Statement

When working with the if statement, you will often want to define an alternative block of code that should be executed if the expression you are testing evaluates to false. You can do this by adding else to the if statement followed by a further block of code:

```
if ( expression ) {
    // code to execute if the expression evaluates to true
} else {
    // code to execute in all other cases
}
```

Listing 5.2 amends the example in Listing 5.1 so that a default block of code is executed if $mood is not equivalent to "happy".

LISTING 5.2　An if Statement That Uses else

```
 1: <html>
 2: <head>
 3: <title>Listing 5.2</title>
 4: </head>
 5: <body>
 6: <?php
 7: $mood = "sad";
 8: if ( $mood == "happy" ) {
 9:     print "Hooray, I'm in a good mood";
10: } else {
11:     print "Not happy but $mood";
12: }
13: ?>
14: </body>
15: </html>
```

Notice in line 7 that $mood contains the string "sad", which is not equivalent to "happy", so the expression in the if statement in line 8 evaluates to false. This means that the first block of code (line 9) is skipped. The block of code after else, therefore, is executed, and the message "Not happy but sad" is printed to the browser.

Using the else clause with the if statement allows scripts to make sophisticated decisions, but you currently are limited to an either-or branch. PHP 4 allows you to evaluate multiple expressions one after the other.

5

Using the `elseif` Clause with the `if` Statement

You can use an `if`-`elseif`-`else` construct to test multiple expressions before offering a default block of code:

```
if ( expression ) {
    // code to execute if the expression evaluates to true
} elseif ( another expression ) {
    // code to execute if the previous expression failed
    // and this one evaluates to true
} else {
    // code to execute in all other cases
}
```

If the first expression does not evaluate to `true`, then the first block of code is ignored. The `elseif` clause then causes another expression to be evaluated. Once again, if this expression evaluates to `true`, then the second block of code is executed. Otherwise, the block of code associated with the `else` clause is executed. You can include as many `elseif` clauses as you want, and if you don't need a default action, you can omit the `else` clause.

 The `elseif` clause can also be written as two separate words: `else if`. The syntax you employ is a matter of taste.

Listing 5.3 adds an `elseif` clause to the previous example.

LISTING 5.3   An `if` Statement that Uses `else` and `elseif`

```
 1: <html>
 2: <head>
 3: <title>Listing 5.3</title>
 4: </head>
 5: <body>
 6: <?php
 7: $mood = "sad";
 8: if ( $mood == "happy" ) {
 9:     print "Hooray, I'm in a good mood";
10: } elseif ( $mood == "sad" ) {
11:     print "Awww. Don't be down!";
12: } else {
13:     print "Neither happy nor sad but $mood";
14: }
15: ?>
16: </body>
17: </html>
```

Once again, $mood holds a string, "sad" in line 7. This is not equivalent to "happy", so the first block in line 9 is ignored. The elseif clause in line 10 tests for equivalence between the contents of $mood and "sad", which evaluates to true. This block of code is therefore executed. In lines 12, 13 and 14 we provide default behavior. If none of the test conditions have been fulfilled we simply print out a message including the actual value of the $mood variable.

The switch Statement

The switch statement is an alternative way of changing program flow according to the evaluation of an expression. There are some key differences between the switch and if statements. Using the if statement in conjunction with elseif, you may evaluate multiple expressions. switch evaluates only one expression, executing different code according to the result of that expression, as long as the expression evaluates to a simple type (a number, a string, or a boolean). The result of an expression evaluated as part of an if statement is read as either true or false. The expression of a switch statement yields a result that is tested against any number of values.

```
switch ( expression ) {
    case result1:
        // execute this if expression results in result1
        break;
    case result2:
        // execute this if expression results in result2
        break;
    default:
        // execute this if no break statement
        // has been encountered hitherto
}
```

The switch statement's expression is often simply a variable. Within the switch statement's block of code, you find a number of case statements. Each of these tests a value against the result of the switch statement's expression. If these are equivalent, then the code after the case statement is executed. The break statement ends execution of the switch statement altogether. If this is left out, the next case statement's expression is evaluated. If the optional default statement is reached, its code is executed.

Don't forget to include a break statement at the end of any code that will be executed as part of a case statement. Without break, the program flow will continue to the next case statement and ultimately to the default statement. In most cases, this will not be the behavior that you will be expecting.

Listing 5.4 re-creates the functionality of the if statement example, using the switch statement.

LISTING 5.4   A switch Statement

```
 1: <html>
 2: <head>
 3: <title>Listing 5.4</title>
 4: </head>
 5: <body>
 6: <?php
 7: $mood = "sad";
 8: switch ( $mood ) {
 9:     case "happy":
10:         print "Hooray, I'm in a good mood";
11:         break;
12:     case "sad":
13:         print "Awww. Don't be down!";
14:         break;
15:     default:
16:         print "Neither happy nor sad but $mood";
17: }
18: ?>
19: </body>
20: </html>
```

Once again, in line 7 the $mood variable is initialized to "sad". The switch statement in line 8 uses this variable as its expression. The first case statement in line 9 tests for equivalence between "happy" and the value of $mood. There is no match, so script execution moves on to the second case statement in line 12. The string "sad" is equivalent to the value of $mood, so this block of code is executed. The break statement in line 14 ends the process.

Using the ? Operator

The ? or ternary operator is similar to the if statement but returns a value derived from one of two expressions separated by a colon. Which expression is used to generate the value returned depends on the result of a test expression:

```
( expression )?returned_if_expression_is_true:returned_if_expression_is_false;
```

If the test expression evaluates to true, the result of the second expression is returned; otherwise, the value of the third expression is returned. Listing 5.5 uses the ternary operator to set the value of a variable according to the value of $mood.

LISTING 5.5   Using the ? Operator

```
 1: <html>
 2: <head>
 3: <title>Listing 5.5</title>
 4: </head>
 5: <body>
 6: <?php
 7: $mood = "sad";
 8: $text = ( $mood=="happy" )?"Hooray, I'm in a good mood":"Not happy but
➥$mood";
 9: print "$text";
10: ?>
11: </body>
12: </html>
```

In line 7, $mood is set to "sad". In line 8, $mood is tested for equivalence to the string "happy". Because this test returns false, the result of the third of the three expressions is returned.

The ternary operator can be difficult to read but is useful if you are dealing with only two alternatives and like to write compact code.

Loops

So far you've looked at decisions that a script can make about what code to execute. Scripts can also decide how many times to execute a block of code. Loop statements are designed to enable you to achieve repetitive tasks. Almost without exception, a loop continues to operate until a condition is achieved, or you explicitly choose to exit the loop.

The while Statement

The while statement looks similar in structure to a basic if statement:

```
while ( expression ) {
    // do something
}
```

As long as a while statement's expression evaluates to true, the code block is executed over and over again. Each execution of the code block in a loop is often called an 'iteration.' Within the block, you usually change something that affects the while statement's expression; otherwise, your loop continues indefinitely. Listing 5.6 creates a while loop that calculates and prints multiples of two up to 24.

5

LISTING 5.6   A while Statement

```
 1: <html>
 2: <head>
 3: <title>Listing 5.6</title>
 4: </head>
 5: <body>
 6: <?php
 7: $counter = 1;
 8: while ( $counter <= 12 ) {
 9:     print "$counter times 2 is ".($counter*2)."<br>";
10:     $counter++;
11: }
12: ?>
13: </body>
14: </html>
```

In this example, we initialize a variable $counter in line 7. The while statement in line 8 tests the $counter variable. As long as the integer contained by $counter is smaller than or equal to 12, the loop continues to run. Within the while statement's code block, the value contained by $counter is multiplied by two, and the result is printed to the browser. Then in line 10, $counter is incremented. This last stage is extremely important. If you were to forget to change $counter, the while expression would never resolve to false, and the loop would never end.

The do...while Statement

A do...while statement looks a little like a while statement turned on its head. The essential difference between the two is that the code block is executed before the truth test and not after it:

```
do   {
    // code to be executed
} while ( expression );
```

> The test expression of a do...while statement should always end with a semicolon.

This statement might be useful if you want the code block to be executed at least once even if the while expression evaluates to false. Listing 5.7 creates a do...while statement. The code block is executed a minimum of one time.

LISTING 5.7 The do...while Statement

```
 1: <html>
 2: <head>
 3: <title>Listing 5.7</title>
 4: </head>
 5: <body>
 6: <?php
 7: $num = 1;
 8: do {
 9:     print "Execution number: $num<br>\n";
10:     $num++;
11: } while ( $num > 200 && $num < 400 );
12: ?>
13: </body>
14: </html>
```

The do...while statement tests whether the variable $num contains a value that is greater than 200 and smaller than 400. In line 7, we have initialized $num to 1 so this expression returns false. Nonetheless, the code block is executed before the expression is evaluated, so the statement will print a single line to the browser.

The for Statement

You cannot achieve anything with a for statement that you cannot do with a while statement. On the other hand, the for statement is often a neater and safer way of achieving the same effect. Earlier, Listing 5.6 initialized a variable outside the while statement. The while statement then tested the variable in its expression. The variable was incremented within the code block. The for statement allows you to achieve this on a single line. This allows for more compact code and makes it less likely that you forget to increment a counter variable, thereby creating an infinite loop.

```
for ( initialization expression; test expression; modification expression ) {
    // code to be executed
}
```

Each of the expressions within the parentheses of the for statement is separated by semicolons. Usually, the first expression initializes a counter variable, the second expression is the test condition for the loop, and the third expression increments the counter. Listing 5.8 shows a for statement that re-creates the example in Listing 5.6, which multiplies 12 numbers by 2.

5

LISTING 5.8   Using the `for` Statement

```
 1: <html>
 2: <head>
 3: <title>Listing 5.8</title>
 4: </head>
 5: <body>
 6: <?php
 7: for ( $counter=1; $counter<=12; $counter++ ) {
 8:     print "$counter times 2 is ".($counter*2)."<br>";
 9: }
10: ?>
11: </body>
12: </html>
```

The results of Listings 5.6 and 5.8 are exactly the same. The `for` statement, though, makes the code more compact. Because `$counter` is initialized and incremented at the top of the statement, the logic of the loop is clear at a glance. In line 7, within the `for` statement's parentheses, the first expression initializes the `$counter` variable and sets it to 1. The test expression checks that `$counter` contains a value that is less than or equal to 12. The final expression increments the `$counter` variable.

When program flow reaches the `for` loop, the `$counter` variable is initialized, and the test expression is evaluated. If the expression evaluates to `true`, the code block is executed. The `$counter` variable is then incremented and the test expression evaluated again. This process continues until the test expression evaluates to `false`.

Breaking Out of Loops with the `break` Statement

Both `while` and `for` statements incorporate a built-in test expression with which you can end a loop. The `break` statement, though, enables you to break out of a loop according to additional tests. This can provide a safeguard against error. Listing 5.9 creates a simple `for` statement that divides a large number by a variable that is incremented, printing the result to the screen.

LISTING 5.9   A `for` Loop That Divides 4000 by Ten Incremental Numbers

```
 1: <html>
 2: <head>
 3: <title>Listing 5.9</title>
 4: </head>
 5: <body>
 6: <?php
 7: for ( $counter=1; $counter <= 10; $counter++ ) {
 8:     $temp = 4000/$counter;
```

LISTING 5.9   continued

```
 9:     print "4000 divided by $counter is... $temp<br>";
10: }
11: ?>
12: </body>
13: </html>
```

In line 7, this example initializes the variable $counter to 1. The for statement's test expression checks that $counter is smaller than or equal to 10. Within the code block, 4000 is divided by $counter, printing the result to the browser.

This seems straightforward enough. What, though, if the value you place in $counter comes from user input? The value could be a minus number, or even a string. Let's take the first instance. Changing the initial value of $counter from 1 to –4 causes 4000 to be divided by zero as the code block is executed for the fifth time, which is not advisable. Listing 5.10 guards against this by breaking out of the loop if the $counter variable contains zero.

LISTING 5.10   Using the break Statement

```
 1: <html>
 2: <head>
 3: <title>Listing 5.10</title>
 4: </head>
 5: <body>
 6: <?php
 7: $counter = -4;
 8: for ( ; $counter <= 10; $counter++ ) {
 9:     if ( $counter == 0 )
10:         break;
11:     $temp = 4000/$counter;
12:     print "4000 divided by $counter is... $temp<br>";
13: }
14: ?>
15: </body>
16: </html>
```

Dividing a number by zero does not cause a fatal error in PHP 4. Instead, a warning is generated and execution continues.

Use an `if` statement, shown in line 9, to test the value of $counter. If it is equivalent to zero, the `break` statement immediately halts execution of the code block, and program flow continues after the `for` statement.

Notice that we initialized the $counter variable in line 7, outside the `for` statement's parentheses, to simulate a situation in which the value of $counter is set according to form input or a database look up.

> You can omit any of the expressions of a `for` statement, but you must remember to retain the semicolons.

Skipping an Iteration with the `continue` Statement

The `continue` statement ends execution of the current iteration but doesn't cause the loop as a whole to end. Instead, the next iteration is immediately begun. Using the `break` statement in Listing 5.10 was a little drastic. With the `continue` statement in Listing 5.11, you can avoid a divide by zero error without ending the loop completely.

LISTING 5.11   Using the `continue` Statement

```
 1: <html>
 2: <head>
 3: <title>Listing 5.11</title>
 4: </head>
 5: <body>
 6: <?php
 7: $counter = -4;
 8: for ( ;  $counter <= 10; $counter++ ) {
 9:     if ( $counter == 0 )
10:         continue;
11:     $temp = 4000/$counter;
12:     print "4000 divided by $counter is... $temp<br>";
13: }
14: ?>
15: </body>
16: </html>
```

In line 10, we have swapped the `break` statement for a `continue` statement. If the $counter variable is equivalent to zero, the iteration is skipped, and the next one immediately is started.

The break and continue statements can make code more difficult to read. Because they often add layers of complexity to the logic of the loop statements that contain them they are best used with care.

Nesting Loops

Loop statements can contain other loop statements. This combination is particularly useful when working with dynamically created HTML tables. Listing 5.12 uses two for statements to print a multiplication table to the browser.

LISTING 5.12   Nesting Two for Loops

```
 1: <html>
 2: <head>
 3: <title>Listing 5.12</title>
 4: </head>
 5: <body>
 6: <?php
 7: print "<table border=\"1\">\n";
 8: for ( $y=1; $y<=12; $y++ ) {
 9:     print "<tr>\n";
10:     for ( $x=1; $x<=12; $x++ ) {
11:         print "\t<td>";
12:         print ($x*$y);
13:         print "</td>\n";
14:     }
15:     print "</tr>\n";
16: }
17: print "</table>";
18: ?>
19: </body>
20: </html>
```

Before we examine the for loops, let's take a closer look at line 7 in Listing 5.12.

```
print "<table border=\"1\">\n";
```

Notice that we have used the backslash character ('\') before each of the quotation marks within the string. This is necessary in order to tell the PHP engine that we wish to quote the quotation character, rather than interpret it as the beginning or end of a string. If we did not do this, the statement would not make sense to the engine, consisting as it would of a string, followed by a number followed by another string. This would generate an error. We will encounter this backslash technique, known as *escaping*, once again in Hour 7, "Arrays."

The outer `for` statement (line 8) initializes a variable called $y, setting its starting value to 1. It defines an expression that tests that $y is smaller or equal to 12 and defines the increment for $y. For each iteration, the code block prints a TR (table row) HTML element (line 9) and defines another `for` statement (line 10). This inner loop initializes a variable called $x and defines expressions along the same lines as for the outer loop. For each iteration, the inner loop prints a TD (table cell) element to the browser (line 11), as well as the result of $x multiplied by $y (line 12). In line 13 we close the table cell. After the inner loop has completed we fall back through to the outer loop where we close the table row on line 15, ready for the process to begin again. When the outer loop has finished the result is a neatly formatted multiplication table. We wrap things up by closing the table on line 17.

Codeblocks and Browser Output

In Hour 3 we established that we can slip in and out of HTML mode at will, using the PHP start and end tags. In this chapter we have discovered that we can present distinct output to the user according to a decision-making process that we can control with `if` and `switch` statements. In this section we will combine these two techniques.

Imagine a script that outputs a table of values only when a variable is set to the boolean value `true`. Listing 5.13 shows a simplified HTML table constructed with the code block of an `if` statement.

LISTING 5.13   A code block containing multiple print() statements

```
 1: <html>
 2: <head>
 3: <title>Listing 5.13</title>
 4: </head>
 5: <body>
 6: <?php
 7: $display_prices = true;
 8: if ( $display_prices ) {
 9:     print "<table border=\"1\">";
10:     print "<tr><td colspan=\"3\">";
11:     print "todays prices in dollars";
12:     print "</td></tr>";
13:     print "<td>14</td><td>32</td><td>71</td>";
14:     print "</tr></table>";
15: }
16: ?>
17: </body>
18: </html>
```

If `$display_prices` is set to `true` in line 7, then the table is printed. For the sake of readability we split the output into multiple `print()` statements, and once again we escape any quotation marks. There's nothing wrong with that, but we can save ourselves some typing by simply slipping back into HTML mode within the code block. In Listing 5.14 we do just that.

LISTING 5.14　Returning to HTML mode within a code block

```
 1: <html>
 2: <head>
 3: <title>Listing 5.14</title>
 4: </head>
 5: <body>
 6: <?php
 7: $display_prices = true;
 8: if ( $display_prices ) {
 9: ?>
10:     <table border="1">
11:     <tr><td colspan="3">todays prices in dollars</td></tr>
12:     <td>14</td><td>32</td><td>71</td>
13:     </tr></table>
14: <?php
15: }
16: ?>
17: </body>
18: </html>
```

The important thing to note here is that the shift to HTML mode on line 9 only occurs if the condition of the `if` statement is fulfilled. This can save us the bother of escaping quotation marks and of wrapping our output in `print()` statements. It might, however, affect the readability of our code in the long run, especially as our script begins to grow.

Summary

In this hour, you learned about control structures and the ways in which they can help to make your scripts flexible and dynamic. Most of these structures will reappear regularly throughout the rest of the book.

You learned how to define an `if` statement and how to provide for alternative actions with the `elseif` and `else` clauses. You learned how to use the `switch` statement to change flow according to multiple equivalence tests on the result of an expression. You learned about loops, in particular, the `while` and `for` statements, and you learned how to use `break` and `continue` to prematurely end the execution of a loop or to skip an iteration. You learned how to nest one loop within another and saw a typical use for this

5

structure. Finally you looked at a technique for using PHP start and end tags in conjunction with conditional code blocks.

You should now have enough information to write scripts of your own. Your scripts can now make decisions and perform repetitive tasks. In the next hour we will be looking at a way of adding even more power to your applications. Functions will enable you to organize your code, preventing duplication and improving reusability.

Q&A

Q Must a control structure's test expression result in a boolean value?

A Ultimately, yes, but in the context of a test expression zero, an undefined variable, or an empty string will be converted to `false` for the purposes of the test. All other values will evaluate to `true`.

Q Must I always surround a code block in a control statement with brackets?

A If the code you want executed as part of a control structure consists of only a single line, you can omit the brackets.

Q Does this hour cover every kind of loop there is?

A In Hour 7, "Arrays," you encounter the `foreach` statement, which enables you to loop through every element in an array.

Workshop

Quiz

1. How would you use an `if` statement to print the string `"Youth message"` to the browser if an integer variable, `$age`, is between 18 and 35? If `$age` contains any other value, the string `"Generic message"` should be printed to the browser.

2. How would you extend your code in question 1 to print the string `"Child message"` if the `$age` variable is between 1 and 17?

3. How would you create a `while` statement that prints every odd number between 1 and 49?

4. How would you convert the `while` statement you created in question 3 into a `for` statement?

Quiz Answers

1.
```
$age = 22;

if ( $age >= 18 && $age <= 35 )
    print "Youth message<BR>\n";
else
    print "Generic message<BR>\n";
```

2.
```
$age = 12;

if ( $age >= 18 && $age <= 35 )
    print "Youth message<BR>\n";
elseif ( $age >= 1 && $age <= 17 )
    print "Child message<BR>\n";
else
    print "Generic message<BR>\n";
```

3.
```
$num = 1;
while ( $num <= 49 )
    {
    print "$num<BR>\n";
    $num += 2;
    }
```

4.
```
for ( $num = 1; $num <= 49; $num += 2 )

    print "$num<BR>\n";
```

Activities

1. Review the syntax for control structures. Think about how these techniques will help you in your scripting. Perhaps some of the script ideas you are developing will be able to behave in different ways according to user input, or will loop to display an HTML table. Start to build the control structures you will be using. Use temporary variables to mimic user input or database queries for the time being.

2. Review the section on the ternary operator. What distinguishes it from the control structures covered in the rest of the chapter? Why might it be useful?

5

HOUR 6

Functions

Functions are the heart of a well-organized script, making code easy to read and reuse. No large project would be manageable without them.

Throughout this hour, we will investigate functions and demonstrate some of the ways in which they can save you from repetitive work. In this hour, you will learn:

- How to define and call functions
- How to pass values to functions and receive values in return
- How to call a function dynamically using a string stored in a variable
- How to access global variables from within a function
- How to give a function a "memory"
- How to pass data to functions by reference
- How to create anonymous functions
- How to check that a function exists before calling it

What Is a Function?

You can think of a function as a machine. A machine takes the raw materials you feed it and works with them to achieve a purpose or to produce a product. A function accepts values from you, processes them, and then performs an action (printing to the browser, for example) or returns a new value, possibly both.

If you needed to bake a single cake, you would probably do it yourself. If you needed to bake thousands of cakes, you would probably build or acquire a cake-baking machine. Similarly, when deciding whether to create a function, the most important factor to consider is the extent to which it can save you from repetition.

A function, then, is a self-contained block of code that can be called by your scripts. When called, the function's code is executed. You can pass values to functions, which they will then work with. When finished, a function can pass a value back to the calling code.

Calling Functions

Functions come in two flavors—those built into the language and those you define yourself. PHP 4 has hundreds of built-in functions. The very first script in this book consisted of a single function call:

```
print("Hello Web");
```

In this example, we called the `print()` function, passing it the string `"Hello Web"`. The function then went about the business of writing the string. A function call consists of the function name, `print` in this case, followed by parentheses. If you want to pass information to the function, you place it between these parentheses. A piece of information passed to a function in this way is called an argument. Some functions require that more than one argument be passed to them. Arguments in these cases must be separated by commas:

```
some_function( $an_argument, $another_argument );
```

`print()` is typical in that it returns a value. Most functions give you some information back when they've completed their task, if only to tell whether their mission was successful. `print()` returns a boolean, therefore.

print() is not a typical function in that it does not require parentheses in order to run successfully.

print("Hello Web");

and

print "Hello Web";

are equally valid. This is an exception. All other functions require parentheses, whether or not they accept arguments.

The abs() function, for example, requires a signed numeric value and returns the absolute value of that number. Let's try it out in Listing 6.1.

LISTING 6.1 Calling the Built in abs() Function.

```
 1: <html>
 2: <head>
 3: <title>Listing 6.1</title>
 4: </head>
 5: <body>
 6: <?php
 7: $num = -321;
 8: $newnum = abs( $num );
 9: print $newnum;
10: // prints "321"
11: ?>
12: </body>
13: </html>
```

In this example, we assign the value -321 to a variable $num. We then pass that variable to the abs() function, which made the necessary calculation and returned a new value. We assign this to the variable $newnum and print the result. In fact, we could have dispensed with temporary variables altogether, passing our number straight to abs(), and directly printing the result:

print(abs(-321));

We used the temporary variables $num and $newnum though, to make each step of the process as clear as possible. Sometimes your code can be made more readable by breaking it up into a greater number of simple expressions.

You can call user-defined functions in exactly the same way as we have been calling built-in functions.

6

Defining a Function

You can define a function using the `function` statement:

```
function some_function( $argument1, $argument2 ) {
    // function code here
}
```

The name of the function follows the `function` statement and precedes a set of parentheses. If your function is to require arguments, you must place comma-separated variable
names within the parentheses. These variables will be filled by the values passed to your
function. If your function requires no arguments, you must nevertheless supply the
parentheses.

Listing 6.2 declares a function.

LISTING 6.2   Declaring a Function

```
 1: <html>
 2: <head>
 3: <title>Listing 6.2</title>
 4: </head>
 5: <body>
 6: <?php
 7: function bighello() {
 8:     print "<h1>HELLO!</h1>";
 9: }
10: bighello();
11: ?>
12: </body>
13: </html>
```

The script in Listing 6.2 will simply output the string "HELLO" wrapped in an HTML
<H1> element. We declare a function `bighello()` that requires no arguments. Because of
this, we leave the parentheses empty. `bighello()` is a working function but not terribly
useful. Listing 6.3 creates a function that requires an argument and actually does something helpful with it.

LISTING 6.3   Declaring a Function That Requires Arguments

```
 1: <html>
 2: <head>
 3: <title>Listing 6.3</title>
 4: </head>
 5: <body>
 6: <?php
```

LISTING 6.3   continued

```
 7: function printBR( $txt ) {
 8:     print ("$txt<br>\n");
 9: }
10: printBR("This is a line");
11: printBR("This is a new line");
12: printBR("This is yet another line");
13: ?>
14: </body>
15: </html>
```

FIGURE 6.1

A function that prints a string with an appended <BR> tag.

You can see the output from the script in Listing 6.3 in Figure 6.1. In line 7, the printBR() function expects a string, so we place the variable name $txt between the parentheses when we declare the function. Whatever is passed to printBR() will be stored in $txt. Within the body of the function, in line 8, we print the $txt variable, appending a <br> element and a newline character to it.

Now when we want to write a line to the browser, such as in line 10, 11 or 12, we can call printBR() instead of the built-in print(), saving us the bother of typing the <br> element.

6

Returning Values from User-Defined Functions

In our previous example we output an amended string to the browser within the printBR() function. Sometimes, however, you will want a function to provide you with a value that you can work with yourself. If your function has transformed a string that you have provided, you may wish to get the amended string back so that you can pass it to other functions. A function can return a value using the `return` statement in conjunction with a value. `return` stops the execution of the function and sends the value back to the calling code.

Listing 6.4 creates a function that returns the sum of two numbers.

LISTING 6.4   A Function That Returns a Value

```
 1: <html>
 2: <head>
 3: <title>Listing 6.4</title>
 4: </head>
 5: <body>
 6: <?php
 7: function addNums( $firstnum, $secondnum ) {
 8:     $result = $firstnum + $secondnum;
 9:     return $result;
10: }
11: print addNums(3,5);
12: // will print "8"
13: ?>
14: </body>
15: </html>
```

The script in Listing 6.4 will print the number '8.' Notice in line 7 that `addNums()` should be called with two numeric arguments (line 11 shows those to be 3 and 5 in this case). These are stored in the variables `$firstnum` and `$secondnum`. Predictably, `addNums()` adds the numbers contained in these variables together and stores the result in a variable called `$result`.

The `return` statement can return a value or nothing at all. How a value passed by `return` is arrived at can vary. The value could be hard-coded:

```
return 4;
```

It could be the result of an expression:

```
return ( $a/$b );
```

It could be the value returned by yet another function call:

```
return ( another_function( $an_argument ) );
```

Dynamic Function Calls

It is possible to assign function names as strings to variables and then treat these variables exactly as you would the function name itself. Listing 6.5 creates a simple example of this.

LISTING 6.5 Calling a Function Dynamically

```
 1: <html>
 2: <head>
 3: <title>Listing 6.5</title>
 4: </head>
 5: <body>
 6: <?php
 7: function sayHello() {
 8:     print "hello<br>";
 9: }
10: $function_holder = "sayHello";
11: $function_holder();
12: ?>
13: </body>
14: </html>
```

A string identical to the name of the sayHello() function is assigned to the $function_holder variable on line 10. Once this is done, we can use this variable in conjunction with parentheses to call the sayHello() function. We do this on line 11.

Why would we want to do this? In the example, we simply made more work for ourselves by assigning the string "sayHello" to $function_holder. Dynamic function calls are useful when you want to alter program flow according to changing circumstances. We might want our script to behave differently according to a parameter set in a URL's query string, for example. We could extract the value of this parameter and use it to call one of a number of functions.

PHP's built-in functions also make use of this feature. The array_walk() function, for example, uses a string to call a function for every element in an array. You can see an example of array walk() in action in Hour 1.

6

Variable Scope

A variable declared within a function remains local to that function. In other words, it will not be available outside the function or within other functions. In larger projects, this can save you from accidentally overwriting the contents of a variable when you declare two variables of the same name in separate functions.

Listing 6.6 creates a variable within a function and then attempts to print it outside the function.

LISTING 6.6   Variable Scope: A Variable Declared Within a Function Is Unavailable Outside the Function

```
 1: <html>
 2: <head>
 3: <title>Listing 6.6</title>
 4: </head>
 5: <body>
 6: <?php
 7: function test() {
 8:      $testvariable = "this is a test variable";
 9: }
10: print "test variable: $testvariable<br>";
11: ?>
12: </body>
13: </html>
```

FIGURE 6.2

Attempting to reference a variable defined within a function.

You can see the output of the script in Listing 6.6 in Figure 6.2. The value of the variable $testvariable is not printed. This is because no such variable exists outside the test() function. Note that the attempt in line 10 to access a nonexistent variable does not cause an error.

Similarly, a variable declared outside a function will not automatically be available within it.

Accessing Variables with the `global` Statement

From within a function, it is not possible by default to access a variable that has been defined elsewhere. If you attempt to use a variable of the same name, you will set or access a local variable only. Let's put this to the test in Listing 6.7.

LISTING 6.7 Variables Defined Outside Functions Are Inaccessible from Within a Function by Default

```
 1: <html>
 2: <head>
 3: <title>Listing 6.7</title>
 4: </head>
 5: <body>
 6: <?php
 7: $life = 42;
 8: function meaningOfLife() {
 9:     print "The meaning of life is $life<br>";
10: }
11: meaningOfLife();
12: ?>
13: </body>
14: </html>
```

FIGURE 6.3

Attempting to print a global variable from within a function.

You can see the output from the script in Listing 6.7 in Figure 6.3. As you might expect, the meaningOfLife() function has no access to the $life variable from line 7; $life is empty when the function attempts to print it. On the whole, this is a good thing. We're saved from potential clashes between identically named variables, and a function can always demand an argument if it needs information about the outside world.

Occasionally, however, you may want to access an important global variable from within a function without passing it in as an argument. This is where the `global` statement comes into its own. Listing 6.8 uses `global` to restore order to the universe.

LISTING 6.8 Accessing Global Variables with the `global` Statement

```
 1: <html>
 2: <head>
 3: <title>Listing 6.8</title>
 4: </head>
 5: <body>
 6: <?php
 7: $life=42;
 8: function meaningOfLife() {
 9:      global $life;
10:      print "The meaning of life is $life<br>";
11: }
12: meaningOfLife();
13: ?>
14: </body>
15: </html>
```

FIGURE 6.4

Successfully accessing a global variable from within a function using the `global` *keyword.*

You can see the output from the script in Listing 6.8 in Figure 6.4. By placing `global` in front of the `$life` variable when we declare it in the `meaning_of_life()` function (line 9), we make it refer to the `global $life` variable declared outside the function (line 7).

You will need to use the global statement for every function that wishes to access a particular global variable.

Be careful, though. If we manipulate the contents of the variable within the function, `$life` will be changed for the script as a whole.

You can declare more than one variable at a time with the `global` statement, simply separate each of the variables you wish to access with commas.

```
global $var1, $var2, $var3;
```

In Hour 9, "Working with Forms" we will encounter the `$GLOBALS` array, a way of accessing global variables from anywhere in your script.

> Usually, an argument is a copy of whatever value is passed by the calling code; changing it in a function has no effect beyond the function block. Changing a global variable within a function on the other hand changes the original and not a copy. Use the `global` statement sparingly.

Saving State Between Function Calls with the `static` Statement

Variables within functions have a short but happy life on the whole. They come into being when the function is called and die when execution is finished. Once again, this is as it should be. It is usually best to build a script as a series of self-contained blocks, each with as little knowledge of others as possible. Occasionally, however, you may want to give a function a rudimentary memory.

Let's assume that we want a function to keep track of the number of times it has been called. Why? In our examples, the function is designed to create numbered headings in a script that dynamically builds online documentation.

We could, of course use our newfound knowledge of the `global` statement to do this. We have a crack at this in Listing 6.9.

LISTING 6.9 Using the `global` Statement to Remember the Value of a Variable Between Function Calls

```
 1: <html>
 2: <head>
 3: <title>Listing 6.9</title>
 4: </head>
 5: <body>
 6: <?php
 7: $num_of_calls = 0;
 8: function numberedHeading( $txt ) {
 9:     global $num_of_calls;
10:     $num_of_calls++;
```

6

LISTING 6.9   continued

```
11:     print "<h1>$num_of_calls. $txt</h1>";
12: }
13: numberedHeading("Widgets");
14: print("We build a fine range of widgets<p>");
15: numberedHeading("Doodads");
16: print("Finest in the world<p>");
17: ?>
18: </body>
19: </html>
```

FIGURE 6.5

Using the global *statement to keep track of the number of times a function has been called.*

This does the job. We declare a variable, $num_of_calls, in line 7, outside the function numberedHeading(). We make this variable available to the function with the global statement in line 9. You can see the output of Listing 6.9 in Figure 6.5.

Every time numberedHeading() is called, $num_of_calls is incremented (line 10). We can then print out a heading complete with a heading number.

This is not the most elegant solution, however. Functions that use the global statement cannot be read as standalone blocks of code. In reading or reusing them, we need to look out for the global variables that they manipulate.

This is where the static statement can be useful. If you declare a variable within a function in conjunction with the static statement, the variable remains local to the function. On the other hand, the function "remembers" the value of the variable from execution to execution. Listing 6.10 adapts the code from Listing 6.9 to use the static statement.

LISTING 6.10   Using the `static` Statement to Remember the Value of a Variable Between Function Calls

```
 1: <html>
 2: <head>
 3: <title>Listing 6.10</title>
 4: </head>
 5: <body>
 6: <?php
 7: function numberedHeading( $txt ) {
 8:     static $num_of_calls = 0;
 9:     $num_of_calls++;
10:     print "<h1>$num_of_calls. $txt</h1>";
11: }
12: numberedHeading("Widgets");
13: print("We build a fine range of widgets<p>");
14: numberedHeading("Doodads");
15: print("Finest in the world<p>");
16: ?>
17: </body>
18: </html>
```

numberedHeading() has become entirely self-contained. When we declare the $num_of _calls variable on line 8, we assign an initial value to it. This assignment is made when the function is first called on line 12. This initial assignment is ignored when the function is called a second time on line 14. Instead, the previous value of $num_of_calls is remembered. We can now paste the numberedHeading() function into other scripts without worrying about global variables. Although the output of Listing 6.10 is exactly the same as that for Listing 6.9, we have made the code more elegant.

More About Arguments

You've already seen how to pass arguments to functions, but there's more to cover yet. In this section, you'll look at a technique for giving your arguments default values and explore a method of passing variables by reference rather than by value. This means that the function is given an 'alias' to the original value rather than a copy of it.

Setting Default Values for Arguments

PHP gives you a nifty feature to help build flexible functions. Until now, we've said that some functions "demand" one or more arguments. By making some arguments optional, you can render your functions a little less autocratic.

6

Listing 6.11 creates a useful little function that wraps a string in an HTML font element. We want to give the user of the function the chance to change the font element's size attribute, so we demand a $size argument in addition to the string (line 7).

LISTING 6.11   A Function Requiring Two Arguments

```
 1: <html>
 2: <head>
 3: <title>Listing 6.11</title>
 4: </head>
 5: <body>
 6: <?php
 7: function fontWrap( $txt, $size ) {
 8:     print "<font size=\"$size\"
 9:         face=\"Helvetica,Arial,Sans-Serif\">
10:         $txt</font>";
11: }
12: fontWrap("A heading<br>",5);
13: fontWrap("some body text<br>",3);
14: fontWrap("some more body text<BR>",3);
15: fontWrap("yet more body text<BR>",3);
16: ?>
17: </body>
18: </html>
```

FIGURE 6.6

A function that formats and outputs strings.

You can see the output from the script in Listing 6.11 in Figure 6.6. Useful though this function is, we really only need to change the font size occasionally. Most of the time we default to 3. By assigning a value to an argument variable within the function definition's parentheses, we can make the $size argument optional. If the function call doesn't define an argument for this, the value we have assigned to the argument is used instead. Listing 6.12 uses this technique to make the $size argument optional.

LISTING 6.12   A Function with an Optional Argument

```
 1: <html>
 2: <head>
 3: <title>Listing 6.12</title>
 4: </head>
 5: <body>
 6: <?php
 7: function fontWrap( $txt, $size=3 ) {
 8:     print "<font size=\"$size\"
 9:         face=\"Helvetica,Arial,Sans-Serif\">
10:         $txt</font>";
11: }
12: fontWrap("A heading<br>",5);
13: fontWrap("some body text<br>");
14: fontWrap("some more body text<br>");
15: fontWrap("yet more body text<br>");
16: ?>
17: </body>
18: </html>
```

When the fontWrap() function is called with a second argument, as in line 12, this value is used to set the size attribute of the font element. When we omit this argument, as in lines 13, 14 and 15, the default value of 3 is used instead. You can create as many optional arguments as you want, but when you've given an argument a default value, all subsequent arguments should also be given defaults.

Passing References to Variables to Functions

When you pass arguments to functions they are stored as copies in parameter variables. Any changes made to these variables in the body of the function are local to that function and are not reflected beyond it. This is illustrated in Listing 6.13.

LISTING 6.13   Passing an Argument to a Function by Value

6

```
 1: <html>
 2: <head>
 3: <title>Listing 6.13</title>
 4: </head>
 5: <body>
 6: <?php
 7: function addFive( $num ) {
 8:     $num += 5;
 9: }
10: $orignum = 10;
11: addFive( $orignum );
12: print( $orignum );
```

LISTING 6.13   continued

```
13: ?>
14: </body>
15: </html>
```

The addFive() function accepts a single numeric value and adds 5 to it. It returns nothing. We assign a value to a variable $orignum in line 10, and then pass this variable to addFive() in line 11. A copy of the contents of $orignum is stored in the variable $num. Although we increment $num by 5, this has no effect on the value of $orignum. When we print $orignum, we find that its value is still 10. By default, variables passed to functions are passed by value. In other words, local copies of the values of the variables are made.

We can change this behavior by creating a reference to our original variable. You can think of a reference as a signpost that points to a variable. In working with the reference you are manipulating the value to which it points.

Listing 6.14 shows this technique in action. When you pass an argument to a function by reference, as in line 11, the contents of the variable you pass ($orignum) are accessed by the argument variable and manipulated within the function, rather than just a copy of the variable's value (10). Any changes made to an argument in these cases will change the value of the original variable. You can pass an argument by reference by adding an ampersand to the argument name in the function definition, as shown in line 7.

LISTING 6.14   Using a Function Definition to Pass an Argument to a Function by Reference

```
 1: <html>
 2: <head>
 3: <title>Listing 6.14</title>
 4: </head>
 5: <body>
 6: <?php
 7: function addFive( &$num ) {
 8:     $num += 5;
 9: }
10: $orignum = 10;
11: addFive( $orignum );
12: print( $orignum );
13: ?>
14: </body>
15: </html>
```

Until recently it was also usual to set up pass by reference from within the calling code rather than at the function declaration. This technique 'call-time pass-by-reference' involved prepending an ampersand to the variable in the function call rather than in the function declaration. This technique has been deprecated, and so should not be used.

If you are using library code that falls foul of this deprecation, you can temporarily suppress PHP's warning messages by setting the allow_call_time_pass_reference directive to on in your php.ini file.

Creating Anonymous Functions

It is possible to create functions 'on the fly' during script execution. Because such functions are not themselves given a name, but are stored in variables or passed to other functions, they are known as anonymous functions. PHP 4 provides the create_function() function for creating anonymous functions. create_function() requires two string arguments. The first argument should contain a comma delimited list of argument variables, exactly the same as the argument variables you would include in a standard function declaration. The second argument should contain our function body.

In Listing 6.15 we create a simple anonymous function to add two numbers together.

LISTING 6.15   A simple anonymous function

```
 1: <html>
 2: <head>
 3: <title>Listing 6.15</title>
 4: </head>
 5: <body>
 6: <?php
 7: $my_anon = create_function( '$a, $b', 'return $a+$b;' );
 8: print $my_anon( 3, 9 );
 9: // prints 12
10: ?>
11: </body>
12: </html>
```

6

Note that we used single quotes when passing arguments to create_function(). That saved us from having to escape the variable names within the arguments. We could have used double quotes but the function call would have been a little more involved:

```
$my_anon = create_function( "\$a, \$b", "return \$a+\$b;" );
```

So what use are anonymous functions? In practical terms you will probably only use them when built-in functions need to be passed as 'callback' functions. A callback function is generally written by the user and designed to be invoked (usually repeatedly) by the function to which it is passed. You will see examples of this in Hour 16, "Working With Data".

The second argument to `create_function()` is the function body. Don't forget to end the last statement in this string with a semi-colon. The interpreter will complain and your anonymous function will not be executed if you omit it.

Testing for Function Existence

We have seen that we do not always know that a function exists before we try to invoke it. If our code were to work with a function name stored in a variable, for example, it would be useful for us to be able to test whether or not the function exists before we attempt to call it. Furthermore, different builds of the PHP engine may include different functionality. If you are writing a script that may be run on multiple servers, you might want to check that key features are available. You might write code that will use MySQL if `mysql` functions are available, but simply log data to a text file otherwise.

You can use `function_exists()` to check for the availability of a function. `function_exists()` requires a string representing a function name. It will return `true` if the function can be located and `false` otherwise.

Listing 6.16 shows `function_exists()` in action, and illustrates some of the other topics we have covered in this chapter.

LISTING 6.16   Testing for a Function's Existence

```
 1: <html>
 2: <head>
 3: <title>Listing 6.16</title>
 4: </head>
 5: <body>
 6: <?php
 7:
 8: function tagWrap( $tag, $txt, $func="" ) {
 9:     if ( ! empty( $txt ) && function_exists( $func ) )
10:         $txt = $func( $txt );
11:     return "<$tag>$txt</$tag>\n";
12: }
```

LISTING 6.16 continued

```
13:
14: function underline( $txt ) {
15:     return "<u>$txt</u>";
16: }
17:
18: print tagWrap('b', 'make me bold');
19: // <b>make me bold</b>
20:
21: print tagWrap('i', 'underline me too', "underline");
22: // <i><u>underline me too</u></i>
23:
24: print tagWrap('i', 'make me italic and quote me',
25:     create_function('$txt', 'return "&quot;$txt&quot;";'));
26: // <i>&quot;make me italic and quote me&quot;</i>
27:
28: ?>
29: </body>
30: </html>
```

We define two functions, tagWrap() (line 9) and underline() (line 14). TagWrap() accepts three strings, a tag, the text to be formatted, and an optional function name. It returns a formatted string. underline() requires a single argument, the text to be formatted, and returns the text wrapped in <u> tags.

When we first call tagWrap() on line 18 we pass it the character 'b' and the string 'make me bold'. Because we haven't passed a value for the function argument, the default value (an empty string) is used. On line 9 we check whether the $func variable contains characters and, if it is not empty we call function_exists() to check for a function by that name. Of course, the $func variable is empty, so we wrap the $txt variable in <b> tags on line 11 and return the result.

We next call tagWrap() on line 21 with the string 'i', some text, and a third argument: "underline". function_exists() does find a function called underline() (line 14), so this is called and passed the $txt argument variable before any further formatting is done. The result is an italicized, underlined string.

Finally, we call tagWrap() on line 24 with an anonymous function (which wraps text in quotation entities). Of course, it would be quicker for us to simply add the entities to the text to be transformed ourselves, but this does illustrate the point that function_exists() works as well on anonymous functions as it does on strings representing function names.

6

Summary

In this hour, you learned about functions and how to deploy them. You learned how to define and pass arguments to a function. You learned how to use the `global` and `static` statements. You learned how to pass references to functions and how to create default values for function arguments. Finally, you learned how to create anonymous functions and to test for function existence.

Q&A

Q **Apart from the `global` keyword, is there any way that a function can access and change global variables?**

A You can also access global variables anywhere in your scripts with a built-in associative array called `$GLOBALS`. To access a global variable called `$test` within a function, you could reference it as `$GLOBALS['test']`. You can learn more about associative arrays in the next hour.

You can also change global variables from within a function if it has been passed in by reference.

Q **Can you include a function call within a string, as you can with a variable?**

A No. You must call functions outside quotation marks.

Workshop

Quiz

1. True or False: If a function doesn't require an argument, you can omit the parentheses in the function call.

2. How do you return a value from a function?

3. What would the following code fragment print to the browser?

```
$number = 50;

function tenTimes() {
      $number = $number * 10;
}

tenTimes();
print $number;
```

4. What would the following code fragment print to the browser?

```
$number = 50;

function tenTimes() {
    global $number;
    $number = $number * 10;
}

tenTimes();
print $number;
```

5. What would the following code fragment print to the browser?

```
$number = 50;

function tenTimes( $n ) {
    $n = $n * 10;
}

tenTimes( $number );
print $number;
```

6. What would the following code fragment print to the browser?

```
$number = 50;

function tenTimes( &$n ) {
    $n = $n * 10;
}

tenTimes( $number );
print $number;
```

Quiz Answers

1. The statement is false. You must always include the parentheses in your function calls, whether you are passing arguments to the function or not.

2. You must use the return keyword.

3. It would print 50. The tenTimes() function has no access to the global $number variable. When it is called, it will manipulate its own local $number variable.

4. It would print 500. We have used the global statement, which gives the tenTimes() function access to the $number variable.

5. It would print 50. When we pass an argument to the tenTimes() function, it is passed by value. In other words, a copy is placed in the parameter variable $n. Any changes we make to $n have no effect on the $number variable.

6

6. It would print 500. By adding the ampersand to the parameter variable $n, we ensure that this argument is passed by reference. $n and $number point to the same value, so any changes to $n will be reflected when you access $number.

Activities

1. Create a function that accepts four string variables and returns a string that contains an HTML table element, enclosing each of the variables in its own cell.

Hour 7

Arrays

Arrays, and the tools to manipulate them, greatly enhance the scope and flexibility of PHP 4 scripts. After you've mastered arrays, you will be able to store and organize complex data structures.

This hour introduces arrays and some of the functions that help you work with them. In this hour, you will learn:

- What arrays are and how to create them
- How to access data from and about arrays
- How to access and sort the data contained in arrays
- How to create more flexible functions using arrays

What Is an Array?

You already know that a variable is a "bucket" in which you can temporarily store a value. By using variables, you can create a script that stores, processes, and outputs different information every time it is run. Unfortunately, you can only store one value at a time in a variable. Arrays are special variables that enable you to overcome this limitation. An array enables you to store as many values as you want in the same variable. Each value is indexed within the array by a number or a string. If a variable is a bucket, you can think of an array as a filing cabinet—a single container that can store many discrete items.

Of course, if you have five values to store, you could always define five variables. So, why use an array rather than a variable? First, an array is flexible. It can store two values or two hundred values without the need to define further variables. Second, an array allows you to work easily with all its items. You can loop through each item or pull one out at random. You can sort items numerically, alphabetically, or even according to a system of your own.

Each item in an array is commonly referred to as an element. Each element can be accessed directly via its index. An index to an array element can be either a number or a string.

By default, array elements are indexed by numbers, starting at 0. It's important to remember, therefore, that the index of the last element of a sequential numerically indexed array is always one less than the number of elements the array contains.

For example, Table 7.1 shows the elements in an array called users. Notice that the third element has an index of 2.

TABLE 7.1   The Elements in the users Array

Index Number	Value	Which Element?
0	Bert	First
1	Sharon	Second
2	Betty	Third
3	Harry	Fourth

Indexing arrays by string can be useful in cases where you need to store both names and values.

PHP 4 provides tools to access and manipulate arrays indexed by both name and number. Some of these are covered in this hour, and others will be covered in Hour 16, "Working with Data."

Creating Arrays

By default, arrays are lists of values indexed by number. Values can be assigned to an array in two ways: with the array() construct or directly using the array operator [ ]. You'll meet both of these in the next two sections.

Defining Arrays with the `array()` Construct

The `array()` construct is useful when you want to assign multiple values to an array at one time. Let's define an array called $users and assign four strings to it:

```
$users = array("Bert", "Sharon", "Betty", "Harry" );
```

You can now access the third element in the $user array by using the index "2":

```
print $users[2];
```

This would return the string `"Betty"`. The index of an array element is placed between square brackets directly after the array name. You can use this notation either to set or retrieve a value.

Remember that arrays are indexed from zero by default, so the index of any element in an sequentially indexed array always is one less than the element's place in the list.

Defining or Adding to Arrays with the Array Identifier

You can create a new array (or add to an existing one) by using the array identifier in conjunction with the array name. The array identifier is a set of square brackets with no index number or name inside it.

Let's re-create our $users array in this way:

```
$users[] = " Bert";
$users[] = " Sharon";
$users[] = " Betty";
$users[] = " Harry";
```

Notice that we didn't need to place any numbers between the square brackets. PHP 4 automatically takes care of the index number, which saves you from having to work out which is the next available slot.

We could have added numbers if we wanted, and the result would have been exactly the same. It's not advisable to do this, though. Take a look at the following code:

```
$users[0] = " Bert";
$users[200] = "Sharon";
```

The array has only two elements, but the index of the final element is 200. PHP 4 will not initialize the intervening elements. This could lead to confusion when attempting to access elements in the array. On the other hand, there may be circumstances in which you will want to use arbitrary index numbers in your array.

7

In addition to creating arrays, you can use the array identifier to add new values onto the end of an existing array. In the following code, we define an array with the `array()` construct and use the array identifier to add a new element:

```
$users = array ("Bert", " Sharon", "Betty", "Harry" );
$users[] = "Sally";
```

Associative Arrays

Numerically indexed arrays are useful for storing values in the order they were added or according to a sort pattern. Sometimes, though, you need to access elements in an array by name. An associative array is indexed with strings between the square brackets rather than numbers. Imagine an address book. Which would be easier, indexing the "name" field as 4 or as "name"?

Once again, you can define an associative array using either `array()` or the array operator `[]`.

> The division between an associative array and a numerically indexed array is not absolute in PHP. They are not separate types as arrays and hashes are in Perl. It is a good idea, nevertheless, to treat them separately. Each demands different strategies for access and manipulation.

Defining Associative Arrays with the `array()` Construct

To define an associative array with the `array()` construct, you must define both the key and value for each element. The following code creates an associative array called `$character` with four elements:

```
$character = array (
          "name" => "bob",
          "occupation" => "superhero",
          "age" => 30,
          "special power" => "x-ray vision"
          );
```

We can now access any of the fields of $character:

```
print $character['age'];
```

The keys in an associative array are strings, but in its default error reporting state the engine won't complain if array keys aren't quoted. For this reason, array keys were not quoted in the previous edition of this book.

This is not good practice, however. If your error reporting is set to a higher than standard level, the engine will complain every time an unquoted associative array key is met. Even worse, if an array key happens to coincide with a constant, the value of the constant will be substituted for the key as typed.

You should enclose an associative array key with quotation marks when the key in question is a string literal.

```
print $character[age]; // wrong
print $character["age"]; // right
```

If the key is stored in a variable, you do not need to use quotation marks.

```
$agekey = "age";
print $character[$agekey]; // right
```

Directly Defining or Adding to an Associative Array

You can create or add a name/value pair to an associative array simply by assigning a value to a named element. In the following, we re-create our $character array by directly assigning a value to each key:

```
$character["name"] = "bob";
$character["occupation"] = "superhero";
$character["age"] = 30;
$character["special power"] = "x-ray vision";
```

Multidimensional Arrays

Until now, we've simply said that elements of arrays are values. In our $character array, three of the elements held strings, and one held an integer. The reality is a little more complex, however. In fact, an element of an array could be a value, an object, or even another array. A multidimensional array is an array of arrays. Imagine an array that stores an array in each of its elements. To access the third element of the second element, you would have to use two indices:

```
$array[1][2]
```

The fact that an array element can itself be an array enables you to create sophisticated data structures relatively easily. Listing 7.1 defines an array that has an associative array as each of its elements.

7

LISTING 7.1   Defining a Multidimensional Array

```
 1: <html>
 2: <head>
 3: <title>Listing 7.1</title>
 4: </head>
 5: <body>
 6: <?php
 7:
 8: $characters = array (
 9:             array (
10:                 "name"=> "bob",
11:                 "occupation" => "superhero",
12:                 "age" => 30,
13:                 "specialty" =>"x-ray vision"
14:             ),
15:             array (
16:                 "name" => "sally",
17:                 "occupation" => "superhero",
18:                 "age" => 24,
19:                 "specialty" => "superhuman strength"
20:             ),
21:             array (
22:                 "name" => "mary",
23:                 "occupation" => "arch villain",
24:                 "age" => 63,
25:                 "specialty" =>"nanotechnology"
26:             )
27:         );
28:
29: print $characters[0]['occupation'];
30: // prints "superhero"
31: ?>
32: </body>
33: </html>
```

Notice that we have nested array construct calls within an array construct call. At the first level, we define an array. For each of its elements, we define an associative array.

Accessing $characters[2], therefore, gives us access to the third associative array (beginning on line 21). in the top-level array (beginning on line 8).We can then go ahead and access any of the associative array's fields. $characters[2]['name'] will be "mary," and $characters[2]['age'] will be 63.

When this concept is clear, it will be easy to create complex combinations of associative and numerically indexed arrays.

Accessing Arrays

So far, you've seen the ways in which you can create and add to arrays. In this section, you will examine some of the tools that PHP 4 provides to allow you to acquire information about arrays and access their elements.

Getting the Size of an Array

You can access an element of an array by using its index:

```
print $user[4]
```

Because of the flexibility of arrays, however, you won't always know how many elements a particular array contains. That's where the count() function comes into play. count() returns the number of elements in an array. In the following code, we define a numerically indexed array and use count() to access its last element:

```
$users = array ("Bert", " Sharon", "Betty", "Harry" );
print $users[count($users)-1];
```

Notice that we subtract 1 from the value returned by count(). This is because count() returns the number of elements in an array, not the index of the last element.

Although arrays are indexed from zero by default, it is possible to change this. For the sake of clarity and consistency, however, this is not usually advisable.

Although count() will give you the size of an array, you can only use it to access the last element in the array if you are sure that array elements have been added consecutively. If we had initialized the $user array with values at arbitrary indeces,

```
$users[66] = "Bert";
$users[100] = "Sharon";
$users[556] = "Betty";
$users[703] - "Harry";
```

count() would not be of any use in finding the final element. The array still only contains 4 elements, but there is no element indexed by 3. If you are not certain that your array is consecutively indexed, you can use the end() function to retrieve the final element in the array. end() requires an array as its only argument. It will return the given array's last element. The following statement will print the final element in the $users array no matter how it was initialized.

```
print end($users);
```

7

Looping through an Array

There are many ways of looping through each element of an array. For these examples, you'll use PHP's powerful `foreach` statement. You will examine some other methods in Hour 16, "Working with Data."

In the context of numerically indexed arrays, you would use a `foreach` statement like this:

```
foreach( $array as $temp ) {
    //...
}
```

where `$array` is the array you want to loop through, and `$temp` is a variable in which you will temporarily store each element.

In the following code, we define a numerically indexed array and use `foreach` to access each of its elements in turn:

```
$users = array ("Bert", "Sharon", "Betty", "Harry" );
foreach ( $users as $val ) {
    print "$val<br>";
    }
```

You can see the output from this code fragment in Figure 7.1.

FIGURE 7.1

Looping through an array.

The value of each element is temporarily placed in the variable `$val`, which we then print to the browser. If you are moving to PHP 4 from Perl, be aware of a significant difference in the behavior of `foreach`. Changing the value of the temporary variable in a Perl `foreach` loop changes the corresponding element in the array. Changing the temporary variable in the preceding example would have no effect on the `$users` array. You will look at a way of using `foreach` to change the values of a numerically indexed array in Hour 16.

Looping through an Associative Array

To access both the keys and values of an associative array, you need to alter the use of foreach slightly.

In the context of associative arrays, you would use a foreach statement like this:

```
foreach( $array as $key=>$value ) {
    //...
}
```

where $array is the array we are looping through, $key is a variable that temporarily holds each key, and $value is a variable that temporarily holds each value.

Listing 7.2 creates an associative array and accesses each key and value in turn.

LISTING 7.2   Looping Through an Associative Array with foreach

```
 1: <html>
 2: <head>
 3: <title>Listing 7.2</title>
 4: </head>
 5: <body>
 6: <?php
 7: $character = array (
 8:                 "name" => "bob",
 9:                 "occupation" => "superhero",
10:                 "age" => 30,
11:                 "special power" => "x-ray vision"
12:                 );
13: foreach ( $character as $key=>$val ) {
14:     print "$key = $val<br>";
15: }
16:
17: ?>
18: </body>
19: </html>
```

The array is created on line 7. We use the foreach statement on line 13 to loop through the character array. Each key is placed in a variable called $key and each value placed in a variable called $val. They are printed on line 14. You can see the output from Listing 7.2 in Figure 7.2.

7

FIGURE 7.2

Looping through an associative array.

Outputting a Multidimensional Array

You can now combine these techniques to output the multidimensional array created in Listing 7.1. Listing 7.3 defines a similar array and uses foreach to loop through each of its elements.

LISTING 7.3   Looping Through a Multidimensional Array

```
 1: <html>
 2: <head>
 3: <title>Listing 7.3</title>
 4: </head>
 5: <body>
 6: <?php
 7: $characters = array (
 8:         array (
 9:             "name"=> "bob",
10:             "occupation" => "superhero",
11:             "age" => 30,
12:             "specialty" =>"x-ray vision"
13:         ),
14:         array (
15:             "name" => "sally",
16:             "occupation" => "superhero",
17:             "age" => 24,
18:             "specialty" => "superhuman strength"
19:         ),
20:         array (
21:             "name" => "mary",
22:             "occupation" => "arch villain",
23:             "age" => 63,
24:             "specialty" =>"nanotechnology"
25:         )
```

LISTING 7.3 continued

```
26:         );
27:
28: foreach ( $characters as $val ) {
29:     foreach ( $val as $key=>$final_val ) {
30:         print "$key: $final_val<br>";
31:     }
32:     print "<br>";
33: }
34:
35: ?>
36: </body>
37: </html>
```

FIGURE 7.3

Looping through an multidimensional array.

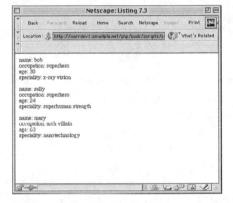

You can see the output from Listing 7.3 in Figure 7.3. We create two foreach loops (lines 28 and 29). The outer loop on line 28 accesses each element in the numerically indexed array $characters, placing each one in $val. Because $val itself then contains an associative array, we can loop through this on line 29, outputting each of its elements (temporarily stored in $key and $final_val) to the browser.

For this technique to work as expected, we need to make sure in advance that $val will always contain an array. To make this code a little more robust, we could use the function is_array() to test that $val. is_array() accepts a variable, returning true if the variable is an array, or false otherwise. Alternatively we could cast the $val variable created on line 29 to an array, thereby ensuring that it is always an array, whatever type it started out as.

```
$val = (array) $val;
```

7

Manipulating Arrays

You can now populate arrays and access their elements, but PHP 4 has functions to help you do much more than that with arrays. If you're used to Perl, you'll find some of these eerily familiar!

Joining Two Arrays with `array_merge()`

`array_merge()` accepts two or more arrays and returns a merged array combining all their elements. In the following example, we create two arrays, joining the second to the first, and loop through the resultant third array:

```
$first = array("a", "b", "c");
$second = array(1,2,3);
$third = array_merge( $first,  $second  );

foreach ( $third as $val ) {
    print "$val<BR>";
}
```

The $third array contains copies of all the elements of both the $first and $second arrays. The `foreach` statement prints this combined array ('a', 'b', 'c', 1, 2, 3) to the browser with a <BR> tag between each element. Remember that the arrays passed to `array_merge()` are not themselves transformed. If two arrays passed to `array_merge()` have elements with the same string index, then those of the first array will be overwritten by their namesakes in the second.

Adding Multiple Variables to an Array with `array_push()`

`array_push()` accepts an array and any number of further parameters, each of which is added to the array. Note that the `array_push()` function is unlike `array_merge()` in that the array passed in as the first argument is transformed. `array_push()` returns the total number of elements in the array. Let's create an array and add some more values to it:

```
$first = array("a", "b", "c");
$total = array_push( $first, 1, 2, 3  );

print "There are $total elements in \$first<P>";
foreach ( $first as $val ) {
    print "$val<BR>";
}
```

Because `array_push()` returns the total number of elements in the array it transforms, we are able to store this value (6) in a variable and print it to the browser. The $first array now contains its original elements as well the three integers we passed to the `array_ push()` function, all of these are printed to the browser within the `foreach` statement.

Notice that we used a backslash character when we printed the string "\$first". If you use a dollar sign followed by numbers and letters within a string, PHP will attempt to insert the value of a variable by that name. In the example above we wished to print the string '$first' rather than the value of the $first variable. To print the special character '$', therefore, we must precede it with a backslash. PHP will now print the character instead of interpreting it. This process is often referred to as "escaping" a character.

Perl users beware! If you're used to working with Perl's push(), you should note that if you pass a second array variable to array_push() it will be added as a single element, creating a multidimensional array. If you want to combine two arrays, use array_merge().

Removing the First Element of an Array with array_shift()

array_shift() removes and returns the first element of an array passed to it as an argument. In the following example, we use array_shift() in conjunction with a while loop. We test the value returned from count() to check whether the array still contains elements:

```php
<?php
$an_array = array("a", "b", "c");

while ( count( $an_array ) ) {
    $val = array_shift( $an_array );
    print "$val<BR>";
    print "there are ".count( $an_array )." elements in \$an_array <br>";
}
?>
```

You can see the output from this fragment of code in Figure 7.4.

7

`array_shift()` is useful when you need to create a queue and act on it until the queue is empty.

Slicing Arrays with `array_slice()`

`array_slice()` enables you to extract a chunk of an array. It accepts an array as an argument, a starting position (offset), and an (optional) length. If the length is omitted, `array_slice()` generously assumes that you want all elements from the starting position onward returned. `array_slice()` does not alter the array you pass to it. It returns a new array containing the elements you have requested.

In the following example, we create an array and extract a new three-element array from it:

```
$first = array("a", "b", "c", "d", "e", "f");
$second = array_slice($first, 2, 3);

foreach ( $second as $var ) {
    print "$var<br>";
}
```

This will print the elements 'c', 'd', and 'e', separating each by a `<BR>` tag. Notice that the offset is inclusive if we think of it as the index number of the first element we are requesting. In other words, the first element of the $second array is equivalent to `$first[2]`.

If we pass `array_slice()` an offset argument that is less than zero, the returned slice will begin that number of elements from the end of the given array.

If we pass `array_slice()` a length argument that is less than zero, the returned slice will contain all elements from the offset position to that number of elements from the end of the given array.

Sorting Arrays

Sorting is perhaps the greatest magic you can perform on an array. Thanks to the functions that PHP 4 offers to achieve just this, you can truly bring order from chaos. This section introduces some functions that allow you to sort both numerically indexed and associative arrays.

Sorting Numerically Indexed Arrays with `sort()`

`sort()` accepts an array as its argument and sorts it either alphabetically if any strings are present or numerically if all elements are numbers. The function doesn't return any data, transforming the array you pass it. Note that it differs from Perl's `sort()` function in this respect. The following fragment of code initializes an array of single character strings, sorts it and outputs the transformed array:

```
$an_array = array("x","a","f","c");
sort( $an_array );

foreach ( $an_array as $var ) {
    print "$var<BR>";
}
```

> Don't pass an associative array to `sort()`. You will find that the values are sorted as expected but that your keys have been lost—replaced by numerical indices that follow the sort order.

You can reverse sort a numerically indexed array by using `rsort()` in exactly the same way as `sort()`.

Sorting an Associative Array by Value with `asort()`

`asort()` accepts an associative array and sorts its values just as `sort()` does. However, it preserves the array's keys:

```
$first = array("first"=>5,"second"=>2,"third"=>1);
asort( $first );

foreach ( $first as $key => $val ) {
    print "$key = $val<BR>";
}
```

You can see the output from this fragment of code in Figure 7.5.

FIGURE 7.5

Sorting an associative array by its values with `asort()`.

You can reverse sort an associative array by value with `arsort()`.

Sorting an Associative Array by Key with `ksort()`

`ksort()` accepts an associative array and sorts its keys. Once again, the array you pass it will be transformed and nothing will be returned:

```
$first = array("x"=>5,"a"=>2,"f"=>1);
ksort( $first );

foreach ( $first as $key => $val ) {
    print "$key = $val<BR>";
}
```

You can see the output from this fragment of code in Figure 7.6.

FIGURE 7.6

Sorting an associative array by its keys with `ksort()`.

You can reverse sort an associative array by key with `krsort()`.

Functions Revisited

Now that we have covered arrays, we can examine some built-in functions that could help you make your own functions more flexible. If you have programmed in Perl before, you will know that you can easily create subroutines that accept a variable number of arguments. PHP 4 provides functions that make it just as easy.

Imagine that you have created a function that accepts three string arguments and returns a single string containing each of the provided arguments wrapped in an HTML table which includes the sum of the numbers in its final row.

```
function addNums( $num1, $num2 ) {
        $result = $num1 + $num2;
        $ret  = "<table border=\"1\">";
        $ret .= "<tr><td>number 1: </td><td>$num1  </td></tr>";
        $ret .= "<tr><td>number 2: </td><td>$num2  </td></tr>";
```

```
        $ret .= "<tr><td>result:    </td><td>$result</td></tr>";
        $ret .= "</table>";
        return $ret;
}

print addNums( 49, 60 );
```

This very simple function does its job well enough, but it is not very flexible. Imagine now that we are asked to amend the function to handle four arguments, or six, or, well, pretty much any number of integers. The simplest solution would be to ask that the calling code provides a single array containing all the numbers rather than two individual integers. This would mean that lots of code would have to be changed in the project as a whole as well as in the function. It would be better, then, to change the function to accept any number of integers.

The tools for this job are `func_num_args()` and `func_get_arg()`. `func_num_args()` returns the number of arguments that have been passed to the function, it does not itself require an argument. `func_get_arg()` requires an integer representing the index of the argument required, and will return its value. As with arrays, arguments are indexed from zero, so to get the first argument passed to a function you would use

```
func get arg(0);
```

It is your responsibility to check that the index you pass to `func_get_arg()` is within the number of arguments that were passed to the function you are testing. If the index is out of range `func_get_arg()` will return `false` and an error will be generated. Now we can rewrite our `addNums()` function:

```
function addNums() {
        $ret  = "<table border=\"1\">";
        for ( $x=0; $x<func_num_args(); $x++ ) {
                $arg = func_get_arg( $x );
                $result += $arg;
                $ret .= "<tr><td>number ".($x+1).": </td><td>$arg</td></tr>";
        }
        $ret .= "<tr><td>result: </td><td>$result</td></tr>";
        $ret .= "</table>";
        return $ret;
}

print addNums( 49, 60, 44, 22, 55 );
```

Notice that we do not provide any argument variables at all in the function declaration. Instead, we use a `for` loop to access each of the arguments in term. The loop will execute just the right number of times because our upper limit is set by `func_num_args()`.

7

So, given that we haven't actually used an array in this example, why is this section in a chapter on arrays? Firstly, the way that arguments to functions are indexed makes them somewhat array-like. Mainly though, we have yet to cover another function: func_get_args(). func_get_args() returns an array containing all the arguments passed to our function. This means that we can rewrite our example to work with a familiar foreach loop

```
function addNums() {
        $args = func_get_args();
        $ret  = "<table border=\"1\">";
        foreach( $args as $key => $val ) {
                $result += $val;
                $ret .= "<tr><td>number ".($key+1).": </td><td>$val</td></tr>";
        }
        $ret .= "<tr><td>result: </td><td>$result</td></tr>";
        $ret .= "</table>";
        return $ret;
}

print addNums( 49, 60, 44, 22, 55 );
```

Rather than access our arguments one at a time we simply decant the lot into an array variable called $args. Then it's simply a matter of looping through the array.

Summary

In this hour, you learned about arrays and some of the many tools that PHP 4 provides to work with them. You should now be able to create both numerically indexed and associative arrays, and output data from them using a foreach loop.

You should be able to combine arrays to create multidimensional arrays and loop through the information they contain. You learned how to manipulate arrays by adding or removing multiple elements and examined some of the techniques that PHP 4 makes available to sort arrays. Finally, you learned about functions that use array-like indexing to help make your own functions more flexible.

In Hour 8 we complete our tour of PHP fundamentals by taking a look at PHP's support for objects. PHP developers are increasingly creating libraries using classes and objects, so this is an area well worth studying.

Q&A

Q If the `foreach` statement was introduced with PHP 4, how did programmers using PHP3 iterate through arrays?

A The PHP3 technique for looping through an array involved a function called `each()`, which was used in conjunction with a `while` statement. You can read about this technique in Hour 16.

Q Are there any functions for manipulating arrays that we have not covered here?

A PHP 4 supports many array functions. You can read about some more of these in Hour 16 and find them all in the official PHP manual at `http://www.php.net/manual/ref.array.php`.

Q I can discover the number of elements in an array, so should I use a `for` statement to loop through an array?

A You should be cautious of this technique. You cannot be absolutely sure that the array you are reading is indexed by consecutively numbered keys.

Workshop

Quiz

1. What construct can you use to define an array?

2. What is the index number of the last element of the array defined below?
   ```
   $users = array("Harry", "Bob", "Sandy");
   ```

3. Without using a function, what would be the easiest way of adding the element "Susan" to the `$users` array defined previously?

4. Which function could you use to add the string "Susan" to the `$users` array?

5. How would you find out the number of elements in an array?

6. In PHP 4, what is the simplest way of looping through an array?

7. What function would you use to join two arrays?

8. How would you sort an associative array by its keys?

7

Quiz Answers

1. You can create an array with the array() construct.

2. The last element is $users[2]. Remember that arrays are indexed from 0 by default.

3. $users[] = "Susan";

4. array_push($users, "Susan");

5. You can count the number of elements in an array with the count() function.

6. You can loop through an array using the foreach statement.

7. You can merge arrays with the array_merge() function.

8. You can sort an associative array by its keys with the ksort() function.

Activities

1. Create a multidimensional array of movies organized by genre. This should take the form of an associative array with genres as keys ("SF", "Action", "Romance", and so on). Each of this associative array's elements should be an array containing movie names ("2001", "Alien", "Terminator", and so on).

2. Loop through the array you created in Activity 1, outputting each genre and its associated movies to the browser.

HOUR **8**

Objects

Object-oriented programming is dangerous. It changes the way you think about coding, and once the concepts have a hold on you, they don't let go. PHP, like Perl before it, has progressively incorporated more object-oriented aspects into its syntax and structure. With the advent of PHP 4, it becomes possible to use object-oriented code at the heart of your projects.

Throughout this hour, you'll take a tour of PHP's object-oriented features and apply them to some real-world code. In this hour, you will learn:

- What objects and classes are
- How to create classes and instantiate objects
- How to create and access properties and methods
- How to create classes that inherit functionality from others
- How to find out about objects in your code
- How to save objects to a string that can be stored in a file or database
- Some of the reasons why object-oriented programming can help you to organize your projects

What Is an Object?

An object is an enclosed bundle of variables and functions forged from a special template called a class. Objects hide a lot of their inner workings away from the code that uses them, providing instead easy interfaces through which you can send them orders and they can return information. These interfaces are special functions called methods. All the methods of an object have access to special variables called properties.

By defining a class, you lay down a set of characteristics. By creating objects of that type, you create entities that share these characteristics but might initialize them as different values. You might create an automobile class, for example. This class would have a color characteristic. All automobile objects would share the characteristic of color, but some would initialize it to "blue," others to "green," and so on.

Perhaps the greatest benefit of object-oriented code is its reusability. Because the classes used to create objects are self-enclosed, they can be easily pulled from one project and used in another. Additionally, it is possible to create child classes that inherit and override the characteristics of their parents. This technique can allow you to create progressively more complex and specialized objects that can draw on base functionality while adding more of their own.

Perhaps the best way to explain object-oriented programming is to do it.

Creating an Object

To create an object, you must first design the template from which it can be instantiated. This template is known as a class, and in PHP 4 it must be declared with the class keyword:

```
class first_class {
    // a very minimal class
}
```

The first_class class is the basis from which you can instantiate any number of first_class objects. To create an instance of an object, you must use the new statement:

```
$obj1 = new first_class();
$obj2 = new first_class();
print "\$obj1 is a ".gettype($obj1)."<br>";
print "\$obj2 is a ".gettype($obj2)."<br>";
```

You can test that $obj1 and $obj2 contain objects with PHP's gettype() function. gettype() accepts any variable and returns a string that should tell you what you are dealing with. In a loosely typed language like PHP, gettype() is useful when checking arguments sent to functions. In the previous code fragment, gettype() returns the string "object", which is then written to the browser.

So, you have confirmed that you have created two objects. Of course they're not very useful yet, but they help to make an important point. You can think of a class as a mold with which you can press as many objects as you want. Let's add some more features to the class to make your objects a little more interesting.

Object Properties

Objects have access to special variables called properties. These can be declared anywhere within the body of your class, but for the sake of clarity should be defined at the top. A property can be a value, an array, or even another object:

```
class first_class
    {
    var $name = "harry";
    }
```

Notice that we declared our variable with the var keyword. This is essential in the context of a class, and you will be rewarded with a parse error if you forget it. Now any first_class object that is created will contain a property called name with the value of "harry". You can access this property from outside the object and even change it:

```
class first_class {
    var $name = "harry";
}

$obj1 = new first_class();
$obj2 = new first_class();
$obj1->name = "bob";
print "$obj1->name<BR>";
print "$obj2->name<BR>";
```

The -> operator allows you to access or change the properties of an object. Although $obj1 and $obj2 were born with the name of "harry", we have helped $obj2 to change its mind by assigning the string "bob" to its name property, before using the -> operator once again to print each object's name property to the screen.

> Object-oriented languages, such as Java, demand that the programmer set a level of privacy for all properties and methods. This means that access can be limited to only those features needed to use the object effectively, and properties meant only for internal use can be safely tucked away. PHP has no such protection. You can access all the fields of an object, which can cause problems if a property isn't meant to be changed.

You can use objects to store information, but that makes them little more interesting than associative arrays. In the next section, you will look at object methods, and your objects can get a little more active.

Object Methods

A method is a function defined within a class. Every object instantiated from the class will have the method's functionality. Listing 8.1 adds a method to the `first_class` class (line 7).

LISTING 8.1   A Class with a Method

```
 1: <html>
 2: <head>
 3: <title>Listing 8.1</title>
 4: <body>
 5: <?php
 6: class first_class {
 7:     function sayHello() {
 8:         print "hello";
 9:     }
10: }
11:
12: $obj1 = new first_class();
13: $obj1->sayHello();
14: // outputs "hello"
15: ?>
16: </body>
17: </html>
```

As you can see, a method looks and behaves much like a normal function. A method is always defined within a class, however. You can call an object method using the -> operator. Importantly, methods have access to the class's member variables. You've already seen how to access a property from outside an object, but how does an object refer to itself? Find out in Listing 8.2.

LISTING 8.2   Accessing a Property from Within a Method

```
 1: <html>
 2: <head>
 3: <title>Listing 8.2</title>
 4: <body>
 5: <?php
 6: class first_class {
```

LISTING 8.2 continued

```
 7:     var $name="harry";
 8:     function sayHello() {
 9:         print "hello my name is $this->name<BR>";
10:     }
11: }
12:
13: $obj1 = new first_class();
14: $obj1->sayHello();
15: // outputs "hello my name is harry"
16: ?>
17: </body>
18: </html>
```

A class uses the special variable $this to refer to the currently instantiated object (line 9). You can think of it as a personal pronoun. Although you refer to an object by the handle you have assigned it to ($obj1, for example), an object must refer to itself by means of the $this variable. Combining the $this variable and the -> operator, you can access any property or method in a class from within the class itself.

Imagine that you want to assign a different value to the name property to every object of type first_class you create. You could do this by manually resetting the name property as you did earlier, or you could create a method to do it for you, as shown in Listing 8.3 on line 10.

LISTING 8.3 Changing the Value of a Property from Within a Method

```
 1: <html>
 2: <head>
 3: <title>Listing 8.3</title>
 4: </head>
 5: <body>
 6: <?php
 7: class first_class {
 8:     var $name="harry";
 9:
10:     function setName( $n ) {
11:         $this->name = $n;
12:     }
13:
14:     function sayHello() {
15:         print "hello my name is $this->name<BR>";
16:     }
17: }
18:
19:
```

LISTING 8.3   continued

```
20: $obj1 = new first_class();
21: $obj1->setName("william");
22: $obj1->sayHello();
23: // outputs "hello my name is william"
24: ?>
25: </body>
26: </html>
```

The name property of the object begins as "harry" (line 10), but after the object's
setName() method is called on line 21, it is changed to "william". Notice how the
object is capable of adjusting its own property. Notice also that you can pass arguments
to the method in exactly the same way as you would to a function.

We're still missing a trick here, however. If you create a method with exactly the same
name as the first_class class, it will automatically be called when a new object is
instantiated. In this way, you can give your objects arguments to process at the moment
you instantiate them. Objects can run code to initialize themselves based on these arguments or other factors. These special methods are called constructors. Listing 8.4 adds a
constructor to the first_class class.

LISTING 8.4   A Class with a Constructor

```
1: <html>
2: <head>
3: <title>Listing 8.4</title>
4: </head>
5: <body>
6: <?php
7: class first_class {
8:     var $name;
9:     function first_class( $n="anon" ) {
10:         $this->name = $n;
11:     }
12:     function sayHello() {
13:         print "hello my name is $this->name<BR>";
14:     }
15: }
16:
17: $obj1 = new first_class("bob");
18: $obj2 = new first_class("harry");
19: $obj1->sayHello();
20: // outputs "hello my name is bob"
21: $obj2->sayHello();
22: // outputs "hello my name is harry"
```

8

LISTING 8.4   continued

```
23: ?>
24: </body>
25: </html>
```

The `first_class()` constructor method on line 9 is automatically called when we instantiate a `first_class` object. We set up a default so that the string `"anon"` is assigned to the parameter if we don't include an argument when we create our object.

An Example

Let's bring these techniques together to create an example that might be a little more useful. We will create a class that can maintain a table of fields, organized in named columns. This data should be built up on a row-by-row basis, and a crude method should be included so that the data can be written to the browser. Neatly formatting the data is not necessary at this stage.

Defining the Class's Properties

First, we must decide what properties we need to store the data in. We will keep the column names in an array and the rows in a multidimensional array. We'll also store an integer so that we can easily keep track of the number of columns we're dealing with:

```
class Table {
    var $table_array = array();
    var $headers = array();
    var $cols;
}
```

Creating a Constructor

We need to get the names of the columns that we'll be working with straight away. We can do this in the constructor by asking for an array of strings as a parameter. Armed with this information, we can calculate the number of columns and assign the result to the `cols` property:

```
function Table( $headers ) {
    $this->headers = $headers;
    $this->cols = count ( $headers );
}
```

Assuming that the correct information is provided when the new `Table` object is created, we will know right away the number of columns we'll be storing and the name of each column. Because this information has been stored in properties, it will be available to all the object's methods.

The addRow() Method

The Table object accepts each row of data in the form of an array, assuming, of course, that this information is provided in the same order as that of the column names:

```
function addRow( $row ) {
    if ( count ($row) != $this->cols )
        return false;
    array_push($this->table_array, $row);
    return true;
}
```

The addRow() method expects an array, which is stored in a parameter variable called $row. We have stored the number of columns that the object expects to handle in the $cols property. We can check that the $row array parameter contains the right number of elements using the count() function. If it doesn't, a boolean false is returned.

We then use PHP's array_push() function to add the row array to the table_array property. array_push() accepts two arguments—an array to add to and the value to push onto it. If the second argument is itself an array, it will be added as a single element of the first array, creating a multidimensional array. In this way, we can build up an array of arrays.

The addRowAssocArray() Method

The addRow() method is fine as long as the elements of the array passed to it are ordered correctly. The addRowAssocArray() method allows for a little more flexibility. It expects an associative array. The keys for each value should match one of the header names we are storing in our headers property, or they'll be ignored:

```
function addRowAssocArray( $row_assoc ) {
    $row = array();
    foreach ( $this->headers as $header ) {
        if ( ! isset( $row_assoc[$header] ))
            $row_assoc[$header] =   "";
        $row[] = $row_assoc[$header];
    }
    array_push($this->table_array, $row);
    return true;
}
```

The associative array passed to addRowAssocArray() is stored in the parameter variable $row_assoc. We create an empty array called $row to store the values that we will eventually add to the table_array property. We loop through the headers array to check that a value corresponding to each string exists in the $row_assoc array. To do this, we use the PHP 4 function isset(), which expects any variable as its argument. It returns true if the variable passed to it has been set and `false` otherwise. We pass `isset()` the element in the `$row_assoc` array whose key is the current value in the headers property we are looping through. If no element indexed by that string exists in `$row_assoc`, we go ahead and create one with the value of an empty string. We can then continue to build up our `$row` array, adding to it the element in `$row_assoc` indexed by the current string in the headers array. By the time we have finished looping through the `headers` array property, `$row` contains an ordered copy of the values passed to us in `$row_assoc`, with empty strings in place of any omissions.

We now have two simple methods to allow the addition of rows of data to a `Table` object's `table_array` property. All we need now is a way of outputting the data.

The `output()` Method

The `output()` method writes both the headers and the `table_array` array properties to the browser. This method is provided mainly for the purpose of debugging. You'll see a more satisfactory solution later in the hour.

```
function output() {
    print "<pre>";
    foreach ( $this->headers as $header )
        print "<B>$header</B>   ";
    print "\n";
    foreach ( $this->table_array as $y ) {
        foreach ( $y as $xcell )
            print "$xcell   ";
        print "\n";
    }
    print "</pre>";
}
```

This code fragment should be fairly self-explanatory. We loop first through the headers_ array property, writing each element to the screen. We then do the same for the `table_array` property. Because the `table_array` property is a two-dimensional array, each of its elements is itself an array that must be looped through within the main loop.

Bringing It All Together

Listing 8.5 includes the entire `Table` class, as well the code that instantiates a `Table` object and calls each of its methods.

LISTING 8.5   The `Table` Class

```
1: <html>
2: <head>
3: <title>Listing 8.5</title>
```

LISTING 8.5   continued

```
 4: </head>
 5: <body>
 6: <?php
 7: class Table {
 8:     var $table_array = array();
 9:     var $headers = array();
10:     var $cols;
11:     function Table( $headers ) {
12:         $this->headers = $headers;
13:         $this->cols = count ( $headers );
14:     }
15:
16:     function addRow( $row ) {
17:         if ( count ($row) != $this->cols )
18:             return false;
19:         array_push($this->table_array, $row);
20:         return true;
21:     }
22:
23:     function addRowAssocArray( $row_assoc ) {
24:         $row = array();
25:         foreach ( $this->headers as $header ) {
26:             if ( ! isset( $row_assoc[$header] ))
27:                 $row_assoc[$header] = "";
28:             $row[] = $row_assoc[$header];
29:         }
30:         array_push($this->table_array, $row);
31:         return true;
32:     }
33:
34:     function output() {
35:         print "<pre>";
36:         foreach ( $this->headers as $header )
37:             print "<B>$header</B>   ";
38:         print "\n";
39:         foreach ( $this->table_array as $y ) {
40:             foreach ( $y as $xcell )
41:                 print "$xcell   ";
42:             print "\n";
43:         }
44:         print "</pre>";
45:     }
46: }
47:
48: $test = new table( array("a","b","c") );
49: $test->addRow( array(1,2,3) );
50: $test->addRow( array(4,5,6) );
51: $test->addRowAssocArray( array ( b=>0, a=>6, c=>3 ) );
```

LISTING 8.5   continued

```
52: $test->output();
53: ?>
54: </body>
55: </html>
```

You can see the output of Listing 8.5 in Figure 8.1.

FIGURE 8.1

The Table *object in action.*

The output looks neat as long as the individual strings are the same length. This will change if we vary the length of any of the elements.

What's Missing?

Although this class will do a job effectively for us, with more time and space, we might have added some features and safeguards.

Because PHP is loosely typed, it is our responsibility to make sure that parameters passed to our methods are the type we are expecting. For this purpose, we can use the data functions covered in Hour 16, "Working with Data." We might also want to make the Table object a little more flexible, adding methods to sort the rows according to the values in any column before we output, for example.

Why a Class?

So, what's better about using an object to achieve this task than simply manipulating arrays ourselves as and when we need to? It certainly isn't efficiency. We've added overheads to the process of storing and retrieving information.

First, this code is reusable. It has a clear purpose—to represent data in a certain way, and we can now slot it into any project that needs data stored and output in this way.

Second, a Table object is active. We can ask it to output its data without bothering to write code to loop through its table_array property.

Third, we've built an interface to the object's functionality. If we decide later to optimize the code in the class, we can do so without disturbing the rest of the project, as long as the same methods remain, expecting the same arguments and returning the same data types.

Finally, we can build classes that inherit, extend, and override its functionality. This makes object-oriented code truly cool.

Inheritance

To create a class that inherits functionality from a parent class, we need to alter our class declaration slightly. Listing 8.6 returns to our simple example.

LISTING 8.6   Creating a Class That Inherits from Another

```
1: <html>
2: <head>
3: <title>Listing 8.6</title>
4: </head>
5: <body>
6: <?php
7: class first_class {
8:     var $name = "harry";
9:     function first_class( $n ) {
10:         $this->name = $n;
11:     }
12:     function sayHello() {
13:         print "Hello my name is $this->name<br>";
14:     }
15: }
16:
17: class second_class extends first_class {
18:
19: }
20:
21: $test = new second_class("son of harry");
22: $test->sayHello();
23: // outputs "Hello my name is son of harry"
24: ?>
25: </body>
26: </html>
```

In addition to the simple `first_class` class defined on line 7, we have created an even more basic `second_class` class on line 17. Notice the `extends` clause in the class declaration. This means that a `second_class` object inherits all the functionality laid down in the `first_class` class. Any `second_class` object will have a `sayHello()` method and a `name` property just as any `first_class` object would.

If that's not enough, there's even more magic to be found in Listing 8.6. Notice that we didn't define a constructor method for the `second_class` class. So, how was the `name` property changed from the default, `"harry"` to the value passed to the `second_class` class, `"son of harry"`? Because we didn't provide a constructor, the `first_class` class's constructor was automatically called.

 If a class extending another doesn't contain a constructor method, the parent class's constructor method will be called automatically when a child object is created. This feature is new in PHP 4.

Overriding the Method of a Parent Class

The `second_class` class currently creates objects that behave in exactly the same way as `first_class` objects. In object-oriented code, child classes can override the methods of their parents, allowing objects instantiated from them to behave differently, while otherwise retaining much of the same functionality. Listing 8.7 gives the `second_class` class its own `sayHello()` method.

LISTING 8.7   The Method of a Child Class Overriding That of Its Parent

```
 1: <html>
 2: <head>
 3: <title>Listing 8.7</title>
 4: </head>
 5: <body>
 6: <?php
 7: class first_class {
 8:     var $name = "harry";
 9:     function first_class( $n ) {
10:         $this->name = $n;
11:     }
12:     function sayHello() {
13:         print "Hello my name is $this->name<br>";
14:     }
15: }
16:
```

LISTING 8.7   continued

```
17: class second_class extends first_class {
18:     function sayHello() {
19:         print "I'm not going to tell you my name<br>";
20:     }
21: }
22:
23: $test = new second_class("son of harry");
24: $test->sayHello();
25: // outputs "I'm not going to tell you my name"
26: ?>
27: </body>
28: </html>
```

The sayHello() method in the second_class class (line 12) is called in preference to that in the parent class.

Calling an Overridden Method

Occasionally, you will want the functionality of a parent class's method, as well as the benefit of your own additions. Object-oriented programming allows you to have your cake and eat it too. In Listing 8.8, the second_class's sayHello() method calls the method in the first_class class that it has overridden.

LISTING 8.8   Calling an Overridden Method

```
 1: <html>
 2: <head>
 3: <title>Listing 8.8</title>
 4: </head>
 5: <body>
 6: <?php
 7: class first_class {
 8:     var $name = "harry";
 9:     function first_class( $n ) {
10:         $this->name = $n;
11:     }
12:     function sayHello() {
13:         print "Hello my name is $this->name<br>";
14:     }
15: }
16:
17: class second_class extends first_class {
18:     function sayHello() {
19:         print "I'm not going to tell you my name — ";
20:         first_class::sayHello();
```

LISTING 8.8   continued

```
21:      }
22: }
23:
24: $test = new second_class("son of harry");
25: $test->sayHello();
26: // outputs "I'm not going to tell you my name — Hello my name is son of
harry"
27: ?>
28: </body>
29: </html>
```

By using the syntax

```
parentclassname::methodname()
```

we can call any method that we have overridden. We demonstrate this on line 20. This syntax is new to PHP 4—the same code will result in a parse error with PHP3.

Inheritance: An Example

You've seen how one class can inherit, override, and extend the functionality of another. Now we can use some of these techniques to create a class that inherits from the Table class created in Listing 8.5. The new class will be called HTMLTable and will be designed to overcome the deficiencies of Table's output() method.

Defining HTMLTable's Properties

HTMLTable will format the data that it stores courtesy of Table's functionality using a standard HTML table. For this example, we will allow an HTMLTable's user to change the CELLPADDING argument of the TABLE element and the BGCOLOR argument of the TD element. A real-world example should allow for many more changes than this.

```
class HTMLTable extends Table {
    var $bgcolor;
    var $cellpadding = "2";
}
```

We have defined a new class and established that it will inherit from Table by using the extends clause. We create two properties, bgcolor and cellpadding, giving cellpadding a default value of 2.

Creating the Constructor

You have already seen that a parent class's constructor is called automatically if you don't define a constructor for a child class. In this case, however, we want to do more work with our constructor than has already been written for the Table class:

```
function HTMLTable( $headers, $bg="#ffffff" ) {
    Table::Table($headers);
    $this->bgcolor=$bg;
}
```

The HTMLTable constructor accepts an array of column names and a string. The string becomes our bgcolor property, and we give it a default value, making it an optional argument. We call the Table class's constructor, passing the $header array to it. Laziness is a virtue in programming, so we let the Table class's constructor do its thing and worry no more about it. We initialize the HTMLObject's bgcolor property.

If a child class is given a constructor method, the parent's constructor is no longer called implicitly. The child class's constructor must explicitly call that of its parent.

The setCellpadding() Method

A child class can of course create its own entirely new methods. setCellpadding() allows a user to change the cellpadding property from the default. Of course, it would be perfectly possible to set the cellpadding property directly from outside the object, but this is not good practice on the whole. As a rule of thumb, it is best to create methods that will change properties on behalf of an object's user. In a more complex version of this class, the setCellpadding() method might need to change other properties to reflect the change made to the cellpadding property. Unfortunately, there is no neat way of enforcing privacy in PHP 4.

```
function setCellpadding( $padding ) {
    $this->cellpadding = $padding;
}
```

The Output() Method

The Output() method completely overrides the equivalent method in the Table class. It outputs data according to exactly the same logic as its parent, adding HTML table formatting:

```
function output() {
    print "<table cellpadding=\"$this->cellpadding\" border=1>";
    foreach ( $this->headers as $header )
        print "<td bgcolor=\"$this->bgcolor\"><b>$header</b></td>";
    foreach ( $this->table_array as $row=>$cells ) {
        print "<tr>";
        foreach ( $cells as $cell )
            print "<td bgcolor=\"$this->bgcolor\">$cell</td>";
        print "</tr>";
    }
    print "</table>";
}
```

The output() method should be fairly clear if you understood the Table class's version. We loop through both the header and table_array arrays, outputting each to the browser. Crucially, though, we format the data into a table, using the cellpadding and bgcolor properties to change the spacing and color of the table that the end user sees.

The Table and HTMLTable Classes in Their Entirety

Listing 8.9 brings the entire Table and HTMLTable examples together. We also instantiate an HTMLTable object, change its cellpadding property, add some data, and call its output() method. In a real-world example, we would probably get our row data directly from a database.

LISTING 8.9   The Table and HTMLTable Classes

```
 1: <html>
 2: <head>
 3: <title>testing objects</title>
 4: </head>
 5: <body>
 6: <?php
 7: class Table {
 8:     var $table_array = array();
 9:     var $headers = array();
10:     var $cols;
11:     function Table( $headers ) {
12:         $this->headers = $headers;
13:         $this->cols = count ( $headers );
14:     }
15:
16:     function addRow( $row ) {
17:         if ( count ($row) != $this->cols )
18:             return false;
19:         array_push($this->table_array, $row);
20:         return true;
21:     }
```

LISTING 8.9   continued

```
22:
23:        function addRowAssocArray( $row_assoc ) {
24:            if ( count ($row_assoc) != $this->cols )
25:                return false;
26:            $row = array();
27:            foreach ( $this->headers as $header ) {
28:                if ( ! isset( $row_assoc[$header] ))
29:                    $row_assoc[$header] = " ";
30:                $row[] = $row_assoc[$header];
31:            }
32:            array_push($this->table_array, $row);
33:        }
34:
35:        function output() {
36:            print "<pre>";
37:            foreach ( $this->headers as $header )
38:                print "<B>$header</B>  ";
39:            print "\n";
40:            foreach ( $this->table_array as $y ) {
41:                foreach ( $y as $xcell )
42:                    print "$xcell   ";
43:                print "\n";
44:            }
45:            print "</pre>";
46:        }
47: }
48:
49: class HTMLTable extends Table {
50:        var $bgcolor;
51:        var $cellpadding = "2";
52:        function HTMLTable( $headers, $bg="#ffffff" ) {
53:            Table::Table($headers);
54:            $this->bgcolor=$bg;
55:        }
56:
57:        function setCellpadding( $padding ) {
58:            $this->cellpadding = $padding;
59:        }
60:        function output() {
61:            print "<table cellpadding=\"$this->cellpadding\" border=1>";
62:            foreach ( $this->headers as $header )
63:                print "<td bgcolor=\"$this->bgcolor\"><b>$header</b></td>";
64:            foreach ( $this->table_array as $row=>$cells ) {
65:                print "<tr>";
66:                foreach ( $cells as $cell )
67:                    print "<td bgcolor=\"$this->bgcolor\">$cell</td>";
68:                print "</tr>";
69:            }
```

LISTING 8.9   continued

```
70:        print "</table>";
71:    }
72: }
73: $test = new HTMLTable( array("a","b","c"), "#00FF00" );
74: $test->setCellpadding( 7 );
75: $test->addRow( array(1,2,3));
76: $test->addRow( array(4,5,6));
77: $test->addRowAssocArray( array ( b=>0, a=>6, c=>3 ));
78: $test->output();
79: ?>
80: </body>
81: </html>
```

You can see the output from Listing 8.9 in Figure 8.2.

FIGURE 8.2

The HTMLTable *object in action.*

Why Use Inheritance?

So, why did we split Table from HTMLTable? Surely we could have saved ourselves time and space by building HTML table capabilities into the Table class? The answer lies in flexibility.

Imagine that a client gave you the brief to create a class that can maintain a table of fields, organized in named columns. If you had built a monolithic class that collected and stored the data, customized HTML, and output the result to the browser, all would seem to be well.

If the same client came back to you and asked whether the code could be adapted additionally to write neatly formatted data to a text file, you could probably add some more methods and properties to make it do this too.

A week or so later, the client realizes that she would like the code to be able to send data out as an email, and while you're at it, the company intranet uses a subset of XML; could this be accommodated too? At this stage, including all the functionality in a single class is beginning to look a little unwieldy, and you would already be considering a complete rewrite of the code.

Let's try this scenario out with our `Table` and `HTMLTable` examples. We have already substantially separated formatting the data from acquiring and preparing it. When our client asks that the code should be capable of outputting to a file, we only need to create a new class that inherits from `Table`. Let's call it `FileTable`. We need make no changes at all to our existing code. The same would be true for `MailTable` and `XMLTable`. Figure 8.3 illustrates the relationship between these classes.

FIGURE 8.3

The relationship between the `Table` *class and multiple child classes.*

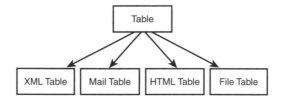

What's more, we know that *any* object that inherits from `Table` will have an `output()` method, so we can group a bunch of them into an array. When we're ready, we can loop through the lot, calling `output()` without worrying about the mechanics. From a single array of `Table`-derived objects, we can write emails, HTML, XML, or plain text, simply by repeatedly calling `output()`!

Testing Classes and Objects

We have already seen how we can use functions like `gettype()` to test data types. This is very useful to ensure that functions are supplied with the right arguments.

All objects belong to the "object" datatype, but we sometimes need more information than this.

Finding the Class of an Object

We have a class that simply outputs a string. Its output method, though, requires an `OutputFilter` object.

```
class SayHello {
        function print_hello( $filter_object ) {
                print $filter_object->filter( "hello you<br>" );
        }
}
```

8

```
class OutputFilter {
        function filter( $txt ) {
                return "<b>$txt</b>";
        }
}
$hello = new SayHello();
$hello->print_hello( new OutputFilter() );
```

As you can see, the sayHello class is betting that the object passed to it has a filter() method. Clearly, we are taking a lot on trust here. We can ensure that the variable passed to the print_hello() function is an OutputFilter object using the get_class() function. get_class() accepts an object and returns the name of its class (in lowercase letters).

```
class sayHello {
        function print_hello( $filter_object ) {
                if ( get_class( $filter_object ) != "outputfilter" )
                    return false;
                print $filter_object->filter( "hello you<br>" );
        }
}
```

Our print_hello() function can now be reasonably sure that it is dealing with an OutputFilter object.

Finding the Family of an Object

In the previous example, you may have wondered about the point of delegating the task of filtering output text to an object provided from outside the SayHello class. Imagine though that we have an entire family of OutputFilter objects.

```
class ItalicFilter extends OutputFilter {
        function filter( $txt ) {
                return "<i>$txt</i>";
        }
}

class UnderlineFilter extends OutputFilter {
        function filter( $txt ) {
                return "<u>$txt</u>";
        }
}

class BlinkFilter extends OutputFilter {
        function filter( $txt ) {
                return "<blink>$txt</blink>";
        }
}
```

As things stand we would not be able to pass a `BlinkFilter` object to `SayHello`. Wouldn't it be nice if we could make `SayHello` relax and accept any object that belongs to the `OutputFilter` family? After all, if it belongs to that family, it is absolutely guaranteed that an object will have a `filter()` method.

The `is_subclass_of()` function is just the thing for this. `is_subclass_of()` accepts an object and the name of the class from which the object should be derived. If the object is a subclass of the class in question the function returns `true`, otherwise it returns `false`. We can now add an additional check to our `print_hello()` method.

Listing 8.10 brings all our fragments together. Note the `print_hello()` method on line 3, and our use of `is_subclass_of()` on line 5.

LISTING 8.10   Testing the Class and Inheritance of an Object

```
1: <?php
2: class SayHello {
3:         function print_hello( $filter_object ) {
4:                 if ( get_class( $filter_object ) != "outputfilter" &&
5:                     ! is_subclass_of( $filter_object,"outputfilter")  )
6:                             return false;
7:                 print $filter_object->filter( "hello you<br>" );
8:         }
9: }
10:
11: class OutputFilter {
12:         function filter( $txt ) {
13:                 return "<b>$txt</b>";
14:         }
15: }
16:
17: class ItalicFilter extends OutputFilter {
18:         function filter( $txt ) {
19:                 return "<i>$txt</i>";
20:         }
21: }
22:
23: class UnderlineFilter extends OutputFilter {
24:         function filter( $txt ) {
25:                 return "<u>$txt</u>";
26:         }
27: }
28:
29: class BlinkFilter extends OutputFilter {
30:         function filter( $txt ) {
31:                 return "<blink>$txt</blink>";
32:         }
33: }
```

LISTING 8.10 continued

```
34:
35: $hello = new SayHello();
36: $hello->print_hello( new OutputFilter() );
37: $hello->print_hello( new ItalicFilter() );
38: $hello->print_hello( new UnderlineFilter() );
39: $hello->print_hello( new BlinkFilter() );
40: ?>
```

Checking for Class and Method Existence

As libraries grow, classes become increasingly interdependent. With this comes the possibility that a class might attempt to invoke another that is not available to the script. PHP provides you with functions for testing both class and method existence.

class_exists() requires a string representing a class name. If the user-defined class is found the function will return true. Otherwise it will return false. class_exists() is especially useful when using class names stored in strings.

```
if ( class_exists( $class_name ) )
    $obj = new $class_name( );
```

method_exists() requires two arguments: an object, and a string containing the name of the method you are checking for.

```
if ( method_exists( $filter_object, "filter" ) )
    print $filter_object->filter( "hello you<br>" );
```

Storing and Retrieving Objects

Usually you will separate your objects from data storage. In other words, you will use saved data to construct objects, and then when you are done, you will store the data again. Occasionally, though, you will want your object and data to persist intact. PHP provides two functions to help you with this.

To 'freeze-dry' an object you should pass it to the serialize() function. serialize() will produce a string that you can then store in a file, a database, or transmit to another script.

```
class apple {
    var $flavor="sweet";
}
$app = new apple();
$stored = serialize( $app );
print $stored;
// prints "O:5:"apple":1:{s:6:"flavor";s:5:"sweet";}"
```

The string produced by serialize() can be converted back into an object with the unserialize() function. If the original class is present at the time unserialize() is called, an exact copy of the original object will be produced.

```
$new_app = unserialize( $stored );
print $new_app->flavor;
// prints "sweet"
```

In some circumstances you will need your objects to clean up a little before storage. This is particularly important if an object has a database connection open, or is working with a file. By the same token, you may want your object to perform some sort on initialization when it is woken up. You can handle these needs by including two special methods in any object that might need to be serialized.

The __sleep() method will automatically be called by serialize() before it packs up the object. This allows you to perform any clean up operations you may need. In order for the serialization to work, your __sleep() method must return an array of the property names that you wish to be saved in the serialized string.

```
class apple {
    var $flavor="sweet";
    var $frozen = 0;
    function __sleep() {
        $this->frozen++;
        // any clean up stuff goes here
        return array_keys( get_object_vars( $this ) );
    }
}
$app = new apple();
$stored = serialize( $app );
print $stored;
// prints "0:5:"apple":2:{s:6:"flavor";s:5:"sweet";s:6:"frozen";i:1;}"
```

Notice the trick we used at the end of the __sleep() method in order to list the names of all the properties in the object. We used the built-in function get_object_vars(). This requires an object and returns an associative array of all the properties belonging to it. We pass the result of our call to get_object_vars() to the array_keys() function. array_keys() accepts an array (usually an associative array) and returns an array of its keys.

PHP also supports a special method called __wakeup(). If this is defined, it will automatically be called by unserialize(). This will enable you to resume database connections, or to provide any other initialization the object might need. We might add the following method to our apple class.

```
function __wakeup() {
    print "This apple has been frozen ".$this->frozen." time(s)";
    // any initialization stuff goes here
}
```

Now that we have added __wakeup() we can call unserialize()

```
$new_app = unserialize( $stored );
// prints "This apple has been frozen 1 time(s)"
```

Summary

It is not possible to introduce you to all the aspects of object-oriented programming in one short hour, but I hope I have introduced you to some of the possibilities.

The extent to which you use objects and classes in your projects is a matter of choice. It is likely that heavily object-oriented projects will be somewhat more resource-intensive at runtime than more traditional code. However, effective deployment of object-oriented techniques can significantly improve the flexibility and organization of your code.

Throughout this hour, you learned how to create classes and instantiate objects from them. You learned how to create and access properties and methods. You learned how to build new classes that inherit and override the features of other classes.

Finally you learned how to determine the class of an object and whether an object's class is a subclass of another.

Now that we have covered the core of the PHP language we are ready to move on and begin to explore some of its wider features. In the next hour we will look at PHP's support for handling HTML forms.

Q&A

Q **This hour introduced some unfamiliar concepts. Do I really need to understand object-oriented programming to become a good PHP programmer?**

A The short answer is no. Most PHP scripts use little or no object-oriented code at all. The object-oriented approach won't help you do things that you couldn't otherwise achieve. The benefits of object-oriented programming lie in the organization of your scripts, their reusability, and their extensibility.

Even if you decide not to produce object-oriented code, however, you may need to decipher third-party programs that contain classes. This hour should help you understand such code.

Q **I'm confused by the special variable `$this`.**

A Within a class, you sometimes need to call the class's methods or access its properties. By combining the `$this` variable and the `->` operator, you can do both. The `$this` variable is the handle a class is automatically given to refer to itself and to its components.

Workshop

Quiz

1. How would you declare a class called `emptyClass()` that has no methods or properties?

2. Given a class called `emptyClass()`, how would you create an object that is an instance of it?

3. How can you declare a property within a class?

4. How would you choose a name for a constructor method?

5. How would you create a constructor method in a class?

6. How would you create a regular method within a class?

7. How can you access and set properties or methods from within a class?

8. How would you access an object's properties and methods from outside the object's class?

9. What should you add to a class definition if you want to make it inherit functionality from another class?

Quiz Answers for Hour 8

1. You can declare a class with the `class` keyword:
```
class emptyClass {

}
```

2. You should use the `new` operator to instantiate an object:
```
$obj = new emptyClass();
```

3. You can declare a property using the `var` keyword:
```
class Point {
    // properties
    var $x = 0;
    var $y = 0;
}
```

4. You can't choose the name of a constructor. It must take the name of a class that contains it.

5. You can create a constructor by declaring a method that has the same name as the class that contains it. The constructor will be called automatically when an object is instantiated from the class.

```
class Point {
    // properties
    var $x = 0;
    var $y = 0;

    // constructor
    function Point( $x, $y ) {
        // set up code goes here
    }
}
```

6. A method is a function of any name declared within a class:

```
class Point {
    // properties
    var $x = 0;
    var $y = 0;

    // constructor
    function Point( $x, $y ) {
        // set up code goes here
    }

    // method
    function moveTo( $x, $y ) {

    }
}
```

7. Within a class, you can access a property or method by combining the $this variable and the -> operator:

```
class Point {
    // properties
    var $x = 0;
    var $y = 0;

    // constructor
    function Point( $x, $y ) {
        // calling a method
        $this->moveTo( $x, $y );
    }

    // method
    function moveTo( $x, $y ) {
```

```
            // setting properties
            $this->x = $x;
            $this->y = $y;
        }
    }
```

8. You can call an object's methods and access its properties using a reference to the object (usually stored in a variable) in conjunction with the `->` operator:

```
// instantiating an object
$p = new Point( 40, 60 );

// calling an object's method
$p->moveTo( 20, 200 );

// accessing an object's property
print $p->x;
```

9. For a class to inherit from another it must be declared with the `extends` keyword and the name of the class from which you want to inherit:

```
class funkyPoint extends Point {
}
```

Activities

1. Create a class called `baseCalc()` that stores two numbers as properties. Give it a `calculate()` method that prints the numbers to the browser.

2. Create a class called `addCalc()` that inherits its functionality from `baseCalc()`. Override the `calculate()` method so that the sum of the properties is printed to the browser.

3. Repeat activity 2, for a class called `minusCalc()`. Give `minusCalc()` a calculate method that subtracts the first property from the second, outputting the result to the browser.

PART III
Working with PHP

Hour

HOUR 9

Working with Forms

Until now, all examples in this book have been missing a crucial dimension.
You can set variables and arrays, create and call functions, and work with
objects. All this is meaningless if users can't reach into a language's environment to offer it information. In this hour, you will look at strategies for
acquiring and working with user input.

On the World Wide Web, HTML forms are the principal means by which
substantial amounts of information can pass from the user to the server. PHP
is designed to acquire and work with information submitted via HTML
forms.

In this hour, you will learn

- How to get and use predefined variables
- How to access information from form fields
- How to work with form elements that allow multiple selections
- How to create a single document that contains both an HTML form
  and the PHP code that handles its submission
- How to save state with hidden fields

- How to redirect the user to a new page
- How to build HTML forms that upload files and how to write the PHP code to handle them

Predefined Variables

Before you actually build a form and use it to acquire data, you need to make a small detour and look again at global variables. You first met these in Hour 6, "Functions." A global variable is any variable declared at the "top level" of a script—that is, declared outside a function. All functions are made available in a built-in associative array called $GLOBALS. This is useful in Listing 9.1 because we can take a peek at all our script's global variables with a single loop.

LISTING 9.1   Looping Through the $GLOBALS Array

```
 1: <html>
 2: <head>
 3: <title>Listing 9.1 Looping through the $GLOBALS array</title>
 4: </head>
 5: <body>
 6: <?php
 7: $user1 = "Bob";
 8: $user2 = "Harry";
 9: $user3 = "Mary";
10: foreach ( $GLOBALS as $key=>$value ) {
11:     print "\$GLOBALS[\"$key\"] == $value<br>";
12: }
13: ?>
14: </body>
15: </html>
```

We declare three variables (lines 7-9) and then loop through the built-in $GLOBALS associative array (lines 10 and 11), writing both array keys and values to the browser. In the output, we are able to locate the variables we defined, but we see an awful lot more besides these. PHP automatically defines global variables that describe both the server and client environments. According to your system, server, and configuration, the availability of these variables will vary, but they can be immensely useful. Table 9.1 lays out some common predefined variables. These can bc accessed as part of the $GLOBALS array, or directly.

TABLE 9.1 Some Predefined Variables

Variable	Contains	Example
$HTTP_USER_AGENT	The name and version of the client	Mozilla/4.6 (X11;I;Linux2.2.6-15apmac ppc)
$REMOTE_ADDR	The IP address of the client	158.152.55.35
$REQUEST_METHOD	Whether the request was GET or POST	POST
$QUERY_STRING	For GET requests, the encoded data send appended to the URL	name=matt&address= unknown
$REQUEST_URI	The full address of the request including query string	/matt/php-book/forms/ eg9.14.html? name=matt
$HTTP_REFERER	The address of the page from which the request was made	http://www.test. com/a_page.html

In addition to these header-oriented variables, PHP makes some other global variables available to you. The variable $GLOBALS["PHP_SELF"], for example, gives you the path to the script currently running. On my system this was as follows:

/dev/php24/ch9/listing9.1.php

This variable can also be directly accessed as the global variable $PHP_SELF.

A Script to Acquire User Input

For now, we'll keep our HTML separate from our PHP code. Listing 9.2 builds a simple HTML form.

LISTING 9.2 A Simple HTML Form

```
1: <html>
2: <head>
3: <title>Listing 9.2 A simple HTML form</title>
```

LISTING 9.2   continued

```
 4: </head>
 5: <body>
 6: <form action="listing9.3.php">
 7: <input type="text" name="user">
 8: <br>
 9: <textarea name="address" rows="5" cols="40">
10: </textarea>
11: <br>
12: <input type="submit" value="hit it!">
13: </form>
14: </body>
15: </html>
```

We define a form that contains a text field with the name "user" on line 7, a text area with the name "address" on line 9, and a submit button on line 12. It is beyond the remit of this book to cover HTML in detail. If you find the HTML in these examples hard going, take a look at *Sams Teach Yourself HTML in 24 Hours* or one of the numerous online HTML tutorials. The FORM element's ACTION argument points to a file called listing9.3.php, which processes the form information. Because we haven't added anything more than a filename to the ACTION argument, the file listing9.3.php should be in the same directory on the server as the document that contains our HTML.

Listing 9.3 creates the code that receives our users' input.

LISTING 9.3   Reading Input from the Form in Listing 9.2

```
 1: <html>
 2: <head>
 3: <title>Listing 9.3 Reading input from the form in Listing 9.2</title>
 4: </head>
 5: <body>
 6: <?php
 7: print "Welcome <b>$user</b><P>\n\n";
 8: print "Your address is:<P>\n\n<b>$address</b>";
 9: ?>
10: </body>
11: </html>
```

This is the first script in this book that is not designed to be called by hitting a link or typing directly into the browser's location field. We include the code from Listing 9.3 in a file called listing9.3.php. This file is called when a user submits the form defined in Listing 9.2.

In the code, we have accessed two variables, $user and $address. It should come as no surprise that these variables contain the values that the user added to the text field named "user" and the text area named "address". Forms in PHP really are as simple as that. Any information submitted by a user will be available to you in global variables that will have the same names as those of the form elements on an HTML page.

Accessing Form Input with User Defined Arrays

The examples so far enable us to gather information from HTML elements that submit a single value per element name. This leaves us with a problem when working with SELECT elements. These elements make it possible for the user to choose multiple items. If we name the SELECT element with a plain name

```
<select name="products" multiple>
```

the script that receives this data will only have access to a single value corresponding to this name. We can change this behavior by renaming any elements of this kind so that its name ends with an empty set of square brackets. We do this in Listing 9.4.

LISTING 9.4   An HTML Form Including a SELECT Element

```
1: <html>
2: <head>
3: <title>Listing 9.4 An HTML form including a SELECT element</title>
4: </head>
5: <body>
6: <form action="listing9.5.php" method="POST">
7: <input type="text" name="user">
8: <br>
9: <textarea name="address" rows="5" cols="40">
10: </textarea>
11: <br>
12: <select name="products[]" multiple>
13: <option>Sonic Screwdriver
14: <option>Tricorder
15: <option>ORAC AI
16: <option>HAL 2000
17: </select>
18: <br>
19: <input type="submit" value="hit it!">
20: </form>
21: </body>
22: </html>
```

In the script that processes the form input, we now find that input from the
"products[]" form element created on line 12 will be available in an array called
$products. products[] is a select element, and we offer the user multiple choices
using the option elements on lines 13 to 16. We demonstrate that the user's choices
are made available in an array in Listing 9.5.

LISTING 9.5   Reading Input from the Form in Listing 9.4

```
 1: <html>
 2: <head>
 3: <title>Listing 9.5 Reading input from the form in Listing 9.4</title>
 4: </head>
 5: <body>
 6: <?php
 7: print "Welcome <b>$user</b><p>\n\n";
 8: print "Your address is:<p>\n\n<b>$address</b><p>\n\n";
 9: print "Your product choices are:<p>\n\n";
10: if ( ! empty( $products ) ) {
11:     print "<ul>\n\n";
12:     foreach ( $products as $value ) {
13:         print "<li>$value<br>\n";
14:     }
15:     print "</ul>";
16: }
17: ?>
18: </body>
19: </html>
```

On line 7 we access the $user variable, which is derived from the user form element.
On line 10 we test for the $products variable. If it is present we loop through it on line
12, outputting each choice to browser on line 13.

Although this technique is particularly useful with the SELECT element, it will in fact
work with any form element at all. By giving a number of check boxes the same name,
for example, you can allow a user to choose many values within a single field name. As
long as the name you choose ends with empty square brackets, PHP compiles the user
input for this field into an array. We can replace the SELECT element from lines 12-17 in
Listing 9.4 with a series of check boxes to achieve exactly the same effect:

```
<input type="checkbox" name="products[]" value="Sonic Screwdriver">Sonic
Screwdriver<br>
<input type="checkbox" name="products[]" value="Tricorder">Tricorder<br>
<input type="checkbox" name="products[]" value="ORAC AI">ORAC AI<br>
<input type="checkbox" name="products[]" value="HAL 2000">HAL 2000<br>
```

In fact, we are not limited to numerically indexed arrays. We can place form input data into associative arrays, and even into multidimensional arrays. To keep our script's data neat, for example, we might wish to place all form input into an associative array called $form. We can do this very simply by constructing our form field names as if they were elements in an associative array (once again, omitting the dollar sign).

```
<input type="text" name="form[user]"><br>
<textarea name="form[address]" rows="5" cols="40">
</textarea>
```

Once submitted we will then be able access 'user' and 'address' as elements in the $form array.

```
print $form[user];
```

To construct a multidimensional array, we can simply extend the associative array naming convention to include another level

```
<input type="checkbox" name="form[products][]" value="Sonic Screwdriver">Sonic
Screwdriver<br>
<input type="checkbox" name="form[products][]" value="Tricorder">Tricorder<br>
<input type="checkbox" name="form[products][]" value="ORAC AI">ORAC AI<br>
<input type="checkbox" name="form[products][]" value="HAL 2000">HAL 2000<br>
```

When submitted, the $form[products] element should contain a numerically indexed array, populated according to the checkboxes clicked by the user.

Accessing Form Input with Built-In Arrays

The techniques you have looked at so far work well but can clutter up your scripts with global variables. To limit the number of globals in your script you can disable the feature that creates variables for each of your form fields by setting the register_globals directive to off in the php.ini file. We discussed the php.ini file in more detail in Hour 2, "Installing PHP".

That will clean up your namespace, but how can you access submitted form elements now?

The global variables that PHP 4 makes available provide the solution to this problem. According to whether or not a submitting form used the GET or POST method, you will have access to one or both of $HTTP_GET_VARS or $HTTP_POST_VARS. These are associative arrays that contain the name/value pairs submitted. Listing 9.6 takes advantage of this to list all the fields submitted from a form via a GET request.

LISTING 9.6　Reading Input from Any Form Using the $HTTP_GET_VARS array

```
 1: <html>
 2: <head>
 3: <title>Listing 9.6 Reading input from any form using the $HTTP_GET_VARS
➥array</title>
 4: </head>
 5: <body>
 6: <?php
 7: foreach ( $HTTP_GET_VARS as $key=>$value ) {
 8:     print "$key == $value<BR>\n";
 9: }
10: ?>
11: </body>
12: </html>
```

This code lists the names and values of all parameters passed to it via a GET transaction. We could also do the very same thing with the $HTTP_POST_VARS array.

Distinguishing Between GET and POST Transactions

To work flexibly, a script that can accept data from any source must be able to decide whether to read the $HTTP_GET_VARS or $HTTP_POST_VARS arrays. On most systems, you can discover whether you are dealing with a GET or POST transaction in the predefined variable $REQUEST_METHOD, which should contain the string "post" or "get". To be absolutely sure that your scripts are entirely portable, however, you can simply test both arrays for elements.

Listing 9.7 amends our form parser script to work with the correct array every time.

LISTING 9.7　Extracting Parameters from Either a <u>GET</u> or <u>POST</u> Request

```
 1: <html>
 2: <head>
 3: <title>Listing 9.7 Extracting parameters from
 4:       either a GET or POST request</title>
 5: </head>
 6: <body>
 7: <?php
 8: $PARAMS = ( count( $HTTP_POST_VARS ) )
 9:         ? $HTTP_POST_VARS : $HTTP_GET_VARS;
```

LISTING 9.7 continued

```
10:
11: foreach ( $PARAMS as $key=>$value ) {
12:    print "$key == $value<BR>\n";
13: }
14:
15: ?>
16: </body>
17: </html>
```

9

We use the ternary operator on line 8 to set a variable called $PARAMS. Using the built-in count() function, we first check whether the $HTTP_POST_VARS array contains elements. If the $HTTP_POST_VARS array is not empty, the ternary expression resolves to this; otherwise, it resolves to $HTTP_GET_VARS. We can now use the $PARAMS array throughout the rest of the script without worrying about whether it has been populated as the result of a GET or a POST request.

Combining HTML and PHP Code on a Single Page

In some circumstances, you may want to include form-parsing code on the same page as a hard-coded HTML form. Such a combination can be useful if you need to present the same form to the user more than once. You would have more flexibility if you were to write the entire page dynamically, of course, but you would miss out on one of the great strengths of PHP. The more standard HTML you can leave in your pages, the easier they will be for designers and page builders to amend without reference to you. You should avoid scattering substantial chunks of PHP code throughout your documents, however. This will make them hard to read and maintain. Where possible you should create functions that can be called from within your HTML code, and can be reused in other projects.

For the following examples, imagine that we are creating a site that teaches basic math to preschool children and have been asked to create a script that takes a number from form input and tells the user whether it is larger or smaller than a predefined integer.

Listing 9.8 creates the HTML. For this example, we need only a single text field, but even so, we'll include a little PHP.

LISTING 9.8   An HTML Form that Calls Itself

```
 1: <html>
 2: <head>
 3: <title>Listing 9.8 An HTML form that calls itself</title>
 4: </head>
 5: <body>
 6: <form method="POST">
 7: Type your guess here: <input type="text" name="guess">
 8: </form>
 9: </body>
10: </html>
```

Whatever we name the page that contains this form, the fact that we have left out the
action attribute of the form element will mean that the form will be submitted back to
its own url.

> Almost all browsers will submit a form to its current page if the form
> element's action attribute is omitted. You can, however, explicitly tell the
> browser to submit a form back to its own document by using the predefined
> $PHP_SELF variable.
>
> <form action="<?php print $PHP_SELF?>">

The script in Listing 9.8 will not produce any output. In Listing 9.9, we begin to build
up the PHP element of the page. First, we need to define the number that the user will
guess. In a fully working version, we would probably randomly generate this, but for
now we will keep it simple. We assign '42' to the $num_to_guess variable on line 2.
Next, we need to decide whether the form has been submitted; otherwise, we will
attempt to assess variables that have not yet been made available. We can test for submission by testing for the existence of the variable $guess. $guess will have been made
available as a global variable if your script has been sent a "guess" parameter. If this
isn't present, we can safely assume that the user has arrived at the page without submitting a form. If the value *is* present, we can go ahead and test the value it contains. The
test for the presence of the $guess variable takes place on line 4.

LISTING 9.9   A PHP Number Guessing Script

```
 1: <?php
 2: $num_to_guess = 42;
 3: $message = "";
 4: if ( ! isset( $guess ) )
```

LISTING 9.9 continued

```
 5:    $message = "Welcome to the guessing machine!";
 6: elseif   ( $guess > $num_to_guess )
 7:    $message = "$guess is too big! Try a smaller number";
 8: elseif   ( $guess < $num_to_guess )
 9:    $message = "$guess is too small! Try a larger number";
10: else // must be equivalent
11:    $message = "Well done!";
12:
13: ?>
14: <html>
15: <head>
16: <title>Listing 9.9 A PHP number guessing script</title>
17: </head>
18: <body>
19: <h1>
20: <?php print $message ?>
21: </h1>
22: <form method="POST">
23: Type your guess here: <input type="text" name="guess">
24: </form>
25: </body>
26: </html>
```

The bulk of this script consists of an if statement that determines which string to assign to the variable $message. If the $guess variable has not been set, we assume that the user has arrived for the first time and assign a welcome string to the $message variable on line 5.

Otherwise, we test the $guess variable against the number we have stored in $num_to_guess, and assign advice to $message accordingly. We test whether $guess is larger than $num_to_guess on line 6, and whether it is smaller than $num_to_guess on line 8. If $guess is neither larger nor smaller than $num_to_guess, we can assume that it is equivalent and assign a congratulations message to the variable (line 11). Now all we need to do is print the $message variable within the body of the HTML.

There are a few more additions yet, but you can probably see how easy it would be to hand this page over to a designer. He can make it beautiful without having to disturb the programming in any way.

Using Hidden Fields to Save State

The script in Listing 9.9 has no way of knowing how many guesses a user has made. We can use a hidden field to keep track of this. A hidden field behaves exactly the same as a text field, except that the user cannot see it, unless he views the HTML source of the document that contains it. Listing 9.10 adds a hidden field to the number guessing script and some PHP to work with it.

LISTING 9.10 Saving State with a Hidden Field

```
 1: <?php
 2: $num_to_guess = 42;
 3: $num_tries = ( isset( $num_tries ) ) ? ++$num_tries : 0;
 4: $message = "";
 5: if ( ! isset( $guess ) )
 6:    $message = "Welcome to the guessing machine!";
 7: elseif   ( $guess > $num_to_guess )
 8:    $message = "$guess is too big! Try a smaller number";
 9: elseif   ( $guess < $num_to_guess )
10:    $message = "$guess is too small! Try a larger number";
11: else // must be equivalent
12:    $message = "Well done!";
13:
14: $guess = (int) $guess;
15: ?>
16: <html>
17: <head>
18: <title>Listing 9.10 Saving state with a hidden field</title>
19: </head>
20: <body>
21: <h1>
22: <?php print $message ?>
23: </h1>
24: Guess number: <?php print $num_tries?>
25: <form method="POST">
26: Type your guess here:
27: <input type="text" name="guess" value="<?php print $guess?>">
28: <input type="hidden" name="num_tries" value="<?php print $num_tries?>">
29: </form>
30: </body>
31: </html>
```

The hidden field on line 28 is given the name "num_tries". We also use PHP to write its value. While we're at it, we do the same for the "guess" field on line 27, so that the user can always see his last guess. This technique is useful for scripts that parse user input. If we were to reject a form submission for some reason we can at least allow our user to edit his previous query.

9

When you need to output the value of an expression to the browser, you can of course use print() or echo(). When you are entering PHP mode explicitly to output such a value you can also take advantage of a special extension to PHP's short opening tags. If you add an equals (=) sign to the short PHP opening tag, the value contained will be printed to the browser. So

```
<? print $test;?>
```

is equivalent to

```
<?=$test?>
```

Within the main PHP code, we use a ternary operator to increment the $num_tries variable. If the $num_tries variable is set, we add one to it and reassign this incremented value; otherwise, we initialize $num_tries to 0. Within the body of the HTML, we can now report to the user how many guesses he has made.

Don't entirely trust hidden fields. You don't know where their values have been! This isn't to say that you shouldn't use them, just be aware that your users are capable of viewing and amending source code should they want to cheat your scripts.

Redirecting the User

Our simple script still has one major drawback. The form is rewritten whether or not the user guesses correctly. The fact that the HTML is hard-coded makes it difficult to avoid writing the entire page. We can, however, redirect the user to a congratulations page, thereby sidestepping the issue altogether.

When a server script communicates with a client, it must first send some headers that provide information about the document to follow. PHP usually handles this for you automatically, but you can choose to send your own header lines with PHP's header() function.

To call the header() function, you must be sure that no output has been sent to the browser. The first time that content is sent to the browser, PHP will send out headers and it will be too late for you to send your own. Any output from your document, even a line break or a space outside of your script tags will cause headers to be sent. If you intend to use the header() function in a script you must make certain that nothing precedes the PHP code that contains the function call. You should also check any libraries that you might be using.

Listing 9.11 shows typical headers sent to the browser by PHP.

LISTING 9.11   Typical Server Headers Sent from a PHP Script

```
1: HEAD /dev/php24/ch9/listing9.1.php HTTP/1.0
2:
3: HTTP/1.1 200 OK
4: Date: Mon, 24 Sep 2001 14:32:28 GMT
5: Server: Apache/1.3.12 Cobalt (Unix) PHP/4.0.6 mod_perl/1.24
6: X-Powered-By: PHP/4.0.6
7: Connection: close
8: Content-Type: text/html
```

You can see headers sent in response to a request by using a telnet client. Connect to a Web host at port 80 and then type

HEAD /path/to/file.html HTTP/1.0

followed by two returns. The headers should be displayed on your client.

By sending a "Location" header instead of PHP's default, you can cause the browser to be redirected to a new page:

header("Location: http://www.corrosive.co.uk");

Assuming that we have created a suitably upbeat page called "congrats.html", we can amend our number guessing script to redirect the user if she guesses correctly, as shown in Listing 9.12.

LISTING 9.12   Using header() to Send Raw Headers

```
 1: <?php
 2: $num_to_guess = 42;
 3: $message = "";
 4: $num_tries = ( isset( $num_tries ) ) ? ++$num_tries : 0;
 5: if ( ! isset( $guess ) )
 6:    $message = "Welcome to the guessing machine!";
 7: elseif   ( $guess > $num_to_guess )
 8:    $message = "$num is too big! Try a smaller number";
 9: elseif   ( $guess < $num_to_guess )
10:    $message = "$num is too small! Try a larger number";
```

LISTING 9.12 continued

```
11: else { // must be equivalent
12:    header( "Location: congrats.html" );
13:    exit;
14: }
15: $guess = (int)$guess;
16: ?>
17: <html>
18: <head>
19: <title>Listing 9.12 Using header() to send raw headers</title>
20: </head>
21: <body>
22: <h1>
23: <?php print $message ?>
24: </h1>
25: Guess number: <?php print $num_tries?>
26: <form method="POST">
27: Type your guess here:
28: <input type-"text" name="guess" value="<?php print $guess?>">
29: <input type="hidden" name="num_tries"
30:     value="<?php print $num_tries ?>">
31: </form>
32: </body>
33: </html>
```

The else clause of our if statement on line 11 now causes the browser to request
"congrats.html". We ensure that all output from the current page is aborted with the
exit statement on line 13, which immediately ends execution and output, whether
HTML or PHP.

File Upload Forms and Scripts

So far we've looked at simple form input. Browsers Netscape 2 or better and Internet
Explorer 4 or better all support file uploads, and so, of course, does PHP. In this section,
you will examine the features that PHP makes available to deal with this kind of input.

First, we need to create the HTML. HTML forms that include file upload fields must
include an ENCTYPE argument:

ENCTYPE="multipart/form-data"

PHP also works with an optional hidden field that can be inserted before the file upload
field. This should be called MAX_FILE_SIZE and should have a value representing the
maximum size in bytes of the file that you are willing to accept. This size cannot override the maximum size set in the upload_max_filesize field in your php.ini file that

defaults to 2 megabytes. The MAX_FILE_SIZE field will be obeyed at the browser's discretion, so you should rely upon the php.ini setting to cap unreasonable uploads. After the MAX_FILE_SIZE field has been entered, you are ready to add the upload field itself. This is simply an INPUT element with a TYPE argument of "file". You can give it any name you want. Listing 9.13 brings all this together into an HTML upload form.

LISTING 9.13   A Simple File Upload Form

```
 1: <html>
 2: <head>
 3: <title>Listing 9.13 A simple file upload form</title>
 4: </head>
 5: <body>
 6: <form enctype="multipart/form-data" method="POST">
 7: <input type="hidden" name="MAX_FILE_SIZE" value="51200">
 8: <input type="file" name="fupload"><br>
 9: <input type="submit" value="upload!">
10: </form>
11: </body>
12: </html>
```

Notice that once again this form calls the page that contains it. This is because we are going to add some PHP code to handle the uploaded file. We limited file uploads to 50KB on line 7 and named our upload field "fupload" on line 8. As you might expect, this name will soon become important.

When a file is successfully uploaded, it is given a unique name and stored in a temporary directory. On UNIX systems the default temporary directory is /tmp, but you can set it with the upload_tmp_dir directive in php.ini.

Information about the uploaded file will become available to you in the $HTTP_POST_FILES array which will be indexed by the names of each upload field in the form. The corresponding value for each of these keys will itself be an associative array. These fields are described in Table 9.2.

TABLE 9.2   File Upload Global Variables

Element	Contains	Example
$HTTP_POST_FILES['fupload']['name']	Name of uploaded file	test.gif
$HTTP_POST_FILES['fupload']['tmp_name']	Path to temporary file	/tmp/phprDfZvN
$HTTP_POST_FILES['fupload']['size']	Size (in bytes) of uploaded file	6835
$HTTP_POST_FILES['fupload']['type']	Mime type of uploaded file (where given by client)	image/gif

Armed with this information, we can write a quick and dirty script that displays information about uploaded files (see Listing 9.14). If the uploaded file is in GIF format, the script will even attempt to display it.

LISTING 9.14 A File Upload Script

```
 1: <html>
 2: <head>
 3: <title>Listing 9.14 A file upload script</title>
 4: </head>
 5: <?php
 6: $file_dir = "/home/corrdev/htdocs/php24/scrap/uploads";
 7: $file_url = "http://corros.colo.hosteurope.com/dev/php24/scrap/uploads";
 8:
 9: foreach( $HTTP_POST_FILES as $file_name => $file_array ) {
10:     print "path: ".$file_array['tmp_name']."<br>\n";
11:     print "name: ".$file_array['name']."<br>\n";
12:     print "type: ".$file_array['type']."<br>\n";
13:     print "size: ".$file_array['size']."<br>\n";
14:
15:     if ( is_uploaded_file( $file_array['tmp_name'] )
16:         && $file_array['type'] == "image/gif" ) {
17:         move_uploaded_file( $file_array['tmp_name'], "$file_dir/$file_name")
18:             or die ("Couldn't copy");
19:         print "<img src=\"$file_url/$file_name\"><p>\n\n";
20:     }
21: }
22:
23: ?>
24: <body>
25: <form enctype="multipart/form-data" method="POST">
26: <input type="hidden" name="MAX_FILE_SIZE" value="51200">
27: <input type="file" name="fupload"><br>
28: <input type="submit" value="Send file!">
29: </form>
30: </body>
31: </html>
```

In Listing 9.14, we first create the $file_dir and $file_url variables on lines 6 and 7 to store path information. Then we use a foreach statement to loop through every element in the $HTTP_POST_FILES array on line 9. This will be empty the first time the page is loaded, so nothing in the loop will be executed and our script will default to writing the upload form.

Once the form has been submitted the $HTTP_POST_FILES array will be populated. We are using a loop rather than an if statement in order to make our script capable of scaling to deal with multiple uploads on the same page. The foreach loop on line 9 stores the upload file's name in the $file_name variable and the file information in the $file_ array variable. We can then output the information we have about the upload.

To move the uploaded file to a directory within our web space, we need to run a couple of checks first. We are only dealing with GIF files in this example so test the mime type on line 16.

Also, use a new function to verify the file on line 15. The is_uploaded_file() function was re-introduced with PHP 4.03. It accepts a path to an uploaded file and returns true only if the file in question is a valid upload file. This function therefore enhances the security of your scripts.

Assuming that all is well, copy the file from its temporary home to a new directory on line 17. We use another function, move_uploaded_file() for this purpose. This will copy a file from one place to another, first performing the same security checks as those performed by is_uploaded_file(). move_uploaded_file() requires a path to the source file and a path to the destination. It will return true if the move was successful and false if the file was not a valid upload file, or if it could not be found.

Beware of the names of uploaded files. Operating systems such as MacOS and Windows are pretty relaxed when it comes to file naming, so expect uploaded files to come complete with spaces, quotation marks and all manner of other unexpected characters. It is therefore a good idea to filter file names. You can learn more about techniques for testing and checking strings in Hour 17 "Working with Strings" and Hour 18 "Working with Regular Expressions".

When we created the $file_dir variable on line 6 to store the file path to our upload directory, we also created a variable called $file_url on line 7 to store the URL of the same directory. We wrap up the script by writing an HTML image element that references our newly written image.

Summary

If you've kept up so far, things should be getting exciting now. You have the tools to create truly sophisticated and interactive environments. There are still a few things missing, of course. Now that you can get information from the user, it would be nice to be able to do something with it. Write it to a file, perhaps. That is the subject of the next hour.

Throughout this hour, you have learned how to work with the $GLOBALS associative array and acquire predefined variables, form input, and uploaded files using global variables. You have also learned how to send raw headers to the client to redirect a browser. You have learned how to acquire list information from form submissions and how to pass information from script call to script call using hidden fields.

Q&A

Q **Can I create arrays for values entered into elements other than select and check box fields?**

A Yes, in fact any element name ending with empty square brackets in a form will resolve to an array element when the form is submitted. You can use this fact to group values submitted from multiple fields of any type into an array.

Q **The header() function seems powerful. Will we look at HTTP headers in more detail?**

A We cover HTTP (Hypertext Transfer Protocol) in more detail in Hour 13, "Beyond the Box."

Q **Automatically converting form element names into variables seems a little risky. Can I disable this feature?**

A Yes, you can ensure that submitted form element names are not converted into global variables by setting the register_globals directive to "off" in the php.ini file.

Workshop

Quiz

1. Which predefined variable could you use to determine the IP address of a user?

2. Which predefined variable could you use to find out about the browser that called your script?

3. What should you name your form fields to access their submitted values from an array variable called $form_array?

4. Which built-in associative array contains all values submitted as part of a GET request?

5. Which built-in associative array contains all values submitted as part of a POST request?

6. What function would you use to redirect the browser to a new page? What string would you pass it?

7. How can you limit the size of a file that a user can submit via a particular upload form?

8. How can you set a limit to the size of upload files for all forms and scripts?

Quiz Answers

1. The variable $REMOTE_ADDR should store the user's IP address.

2. Browser type and version, as well as the user's operating system, are usually stored in a variable called $HTTP_USER_AGENT.

3. Creating multiple fields with the name form_array[] creates a populated array called $form_array when the form is submitted.

4. The built-in array $HTTP_GET_VARS contains all values submitted as part of a GET request.

5. The built-in array $HTTP_POST_VARS contains all values submitted as part of a POST request.

6. You can redirect a user by calling the header() function. You should pass it a Location header:

   ```
   header("Location: anotherpage.html");
   ```

7. When creating upload forms in PHP 4, you can include a hidden field called MAX_FILE_SIZE:

   ```
   <INPUT TYPE="hidden" NAME="MAX_FILE_SIZE" VALUE="51200">
   ```

8. The php.ini option upload_max_filesize determines the maximum size of an upload file that any script will accept. This is set to 2 megabytes by default.

Activities

1. Create a calculator script that allows the user to submit two numbers and choose an operation to perform on them (addition, multiplication, division, subtraction).

2. Use hidden fields with the script you created in activity 1 to store and display the number of requests that the user has submitted.

Hour 10

Working with Files

Testing, reading, and writing to files are staple activities for any full-featured programming language. PHP is no exception, providing you with functions that make the process straightforward. In this hour, you will learn

- How to include files in your documents
- How to test files and directories
- How to open a file before working with it
- How to read data from files
- How to write or append to a file
- How to lock a file
- How to work with directories

Including Files with `include()`

The `include()` statement enables you to incorporate files into your PHP documents. PHP code in these files can be executed as if it were part of the main document. This can be useful for including library code in multiple pages.

Having created a killer function, your only option until now would have been to paste it into every document that needs to use it. Of course, if you discover a bug, or want to add a feature, you will have to find every page that uses the function to make the change. The include() statement can save you from this chore. You can add the function to a single document and, at runtime, read this into any page that needs it. The include() statement requires a single argument, a relative path to the file to be included. Listing 10.1 creates a simple PHP script that uses include() to incorporate and output the contents of a file.

LISTING 10.1 Using include()

```
 1: <html>
 2: <head>
 3: <title>Listing 10.1 Using include()</title>
 4: </head>
 5: <body>
 6: <?php
 7: include("listing10.2.php");
 8: ?>
 9: </body>
10: </html>
```

The include() statement in Listing 10.1 incorporates the document listing10.2.php, the contents of which you can see in Listing 10.2. When run, Listing 10.1 outputs the string "I have been included!!", which may seem strange, given that we have included plain text within a block of PHP code. Shouldn't this cause an error? In fact, the contents of an included file are displayed as HTML by default. If you want to execute PHP code in an included file, you must enclose it in PHP start and end tags. In Listings 10.3 and 10.4, we amend the previous example so that code is executed in the included file.

LISTING 10.2 The File Included in Listing 10.1

```
1: I have been included!!
```

LISTING 10.3 Using the include() statement to Execute PHP in Another File

```
1: <html>
2: <head>
3: <title>Listing 10.3 Using include to execute PHP in another file</title>
4: </head>
5: <body>
6: <?php
```

LISTING 10.3   continued

```
7:  include("listing10.4.php");
8:  ?>
9:  </body>
10: </html>
```

LISTING 10.4   An Include File Containing PHP Code

```
1:  <?php
2:  print "I have been included!!<BR>";
3:  print "But now I can add up...  4 + 4 = ".(4 + 4);
4:  ?>
```

Returning a Value From an Included Document

Included files in PHP4 can return a value in the same way as functions do. As in a function, using the `return` statement ends the execution of code within the included file. Additionally, no further HTML will be included. In Listings 10.5 and 10.6, we include a file, assigning its return value to a variable.

LISTING 10.5   Using `include()` to Execute PHP and Assign the Return Value

```
1:  <html>
2:  <head>
3:  <title>Listing 10.5 Using include() to execute PHP and assign the return
➥value</title>
4:  </head>
5:  <body>
6:  <?php
7:  $addResult = include("listing10.6.php");
8:  print "The include file returned $addResult";
9:  ?>
10: </body>
11: </html>
```

LISTING 10.6   An Include File that Returns a Value

```
1:  <?php
2:  $retval = ( 4 + 4 );
3:  return $retval;
4:  ?>
5:  This HTML should never be displayed because it comes after a return
➥statement!
```

Returning values from included files would only work in PHP3 if the return statement was contained in a function. The code in Listing 10.6 would cause an error.

Using `include()` Within Control Structures

You can use an `include()` statement in a conditional statement, and the referenced file will only be read if the condition is met. The `include()` statement in the following fragment will never be called, for example

```
$test = false;
if ( $test ) {
    include( "a_file.txt" ); // won't be included
}
```

If you use an `include()` statement within a loop, it will be replaced with the contents of the referenced file each time the `include()` statement is called. This content will be executed for every call. Listing 10.7 illustrates this by using an `include()` statement in a `for` loop. The `include()` statement references a different file for each iteration.

LISTING 10.7 Using `include()` Within a Loop

```
1: <html>
2: <head>
3: <title>Listing 10.7 Using include() within a loop</title>
4: </head>
5: <body>
6: <?php
7: for ( $x = 1; $x<=3; $x++ ) {
8:     $incfile = "incfile$x".".txt";
9:     print "Attempting include $incfile<br>";
10:    include( "$incfile" );
11:    print "<p>";
12: }
13: ?>
14: </body>
15: </html>
```

When Listing 10.7 is run, it includes the content of three different files, `"incfile1.txt"`, `"incfile2.txt"`, and `"incfile3.txt"`. Assuming that each of these files simply contains a confirmation of its own name, the output should look something like this:

```
Attempting include incfile1.txt
This is incfile1.txt
```

```
Attempting include incfile2.txt
This is incfile2.txt

Attempting include incfile3.txt
This is incfile3.txt
```

include_once()

One of the problems caused by using multiple libraries within your code is the danger of calling include() twice on the same file. This can occur in larger projects when different library files call include() on a common file. Including the same file twice will often result in the repeated declaration of functions and classes, thereby causing the PHP engine great unhappiness.

The situation is saved by the include_once() statement. include_once() requires the path to an include file and will behave the same way as include() the first time it is called. If include_once() is called again for the same file during script execution, however, the file will *not* be included again.

This makes include_once() an excellent tool for the creation of reusable code libraries.

The include_path directive

Using include() and include_once() to access libraries can increase the flexibility and reusability of your projects. However there are still headaches to overcome. Portability in particular can suffer if you hardcode the paths to included files. Imagine that you create a 'lib' directory and reference it throughout your project:

```
include_once("/home/user/bob/htdocs/project4/lib/mylib.inc.php");
```

When you come to move your project to a new server you may find that you have to change a hundred or more include paths. You can escape this fate by setting the include_path directive in your php.ini file.

```
include_path   .:/home/user/bob/htdocs/project4/lib/
```

include_path can include as many directories as you want separated by colons (semicolons in Windows). You can then reference your library file only by its name

```
include_once("mylib.inc.php");
```

When you move your project you will only need to change the include_path directive.

10

PHP4 has a `require()` statement, which performs a similar function to `include()`. There is also a `require_once()` statement.

`require()` is executed regardless of a script's flow, and should not therefore be used as part conditional or loop structures.

A file included as a result of a `require()` statement cannot return a value.

Testing Files

Before you work with a file or directory, it is often a good idea to learn more about it. PHP4 provides many functions that help you to discover information about files on your system. This section briefly covers some of the most useful.

Checking for Existence with `file_exists()`

You can test for the existence of a file with the `file_exists()` function. This requires a string representing an absolute or relative path to a file that may or may not be there. If the file is found, it returns `true`; otherwise, it returns `false`.

```
if ( file_exists("test.txt") )
   print "The file exists!";
```

A File or a Directory?

You can confirm that the entity you are testing is a file, as opposed to a directory, with the `is_file()` function. `is_file()` requires the file path and returns a Boolean value:

```
if ( is_file( "test.txt" ) )
   print "test.txt is a file!";
```

Conversely, you might want to check that the entity you are testing is a directory. You can do this with the `is_dir()` function. `is_dir()` requires the path to the directory and returns a Boolean value:

```
if ( is_dir( "/tmp" ) )
   print "/tmp is a directory";
```

Checking the Status of a File

When you know that a file exists, and it is what you expect it to be, you can then find out some things that you can do with it. Typically, you might want to read, write to, or execute a file. PHP can help you with all of these.

is_readable() tells you whether you can read a file. On UNIX systems, you may be able to see a file but still be barred from reading its contents. is_readable() accepts the file path as a string and returns a Boolean value:

```
if ( is_readable( "test.txt" ) )
   print "test.txt is readable";
```

is_writable() tells you whether you can write to a file. Once again it requires the file path and returns a Boolean value:

```
if ( is_writable( "test.txt" ) )
   print "test.txt is writable";
```

is_executable() tells you whether you can run a file, relying on either the file's permissions or its extension depending on your platform. It accepts the file path and returns a Boolean value:

```
if ( is_executable( "test.txt" )
   print "test.txt is executable";
```

Determining File Size with `filesize()`

Given the path to a file, filesize() attempts to determine and return its size in bytes. It returns false if it encounters problems.

```
print "The size of test.txt is.. ";
print filesize( "test.txt" );
```

Getting Date Information About a File

Sometimes you will need to know when a file was last written to or accessed. PHP provides several functions that can provide this information.

You can find out when a file was last accessed with fileatime(). This function requires the file path and returns the date that the file was last accessed. To access a file means either to read or write to it. Dates are returned from all these functions in UNIX epoch format. That is, the number of seconds since 1 January 1970. In our examples, we use the date() function to translate this into human readable form. You learn more about date functions in Hour 15, "Working with Dates and Times."

```
$atime = fileatime( "test.txt" );
print "test.txt was last accessed on ";
print date("D d M Y g:i A", $atime);
// Sample output: Thu 13 Jan 2000 2:26 PM
```

You can discover the modification date of a file with the function filemtime(), which requires the file path and returns the date in UNIX epoch format. To modify a file means to change its contents in some way.

```
$mtime = filemtime( "test.txt" );
print "test.txt was last modified on ";
print date("D d M Y g:i A", $mtime);
// Sample output: Thu 13 Jan 2000 2:26 PM]
```

PHP also allows you to test the change time of a document with the filectime() function. On UNIX systems, the change time is set when a file's contents are modified or changes are made to its permissions or ownership. On other platforms, the filectime() returns the creation date.

```
$ctime = filectime( "test.txt" );
print "test.txt was last changed on ";
print date("D d M Y g:i A", $ctime);
// Sample output: Thu 13 Jan 2000 2:26 PM]
```

Creating a Function that Performs Multiple File Tests

Listing 10.8 creates a function that brings the file test functions we have looked at together into one script.

LISTING 10.8   A Function to Output the Results of Multiple File Tests

```
 1: <html>
 2: <head>
 3: <title>Listing 10.8 A function to output the results of multiple file
➥tests</title>
 4: </head>
 5: <body>
 6: <?php
 7: $file = "test.txt";
 8: outputFileTestInfo( $file );
 9:
10: function outputFileTestInfo( $f ) {
11:     if ( ! file_exists( $f ) ) {
12:         print "$f does not exist<BR>";
13:         return;
14:     }
15:     print "$f is ".(is_file( $f )?"":"not ")."a file<br>";
16:     print "$f is ".(is_dir( $f )?"":"not ")."a directory<br>";
17:     print "$f is ".(is_readable( $f )?"":"not ")."readable<br>";
18:     print "$f is ".(is_writable( $f )?"":"not ")."writable<br>";
19:     print "$f is ".(is_executable( $f )?"":"not ")."executable<br>";
20:     print "$f is ".(filesize($f))." bytes<br>";
21:     print "$f was accessed on ".date( "D d M Y g:i A", fileatime( $f )
➥)."<br>";
22:     print "$f was modified on ".date( "D d M Y g:i A", filemtime( $f )
)."<br>";
23:     print "$f was changed on ".date( "D d M Y g:i A", filectime( $f )
➥)."<br>";
```

LISTING 10.8   continued

```
24: }
25:
26: ?>
27: </body>
28: </html>
```

Notice that we have used the ternary operator as a compact way of working with some of these tests. Let's look at one of these, found in line 15, in more detail:

```
print "$f is ".(is_file( $f )?"":"not ")."a file<br>";
```

We use the is_file() function as the right-hand expression of the ternary operator. If this returns true, an empty string is returned. Otherwise, the string "not " is returned. The return value of the ternary expression is added to the string to be printed with concatenation operators. This statement could be made clearer but less compact, as follows:

```
$is_it = is_file( $f )?"":"not ";
print "$f is $isit a file";
```

We could, of course, be even clearer with an if statement, but imagine how large the function would become if we had used the following:

```
if ( is_file( $f ) )
    print "$fi is a file<br>";
else
    print "$f is not a file<br>";
```

Because the result of these three approaches is the same, the approach you take becomes broadly a matter of preference.

Creating and Deleting Files

If a file does not yet exist, you can create one with the touch() function. Given a string representing a file path, touch() attempts to create an empty file of that name. If the file already exists, the contents are not disturbed, but the modification date is updated to the time at which the function executed.

```
touch("myfile.txt");
```

You can remove an existing file with the unlink() function. Once again, unlink() accepts a file path:

```
unlink("myfile.txt");
```

10

All functions that create, delete, read, write, or modify files on Unix systems require that the correct file or directory permissions are set.

Opening a File for Writing, Reading, or Appending

Before you can work with a file, you must first open it for reading, writing, or both. PHP provides the `fopen()` function for this. `fopen()` requires a string containing the file path, followed by a string containing the mode in which the file is to be opened. The most common modes are read (`'r'`), write (`'w'`), and append (`'a'`). `fopen()` returns a file resource you will later use to work with the open file. To open a file for reading, you would use the following:

```
$fp = fopen( "test.txt", 'r' );
```

You would use the following to open a file for writing:

```
$fp = fopen( "test.txt", 'w' );
```

To open a file for appending (that is, to add data to the end of a file), you would use this:

```
$fp = fopen( "test.txt", 'a' );
```

`fopen()` returns `false` if the file cannot be opened for any reason. It is a good idea, therefore, to test the function's return value before proceeding to work with it. You can do this with an `if` statement:

```
if ( $fp = fopen( "test.txt", "w" ) ) {
    // do something with $fp
}
```

Or you can use a logical operator to end execution if an essential file can't be opened:

```
( $fp = fopen( "test.txt", "w" ) ) or die ("Couldn't open file, sorry");
```

If the `fopen()` function returns `true`, the rest of the expression won't be parsed, and the `die()` function (which writes a message to the browser and ends the script) will never be reached. Otherwise, the right-hand side of the `or` operator will be parsed, and the `die()` function will be called.

Assuming that all is well and you go on to work with your open file, you should remember to close it when you have finished. You can do this by calling `fclose()`, which requires the file resource returned from a successful `fopen()` call as its argument:

```
fclose( $fp );
```

Reading from Files

PHP provides a number of functions for reading data from files. These enable you to read by the byte, the line, or even the character.

Reading Lines from a File with `fgets()` and `feof()`

After you have opened a file for reading, you will often need to access it line by line. To read a line from an open file, you can use `fgets()`, which requires the file resource returned from `fopen()` as an argument. You must also pass it an integer as a second argument. This specifies the number of bytes the function should read if it doesn't first encounter a line end or the end of the file. The `fgets()` function reads the file until it reaches a newline character (`"\n"`), the number of bytes specified in the length argument, or the end of the file.

```
$line = fgets( $fp, 1024 ); // where $fp is the file resource returned by
fopen()
```

Although you can read lines with `fgets()`, you need some way of telling when you have reached the end of the file. The `feof()` function does this, returning `true` when the end of the file has been reached and `false` otherwise. Once again this function requires a file resource as its argument:

```
feof( $fp ); // where $fp is the file resource returned by fopen()
```

You now have enough information to read a file line by line, as shown in Listing 10.9.

LISTING 10.9   Opening and Reading a File Line by Line

```
 1: <html>
 2: <head>
 3: <title>Listing 10.9 Opening and reading a file line by line</title>
 4: </head>
 5: <body>
 6: <?php
 7: $filename = "test.txt";
 8: $fp = fopen( $filename, "r" ) or die("Couldn't open $filename");
 9: while ( ! feof( $fp ) ) {
10:     $line = fgets( $fp, 1024 );
11:     print "$line<br>";
12: }
13: ?>
14: </body>
15: </html>
```

10

We call `fopen()` on line 8 with the name of the file that we want to read, using the `or` operator to ensure that script execution ends if the file cannot be read. This usually occurs if the file does not exist, or (on a UNIX system) if the file's permissions won't allow the script read access to the file. The actual reading takes place in the `while` statement on line 9. The `while` statement's test expression calls `feof()` for each iteration, ending the loop when it returns `true`. In other words, the loop continues until the end of the file is reached. Within the code block, we use `fgets()` on line 10 to extract a line (or 1024 bytes) of the file. We assign the result to `$line` and then print it to the browser on line 11, appending a `<BR>` tag for the sake of readability.

Reading Arbitrary Amounts of Data from a File with `fread()`

Rather than reading text by the line, you can choose to read a file in arbitrarily defined chunks. The `fread()` function accepts a file resource as an argument, as well as the number of bytes you want to read. It returns the amount of data you have requested unless the end of the file is reached first.

```
$chunk = fread( $fp, 16 );
```

Listing 10.10 amends our previous example so that it reads data in chunks of 16 bytes rather than by the line.

LISTING 10.10   Reading a File with `fread()`

```
 1: <html>
 2: <head>
 3: <title>Listing 10.10 Reading a file with fread()</title>
 4: </head>
 5: <body>
 6: <?php
 7: $filename = "test.txt";
 8: $fp = fopen( $filename, "r" ) or die("Couldn't open $filename");
 9: while ( ! feof( $fp ) ) {
10:     $chunk = fread( $fp, 16 );
11:     print "$chunk<br>";
12: }
13: ?>
14: </body>
15: </html>
```

Although `fread()` allows you to define the amount of data acquired from a file, it won't let you decide the position from which the acquisition begins. You can set this manually with the `fseek()` function. `fseek()` enables you to change your current position within a file. It requires a file resource and an integer representing the offset from the start of the file (in bytes) to which you want to jump:

```
fseek( $fp, 64 );
```

Listing 10.11 uses fseek() and fread() to output the second half of a file to the browser.

LISTING 10.11   Moving Around a File with fseek()

```
 1: <html>
 2: <head>
 3: <title>Listing 10.11 Moving around a file with fseek()</title>
 4: </head>
 5: <body>
 6: <?php
 7: $filename = "test.txt";
 8: $fp = fopen( $filename, "r" ) or die("Couldn't open $filename");
 9: $fsize = filesize($filename);
10: $halfway = (int)( $fsize / 2 );
11: print "Halfway point: $halfway <BR>\n";
12: fseek( $fp, $halfway );
13: $chunk = fread( $fp, ($fsize - $halfway) );
14: print $chunk;
15: ?>
16: </body>
17: </html>
```

We calculate the halfway point of our file by dividing the return value of filesize() by 2 on line 10. We can then use this as the second argument to fseek() on line 12, jumping to the halfway point. Finally, we call fread() on line 13 to extract the second half of the file, printing the result to the browser.

Reading Characters from a File with fgetc()

fgetc() is similar to fgets() except that it returns only a single character from a file every time it is called. Because a character is always 1 byte in size, fgetc() doesn't require a length argument. You simply need to pass it a file resource:

```
$char = fgetc( $fp );
```

Listing 10.12 creates a loop that reads the file "test.txt" a character at a time, outputting each character to the browser on its own line.

10

LISTING 10.12 Moving Around a File with `fseek()`

```
 1: <html>
 2: <head>
 3: <title>Listing 10.12</title>
 4: </head>
 5: <body>
 6: <?php
 7: $filename = "test.txt";
 8: $fp = fopen( $filename, "r" ) or die("Couldn't open $filename");
 9: while ( ! feof( $fp ) ) {
10:     $char = fgetc( $fp );
11:     print "$char<BR>";
12: }
13: ?>
14: </body>
15: </html>
```

Writing or Appending to a File

The processes for writing to or appending to a file are the same. The difference lies in the `fopen()` call. When you write to a file, you should use the mode argument `"w"` when you call `fopen()`:

```
$fp = fopen( "test.txt", "w" );
```

All subsequent writing will occur from the start of the file. If the file doesn't already exist, it will be created. If the file already exists, any prior content will be destroyed and replaced by the data you write.

When you append to a file, you should use mode `"a"` in your `fopen()` call:

```
$fp = fopen( "test.txt", "a" );
```

Any subsequent writes to your file are added to the existing content.

Writing to a File with `fwrite()` or `fputs()`

`fwrite()` accepts a file resource and a string. It then writes the string to the file. `fputs()` works in exactly the same way.

```
fwrite( $fp, "hello world" );
fputs( $fp, "hello world" );
```

Writing to files is as straightforward as that. Listing 10.13 uses `fwrite()` to print to a file. We then append a further string to the same file using `fputs()`.

LISTING 10.13   Writing and Appending to a File

```
 1: <html>
 2: <head>
 3: <title>Listing 10.13 Writing and appending to a file</title>
 4: </head>
 5: <body>
 6: <?php
 7: $filename = "test.txt";
 8: print "Writing to $filename<br>";
 9: $fp = fopen( $filename, "w" ) or die("Couldn't open $filename");
10: fwrite( $fp, "Hello world\n" );
11: fclose( $fp );
12: print "Appending to $filename<br>";
13: $fp = fopen( $filename, "a" ) or die("Couldn't open $filename");
14: fputs( $fp, "And another thing\n" );
15: fclose( $fp );
16: ?>
17: </body>
18: </html>
```

10

Locking Files with `flock()`

The techniques you have learned for reading and amending files will work fine if you are only presenting your script to a single user. In the real world, however, you would expect many users to access your projects more or less at the same time. Imagine what would happen if two users were to execute a script that writes to one file at the same moment. The file will quickly become corrupt.

PHP 4 provides the `flock()` function to forestall this eventuality. `flock()` will lock a file to warn other process against writing to or reading from a file while the current process is working with it. `flock()` requires a valid file resource, and an integer representing the kind of lock you would like to set. PHP 4 provides predefined constants for each of the integers you are likely to need. In Table 10.1 we list three kinds of locks you can apply to a file.

TABLE 10.1   Integer arguments to the `flock()` function

Constant	Integer	Lock type	Description
LOCK_SH	1	Shared	Allows other processes to read the file but prevents writing (used when reading a file)
LOCK_EX	2	Exclusive	Prevents other processes from either reading from or writing to a file (used when writing to a file)
LOCK_UN	3	Release	Releases a shared or exclusive lock

You should call `flock()` directly after calling `fopen()` and then call it again to release the lock before closing the file.

```
$fp = fopen( "test.txt", "a" ) or die("couldn't open");
flock( $fp, LOCK_EX ); // exclusive lock
// write to the file
flock( $fp, LOCK_UN ); // release the lock
fclose( $fp );
```

> Locking with `flock()` is advisory. Only other scripts that use `flock()` will respect a lock that you set.

Working with Directories

Now that you can test, read, and write to files, turn your attention to directories. PHP provides many functions to work with directories. You will look at how to create, remove, and read them.

Creating Directories with `mkdir()`

`mkdir()` enables you to create a directory. `mkdir()` requires a string representing the path to the directory you want to create and an integer that should be an octal number representing the mode you want to set for the directory. You specify an octal (base 8) number with a leading 0. The mode argument will only have an effect on Unix systems. The mode should consist of three numbers between 0 and 7, representing permissions for the directory owner, group, and everyone, respectively. This function returns `true` if it successfully creates a directory, or `false` if it doesn't. If `mkdir()` fails, this will usually be because the containing directory has permissions that preclude processes with the script's user ID from writing. If you are not comfortable with setting Unix directory permissions, you should find that one of the examples below fits your needs. Unless you really need your directory to be world writable, you should probably use 0755, which allows the world to read your directory but not write to it.

```
mkdir( "testdir", 0777 ); // global read/write/execute permissions
mkdir( "testdir", 0755 ); // world and group: read/execute only
                          // owner: read/write/execute
```

Removing a Directory with `rmdir()`

`rmdir()` enables you to remove a directory from the file system, if the process running your script has the right to do so, and if the directory is empty. `rmdir()` requires only a string representing the path to the directory you want to create.

```
rmdir( "testdir" );
```

Opening a Directory for Reading with `opendir()`

Before you can read the contents of a directory, you must first obtain a directory resource. You can do this with the `opendir()` function. `opendir()` requires a string representing the path to the directory you want to open. `opendir()` returns a directory handle unless the directory is not present or readable, in which case it returns `false`.

```
$dh = opendir( "testdir" );
```

Reading the Contents of a Directory with `readdir()`

Just as you use `gets()` to read a line from a file, you can use `readdir()` to read a file or directory name from a directory. `readdir()` requires a directory handle and returns a string containing the item name. If the end of the directory has been reached, `readdir()` returns `false`. Note that `readdir()` returns only the names of its items, rather than full paths. Listing 10.14 shows the contents of a directory.

LISTING 10.14   Listing the Contents of a Directory with `readdir()`

```
 1: <html>
 2: <head>
 3: <title>Listing 10.14 Listing the contents
 4: of a directory with readdir()</title>
 5: </head>
 6: <body>
 7: <?php
 8: $dirname = ".";
 9: $dh = opendir( $dirname ) or die("couldn't open directory");
10:
11: while ( ! ( ( $file = readdir( $dh ) ) === false ) ) {
12:     if ( is_dir( "$dirname/$file" ) )
13:         print " ";
14:     print "$file<br>";
15: }
16: closedir( $dh );
17: ?>
18: </body>
19: </html>
```

We open our directory for reading with the `opendir()` function on line 9 and use a `while` statement to loop through each of its elements on line 11. We call `readdir()` as part of the `while` statement's test expression, assigning its result to the `$file` variable. Within the body of the `while` statement, we use the `$dirname` variable in conjunction with the `$file` variable to create a full file path, which we can then test on line 12. If the path leads to a directory, we print " " to the browser on line 13. Finally, we print the filename on line 15.

10

We have used a cautious construction in the test of the `while` statement. Most PHP programmers (myself included) would use something like the following:

```
while ( $file = readdir( $dh ) ) {
      print "$file<BR>\n";
}
```

The value returned by `readdir()` will be tested. Because any string other than "0" will resolve to `true`, there should be no problem. Imagine, however, a directory that contains four files, `"0"`, `"1"`, `"2"`, and `"3"`. The output from the preceding code on my system is as follows:

```
.
..
```

When the loop reaches the file named `"0"`, the string returned by `readdir()` resolves to `false`, causing the loop to end. The approach in Listing 10.14 uses === to check that the return value returned by `readdir()` is not *exactly* equivalent to false. 0 only *resolves* to false in the test, so we circumvent the problem.

Summary

In this hour, you learned how to use `include()` to incorporate files into your documents and to execute any PHP code contained in include files. You learned how to use some of PHP's file test functions. You explored functions for reading files by the line, by the character, or in arbitrary chunks. You learned how to write to files, either replacing or appending to existing content. Finally, you learned how to create, remove, and read directories.

Now that we can work with files, we can save and access substantial amounts of data. If we need to look up data from large files, however, our scripts will begin to slow down quite considerably. What we need is some kind of database. In the next hour we will look at PHP's DBA functions, which give us relatively fast access to data on our filesystem.

Q&A

Q Will the `include()` statement slow down my scripts?

A Because an included file must be opened and parsed by the engine, it will add some overhead. The benefits of reusable code libraries often outweigh the relatively low performance overhead, however.

Q Should I always end script execution if a file cannot be opened for writing or reading?

A You should always allow for this possibility. If your script absolutely depends on the file you want to work with, you might want to use the die() function, writing an informative error message to the browser. In less critical situations, you will still need to allow for the failure, perhaps adding it to a log file. You can read more about logging in Hour 22, "Debugging."

Workshop

Quiz

1. What functions could you use to add library code to the currently running script?
2. What function would you use to find out whether a file is present on your file system?
3. How would you determine the size of a file?
4. What function would you use to open a file for reading or writing?
5. What function would you use to read a line of data from a file?
6. How can you tell when you have reached the end of a file?
7. What function would you use to write a line of data to a file?
8. How would you open a directory for reading?
9. What function would you use to read the name of a directory item after you have opened a directory for reading?

Quiz Answers

1. You can use the require() or include() statements to incorporate PHP files into the current document. You could also use include_once() or require_once().
2. You can test for the existence of a file with the file_exists() function.
3. The filesize() function returns a file's size in bytes.
4. The fopen() function opens a file. It accepts the path to a file and a character representing the mode. It returns a file resource.
5. The fgets() function reads data up to the buffer size you pass it, the end of the line, or the end of the document, whichever comes first.
6. The feof() function returns true when the file resource it is passed has reached the end of the file.

10

7. You can write data to a file with the `fputs()` function.

8. The `opendir()` function enables you to open a directory for reading.

9. The `readdir()` function returns the name of a directory item from an opened directory.

Activities

1. Create a form that accepts a user's first and second name. Create a script that saves this data to a file.

2. Create a script that reads the data file you created in activity 1. As well as writing its contents to the browser (adding a `<BR>` tag to each line), print a summary that includes the number of lines in the file and the file's size.

HOUR 11

Working with the DBA Functions

If you don't have access to a SQL database such as MySQL or Oracle, you will almost certainly have a DBM-style database system available to you. DBM stands for database manager and DBM-like systems allow you to store and manipulate name/value pairs on your system.

DBA stands for Database abstraction layer, and these functions are designed to provide a common interface to a range of file-based database systems.

Although DBA functions do not offer you the power of a SQL database, they are flexible and easy to use. The fact that DBA functions stand above a range of common database systems, means that your code is likely to be portable even if the database files themselves might not be.

In this hour, you will learn:

- How to open a database
- How to add data to the database
- How to extract data from the database

- How to change and delete items
- How to store more complex kinds of data in DBM-style databases

Beneath the Abstraction

In order to use the DBA functions, you need to have one of the supported database systems installed. If you are running Linux, it is likely that you will have GDBM (the GNU Database Manager installed). For each system there is a corresponding compile option which should have been used when PHP was installed. You can see the supported databases and their corresponding compile options in Table 11.1.

TABLE 11.1   DBM systems supported by the DBA functions

Type	Compile option	Further information
cdbm	--with-cdbm	Read-only database system
db2	--with-db2	http://www.sleepycat.com/
db3	--with-db3	http://www.sleepycat.com/
dbm	--with-dbm	The original DBM. Deprecated
gdbm	--with-gdbm	GNU Database Manager
ndbm	--with-ndbm	Deprecated

If your system and PHP installation supports one of these systems you will be able to use the DBA functions with no problems. Note that support for the cdbm system (which is designed for fast access to static databases) is read-only.

Opening a Database

You can open a DBM-like database with the function dba_open(). This function requires three arguments: The path to the database file, a string containing the flags with which you want to open the database, and a string representing the database manager you want to work with (the 'type' column in Table 11.1). dba_open() returns a DBA resource that you can then pass to other DBA functions to access or manipulate your database. Because dba_open() involves reading from and writing to files, PHP must have permission to write to the directory that will contain your database.

The flags that you pass to dba_open() determine the way in which you can work with your database. They are listed in Table 11.2

TABLE 11.2 Flags for Use with dba_open()

Flag	Description
r	Opens database reading only
w	Opens database for writing and reading
c	Creates database (or open for read/write access if it exists)
n	Creates new database (truncate old version if it exists)

The following code fragment opens a database, creating a new one if it does not already exist:

```
$dbh = dba_open( "./data/products", "c", "gdbm" )
           or die( "Couldn't open Database" );
```

Notice that we use a die() statement to end script execution if our attempt to open the database fails.

When you finish working with a database, close it using the function dba_close(). This is because PHP locks a database that you are working with so that other processes cannot attempt to modify the data you are reading or writing. If you don't close the database, then other processes are going to have to wait longer before getting their bite of the cherry. dba_close() requires a valid DBA resource:

```
dba_close( $dbh );
```

Adding Data to the Database

You can add name/value pairs to your open database with the function dba_insert(), which requires the name of a key, the value that you want to store, and a valid DBA resource (as returned by dba_open()). This function returns true if all is well and false if an error occurs (such as an attempt to write to a database opened in read-only mode, or to overwrite an element of the same name). If the element you are attempting to insert already exists, then the data is not overwritten.

Listing 11.1 creates or opens a database called products and adds some data to it.

LISTING 11.1 Adding Items to a Database

```
1: <html>
2: <head>
3: <title>Listing 11.1 Adding items to a database</title>
4: </head>
5: <body>
```

LISTING **11.1**   continued

```
 6: Adding products now...
 7:
 8: <?php
 9: $dbh = dba_open( "./data/products", "c", "gdbm" )
10:              or die( "Couldn't open database" );
11:
12: dba_insert( "Sonic Screwdriver", "23.20", $dbh);
13: dba_insert( "Tricorder", "55.50", $dbh);
14: dba_insert( "ORAC AI", "2200.50", $dbh);
15: dba_insert( "HAL 2000", "4500.50", $dbh);
16:
17: dba_close( $dbh );
18: ?>
19: </body>
20: </html>
```

In order to add values to the database we use the dba_insert() functions (lines 12 to 15). All values are converted to strings when added to the database, so we add quotes to the product prices to maintain their format. We can treat these strings as doubles when we extract them from the database if we need to. We covered the double data type in Hour 4 "The Building Blocks." Notice also that we can use keys that have more than one word.

If we now attempt to call dba_insert() with the same key argument as one of the keys we have already used, dba_insert() returns false and makes no change to the database. In some circumstances, this might be what you want; but in others, you will want to amend existing data, as well as create new elements.

Amending Elements in a Database

You can amend an entry in a database with the dba_replace() function. dba_replace() requires the name of a key, the new value to add, and a valid DBA resource. It returns true if all goes well and false if an error occurs. Listing 11.2 amends the code in Listing 11.1 so that keys are added regardless of existence.

LISTING **11.2**   Adding or Changing Items belonging to a Database

```
1: <html>
2: <head>
3: <title>Listing 11.2 Adding or changing items
4:        belonging to database</title>
5: </head>
6: <body>
```

LISTING 11.2   continued

```
 7: Adding products now...
 8: <?php
 9: $dbh = dba_open( "./data/products", "c", "gdbm" )
10:             or die( "Couldn't open database" );
11: dba_replace( "Sonic Screwdriver", "25.20", $dbh );
12: dba_replace( "Tricorder", "56.50", $dbh );
13: dba_replace( "ORAC AI", "2209.50", $dbh );
14: dba_replace( "HAL 2000", "4535.50", $dbh );
15: dba_close( $dbh );
16: ?>
17: </body>
18: </html>
```

We have only had to change the function calls from dba_insert() to dba_replace() to change the functionality of the script.

Reading from a Database

Now that we can add data to our database, we need to find a way to fetch it. We can extract an individual element from the database with the dba_fetch() function. dba_fetch() requires the name of the element you want to access and a valid DBA resource. The function returns the value you are accessing as a string. So to access the price of the "Tricorder" item, we would use the following code:

```
$price = dba_fetch( "Tricorder", $dbh );
```

If the "Tricorder" element does not exist in the database, then dba_fetch() returns false.

You won't always know the names of all the keys in the database, however. What would you do if you needed to output every product and price to the browser without hard-coding the product names into your script? PHP provides a mechanism by which you can loop through every element in a database.

You can get the first key in a database with the dba_firstkey() function. This requires a DBA resource and returns the first key. Note that this won't necessarily be the first element that you added because DBM-like databases often maintain their own ordering systems. After you've retrieved the first key, you can access each subsequent key with the dba_nextkey() function. Once again dba_nextkey() requires a DBA resource and returns an element's key. By combining these functions with dba_fetch(), you can now list an entire database.

11

Listing 11.3 outputs the products database to the browser. We acquire the first key in the database on line 19 using the `dba_firstkey()` function. We then use a while loop on line 20 to work our way through all the elements in the database. Elements are acquired with the call to `dba_fetch()` on line 21. Once we have written the element to the browser we use `dba_nextkey()` on line 24 to acquire the next key and assign it to the `$key` variable. When there are no more keys to acquire, `dba_nextkey()` will return `false`, and the test expression on line 20 will halt the loop.

LISTING 11.3 Reading All Records from a Database

```
 1: <html>
 2: <head>
 3: <title>Listing 11.3 Reading all
 4:        records from a Database </title>
 5: </head>
 6: <body>
 7:    Here at the Impossible Gadget Shop
 8:    we're offering the following exciting
 9:    products:
10: <p>
11: <table border=1 cellpadding ="5">
12: <tr>
13: <td align="center"> <b>product</b></td>
14: <td align="center"> <b>price</b> </td>
15: </tr>
16: <?php
17: $dbh = dba_open( "./data/products", "c", "gdbm" )
18:               or die( "Couldn't open database" );
19: $key = dba_firstkey( $dbh );
20: while ( $key != false ) {
21:     $value = dba_fetch( $key, $dbh);
22:     print "<tr><td align = \"left\"> $key </td>";
23:     print "<td align = \"right\"> \$$value </td></tr>";
24:     $key = dba_nextkey( $dbh);
25: }
26: dba_close( $dbh );
27: ?>
28: </table>
29: </body>
30: </html>
```

Figure 11.1 shows the output from Listing 11.3.

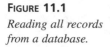

FIGURE 11.1

Reading all records from a database.

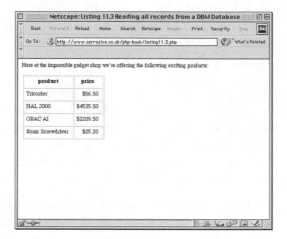

Determining Whether an Item Exists in a Database

Before reading or setting an element in a database, it is sometimes useful to know whether the element exists. You can do this with the dba_exists() function. dba_exists() requires the name of the element for which you are testing and a valid DBA resource. It returns true if the element exists.

```
if ( dba_exists("Tricorder", $dbh ) )
    print dba_fetch( "Tricorder", $dbh );
```

Deleting an Item from a Database

You can delete an item from a database using the dba_delete() function. dba_delete() requires the name of the element you want to remove from the database and a valid DBA resource. It returns true if the item was successfully deleted, and false if the element did not exist to be deleted.

```
dba_delete( "Tricorder", $dbh );
```

Adding Complex Data Structures to a Database

All data in a DBM-like database is extracted in string format, so you are limited to storing integers, strings, and doubles. Any other data type will be lost. Let's try to store an array, for example:

11

```
$array = array( 1, 2, 3, 4 );
$dbh = dba_open( "./data/test", "c", "gdbm" ) or die("Couldn't open test");
dba_insert("arraytest", $array, $dbh );
print gettype( dba_fetch("arraytest", $dbh) );
// prints "string"
```

We create an array and store it in the variable $array. We then open a database and attempt to insert an element called "arraytest", passing it the $array variable as the value. We then test the return type from dba_fetch() when attempting to access "arraytest" and ascertain that a string has been returned. In fact, if we printed the value stored in the "arraytest" record, we would get the string "Array". That would seem to wrap up any hopes for storing arrays and objects.

Fortunately, PHP provides a feature that allows you to "freeze-dry" values of any data type in string format. The data can then be stored in a database or file until it is needed. You can use this technique to store arrays and even objects in a database.

To convert the array in the previous example to a string, we must use the serialize() function. serialize() requires a value of any type and returns a string:

```
$array = array( 1, 2, 3, 4 );
print serialize( $array );
// prints a:4:{i:0;i:1;i:1;i:2;i:2;i:3;i:3;i:4;}
```

We can now store this string in the database. When we want to resurrect it, we can use the unserialize() function. unserialize() requires a serialized string and returns a value of the appropriate data type.

This allows you to store complex data structures within the relatively simple format allowed by DBM-like databases. Listing 11.4 serializes an associative array for each of the items in our list of products and adds the result to a database.

LISTING 11.4   Adding Complex Data to a Database

```
 1: <html>
 2: <head>
 3: <title>Listing 11.4 Adding complex data to a database</title>
 4: </head>
 5: <body>
 6: Adding complex data to database
 7: <?php
 8: $products = array(
 9:        "Sonic Screwdriver" => array( price=>"22.50",
10:                                      shipping=>"12.50",
11:                                      color=>"green" ),
12:        "Tricorder"         => array( price=>"55.50",
13:                                      shipping=>"7.50",
```

LISTING 11.4   continued

```
14:                                         color=>"red" ),
15:         "ORAC AI"          => array( price=>"2200.50",
16:                                         shipping=>"34.50",
17:                                         color=>"blue" ),
18:         "HAL 2000"         => array( price=>"4500.50",
19:                                         shipping=>"18.50",
20:                                         color=>"pink" )
21:         );
22: $dbh = dba_open( "./data/products2", "c", "gdbm" )
23:             or die( "Couldn't open database" );
24: while ( list ( $key, $value ) = each ( $products ) )
25:     dba_replace( $key,  serialize( $value ), $dbh );
26: dba_close( $dbh );
27: ?>
28: </body>
29: </html>
```

We build a multidimensional array beginning on line 8, containing the product names as keys and four arrays of product information as values. We then open the database on line 22 and loop through the array on line 24. For each element, we pass the product name and a serialized version of the product array to dba_replace() (line 25). We then close the database (line 26).

Listing 11.5 writes the code that extracts this data.

LISTING 11.5   Retrieving Serialized Data from a Database

```
 1: <html>
 2: <head>
 3: <title>Listing 11.5 Retrieving serialized
 4:        data from a database</title>
 5: </head>
 6: <body>
 7:     Here at the Impossible Gadget Shop
 8:     we're offering the following exciting
 9:     products:
10: <p>
11: <table border=1 cellpadding ="5">
12: <tr>
13: <td align="center"> <b>product</b></td>
14: <td align="center"> <b>color</b> </td>
15: <td align="center"> <b>shipping</b> </td>
16: <td align="center"> <b>price</b> </td>
17: </tr>
18: <?php
```

11

LISTING **11.5**   continued

```
19: $dbh = dba_open( "./data/products2", "c", "gdbm" )
20:            or die( "Couldn't open database" );
21: $key = dba_firstkey( $dbh );
22: while ( $key != false ) {
23:     $prodarray = unserialize( dba_fetch( $key, $dbh) );
24:     print "<tr><td align=\"left\"> $key </td>";
25:     print "<td align=\"left\">".$prodarray['color']." </td>\n";
26:     print "<td align=\"right\">\$".$prodarray['shipping']." </td>\n";
27:     print "<td align=\"right\">\$".$prodarray['price']." </td></tr>\n";
28:     $key = dba_nextkey( $dbh );
29: }
30: dba_close( $dbh );
31: ?>
32: </table>
33: </body>
34: </html>
```

Listing 11.5 is similar to the example in Listing 11.3. In this case though, we are displaying more fields. We open the database on line 19 and then use dba_firstkey() (line 21) and dba_nextkey() (line 28) to loop through each item in the database. We extract the value and use unserialize() to reconstruct the product array on line 23. It is then simple to print each element of the product array to the browser. Figure 11.2 shows the output from Listing 11.5.

FIGURE **11.2**

Retrieving serialized data from a database.

An Example

We now have enough information to build an example using some of the techniques discussed in this hour. Our brief is to build an administration page to enable a site editor to change the prices in the products database created in Listing 11.2. The administrator should also be able to remove elements from the database and add new ones. The page will not be hosted on a publicly available server, so security is not a problem for this project.

First, we must build a form that incorporates all the elements in the database. The user will be able to change any price using a text field and choose which items to delete using a check box. She will also have two text fields for adding a new item to the database. Listing 11.6 shows the code to create the form.

LISTING 11.6   Building an HTML Form Based on Content from a Database

```
 1: <?php
 2: $dbh = dba_open( "./data/products", "c", "gdbm" )
 3:              or die( "Couldn't open database" );
 4: ?>
 5: <html>
 6: <head>
 7: <title>Listing 11.6 Building an html form based
 8:        on content from a database</title>
 9: </head>
10: <body>
11: <form action="POST">
12: <table border="1">
13: <tr>
14: <td>delete</td>
15: <td>product</td>
16: <td>price</td>
17: </tr>
18: <?php
19: $key = dba_firstkey( $dbh );
20: while ( $key != false ) {
21:     $price = dba_fetch( $key,  $dbh );
22:     print "<tr><td><input type='checkbox' name=\"delete[]\" ";
23:     print "value=\"$key\"></td>";
24:     print "<td>$key</td>";
25:     print "<td> <input type=\"text\" name=\"prices[$key]\" ";
26:     print "value=\"$price\"> </td></tr>";
27:     $key = dba_nextkey( $dbh );
28: }
29: dba_close( $dbh );
30: ?>
31: <tr>
32: <td> </td>
33: <td><input type="text" name="name_add"></td>
34: <td><input type="text" name="price_add"></td>
35: </tr>
36: <tr>
```

LISTING **11.6**   continued

```
37: <td colspan=3 align="right">
38: <input type="submit" value="amend">
39: </td>
40: </tr>
41: </table>
42: </form>
43: </body>
44: </html>
```

We start by opening the database as usual (line 2). We then begin an HTML form that points back to the current page (line 11).

Having written some table headers to the screen on lines 13 to 17, we loop through the contents of our database using dba_firstkey() (line 19) and dba_nextkey() (line 27) to get each key in turn, and dba_fetch() on line 21 to extract the value.

In the first table cell of each row, we create a checkbox (line 22). Notice that we give all these the name "delete[]". This instructs PHP to construct an array called $delete of all submitted values that share this name. We use the database element name (stored in $key) as the value for each check box. When the form is submitted, therefore, we should have a $delete array with the names of all the database elements that we want to delete.

We then print the element name to the browser on line 24 and create another text field (line 25). This field presents the product price to the user, ready for amendment. We name the field using a similar technique as we did for the previous field. This time, however, we include the name of the database element in the square brackets of the field name. PHP constructs an associative array called $prices from these submitted fields with the element names as keys.

We close the database on line 29 and revert to HTML mode to write the final fields (lines 33 and 34). These allow the user to add new product and price combinations. Only two fields are required, and we give them the names name_add and price_add.

Figure 11.3 shows the output from Listing 11.6.

Now that we have created the form, we need to write code to deal with the user input. This is not as difficult as it sounds. There are three possible actions we can take. First, we can delete items from the database; second, we can amend prices in the database; and third, we can add new elements to the database.

FIGURE 11.3

Building an HTML form based on content from a database.

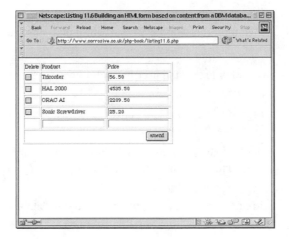

If the form has been submitted, we know which items we need to delete because a
$delete array variable will have been made available. We need to loop through this array
and delete the elements whose names it contains.

```
if ( ! empty( $delete ) ) {
    while ( list ( $key, $val ) = each ( $delete ) ) {
        unset( $prices[$val] );
        dba_delete( $val, $dbh );
    }
}
```

First we test that the $delete array exists and has elements. If the user has only just
arrived at the page, or if she has not chosen to delete any items, the variable will not
exist. If the variable exists, we can go ahead and loop through it. For each string held in
the $delete array, we call dba_delete() removing the element by that name from the
database. We also interfere with another array variable. The $prices array contains all
the key value pairs in the database, although some of the values might have been
changed by the user. If we do not remove the elements, we delete from the database the
$price array as well. The next block of code adds them to the database once again.

To update the database according to the user amendments, we have a choice. We could
only update those elements that the user has elected to change. We would choose this
option if we expected many users to be using the script at the same time or if the database was likely to grow significantly. As it is, this script will be run by a single administrator and is only expected to deal with a few products, so we opt to update every
element in the database:

```
if ( ! empty( $prices ) ) {
    while ( list ( $key, $val ) = each ( $prices ) )
        dba_replace( $key, $val, $dbh );
}
```

11

We test for the existence of the $prices array. This should contain a new version of the entire database. We loop through the array, calling dba_replace() for each of its elements.

Finally, we need to check whether the user has submitted a new product for inclusion in the database:

```
if ( ! empty( $name_add ) && ! empty( $price_add ) )
    dba_replace( "$name_add", "$price_add", $dbh );
```

Instead of testing whether the $name_add and $price_add variables are set, we test whether they are empty. This is a subtle but important difference. When the user submits the form we have built, these variables will always be set. They may, however, contain empty strings. We do not want to add empty strings to our database, so we only execute the code to insert new values if neither variable is empty:

```
if ( ! empty( $name_add ) && ! empty( $price_add ) )
    dba_insert("$name_add", "$price_add", $dbh );
```

We use dba_insert() rather than dba_replace() to guard against the user inadvertently overwriting an element that has already been defined.

You can see the complete code in Listing 11.7. You can find the code that handles deletions on lines 5 to 9. The code to update the database is on lines 12 through 15. We handle the insertion of new elements on lines 17 and 18.

LISTING 11.7 The Complete Product Maintenance Code

```
 1: <?php
 2: $dbh = dba_open( "./data/products", "c", "gdbm" )
 3:               or die( "Couldn't open database" );
 4:
 5: if ( ! empty( $delete ) ) {
 6:     while ( list ( $key, $val ) = each ( $delete ) )  {
 7:         unset( $prices[$val]);
 8:         dba_delete( $val, $dbh  );
 9:     }
10: }
11:
12: if ( ! empty( $prices ) ) {
13:     while ( list ( $key, $val ) = each ( $prices ) )
14:         dba_replace( $key, $val, $dbh );
15: }
16:
17: if ( ! empty( $name_add ) && ! empty( $price_add ) )
18:     dba_insert( "$name_add", "$price_add", $dbh );
19: ?>
20:
```

LISTING 11.7 continued

```
21: <html>
22: <head>
23: <title>Listing 11.7 The complete product maintenance code</title>
24: </head>
25: <body>
26:
27: <form action="<? print $PHP_SELF; ?>" action="POST">
28:
29: <table border="1">
30: <tr>
31: <td>delete</td>
32: <td>product</td>
33: <td>price</td>
34: </tr>
35:
36: <?php
37: $key = dba_firstkey( $dbh );
38: while ( $key != false ) {
39:     $price = dba_fetch( $key, $dbh );
40:     print "<tr><td><input type='checkbox' name=\"delete[]\" ";
41:     print "value=\"$key\"></td>";
42:     print "<td>$key</td>";
43:     print "<td> <input type=\"text\" name=\"prices[$key]\" ";
44:     print "value=\"$price\"> </td></tr>";
45:     $key = dba_nextkey( $dbh );
46: }
47:
48: dba_close( $dbh );
49: ?>
50:
51: <tr>
52: <td> </td>
53: <td><input type="text" name="name_add"></td>
54: <td><input type="text" name="price_add"></td>
55: </tr>
56:
57: <tr>
58: <td colspan=3 align="right">
59: <input type="submit" value="amend">
60: </td>
61: </tr>
62:
63: </table>
64: </form>
65:
66: </body>
67: </html>
```

11

Summary

In this hour, you learned how to use PHP's powerful DBA functions to store and retrieve data. You learned how to use dba_open() to acquire a DBA resource, which you can use with other DBA functions. You learned how to add data to a database with dba_insert(), alter it with dba_replace(), and delete data with dba_delete(). You learned how to use dba_fetch() to retrieve data. You learned how to use serialize() and unserialize() to save complex data structures to a database. Finally, you worked through an example that uses many of the techniques we have examined.

The DBA functions are useful for storing relatively small amounts of data that only needs to be queried in a simple way. Inevitably, our needs will occasionally be more demanding than this. In the next chapter we will cover MySQL, an open source SQL database.

Q&A

Q When should I use a DBM-like database as opposed to a SQL database?

A A DBM-like database is a good option when you want to store small amounts of relatively simple data (typically name/value pairs). Scripts built to use a DBM database have the virtue of portability. If you intend to store large amounts of data or many fields, consider using a SQL database, such as MySQL.

Workshop

Quiz

1. What function would you use to open a database using the DBA functions?

2. What function would you use to insert a record into a database?

3. What function would you use to replace a record in a database?

4. How would you access a record from a database by name?

5. How would you get the name (as opposed to the value) of the first element in a database?

6. How would you get subsequent element names?

7. How would you delete a named element from a database?

Quiz Answers

1. You can open a database with the dba_open() function.

2. The dba_insert() function adds a record to a database.

3. The dba_replace() function replaces a record in a database.

4. The dba_fetch() function returns an element given a DBA resource and the element's name.

5. dba_firstkey() returns the name of the first element in a DBM-like database.

6. After calling dba_firstkey(), you can get subsequent element names by calling dba_nextkey().

7. You can delete an element with dba_delete().

Activities

1. Create a database to keep track of user names and passwords. Create a script that allows users to register their combinations. Don't forget to check for duplications.

2. Create an authentication script that checks a user name and password. If the user input matches an entry in the database, present the user with a special message. Otherwise, re-present the login form to the user.

11

Hour **12**

Database Integration— SQL

One of the defining features of PHP is the ease with which you can connect to and manipulate databases. In this hour, we will concentrate on MySQL, but you will find similar functions for many of the databases that PHP supports. Why MySQL? It fits well with the spirit of PHP in that it is free to the individual user, yet remains a powerful tool that can be used as the basis of demanding real-world projects. Furthermore, versions of MySQL are available for multiple platforms. You can download MySQL from `http://www.mysql.com`.

In this hour, you will learn:

- A few SQL samples
- How to connect to the MySQL database server
- How to select a database
- About error handling
- How to add data to a table
- How to retrieve data from a table

- How to alter data in a table
- About the structure of databases
- An approach to automating database queries

A (Very) Brief Introduction to SQL

SQL stands for *Structured Query Language*. It provides a standardized syntax by which different types of database can be queried. Most SQL database products provide their own extensions to the language, just as many browsers provide their own extensions to HTML. Nonetheless, an understanding of SQL enables you to work with a wide range of database products across multiple platforms.

This book cannot even begin to describe all the intricacies of SQL. Nonetheless, we can fill in some background about MySQL and SQL in general.

MySQL is an open source database server that can be queried using SQL. MySQL runs as a server daemon to which users on the same or even remote machines can connect. Once connected to the server, you can select a database if you have the privileges to do so.

Within a database, there will be a varying number of tables of data. Each table is arranged in rows and columns. The intersection between a row and a column is the point at which each item of data you want to store and access sits. Each column only accepts a predefined type of data, INT for integer, for example, or VARCHAR for a variable number of characters up to a defined limit.

To create a new table within a database we have selected, we might use a SQL query like the following:

```
CREATE TABLE mytable (  first_name VARCHAR(30), second_name VARCHAR(30), age
INT);
```

Our new table has three columns. first_name and second_name can contain strings of up to 30 characters. age can contain any integer.

To add data to this table, we could use an INSERT statement:

```
INSERT INTO mytable ( first_name, second_name, age ) VALUES ( 'John', 'Smith',
36 );
```

The field names to which we want to add data are defined in the first set of parentheses. The values we want to insert are defined in the second.

To acquire all the data in a table, we would use a SELECT statement:

```
SELECT * FROM mytable;
```

The "*" symbol represents a wildcard which means "all fields." To acquire the information from a single field, you can use the column name in place of the wildcard:

```
SELECT age FROM mytable;
```

To change the values already stored in a table, you can use an UPDATE statement:

```
UPDATE mytable SET first_name = 'Bert';
```

This changes the first_name field in every row to "Bert". We can narrow the focus of SELECT and UPDATE statements with a WHERE clause. For example,

```
SELECT * FROM mytable WHERE first_name = 'Bert';
```

returns only those rows whose first_name fields contain the string "Bert". This next example

```
UPDATE mytable SET first_name = "Bert" WHERE second_name = "Baker";
```

changes the first_name fields of all rows whose second_name fields contain "Baker".

For more information on SQL, see *Sams Teach Yourself SQL in 21 Days* by Ryan K. Stephens et. al.

Connecting to the Database Server

12

Before you can begin working with your database, you must first connect to the server. PHP provides the mysql_connect() function to do just this. mysql_connect() does not require any arguments but accepts up to three strings: the hostname, a username, and a password. If you omit any or all of these arguments, the function assumes localhost as the host and that no password or username has been set up in the mysql user table, unless defaults have been set up in the php.ini file. Naturally, this is unwise for anything but a test database, so we will always include a username and password in our examples. mysql_connect() returns a link resource if the connection is successful. You can store this return value in a variable so that you can continue to work with the database server.

The following code fragment uses mysql_connect() to connect to the MySQL database server:

```
$link = mysql_connect( "localhost", "root", "n1ckel" );
if ( ! $link )
   die( "Couldn't connect to MySQL" );
```

If you are using PHP in conjunction with Apache, you could also connect to the database server with `mysql_pconnect()`. From the coder's perspective, this function works in exactly the same way as `mysql_connect()`. In fact, there is an important difference. If you use this function, the connection does not die when your script stops executing or if you call `mysql_close()` (which ends a standard connection to the MySQL server). Instead, the connection is left active, waiting for another process to call `mysql_pconnect()`. In other words, the overhead of opening a new connection to the server can be saved if you use `mysql_pconnect()` and a previous call to the script has left the connection open.

Selecting a Database

Now that we have established a connection to the MySQL daemon, we must choose which database we want to work with. You can select a database with the `mysql_select_db()` function. `mysql_select_db()` requires a database name and optionally accepts a link resource. If you omit this, the resource returned from the last connection to the server will be assumed. `mysql_select_db()` returns `true` if the database exists and you are able to access it. In the following fragment, we select a database called `sample`.

```
$database = "sample";
mysql_select_db( $database ) or die ( "Couldn't open $database );
```

Finding Out About Errors

So far we have tested the return values of the MySQL functions that we have used and called `die()` to end script execution if a problem occurs. You might, however, want to print more informative error messages to the browser to aid debugging. MySQL sets an error number and an error string whenever an operation fails. You can access the error number with `mysql_errno()`, and the error string with `mysql_error()`. Listing 12.1 brings our previous examples together into a simple script that connects to the server and selects a database. We use `mysql_error()` to make our error messages more useful. On line 11 we connect to the database. If this is successful we then select a database on line 15 before closing the connection on line 18.

LISTING 12.1   Opening a Connection and Selecting a Database

```
1: <html>
2: <head>
3: <title>Listing 12.1 Opening a connection and
4: selecting a database</title>
```

LISTING 12.1   continued

```
 5: </head>
 6: <body>
 7: <?php
 8: $user = "harry";
 9: $pass = "elbomonkey";
10: $db = "sample";
11: $link =  mysql_connect( "localhost", $user, $pass  );
12: if ( ! $link )
13:     die( "Couldn't connect to MySQL" );
14: print "Successfully connected to server<P>";
15: mysql_select_db( $db )
16:     or die ( "Couldn't open $db: ".mysql_error() );
17: print "Successfully selected database \"$db\"<P>";
18: mysql_close( $link );
19: ?>
20: </body>
21: </html>
```

If we change the value of the $db variable in Line 10 to "notthere", we will be attempting to open a nonexistent database. The output of our die() function call will look something like the following:

```
Couldn't open sample2: Access denied for user: 'harry@localhost' to database
'notthere'
```

Adding Data to a Table

Now that we have access to our database, we can add information to one of its tables. For the following examples, imagine that we are building a site that allows people to buy domain names.

We have created a table within the sample database called domains. The table was created with five columns: a primary key field called id that will automatically increment an integer as data is added, a domain field that will contain a variable number of characters (VARCHAR), a sex field that will contain a single character, and a mail field that will contain a user's email address. The following SQL statement was used in the MySQL client to create the table:

```
create table domains ( id INT NOT NULL AUTO_INCREMENT,
            PRIMARY KEY( id ),
            domain VARCHAR( 20 ),
            sex CHAR(1),
            mail VARCHAR( 20 ) );
```

12

To add data to this table, we will need to construct and execute a SQL query. PHP provides the `mysql_query()` function for this purpose. `mysql_query()` requires a string containing a SQL query and, optionally, a link resource. If the resource is omitted, the query is sent to the database server to which you last connected. `Mysql_query()` returns a positive value if the query is successful. If your query contains a syntax error, or if you don't have permission to access the database in question, then `query()` returns `false`. Note that a successful query does not necessarily result in any altered rows. Listing 12.2 extends our previous examples starting at line 15 and uses `mysql_query()` (line 17) to send an `INSERT` statement to the `domains` table in the `sample` database.

LISTING 12.2   Adding a Row to a Table

```
 1: <html>
 2: <head>
 3: <title>Listing 12.2 Adding a row to a table</title>
 4: </head>
 5: <body>
 6: <?php
 7: $user = "harry";
 8: $pass = "elbomonkey";
 9: $db = "sample";
10: $link =  mysql_connect( "localhost", $user, $pass  );
11: if ( ! $link )
12:     die( "Couldn't connect to MySQL" );
13: mysql_select_db( $db, $link )
14:         or die ( "Couldn't open $db: ".mysql_error() );
15: $query = "INSERT INTO domains ( domain, sex, mail )
16:         values( '123xyz.com', 'F', 'sharp@adomain.com' )";
17: mysql_query( $query, $link )
18: or die ( "Couldn't add data to \"domains\" table: "
19: .mysql_error() );
20: mysql_close( $link );
21: ?>
22: </body>
23: </html>
```

Notice that we did not insert a value for the `id` column in line 15. This field will auto-increment.

Of course, every time we reload the script in Listing 12.2, the same data is added to a new row. Listing 12.3 creates a script that will enter user input into our database.

LISTING 12.3   Adding User Input to a Database

```
 1: <html>
 2: <head>
 3: <title>Listing 12.3 Adding user input to a database</title>
 4: </head>
 5: <body>
 6: <?php
 7: if ( isset( $domain ) && isset( $sex ) && isset( $domain ) ) {
 8:     // check user input here!
 9:     $dberror = "";
10:     $ret = add_to_database( $domain, $sex, $mail, $dberror );
11:     if ( ! $ret )
12:         print "Error: $dberror<BR>";
13:     else
14:         print "Thank you very much";
15: } else {
16:     write_form();
17: }
18:
19: function add_to_database( $domain, $sex, $mail, &$dberror ) {
20:     $user = "harry";
21:     $pass = "elbomonkey";
22:     $db = "sample";
23:     $link = mysql_pconnect( "localhost", $user, $pass );
24:     if ( ! $link ) {
25:         $dberror = "Couldn't connect to MySQL server";
26:         return false;
27:     }
28:     if ( ! mysql_select_db( $db, $link ) ) {
29:         $dberror = mysql_error();
30:         return false;
31:     }
32:     $query = "INSERT INTO domains ( domain, sex, mail )
33:             values( '$domain', '$sex', '$mail' )";
34:     if ( ! mysql_query( $query, $link ) ) {
35:         $dberror = mysql_error();
36:         return false;
37:     }
38:     return true;
39: }
40:
41: function write_form() {
42:     global $PHP_SELF;
43:     print "<form method=\"POST\">\n";
44:     print "<input type=\"text\" name=\"domain\"> ";
45:     print "The domain you would like<p>\n";
46:     print "<input TYPE=\"text\" name=\"mail\"> ";
47:     print "Your mail address<p>\n";
48:     print "<select name=\"sex\">\n";
```

12

LISTING 12.3   continued

```
49:      print "\t<option value=\"F\"> Female\n";
50:      print "\t<option value=\"M\"> Male\n";
51:      print "</select>\n";
52:      print "<input type=\"submit\" value=\"submit!\">\n</form>\n";
53: }
54: ?>
55: </body>
56: </html>
```

To keep the example brief, we have left out one important process in Listing 12.3, testing user input. We are trusting our users. We should in fact check any kind of user input. We deal with the string functions that help you test user input in Hour 17, "Working with Strings."

We check for the variables $domain, $sex, and $mail on line 7. If they exist, we can be fairly certain that the user has submitted data, and we call the add_to_database() function on line 10.

The add_to_database() function declared on line 19 requires four arguments: the $domain, $sex, and $mail variables submitted by the user, and a string variable called $dberror. We populate this last argument with any error strings we encounter. For this reason, we accept $dberror as a reference to a variable. Any changes made to this string within the function will change the original argument rather than a copy.

We attempt to open a connection to the MySQL server on line 23. If this fails, we assign an error string to $dberror and end the execution of the function by returning false on line 26. We select the database that contains the domains table on line 28 and build an SQL query to insert the user-submitted values. We pass this to mysql_query() on line 34, which makes the query for us. If either mysql_select_db() or mysql_query() fail, we assign the value returned by mysql_error() to $dberror and return false. Assuming that all went well, the function returns true on line 38.

Back in the calling code, we can test the return value from add_to_database() on line 11. If the function returns true, we can be sure that we have added to the database and thank the user on line 14. Otherwise, we write an error message to the browser. We know that the $dberror variable that we passed to add_to_database() will now contain useful information, so we include it in our error message.

If our initial if statement fails to find $domain, $sex, or $mail variables, we can assume that no data has been submitted and call another user-defined function, write_form() on line 16, which outputs an HTML form to the browser.

Acquiring the Value of an Automatically Incremented Field

In our previous examples, we have added data to our database without worrying about the id column, which automatically increments as data is inserted. If we need the value of this field for a record at a later date, we can always extract it with a SQL query. What if we need the value straight away, though? It would be wasteful to look it up. Luckily, PHP provides mysql_insert_id(), a function that returns the value of an auto-incremented key field after a SQL INSERT statement has been performed. mysql_insert_id() optionally accepts a link resource as an argument. With no arguments, it works with the most recent link established.

So, if we want to tell a user the number we have allocated to her order, we could call mysql_insert_id() directly after adding the user's data to our database.

```
$query = "INSERT INTO domains ( domain, sex, mail ) values( '$domain', '$sex',
'$mail' )";
mysql_query( $query, $link );
$id =  mysql_insert_id();
print "Thank you. Your transaction number is $id. Please quote it in any
queries.";
```

Accessing Information

Now that we can add information to a database, we need to look at strategies for retrieving the information that it contains. As you might guess, you can use mysql_query() to make a SELECT query. How do you use this to look at the returned rows, though? When you perform a successful SELECT query, mysql_query() returns a result resource. You can pass this resource to other functions to access and gain information about a result set.

Finding the Number of Rows Found by a Query

You can find the number of rows returned as a result of a SELECT query using the mysql_num_rows() function. mysql_num_rows() requires a result resource and returns a count of the rows in the set. Listing 12.4 uses a SQL SELECT statement to request all rows in the domains table and then uses mysql_num_rows() to determine the table's size. If all we wanted to do was to find the number of rows in the table then the approach in listing 12.4 would be very wasteful. We would do better to use MySQL's COUNT function. Imagine however, that we intend to work with the rows we have found in any case. Perhaps we wish to write the contents of the table to the browser. Having used SELECT for this purpose, we can use mysql_num_rows() to find some useful summary information about the request.

12

LISTING 12.4   Finding the Number of Rows Returned by a SELECT Statement with
mysql_num_rows()

```
 1: <html>
 2: <head>
 3: <title>Listing 12.4 Using mysql_num_rows()</title>
 4: </head>
 5: <body>
 6: <?php
 7: $user = "harry";
 8: $pass = "elbomonkey";
 9: $db = "sample";
10: $link =  mysql_connect( "localhost", $user, $pass  );
11: if ( ! $link )
12:     die( "Couldn't connect to MySQL" );
13: mysql_select_db( $db, $link )
14:     or die ( "Couldn't open $db: ".mysql_error() );
15: $result = mysql_query( "SELECT * FROM domains" );
16: $num_rows = mysql_num_rows( $result );
17: print "There are currently $num_rows rows in the table<P>";
18: //
19: // Further work with the $result resource here
20: //
21: mysql_close( $link );
22: ?>
23: </body>
24: </html>
```

The mysql_query() function returns a result resource. We then pass this to mysql_num_rows(), which returns the total number of rows found.

We connect to the database on line 10 and select the database on line 13. On line 15 we call mysql_query(), passing it our SQL query. The function returns a result resource that we can then use with mysql_num_rows() on line 16. Having output summary information on line 17 we are ready to begin to do some more substantial work with our results. We go on to do this in the next section.

Accessing a Resultset

After you have performed a SELECT query and gained a result resource, you can use a loop to access each found row in turn. PHP maintains an internal pointer that keeps a record of your position within a found set. This moves on to the next row as each one is accessed.

You can easily get an array of the fields in each found row with mysql_fetch_row(). This function requires a result resource, returning an array containing each field in the row. When the end of the found set is reached, `mysql_fetch_row()` returns `false`. Listing 12.5 outputs the entire `domains` table to the browser.

LISTING 12.5 Listing All Rows and Fields in a Table

```
 1: <html>
 2: <head>
 3: <title>Listing 12.5 Listing all rows and fields in a table</title>
 4: </head>
 5: <body>
 6: <?php
 7: $user = "harry";
 8: $pass = "elbomonkey";
 9: $db = "sample";
10: $link =  mysql_connect( "localhost", $user, $pass  );
11: if ( ! $link )
12:     die( "Couldn't connect to MySQL" );
13: mysql_select_db( $db, $link )
14:     or die ( "Couldn't open $db: ".mysql_error() );
15: $result = mysql_query( "SELECT * FROM domains" );
16: $num_rows = mysql_num_rows( $result );
17: print "There are currently $num_rows rows in the table<P>";
18: print "<table border=1>\n";
19: while ( $a_row = mysql_fetch_row( $result ) ) {
20:     print "<tr>\n";
21:     foreach ( $a_row as $field )
22:         print "\t<td>$field</td>\n";
23:     print "</tr>\n";
24: }
25: print "</table>\n";
26: mysql_close( $link );
27: ?>
28: </body>
29: </html>
```

12

After we have connected to the server and selected the database, we use `mysql_query()` on line 15 to send a `SELECT` statement to the database server. We store the returned result resource in a variable called `$result`. We use this to acquire the number of found rows as before.

In the test expression of our `while` statement on line 19, we assign the result of `mysql_fetch_row()` to the variable `$a_row`. Remember that an assignment operator returns the value of its right-hand operand, so the assignment resolves to `true` as long as `mysql_fetch_row()` returns a positive value. Within the body of the `while` statement, we loop through the row array contained in `$a_row` on line 21, outputting each element to the browser embedded in a table cell.

You can also access fields by name in one of two ways. mysql_fetch_array() returns a numeric array, as does mysql_fetch_row(). It also returns an associative array, with the names of the fields as the keys. The following fragment rewrites the while statement from Listing 12.5, incorporating mysql_fetch_array() (this replaces lines 18 to 25):

```
print "<TABLE BORDER=1>\n";
while ( $a_row = mysql_fetch_array( $result ) ) {
    print "<TR>\n";
    print "<TD>".$a_row['mail']."</TD><TD>".$a_row['domain']."</TD>\n";
    print "</TR>\n";
}
print "</TABLE>\n";
```

The default behavior of mysql_fetch_array() is to return an array indexed by string which also contains the same values indexed numerically. This is fine if you want to refer to your fields individually. If, however you need to dump all the array values and keys, you will not want this duplication. mysql_fetch_array() accepts an optional second argument. This integer should be one of three built-in constants. MYSQL_ASSOC, MYSQL_NUM, or MYSQL_BOTH. Passing MYSQL_BOTH is redundant in that it will enforce the default behavior. Passing MYSQL_ASSOC to mysql_fetch_array() will ensure that the return array is indexed by strings only. Passing MYSQL_NUM to mysql_fetch_array() will ensure that the return array is numerically indexed.

If you are seeking the functionality provided by

```
mysql_fetch_array( $result, MYSQL_ASSOC );
```

you can use a shortcut function which was introduced with PHP 4.03. mysql_fetch_assoc() is functionally identical to a call to mysql_fetch_array() with MYSQL_ASSOC.

You can also extract the fields from a row as properties of an object with mysql_fetch_object(). The field names become the names of the properties. The following fragment once again rewrites the while statement from Listing 12.5, this time incorporating mysql_fetch_object() (this replaces lines 18 to 25):

```
print "<table border=1>\n";
while ( $a_row = mysql_fetch_object( $result ) ) {
    print "<tr>\n";
    print "<td>$a_row->mail</td><td>$a_row->domain</td>\n";
    print "</tr>\n";
}
print "</table>\n";
```

Both mysql_fetch_array() and mysql_fetch_object() make it easier for you to selectively extract information from a row. Neither of these functions takes much longer than mysql_fetch_row() to execute. Which you choose to use is largely a matter of preference, although mysql_fetch_array() is more commonly used.

Changing Data

You can change data using the mysql_query() function in conjunction with an UPDATE statement.

A successful UPDATE statement does not necessarily change any rows. You need to use a function to call mysql_affected_rows() to discover whether you have changed data in your table. mysql_affected_rows() optionally accepts a link resource. If this is missing, the most recent connection is assumed. This function can be used with any SQL query that can alter data in a table row.

Listing 12.6 builds a script that allows an administrator to change any of the values in the domain column of our example table.

LISTING 12.6   Using mysql_query() to Alter Rows in a Database

```
1: <html>
2: <head>
3: <title>Listing 12.6 Using mysql_query()
4: to alter rows in a database</title>
5: </head>
6: <body>
7: <?php
8: $user = "harry";
9: $pass = "elbomonkey";
10: $db = "sample";
11: $link =  mysql_connect( "localhost", $user, $pass  );
12: if (  ! $link )
13:     die( "Couldn't connect to MySQL" );
14: mysql_select_db( $db, $link )
15:     or die ( "Couldn't open $db: ".mysql_error() );
16:
17: if ( isset( $domain ) && isset( $id ) ) {
18:     $query = "UPDATE domains SET domain = '$domain' where id=$id";
19:     $result = mysql_query( $query );
20:     if ( ! $result )
21:         die ("Couldn't update: ".mysql_error());
22:     print "<h1>Table updated ". mysql_affected_rows() .
23:     " row(s) changed</h1><p>";
24: }
25: ?>
26: <form action="<? print $PHP_SELF ?>" method="POST">
27: <select name="id">
```

12

LISTING 12.6   continued

```
28: <?
29: $result = mysql_query( "SELECT domain, id  FROM domains" );
30: while( $a_row = mysql_fetch_object( $result ) ) {
31:     print "<OPTION VALUE=\"$a_row->id\"";
32:     if ( isset($id) && $id == $a_row->id )
33:         print " SELECTED";
34:     print "> $a_row->domain\n";
35: }
36: mysql_close( $link );
37: ?>
38: </select>
39: <input type="text" name="domain">
40: </form>
41: </body>
42: </html>
```

We open a connection to the database server and select a database as normal. We then
test for the presence of the variables $domain and $id on line 17. If these are present, we
build a SQL UPDATE query on line 18 that changes the value of the domain field where
the id field contains the same value as our $id variable. We do not get an error if a
nonexistent id is used or if the $domain variable is the same as the current value for
domain in the relevant row. Instead, the mysql_affected_rows() simply returns 0. We
print this return value (usually 1 in this example) to the browser on lines 22 and 23.

Starting on line 26, we print an HTML form to allow the administrator to make her
changes. Note that we use mysql_query() (line 29) once again to extract the values of
the id and domain column and incorporate them in an HTML SELECT element (lines 27
to 38). The administrator will use this pop-up menu to choose which domain to change.
If the administrator has already submitted the form and the id value she chose matches
the value of the id field we are currently outputting, we add the string SELECTED to the
OPTION element (line 33). This ensures that her changed value will be instantly visible to
her in the menu.

Building a Database Abstraction Class

Databases can make it hard to create durable and transportable code. If database code is
built tightly into a project it can be difficult to migrate from one database server to another, for example.

In this sample we are going to create a basic utility class that separates a lot of the database facing code from the logic of a project as a whole. The class will broadly achieve

two things. First it will present a conduit between a program and the database via which SQL queries can be passed. Second, it will automate the generation of SQL for a range of frequently performed operations, such as simple SELECT and UPDATE statements. In the case of SELECT queries, the result set will be provided in the form of an array of associative arrays.

The class should provide two main benefits for the client coder. First, in automating simple queries it should save the need to construct SQL statements on the fly. Second, in providing a clear interface to its functionality it should safeguard portability. If the project is to be moved to a different database server, then an alternative class can be written that maintains the same functionality but with a different implementation behind the scene.

It must be noted, however that all database abstraction schemes (including Perl's famous database independent interface or DBI library) suffer from one major drawback. Different database engines tend to support different SQL syntaxes and features. This means that SQL statements written to work with MySQL may not work with Oracle, for example. For simple projects you can go some way towards dealing with this problem by using SQL features that are as 'standard' as possible, and avoiding the use of features specific to a database application.

Connecting to the Database

To start with, let's build the methods to connect to a database server, and select a database. Along the way, we can look at the method we are going to use for reporting errors.

```
class DataLayer {
        var $link;
        var $errors = array();
        var $debug = false;

        function DataLayer( ) {
        }

        function connect( $host, $name, $pass, $db ) {
                $link =  mysql_connect( $host, $name, $pass );
                if ( ! $link )  {
                        $this->setError("Couldn't connect to database server");
                        return false;
                }

                if ( ! mysql_select_db( $db, $this->link ) ) {
                        $this->setError("Couldn't select database: $db");
                        return false;
                }
                $this->link = $link;
```

12

```
                    return true;
            }

            function getError( ) {
                    return $this->errors[count($this->errors)-1];
            }

            function setError( $str ) {
                    array_push( $this->errors, $str );
            }
    ...
```

We have called our class `DataLayer`. We establish three properties; `$link` will store our database resource, `$errors` will store an array of error messages, and `$debug` is another flag which will help us to monitor the behavior of our class.

The `connect()` method simply uses the now familiar `mysql_connect()` and `mysql_select_db()` functions to connect to the server and choose a database. If you implement this class yourself, you might consider storing the `$host`, `$name`, `$pass` and `$db` argument variables in class properties. We have chosen not to in this example. If we encounter any problems with connection we call the `setError()` function which maintains a stack of error messages. If all goes well, however, we store the database resource returned by `mysql_connect` in our `$link` property.

Making the Query

We're now ready to build the query methods. We split these up into three:

```
        function _query( $query ) {
                if ( ! $this->link ) {
                        $this->setError("No active db connection");
                        return false;
                }
                $result = mysql_query( $query, $this->link );
                if ( ! $result )
                        $this->setError("error: ".mysql_error());
                return $result;
        }

        function setQuery( $query ) {
                if (! $result = $this->_query( $query ) )
                        return false;
                return mysql_affected_rows( $this->link );
        }

        function getQuery( $query ) {
                if (! $result = $this->_query( $query ) )
                        return false;
                $ret = array();
```

```
        while ( $row = mysql_fetch_assoc( $result ) )
                $ret[] = $row;
        return $ret;
    }
```

_query() performs some basic checks, but all it really does is to pass a string containing an SQL query to the mysql_query() function, returning a mysql result resource if all goes well. Both setQuery() and getQuery() call _query(), passing it an SQL string. They differ in what they return to the user, however. setQuery() is designed for SQL statements that act upon a database. UPDATE statements, for example. It returns an integer representing the number of affected rows. getQuery() is designed primarily for SELECT statements. It builds an array of the result set which it returns to the calling code. We're now in a position to test our class.

Testing the Basic Class

For the test, we assume the presence of a table called test_table. The CREATE statement illustrates its structure:

```
CREATE TABLE test_table (
            id INT NOT NULL AUTO_INCREMENT,
            PRIMARY KEY( id ),
            name VARCHAR(255),
            age INT,
            description BLOB
            );
```

Our test code simply connects to the database, adds some data, and then requests it back again, looping through the returned array and printing an HTML table to the browser.

```
$dl = new DataLayer( );
$dl->connect( "localhost", "", "", "test" )  or die ( $dl->getError() );
$dl->setQuery("DELETE FROM test_table");
$dl->setQuery("INSERT INTO test_table (name, age, description)
            VALUES('bob', 20, 'student')");
$dl->setQuery("INSERT INTO test_table (name, age, description)
            VALUES('mary', 66, 'librarian')");
$dl->setQuery("INSERT INTO test_table (name, age, description)
            VALUES('su', 31, 'producer')");
$dl->setQuery("INSERT INTO test_table (name, age, description)
            VALUES('percy', 45, 'civil servant')");
$table = $dl->getQuery("SELECT * from test_table");

print "<table border=\"1\">";
foreach( $table as $d_row ) {
        print "<tr>";
        foreach ( $d_row as $field=>$val )
                print "<td>$val</td>";
```

12

```
        print "</tr>";
}
print "</table>";
```

Automating SQL Statements

SQL can be a highly complex affair, and it is not our purpose to reinvent it. However, some fairly basic operations are performed over and over again, SQL statements can be tedious to construct within a script. These methods should simplify some of these tasks.

Let's illustrate the technique by looking at a method for automating basic SELECT statements.

```
        function select( $table,  $condition="", $sort="" ) {
                $query = "SELECT * FROM $table";
                $query .= $this->_makeWhereList( $condition );
                if ( $sort != "" )
                        $query .= " order by $sort";
                $this->debug( $query );
                return $this->getQuery( $query, $error );
        }

        function _makeWhereList( $condition ) {
                if ( empty( $condition ) )
                        return "";
                $retstr = " WHERE ";
                if ( is_array( $condition ) ) {
                        $cond_pairs=array();
                        foreach( $condition  as $field=>$val )
                                array_push( $cond_pairs, "$field=".$this-
>_quote_val( $val ) );
                        $retstr .= implode( " AND ", $cond_pairs );
                } elseif ( is_string( $condition ) && ! empty( $condition ) )
                        $retstr .= $condition;
                return $retstr;
        }
```

The select() method requires at least a table name. It will also optionally accept condition and sort arguments. The sort argument should be a string such as "age DESC, name". The condition argument can be either an associative array or a string. A condition passed as an associative arrays will be used to construct a WHERE clause with the keys representing field names. So

array(name=>"bob", age=>20)

will resolve to

WHERE name='bob' AND age=20

Where more complex conditions are required, such as

```
WHERE name='bob' AND age<25
```

the condition argument should be passed as string containing the valid SQL fragment. The construction of the WHERE clause takes place in the _makeWhereList() method. If no condition is required an empty string is returned. If the condition is a string, it is simply tacked onto the string "WHERE" and returned. If the condition is an array however, the fieldname/value pairs are first constructed and stored in an array called $cond_pairs. The implode() function is then used to join the new array into a single string, the fieldname/value pairs separated by the string " AND ".

Notice that we call a utility method called quote_val() when we are building our string. This is used to add backslashes to special characters (such as single quotes) within values. It also surrounds strings in quotes, though it leaves numbers alone.

```
function _quote_val( $val ) {
        if ( is_numeric( $val ) )
                return $val;
        return "'".addslashes($val)."'";
}
```

The addslashes() function built-in to PHP. It accepts a string and returns another with special characters backslashed. This is useful for us, because we must surround strings sent to MySQL with single quotes.

To get an array containing a complete listing of our table we can now use the select() method.

```
$table = $dl->select("test_table");
```

To get all rows with an age of less than 40:

```
$table = $dl->select("test_table", "age<40");
```

To pull out information about people called bob

```
$table = $dl->select("test_table", array('name'=>"bob") );
```

Bringing It All Together

Listing 12.7 represents the complete DataLayer class. It includes the methods update(), delete(), and insert() that are similar to select() in that they simply construct SQL statements.

12

LISTING 12.7   The DataLayer Class

```
 1: <?
 2: class DataLayer {
 3:     var $link;
 4:     var $errors = array();
 5:     var $debug = false;
 6:
 7:     function DataLayer( ) {
 8:     }
 9:
10:     function connect( $host, $name, $pass, $db ) {
11:         $link =  mysql_connect( $host, $name, $pass );
12:         if ( ! $link )  {
13:             $this->setError("Couldn't connect to database server");
14:             return false;
15:         }
16:
17:             if ( ! mysql_select_db( $db, $link ) ) {
18:             $this->setError("Couldn't select database: $db");
19:             return false;
20:         }
21:         $this->link = $link;
22:         return true;
23:     }
24:
25:     function getError( ) {
26:         return $this->errors[count($this->errors)-1];
27:     }
28:
29:     function setError( $str ) {
30:         array_push( $this->errors, $str );
31:     }
32:
33:     function _query( $query ) {
34:         if ( ! $this->link ) {
35:             $this->setError("No active db connection");
36:             return false;
37:         }
38:         $result = mysql_query( $query, $this->link );
39:         if ( ! $result )
40:             $this->setError("error: ".mysql_error());
41:         return $result;
42:     }
43:
44:     function setQuery( $query ) {
45:             if (! $result = $this->_query( $query ) )
46:             return false;
47:         return mysql_affected_rows( $this->link );
48:     }
```

LISTING 12.7 continued

```
49:
50:     function getQuery( $query ) {
51:             if (! $result = $this->_query( $query ) )
52:             return false;
53:         $ret = array();
54:         while ( $row = mysql_fetch_assoc( $result ) )
55:             $ret[] = $row;
56:         return $ret;
57:     }
58:
59:     function getResource( ) {
60:         return $this->link;
61:     }
62:
63:     function select( $table,  $condition="", $sort="" ) {
64:             $query = "SELECT * FROM $table";
65:         $query .= $this->_makeWhereList( $condition );
66:         if ( $sort != "" )
67:             $query .= " order by $sort";
68:         $this->debug( $query );
69:             return $this->getQuery( $query, $error );
70:     }
71:
72:     function insert( $table, $add_array ) {
73:             $add_array = $this->_quote_vals( $add_array );
74:             $keys = "(".implode( array_keys( $add_array ), ", ").")";
75:             $values = "values (".implode( array_values( $add_array ),
➥", ").")";
76:             $query = "INSERT INTO $table $keys $values";
77:         $this->debug( $query );
78:             return $this->setQuery( $query );
79:     }
80:
81:     function update( $table, $update_array, $condition="" ) {
82:         $update_pairs=array();
83:         foreach( $update_array  as $field=>$val )
84:             array_push( $update_pairs, "$field=".$this->_quote_val( $val )
➥);
85:
86:             $query = "UPDATE $table set ";
87:         $query .= implode( ", ", $update_pairs );
88:         $query .= $this->_makeWhereList( $condition );
89:         $this->debug( $query );
90:             return $this->setQuery( $query );
91:     }
92:
93:     function delete( $table, $condition="" ) {
94:             $query = "DELETE FROM  $table";
```

12

LISTING 12.7 continued

```
 95:            $query .= $this->_makeWhereList( $condition );
 96:            $this->debug( $query );
 97:                    return $this->setQuery( $query, $error );
 98:        }
 99:
100:        function debug( $msg ) {
101:            if ( $this->debug )
102:                print "$msg<br>";
103:        }
104:
105:        function _makeWhereList( $condition ) {
106:            if ( empty( $condition ) )
107:                return "";
108:            $retstr = " WHERE ";
109:            if ( is_array( $condition ) ) {
110:                $cond_pairs=array();
111:                foreach( $condition  as $field=>$val )
112:                    array_push( $cond_pairs, "$field=".$this->_quote_val( $val
) );
113:                $retstr .= implode( " and ", $cond_pairs );
114:            } elseif ( is_string( $condition ) && ! empty( $condition ) )
115:                $retstr .= $condition;
116:            return $retstr;
117:        }
118:
119:        function _quote_val( $val ) {
120:            if ( is_numeric( $val ) )
121:                return $val;
122:            return "'".addslashes($val)."'";
123:        }
124:
125:        function _quote_vals( $array ) {
126:            foreach( $array as $key=>$val )
127:                $ret[$key]=$this->_quote_val( $val );
128:            return $ret;
129:        }
130: }
131: ?>
```

As you should see from the code, update() (line 81), delete() (line 93), and insert() (line 72) provide a similar interface to that provided by select() (line 63).

update() which is declared on line 81 requires a string representing the table to be worked with. It also requires an associative array of keys and values. The keys should be the field name to be altered, and the value should be the new content for the field.

Finally, an optional condition argument is accepted. This follows the same logic as the condition argument in the select() method. It can be a string or an array.

delete() which is declared on line 93 requires a table name, and an optional condition argument.

insert() is declared on line 72 and requires a table name, and an associative array of fields to add to the row. The keys should be the field name to be altered, and the value should be the new content for the field.

We had better see the code in action. Listing 12.8 is a simple test script that populates and manipulates a table in a database.

LISTING 12.8 Working with the DataLayer Class

```
 1: <html>
 2: <head>
 3: <title>Listing 12.8 Working with the DataLayer Class</title>
 4: </head>
 5: <body>
 6: <?php
 7: include("listing12.9.php");
 8: $people = array(
 9:     array( 'name'=>"bob", 'age'=>20, 'description'=>"student" ),
10:     array( 'name'=>"mary", 'age'=>66, 'description'=>"librarian" ),
11:     array( 'name'=>"su", 'age'=>31, 'description'=>"producer" ),
12:     array( 'name'=>"percy", 'age'=>45, 'description'=>"civil servant" )
13:     );
14:
15: $dl = new DataLayer( );
16: $dl->debug=true;
17: $dl->connect( "localhost", "", "", "test" )  or die ( $dl->getError() );
18:
19: $dl->delete( "test_table" );
20:
21: foreach ( $people  as $person ) {
22:     $dl->insert( "test_table", $person ) or die( $dl->getError() );
23: }
24:
25: foreach ( $people as $person ) {
26:     $person['age']++;
27:     $dl->update( "test_table", $person, array( 'name'=>$person['name'] ) );
28: }
29:
30: $dl->delete( "test_table", "age < 25" );
31: $table = $dl->select( "test_table" );
32:
33: print "<table border=\"1\">";
```

12

LISTING **12.8**   continued

```
34: foreach( $table as $d_row ) {
35:     print "<tr>";
36:     foreach ( $d_row as $field=>$val )
37:         print "<td>$val</td>";
38:     print "</tr>";
39: }
40: print "</table>";
41: ?>
42: </body>
43: </html>
```

We initialize our data using an associative array beginning on line 8. We instantiate a DataLayer object on line 15, set the object's $debug property to true on line 16, and connect to the database on line 17. Because the object is in debug mode, all the SQL we generate will be output to the browser after being sent to the database.

We call the delete() method on line 19, to clear any data in the table, before populating it by looping through our $people on line 21 array and calling the insert() method (line 22) for each person. DataLayer is designed to work with associative arrays, so we only need to pass each element of the $people array to insert() in order to populate the table.

We then decide that we wish to alter the age field of each row. Once again we loop through the people array (line 25), incrementing each element before calling update() on line 27. We can pass the entire $person array to update(). Although this will mean that most fields in the row will be updated with their own value, this is quick and easy from the client coder's perspective. The third argument to update() is a condition array containing the name key and value. In a real world example we would probably use the id field to ensure that we are updating only one row.

Finally, we call delete() once again (line 30), this time including a condition argument. Because we wish to delete all rows with an age value of less than 25, we pass a condition string rather than an array. Remember that condition arrays are only useful for demanding equivalence, so we must 'hardcode' the 'less then' comparison into a string.

You can see the output from Listing 12.8 in Figure 12.1. Because the object was in debug mode, notice that the SQL has been output to the browser.

FIGURE 12.1

Working with the DataLayer Class.

Summary

In this hour, we covered some of the basics of storing and retrieving information from a MySQL database.

You should now be able to establish a connection to the MySQL server using `mysql_connect()` or `mysql_pconnect()`.

You should be able to select a database with `mysql_select_db()`. If the selection fails, you should be able to discover more about the error with `mysql_error()`.

You should be able to make SQL queries using `mysql_query()`. With the result resource this function returns, you should be able to access data, or discover the number of rows you have transformed.

You should be able to use PHP's MySQL functions to list the number of databases, tables, and fields accessible to you and to find out more about the attributes of individual fields.

You should be able to use some of the techniques discussed in the creation of our `DataLayer` class to automate SQL queries, and to separate database code from a larger script.

In the next hour we will take a look at PHP in the contexts of the wider world. In particular we will be exploring techniques for learning about and talking to machines other than our own.

12

Q&A

Q **This hour is specific to MySQL. How transferable are these examples to other SQL databases?**

A There are functions for mSQL that mirror those for MySQL almost exactly. Other database servers have corresponding PHP functions that support their features and capabilities. The common feature of many suites of database function is the capability to send SQL queries. If you work with ANSI (standard) SQL, you should have little problem adapting scripts across database servers.

Q **What is the best way of writing code that can be easily adapted to work with different database servers?**

A It is often a good idea to group code that queries a database into a single class or library. If you need to rewrite your project to work with a different database, you will only need to change a discrete portion of your code without disturbing the project as a whole. Don't forget though that SQL varies from database application to database application.

Workshop

Quiz

1. How would you open a connection to a MySQL database server?
2. What function would you use to select a database?
3. What function would you use to send a SQL query to a database?
4. What does the `mysql_insert_id()` function do?
5. Assuming that you have sent a successful SELECT query to MySQL, name three functions that you might use to access each row returned.
6. Assuming that you have sent a successful UPDATE query to MySQL, what function might you use to determine how many rows have been updated?
7. What function would you call if you want to list all databases available from a MySQL server?
8. What function would you use to list all tables within a database?

Quiz Answers

1. You can connect to a MySQL daemon using the `mysql_connect()` function.
2. The `mysql_select_db()` function attempts to select a database.

3. You can send a SQL query to the database server with the `mysql_query()` function.

4. `mysql_insert_id()` returns the value of an automatically incrementing field after a new row has been added to a table.

5. You can use the `mysql_fetch_row()`, `mysql_fetch_array()`, or `mysql_fetch_object()` functions to access each row of a found set.

6. You can discover the number of rows altered by a SQL statement with the `mysql_affected_rows()` function.

7. The `mysql_list_dbs()` function returns a result pointer that can be used to list all the databases available.

8. The `mysql_list_tables()` function returns a result pointer that can be used to list all the tables within a database.

Activities

1. Create a database with three fields: email (up to 70 characters), message (up to 250 characters), and date (an integer that will contain a UNIX timestamp). Build a script to allow users to populate the database.

2. Create a script that displays the information from the database you created in activity 1.

12

HOUR 13

Beyond the Box

In this hour, we will look at some of the functions that allow you to gain information from or interact with the outside world.

In this hour, you will learn:

- More about predefined variables
- The anatomy of an HTTP connection
- How to acquire a document from a remote server
- How to create your own HTTP connection
- How to connect to other network services
- How to send email from your scripts

Server Variables

You have already encountered some of the predefined variables that PHP, in conjunction with your server, makes available for you. In this section we are going to take a closer look at server variables. These are made available to PHP by the server. If you are running Apache it is likely that all the variables we discuss will be accessible to you. If you are running another server, there is no guarantee that you will be able to use these server variables so it is a good idea to check before using them in scripts. Table 13.1 lists some of the variables that you might be able to use to find out more about your visitors.

TABLE 13.1   Some Useful Server Variables

Variable	Description
$HTTP_REFERER	The URL from which the current script was called (the misspelling is deliberate).
$HTTP_USER_AGENT	Information about the browser and platform that the visitor is using.
$REMOTE_ADDR	The visitor's IP address.
$REMOTE_HOST	The visitor's hostname.
$QUERY_STRING	The (encoded) string that may be appended to the URL (in the format ?akey=avalue&anotherkey=anothervalue). These keys and values should become available to your scripts in global variables.
$PATH_INFO	Additional information that may be appended to the URL.

Listing 13.1 builds a script that outputs the contents of these variables to the browser.

LISTING 13.1   Listing Some Server Variables

```
 1: <html>
 2: <head>
 3: <title>Listing 13.1 Listing some server variables</title>
 4: </head>
 5: <body>
 6: <?php
 7: $envs = array(  "HTTP_REFERER", "HTTP_USER_AGENT", "REMOTE_ADDR",
 8:         "REMOTE_HOST", "QUERY_STRING", "PATH_INFO" );
 9: foreach ( $envs as $env )
10:     print "$env: $GLOBALS[$env]<br>";
11: ?>
12: </body>
13: </html>
```

Figure 13.1 shows the output from Listing 13.1. The data in Figure 13.1 was generated as a result of calling the script from a link in another page. The link that called the script looked like this:

```
<A HREF='listing13.1.php/my_path_info?query_key=query_value'>go</A>
```

As you can see, the link uses a relative path to call listing13.1.php.

FIGURE **13.1**

*Printing some Server
Variables to the
Browser.*

Additional path information (my_path_info) is included after the document name, which becomes available in $PATH_INFO.

We have hard-coded a query string (query_key=query_value) into the link, which becomes available in $QUERY_STRING. You will most often encounter a query string when using a form with a GET method argument, but you can also build your own query strings to pass information from page to page. The query string consists of name value pairs separated by ampersand (&) symbols. These pairs are URL encoded, which means that any characters that are illegal or have other meanings in URLs will be converted to their hexadecimal equivalents. Although you have access to the entire query string in the $QUERY_STRING environmental variable, you will rarely need to use this fact. Each key name will be available to you as a global variable ($query_value in our example) that will hold a corresponding decoded value ("query_value"). You can also use the predefined $HTTP_GET_VARS associative array to access query string keys and values.

The $HTTP_REFERER variable can be useful to you if you want to track which hits on your script originate from which links. Beware, though, this and other environmental variables can be easily faked. You will see how later in this hour. Because correcting it would cause compatibility problems, we are stuck with the incorrect spelling of 'referrer'. Not all browsers will supply this header, so you should avoid relying upon it.

You can parse the $HTTP_USER_AGENT variable to work out the platform and browser that the visitor is using. Once again, this can be faked. This variable can be useful if you need to present different HTML code or JavaScript according to the browser type and version the visitor is using. Hour 17, "Working with Strings," and Hour 18, "Working with Regular Expressions," will give you the tools you need to extract any information you want from this string.

13

The $REMOTE_ADDR variable contains the user's IP address and can be used to track unique visitors to your site. Be aware, though, that many Web users do not have a fixed IP address. Instead, their Internet service providers dynamically allocate them an address when they dial up. This means that a single IP address might be used by different visitors to your site, and that a single visitor might enter using different IP addresses from the same account.

The $REMOTE_HOST variable might not be available to you, depending on the configuration of your server. If available, it will hold the hostname of the user. The presence of this variable requires that the server look up the hostname for every request, so it is often disabled for the sake of efficiency. If you don't have access to this variable, you can acquire it yourself using the value of the $REMOTE_ADDR variable. You will see how to do this later in the hour.

A Brief Summary of an HTTP Client/Server Negotiation

It is beyond the scope of this book to explore all the information exchanged between server and client when a request is made, not least because PHP handles most of these details for you. It is a good idea to gain a basic understanding of this process, however, especially if you intend to write scripts that fetch Web pages or check the status of Web addresses.

HTTP stands for *hypertext transfer protocol*. It is essentially a set of rules that define the process by which a client sends a request and a server returns a response. Both client and server provide information about themselves and the data to be transferred. Much of this information becomes available to you in environment variables.

The Request

A client requests data from the server according to a strict set of rules. The request consists of up to three components:

- A request line
- A header section
- An entity body

The request line is mandatory. It consists of a request method, typically GET, HEAD, or POST; the address of the document to required; and the HTTP version to be used (HTTP/1.0 or HTTP/1.1). A typical request for a document called mydoc.html might look like this:

```
GET /mydoc.html HTTP/1.0
```

The client is making a GET request. In other words, it is requesting an entire document but sending no data itself (in fact you *can* send small amounts of data as part of a GET request by adding a query string to the URL. The HEAD method would be used if you only wanted information about a document. The POST method is used to transfer data from a client to the server, usually from an HTML form.

The request line is enough in itself to make a valid GET request. To inform the server that a request is complete, an empty line must be sent.

Most clients will follow the request line with a header section in which name/value pairs can be sent to the server. Some of these will become available to you as environmental variables. Each client header consists of a key and value on one line separated by a colon. Table 13.2 lists a few of these.

TABLE 13.2 Some Client Headers

Name	Description
Accept	The media types that the client can work with.
Accept-Encoding	The types of data compression that the client can handle.
Accept-Charset	The character sets that the client prefers.
Accept-Language	The language that the client prefers ('en' for English).
Host	The host to which a request is being made. Some servers that maintain multiple virtual hosts rely heavily on this header.
Referer	The document from which a request is being made.
User-Agent	Information about the client type and version.

For GET and HEAD methods, the header section ends the request, and an empty line is sent to the server. For requests made using the POST method, an empty line is followed by the entity body. An entity body consists of any data to be sent to the server. This is usually a set of URL-encoded name/value pairs similar to those found in a query string.

Listing 13.2 shows a request sent to a server by Netscape 4.6.

LISTING 13.2 Typical Client Headers Sent by a Netscape Browser

```
1: GET / HTTP/1.0
2: Connection: Keep-Alive
3: User-Agent: Mozilla/4.51 (Macintosh; I; PPC)
4: Host: www.corrosive.co.uk:8080
5: Accept: image/gif, image/x-xbitmap, image/jpeg, image/pjpeg, image/png, */*
6: Accept-Encoding: gzip
7: Accept-Language: en
8: Accept-Charset: iso-8859-1,*,utf-8
```

13

The Response

After a server has received a client's request, it sends a response back to the client. The response usually consists of three parts:

- A status line
- A header section
- An entity body

As you can see, there's a lot of symmetry between a request and a response. In fact, certain headers can be sent by either client or server, especially those that provide information about an entity body.

The status line consists of the HTTP version that the server is using (HTTP/1.0 or HTTP/1.1), a response code, and a text message that clarifies the meaning of the response code.

There are many response codes that a server can send to a browser. Each code provides some information about the success or otherwise of the request. Table 13.3 lists some of the more common response codes.

TABLE 13.3   Some Response Codes

Code	Text	Description
200	OK	The request was successful, and the requested data will follow.
301	Moved Permanently	The requested data no longer exists on the server. A location header will contain a new address.
302	Moved Temporarily	The requested data has been moved. A location header will contain a new address.
404	Not Found	The data could not be found at the supplied address.
500	Internal Server Error	The server or a CGI script has encountered a severe problem in attempting to serve the data.

A typical response line, therefore, might look something like the following:

```
HTTP/1.1 200 OK
```

The header section includes a series of response headers, formatted in the same way as request headers. Table 13.4 lists some headers commonly sent by servers.

TABLE 13.4   Some Common Server Headers

Name	Description
Date	The current date
Server	The server name and version
Content-Type	The MIME type of content in the entity body
Content-Length	The size of the entity in bytes
Location	The full address of an alternative document

Listing 13.3 shows a typical server response. After the headers have been sent (Lines 2–9), the server sends an empty line to the client (Line 10) followed by the entity body (the document originally requested).

LISTING 13.3   A Server Response

```
 1: HTTP/1.1 200 OK
 2: Date: Tue, 25 Sep 2001 16:10:06 GMT
 3: Server: Apache/1.3.12 Cobalt (Unix) PHP/4.0.6 mod_perl/1.24
 4: Last-Modified: Tue, 25 Sep 2001 16:08:29 GMT
 5: ETag: "147829-62-3bb0abfd"
 6: Accept-Ranges: bytes
 7: Content-Length: 98
 8: Connection: close
 9: Content-Type: text/html
10:
11: <html>
12: <head>
13: <title>Listing 13.3 A server response</title>
14: </head>
15: <body>
16: Hello
17: </body>
18: </html>
```

13

Getting a Document from a Remote Address

Although PHP is a server-side language, it can act as a client, requesting data from remote servers and making the output available to your scripts. If you are already comfortable reading files from the server, you will have no problem using PHP to acquire

information from the Web. In fact, the syntax is exactly the same. You can use fopen()
to connect to a Web address in the same way as you would with a file. Listing 13.4 opens
a connection to a remote server and requests a page, printing the result to the browser.

LISTING 13.4   Getting and Printing a Web Page with fopen()

```
 1: <html>
 2: <head>
 3: <title>Listing 13.4 Getting and printing a web page with fopen()</title>
 4: </head>
 5: <body>
 6: <?php
 7: $webpage = "http://www.corrosive.co.uk/php/hello.html";
 8: $fp = fopen( $webpage, "r" ) or die("couldn't open $webpage");
 9: while ( ! feof( $fp ))
10:     print fgets( $fp, 1024 );
11: ?>
12: </body>
13: </html>
```

In order to take advantage of this feature you will need to ensure that the
allow_url_ fopen directive is set to On. This is the default setting.

It is unlikely that you will want to output an entire page to the browser. More commonly,
you would parse the document you download.

> Prior to PHP4.0.5 fopen() did not support HTTP redirects. When most mod-
> ern browsers are sent a 301 or 302 response header they will make a new
> request based upon the contents of the Location header. fopen() now sup-
> ports this, which means that urls that reference directories no longer have
> to end with a forward slash.

fopen() returns a file resource if the connection is successful and false if the connection cannot be established or the page doesn't exist. After you have a file pointer, you
can use it as normal to read the file. PHP introduces itself to the remote server as a
client. On my system, it sends the following request:

```
GET /php/hello.html HTTP/1.0
Host: www.corrosive.co.uk
User-Agent: PHP/4.0.6
```

You can also access remote files using the include() statement. If the allow_url_fopen directive is set to On and a valid URL is passed to include(), then the result of a request for the remote file will be incorporated into the script.

Unless you are very sure what you are doing, however, you should be cautious of this feature. Including source code from third parties in your own project is a big security risk.

This process is simple and is the approach you will use to access a Web page in most instances. You might want to connect to other network services, however, or learn more about a Web document by parsing the server headers. You will look at how to do this later in the hour.

Converting IP Addresses and Hostnames

Even if your server does not provide you with a $REMOTE_HOST variable, you will probably know the IP address of a visitor from the $REMOTE_ADDR environmental variable. You can use this in conjunction with the function gethostbyaddr() to get the user's hostname. gethostbyaddr() requires a string representing an IP address. It returns the equivalent hostname. If an error occurs, it returns the IP address it was given. Listing 13.5 creates a script that uses gethostbyaddr() to acquire the user's hostname if the $REMOTE_HOST variable is not available.

LISTING 13.5   Using gethostbyaddr() to Get a Hostname

```
 1: <html>
 2: <head>
 3: <title>Listing 13.5 Using gethostbyaddr() to get a host name</title>
 4: </head>
 5: <body>
 6: <?php
 7: if ( isset( $REMOTE_HOST ) )
 8:     print "Hello visitor at $REMOTE_HOST<br>";
 9: elseif ( isset ( $REMOTE_ADDR ) )
10:      print "Hello visitor at ".gethostbyaddr( $REMOTE_ADDR )."<br>";
11: else
12:     print "Hello you, wherever you are<br>";
13: ?>
14: </body>
15: </html>
```

13

If we have access to the $REMOTE_HOST variable, we simply print this to the browser on line 8. Otherwise, if we have access to the $REMOTE_ADDR variable, we attempt to acquire the user's hostname using gethostbyaddr() on line 10. If all else fails, we print a generic welcome message on line 12.

To attempt to convert a hostname to an IP address, you can use gethostbyname(). This function requires a hostname as its argument. It returns an IP address or, if an error occurs, the hostname you provided.

Making a Network Connection

So far we have had it easy. This is because PHP makes working with a Web page on a remote server as simple as opening a file on your own system. Sometimes, though, you need to exercise a little more control over a network connection or acquire more information about it.

You can make a connection to an Internet server with fsockopen(), which requires a hostname or IP address, a port number, and two reference variables. The reference variables you passed to fsockopen() are populated to provide more information about the connection attempt should it fail. You can also pass fsockopen() an optional timeout integer, which determines how long fsockopen() will wait (in seconds) before giving up on a connection. If the connection is successful, a file pointer is returned. Otherwise, it returns false.

The following fragment initiates a connection to a Web server:

```
$fp = fsockopen( "www.corrosive.co.uk", 80, $errno, errdesc, 30 );
```

80 is the usual port number that a Web server listens on.

The first reference variable, $errno, contains an error number if the connection is unsuccessful, and $errdesc might contain more information about the failure.

After you have the file pointer, you can both write to the connection with fputs() and read from it with fgets() as you might with a file. When you have finished working with your connection, you should close it with fclose().

We now have enough information to initiate our own connection to a Web server. Listing 13.6 makes an HTTP connection, retrieving a page and storing it in a variable.

LISTING 13.6   Retrieving a Web Page Using fsockopen()

```
1: <html>
2: <head>
3: <title>Listing 13.6 Retrieving a Web page using fsockopen()</title>
```

LISTING 13.6   continued

```
 4: </head>
 5: <body>
 6: <?php
 7: $host = "www.corrosive.co.uk";
 8: $page = "/index.html";
 9: $fp = fsockopen( "$host", 80, $errno, $errdesc);
10: if ( ! $fp )
11:     die ( "Couldn't connect to $host:\nError: $errno\nDesc: $errdesc\n" );
12:
13: $request = "GET $page HTTP/1.0\r\n";
14: $request .= "Host: $host\r\n";
15: $request .= "Referer: http://www.corrosive.co.uk/refpage.html\r\n";
16: $request .= "User-Agent: PHP test client\r\n\r\n";
17:
18: $page = array();
19: fputs ( $fp, $request );
20: while ( ! feof( $fp ) )
21:     $page[] = fgets( $fp, 1024 );
22: fclose( $fp );
23: print "the server returned ".(count($page))." lines!";
24: ?>
25: </body>
26: </html>
```

Notice the request headers (Lines 13–16) that we send to the server in Line 19. The Webmaster at the remote host will see the value you sent in the User-Agent header in her log file. She may also assume that a visitor to our page connected from a link at http://www.corrosive.co.uk/refpage.html. For this reason, you should be cautious of some of the environmental variables available to your scripts. Treat them as an valuable guide, rather than a set of facts.

There are some legitimate reasons why you might want to fake some headers. You might need to parse some data that will only be sent to Netscape compatible browsers. One way you can do this is to include the word "Mozilla" in the User-Agent header. Nevertheless, pity the poor Webmaster. Operational decisions are made as a result of server statistics, so try not to distort the information you provide.

The example in Listing 13.6 adds little to PHP's built-in method of acquiring Web pages. Listing 13.7 uses fsockopen() to check the status codes returned by servers when we request a series of pages.

13

LISTING 13.7   Outputting the Status Lines Returned by Web Servers

```
 1: <html>
 2: <head>
 3: <title>Listing 13.7 Outputting the status lines returned by web encountered a
➥servers</title>
 4: </head>
 5: <body>
 6: <?php
 7: $to_check = array (
 8:                      "www.corrosive.co.uk"  =>  "/index.html",
 9:                      "www.virgin.com"       =>  "/notthere.html",
10:                      "www.4332blah.com"     =>  "/nohost.html"
11:               );
12:
13: foreach ( $to_check as $host => $page ) {
14:     $fp = fsockopen( "$host", 80, $errno, $errdesc, 10);
15:     print "Trying $host<BR>\n";
16:     if ( ! $fp ) {
17:         print "Couldn't connect to $host:\n<br>Error: $errno\n<br>Desc:
➥$errdesc\n";
18:         print "<br><hr><br>\n";
19:         continue;
20:     }
21:     print "Trying to get $page<br>\n";
22:     fputs( $fp, "HEAD $page HTTP/1.0\r\n\r\n" );
23:     print fgets( $fp, 1024 );
24:     print "<br><br><br>\n";
25:     fclose( $fp );
26: }
27:
28: ?>
29: </body>
30: </html>
```

We create an associative array of the server names and page addresses we want to check starting at line 7. We loop through this using a `foreach` statement on line 13. For every element, we initiate a connection using `fsockopen()` (line 14), setting a timeout of 10 seconds. If the connection fails, we print a message to the browser and use `continue` on line 19 to move on to the next pair. If the connection is successful, we send a request to the server on line 22. We use the HEAD method because we are not interested in parsing an entity body. We use `fgets()` on line 23 to get the status line from the server. We are not going to work with server headers for this example, so we close the connection with `fclose()` on line 25 and move on to the next element in the list.

Figure 13.2 shows the output from Listing 13.7.

FIGURE **13.2**

A Script to Print Server Response Headers.

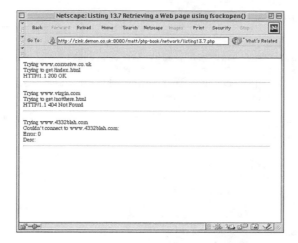

If you are interested in writing sophisticated Web client applications you should look at the CURL package (**http://curl.haxx.se/**). As of PHP 4.02 support was added for CURL which can handle many of HTTP's more tricky aspects including user and password authentication, cookies, and POST form submissions. It can also handle secure transactions with HTTPS and a range of other protocols. You can get more details from the PHP manual at <http://www.php.net/manual/en/ref.curl.php>.

Making an NNTP Connection Using `fsockopen()`

fsockopen() can be used to make a connection to any Internet server. In Listing 13.8, we connect to an NNTP (Usenet) server, select a newsgroup, and list the headers of the first message.

LISTING **13.8** A Basic NNTP Connection Using fsockopen()

```
 1: <html>
 2: <head>
 3: <title>Listing 13.8 A basic NNTP connection using fsockopen()</title>
 4: </head>
 5: <body>
 6: <?php
 7: $server = "news"; // change this to your news server
 8: $group  = "alt.test";
 9: $line = "";
10: print "<pre>\n";
11: print "— Trying to connect to $server\n\n";
```

13

LISTING 13.8   continued

```
12:
13: $fp = fsockopen( "$server", 119, $error, $description, 10 );
14: if ( ! $fp )
15:     die("Couldn't connect to $server\n$errno\n$errdesc\n\n");
16: print "— Connected to $server\n\n";
17:
18: $line = fgets( $fp, 1024 );
19: $status = explode( " ", $line );
20:
21: if ( $status[0] != 200 ) {
22:     fputs( $fp, "close" );
23:     die("Error: $line\n\n");
24: }
25:
26: print "$line\n";
27: print "— Selecting $group\n\n";
28: fputs( $fp, "group alt.test\n" );
29: $line = fgets( $fp, 1024 );
30: $status = explode( " ", $line );
31:
32: if ( $status[0] != 211 ) {
33:     fputs( $fp, "close" );
34:     die("Error: $line\n\n");
35: }
36:
37: print "$line\n";
38: print "— Getting headers for first message\n\n";
39: fputs( $fp, "head\n" );
40: $line = fgets( $fp, 1024 );
41: $status = explode( " ", $line );
42: print "$line\n";
43:
44: if ( $status[0] != 221 ) {
45:     fputs( $fp, "close" );
46:     die("Error: $line\n\n");
47: }
48:
49: while ( ! ( strpos($line, ".")  === 0 ) ) {
50:     $line = fgets( $fp, 1024 );
51:     print $line;
52: }
53:
54: fputs( $fp, "close\n" );
55: print "</pre>";
56: ?>
57: </body>
58: </html>
```

The code in Listing 13.8 does little more than demonstrate that an NNTP connection is possible with `fsockopen()`. In a real-world example, you would want to handle the line parsing in a function to save repetition and to extract more information from the server's output. Rather than reinvent the wheel in this way, you might want to investigate PHP's IMAP functions, which provide POP3 and NNTP connectivity and will automate much of this work for you.

We store the hostname of our server in a variable, `$server` on line 7, and the group we want to select in `$group` on line 8. If you wish to run this script, you should assign the hostname of your Internet Service Provider's news server to the `$server` variable. We use `fsockopen()` on line 13 to connect to the host on port 119, which is the usual port for NNTP connections. If a valid file resource is not returned, we use `die()` on line 15 to print the error number and description to the browser and end script execution. On connection, the server should have sent us a confirmation message, so we attempt to acquire this with `fgets()` on line 18. If all is well, this string begins with the status code 200. To test this, we use `explode()` (line 19) to split the `$line` string into an array using the space character as the delimiter. You can learn more about the `explode()` function in Hour 17. If the first element of this array is 200, we can continue; otherwise, we end the script.

If all is proceeding as expected, we send the news server the "group" command that should select a newsgroup on line 28. If this is successful, the server should return a string beginning with the status code 211. We test this once again on line 32, and end execution if we don't get what we are expecting.

Now that we have selected our newsgroup, we send the "head" command to the server on line 39, which requests the headers for the first message in the group. Again, we test the server response on line 44, looking for the status code 221. Finally, we acquire the header itself. The server's listing of a header will end with a single dot (.) on its own line, so we test for this in a `while` statement on line 49. As long as the server's output line does not begin with a dot, we request and print the next line.

Finally, we close the connection. Figure 13.3 shows a typical output from Listing 13.8.

13

FIGURE **13.3**

Making an NNTP connection.

Sending Mail with the `mail()` Function

PHP can automate the sending of Internet mail for you. The `mail()` function requires three strings representing the recipient of the mail, the mail subject, and the message. `mail()` returns `false` if it encounters an error. In the following fragment, we send an email:

```
$to = "someone@adomain.com";
$subject = "hi";
$message = "just a test message! ";
mail( $to, $subject, $message ) or print "Could not send mail";
```

If you are running PHP on a UNIX system, `mail()` will use a mail application such as Sendmail. On other systems, the function will connect to a local or remote SMTP mail server. You should set this using the SMTP directive in the php.ini file.

You are not limited to the mail headers implied by the `mail()` function's required arguments. You can include as many mail headers as you want in an optional fourth string argument. These should be separated by CRLF characters ('\r\n'). In the following example, we include a From field in our mail message, as well as an X-Priority header that some clients will recognize:

```
$to = "someone@adomain.com";
$from = "book@corrosive.co.uk";
$subject = "hi";
$message = "just a test message! ";
mail( $to, $subject, $message, "$from\r\nX-Priority: 1 (Highest)" )
        or print "Could not send mail";
```

As of PHP 4.0.5 an additional fifth optional parameter can be used. This allows you to pass command line style arguments directly to the mailer.

Summary

In this hour, you learned how to use environmental variables to learn more about your visitors. If you don't have access to a user's hostname, you should now be able to use `gethostbyaddr()` to acquire it.

You learned some of the basics about the negotiation that takes place between client and server when an HTTP connection is made.

You learned how to use `fopen()` to get a document from the Web, and how to use `fsockopen()` to make your own HTTP connection. You should also be able to use `fsockopen()` to make connections to other network services. Finally, you learned how to use `mail()` to send email from your scripts.

So far in this book we have concentrated on text. In the next hour we are going to look at some functions that will allow us to use PHP to construct and manipulate images.

Q&A

Q HTTP seems a little esoteric. Do I really need to know about it to write good PHP code?

A No. You can write excellent code with knowing the intricacies of client/server interaction. On the other hand, a basic understanding of the process is useful if you want to do more than just download pages from remote servers.

Q If I can send fake headers to a remote server, how suspicious should I be of environmental variables myself?

A You should not trust environmental variables such as `$HTTP_REFERER` and `$HTTP_USER_AGENT` if their accuracy is essential to the operation of your script. Remember, though, that the vast majority of clients that you deal with will tell you the truth. If you are merely ensuring a productive user experience by detecting browser type or gathering overall statistical information, there is no need to distrust this data.

13

Workshop

Quiz

1. What server variable might give you the URL of the referring page?
2. Why can you not rely on the $REMOTE_ADDR variable to track an individual user across multiple visits to your script?
3. What does HTTP stand for?
4. What client header line tells the server about the browser that is making the request?
5. What does the server response code 404 mean?
6. Without making your own network connection, what function might you use to access a Web page on a remote server?
7. Given an IP address, what function could you use to get a hostname?
8. What function would you use to make a network connection?
9. What PHP function would you use to send an email?

Quiz Answers

1. You can often find the URL of the referring page in the $HTTP_REFERRER variable.
2. Many service providers allocate a different IP address to their users every time they log on, so you cannot assume that a user will return with the same address.
3. HTTP stands for hypertext transfer protocol.
4. A client might send a User-Agent header, which tells the server about the client version and operating system that are running.
5. The server response 404 means that the requested page or resource cannot be found on the server.
6. The fopen() function can be used for Web pages on remote machines as well as files on your file system.
7. The gethostbyaddr() function accepts an IP address and returns a resolved hostname.
8. The fsockopen() function will establish a connection with a remote server.
9. You can send email with the mail() function.

Activities

1. Create a script that accepts a Web hostname (such as `http://www.microsoft.com`) from user input. Send the host a `HEAD` request using `fsockopen()` to create the connection. Print the response to the browser. Remember to handle the possibility that no connection can be established.

2. Create a script that accepts a message from the user and mails it to you. Add server variables to the user's message to tell you about his or her browser and IP address.

13

HOUR 14

Images On-the-Fly

The functions included in this hour rely on an open source library called GD.

The GD library is a set of tools that enable programmers to create and work with images on-the-fly. You can find out more about GD at http://www. boutell.com/gd/. If you have the GD library installed on your system and PHP was compiled to use it, you will be able to use PHP's image functions to create dynamic images. Many systems will still run the older version of the library, which allows the creation of images in GIF format. Later versions of the library do not support GIFs for licensing reasons. If your system is using a later library, it is possible to compile PHP so that the image functions output images in PNG format, which is supported by the more popular browsers.

If you have the GD library, you will be able to use PHP's image functions to create sophisticated graphics on-the-fly.

In this hour, you will learn:

- How to create and output an image
- How to work with colors

- How to draw shapes, including arcs, rectangles, and polygons
- How to fill areas with color
- How to work with TrueType fonts

Creating and Outputting Images

Before you can begin to work with an image, you must acquire an image resource. You can do this using the `imagecreate()` function. `imagecreate()` requires two arguments, one for the image's height and another for its width. It returns an image resource, which you will use with most of the functions that we will cover in this hour. You should be familiar with resources from your work with files and databases. The image resource returned by `imagecreate()` will be a required argument for most of the functions in this book.

After you have an image resource, you are nearly ready to output your first image to the browser. To do this, you need the `imagegif()` function, which requires the image resource as an argument. Listing 14.1 uses these functions to create and output an image.

LISTING 14.1   A Dynamically Created Image

```
1: <?php
2: header("Content-type: image/gif");
3: $image = imagecreate( 200, 200 );
4: imagegif($image);
5: ?>
```

Notice that we sent a `Content-type` header to the browser (line 2) before doing anything else. We need to tell the browser to expect image information; otherwise, it treats the script's output as HTML. This script can now be called directly by the browser, or as part of an IMG element.

```
<img src="listing14.1.php" alt="a PHP generated image">
```

Figure 14.1 shows the output of Listing 14.1.

We have created a square, but we have no way as yet of controlling its color.

FIGURE **14.1**
A dynamically created image.

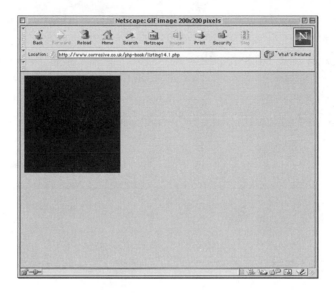

Acquiring Color

To work with color, you need to acquire a color resource. You can do this with the `imagecolorallocate()` function, which requires an image resource and three integers between 0 and 255 representing red, green, and blue. The function returns an image resource that you can use to define the color of shapes, fills, and text.

```
$red = imagecolorallocate($image, 255,0,0);
```

Coincidentally, the first time you call `imagecolorallocate()`, you also set the default color for your image; so by adding the previous code fragment to Listing 14.1, we would create a red square.

Drawing Lines

Before you draw a line on an image, you need to determine the points from and to which you want to draw.

You can think of an image as a block of pixels indexed from 0 on both the horizontal and vertical axes. Their origin is the top left-hand corner of the image.

14

In other words, the pixel with the coordinates 5, 8 is the sixth pixel along and the ninth pixel down, looking from left to right, top to bottom.

The `imageline()` function draws a line between one pixel coordinate and another. It requires an image resource, four integers representing the start and end coordinates of the line, and a color resource.

Listing 14.2 adds to the image created in Listing 14.1, drawing a line from corner to corner.

LISTING 14.2   Drawing a Line with `imageline()`

```
1: <?php
2: header("Content-type: image/gif");
3: $image = imagecreate( 200, 200 );
4: $red = imagecolorallocate($image, 255,0,0);
5: $blue = imagecolorallocate($image, 0,0,255 );
6: imageline( $image, 0, 0, 199, 199, $blue );
7: imagegif($image);
8: ?>
```

We acquire two color resources, one for red (line 4) and one for blue (line 5). We then use the resource stored in the variable `$blue` for the line's color on line 6. Notice that our line ends at the coordinates 199, 199 and not 200, 200. Remember that pixels are indexed from 0. Figure 14.2 shows the output from Listing 14.2.

FIGURE 14.2

Drawing a line with `imageline()`.

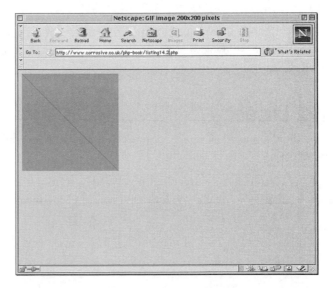

Applying Color Fills

You can fill an area with color using PHP just as you can with your favorite graphics application. The function imagefill() requires an image resource, starting coordinates for the fill it is to perform, and a color resource. It then transforms the starting pixel and all adjacent pixels of the same color. Listing 14.3 adds a call to imagefill() to our script, making the image a little more interesting.

LISTING 14.3 Using imagefill()

```
1: <?php
2: header("Content-type: image/gif");
3: $image = imagecreate( 200, 200 );
4: $red = imagecolorallocate($image, 255,0,0);
5: $blue = imagecolorallocate($image, 0,0,255 );
6: imageline( $image, 0, 0, 199, 199, $blue );
7: imagefill( $image, 0, 199, $blue );
8: imagegif($image);
9: ?>
```

The only change we have made to our example is the call to imagefill() on line 7. Figure 14.3 shows the output from Listing 14.3.

FIGURE 14.3

Using imagefill().

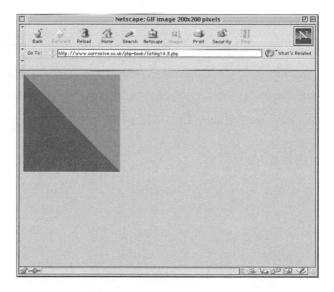

14

Drawing an Arc

You can add partial or complete arcs to your images with the `imagearc()` function. `imagearc()` requires an image object, coordinates for the center point, an integer for width, an integer for height, a start point and an end point (in degrees), and a color resource. Arcs are drawn clockwise starting from 3 o'clock. The following fragment draws a quarter circle:

```
imagearc( $image, 99, 99, 200, 200, 0, 90, $blue );
```

This draws a partial arc, with its center at the coordinates 99, 99. The total height and width will both be 200 pixels. Drawing starts at 3 o'clock and continues for 90 degrees (to 6 o'clock).

Listing 14.4 draws a complete circle and fills it with blue.

LISTING 14.4   Drawing a Circle with `imagearc()`

```
1: <?php
2: header("Content-type: image/gif");
3: $image = imagecreate( 200, 200 );
4: $red = imagecolorallocate($image, 255,0,0);
5: $blue = imagecolorallocate($image, 0,0,255 );
6: imagearc( $image, 99, 99, 180, 180, 0, 360, $blue );
7: imagefill( $image, 99, 99, $blue );
8: imagegif($image);
9: ?>
```

As before we acquire color resources (lines 5 and 5). On line 6 we call `imagearc()` to draw a complete circle. The call to `imagefill()` on line 7 fills our circle with blue.

Figure 14.4 shows the output from Listing 14.4.

Drawing a circle with
imagearc().

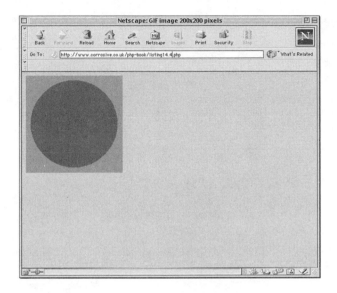

Drawing a Rectangle

You can draw a rectangle in PHP using the imagerectangle() function. imagerectangle() requires an image resource, the coordinates for your rectangle's top-left corner, the coordinates for its bottom right corner, and a color resource. The following fragment draws a rectangle whose top-left coordinates are 19, 19 and bottom-right coordinates are 179, 179:

```
imagerectangle( $image, 19, 19, 179, 179,  $blue );
```

You could then fill this with imagefill(). Because this is such a common operation, however, PHP provides the imagefilledrectangle() function, which expects exactly the same arguments as imagerectangle() but produces a rectangle filled with the color you specify. Listing 14.5 creates a filled rectangle (line 6) and outputs the image to the browser.

14

LISTING 14.5 Drawing a Filled Rectangle with `imagefilledrectangle()`

```
1: <?php
2: header("Content-type: image/gif");
3: $image = imagecreate( 200, 200 );
4: $red = imagecolorallocate($image, 255,0,0);
5: $blue = imagecolorallocate($image, 0,0,255 );
6: imagefilledrectangle( $image, 19, 19, 179, 179,  $blue );
7: imagegif( $image );
8: ?>
```

Figure 14.5 shows the output from Listing 14.5.

FIGURE 14.5

Drawing a filled rectangle with `image-filledrectangle()`.

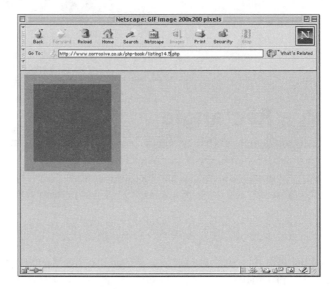

Drawing a Polygon

You can draw more sophisticated shapes using `imagepolygon()`. This function requires an image resource, an array of point coordinates, an integer representing the number of points in the shape, and a color resource. The array passed to `imagepolygon()` should be numerically indexed. The first two elements give the coordinates of the first point, the second two give the coordinates of the second point, and so on. `imagepolygon()` fills in the lines between the points, automatically closing your shape by joining the final point to the first. You can create a filled polygon with the `imagefilledpolygon()` function.

Listing 14.6 draws a filled polygon, outputting the result to the browser.

LISTING 14.6   Drawing a Polygon with `imagefilledpolygon()`

```
 1: <?php
 2: header("Content-type: image/gif");
 3: $image = imagecreate( 200, 200 );
 4: $red = imagecolorallocate($image, 255,0,0);
 5: $blue = imagecolorallocate($image, 0,0,255 );
 6: $points = array (    10, 10,
 7:            190, 190,
 8:            190, 10,
 9:            10, 190
10:            );
11: imagefilledpolygon( $image, $points, count( $points )/2 , $blue );
12: imagegif($image);
13: ?>
```

After acquiring image and color resources (lines 2–5) we create an array of coordinates on line 6. Notice that when we call `imagefilledpolygon()` on line 11 we tell it the number of points we want to connect by counting the number of elements in the `$points` array and dividing the result by 2. Figure 14.6 shows the output from Listing 14.6.

FIGURE 14.6

Drawing a polygon with `imagefilledpolygon()`

.

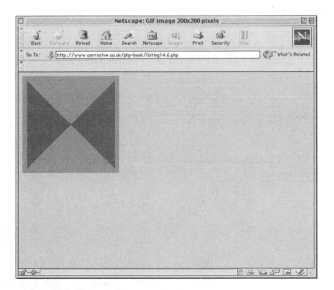

Making a Color Transparent

PHP allows you to make selected colors within your image transparent with `imagecolortransparent()`. This function requires an image resource and a color resource. When you output your image to the browser, the color you pass to

14

`imagecolortransparent()` will be transparent. Listing 14.7 changes our polygon code so that the shape "floats" on the browser instead of sitting against a background color.

LISTING 14.7   Making Colors Transparent with `imagecolortransparent()`

```
 1: <?php
 2: header("Content-type: image/gif");
 3:
 4: $image = imagecreate( 200, 200 );
 5: $red = imagecolorallocate($image, 255,0,0);
 6: $blue = imagecolorallocate($image, 0,0,255 );
 7:
 8: $points = array (      10, 10,
 9:              190, 190,
10:              190, 10,
11:              10, 190
12:              );
13:
14: imagefilledpolygon( $image, $points, count( $points )/2 , $blue );
15: imagecolortransparent( $image, $red );
16: imagegif($image);
17: ?>
```

Listing 14.7 is identical to Listing 14.6 except for the call to `imagecolortransparent()` on line 15. Figure 14.7 shows the output from Listing 14.7.

FIGURE 14.7

Making colors transparent with `imagecolor-transparent()`.

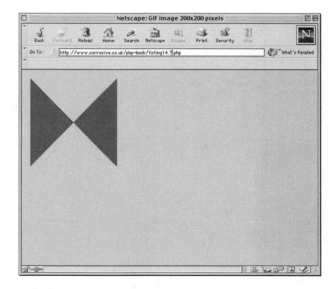

Working with Text

If you have TrueType fonts on your system, you can use these to write text into your images. In addition to the GD library, you need to have the FreeType library installed on your system. If you have this combination, you can create image-based charts or navigation elements. PHP even gives you the tool you need to check that any text that you write will fit within the space available.

Writing a String with `imageTTFtext()`

You can write text to your image with the `imageTTFtext()` function. This requires eight arguments: an image resource, a size argument representing the height of the characters to be written, an angle, the starting coordinates (one argument for the x axis and another for the y axis), a color resource, the path to a TrueType font, and the text you want to write.

The start point for any text you write determines where the baseline of the first character in the string will be.

Listing 14.8 writes a string to an image and outputs the result to the browser.

LISTING 14.8   Writing a String with `imageTTFtext()`

```
 1: <?php
 2: header("Content-type: image/gif");
 3:
 4: $image = imagecreate( 400, 200 );
 5: $red = imagecolorallocate($image, 255,0,0);
 6: $blue = imagecolorallocate($image, 0,0,255 );
 7: $font = "/usr/local/jdk121_pre-v1/jre/lib/fonts/LucidaSansRegular.ttf";
 8:
 9: imageTTFtext( $image, 50, 0, 20, 100, $blue, $font, "Welcome!" );
10:
11: imagegif($image);
12: ?>
```

We create a canvas with a width of 400 pixels and a height of 200 pixels on line 4. We define two colors (lines 5 and 6) and store the path to a TrueType font in a variable called `$font` (line 7). Note that font files are likely to be stored in a different directory on your server. If you are not sure where, you could try searching for files with the `.ttf` extension. We then write the text "Welcome!" to the image on line 9.

For the call to `imageTTFtext()`, we define a size of 50, an angle of 0, a starting position of 20 on the x–axis and 100 on the y–axis. We also pass the function the color resource

14

stored in the $blue variable, the font path stored in $font, and, finally, the text we want to output. You can see the result in Figure 14.8.

FIGURE 14.8

Writing text with imageTTFtext().

Of course, we have to guess where to put the text at the moment. The size argument does not give us an accurate idea of the text's height, and the width is a mystery. In fact, imageTTFtext() will return dimension information, but by then the deed is done. Luckily, PHP provides a function that allows you to try before you buy.

Testing Text Dimensions with imageTTFbox()

You can get information about the dimensions of text using the imageTTFbox() function, which is so called because it tells you about the text's bounding box. imageTTFbox() requires the font size, the angle, a path to a font file, and the text to be written. It is one of the few image functions that do not require an image resource. It returns an eight-element array, which is explained in Table 14.1.

TABLE 14.1 The Array Returned by imageTTFbox()

Index	Description
0	bottom left (horizontal axis)
1	bottom left (vertical axis)
2	bottom right (horizontal axis)
3	bottom right (vertical axis)

TABLE 14.1 continued

Index	Description
4	top right (horizontal axis)
5	top right (vertical axis)
6	top left (horizontal axis)
7	top left (vertical axis)

All figures on the vertical axis are relative to the text's baseline, which is 0. Figures for the vertical axis at the top of the text count down from this figure, and so usually are minus numbers. Figures for the vertical axis at the bottom of the text count up from 0, giving the number of pixels the text drops from the baseline.

So, if you test a string containing a "y" with imageTTFbbox(), for example, the return array might have a figure of 3 for element 1 because the tail of the "y" drops 3 pixels below the baseline. It could have a figure of −10 for element 7 because the text is raised 10 pixels above the baseline.

To complicate matters, there seems to be a 2-pixel difference between the baseline as returned by imageTTFbbox() and the visible baseline when drawing text. You may need to adjust for this, by thinking of the height of the baseline as 2 pixels greater than that returned by the imageTTFbbox().

On the horizontal axis, figures for left-hand side imageTTFbbox() will take account of text that begins before the given start point by returning the offset as a minus number in elements 6 and 0. This usually will be a small number so whether you adjust alignment to take account of this depends on the level of accuracy you require.

You can use the information returned by imageTTFbbox() to align text within an image. Listing 14.9 creates a script that dynamically outputs text, centering it within our image on both the vertical and horizontal planes.

LISTING 14.9 Aligning Text Within a Fixed Space Using imageTTFbbox()

```
1: <?php
2: header("Content-type: image/gif");
3: $height = 100;
4: $width = 200;
5: $fontsize = 50;
6: if ( ! isset ( $text ) )
7:     $text = "Change me!";
8: $image = imagecreate( $width, $height );
9: $red = imagecolorallocate($image, 255,0,0);
```

14

LISTING 14.9   continued

```
10: $blue = imagecolorallocate($image, 0,0,255 );
11: $font = "/home/usr/local/jdk1.3.1/jre/lib/fonts/LucidaSansRegular.ttf";
12: $textwidth = $width;
13: $textheight;
14: while ( true ) {
15:     $box = imageTTFbbox( $fontsize, 0, $font, $text );
16:     $textwidth =  abs( $box[2] );
17:     $textbodyheight = ( abs($box[7]) )-2;
18:     if ( $textwidth < $width - 20 )
19:         break;
20:     $fontsize--;
21: }
22: $gifXcenter = (int) ( $width/2 );
23: $gifYcenter = (int) ( $height/2 );
24: imageTTFtext(    $image, $fontsize, 0,
25:         (int) ($gifXcenter-($textwidth/2)),
26:         (int) ($gifYcenter+(($textbodyheight)/2) ),
27:         $blue, $font, $text );
28: imagegif($image);
29: ?>
```

We store the height and width of the image in the variables $height and $width (lines 3
and 4), and set a default font size of 50 on line 5. On line 6 we test for the presence of a
variable called $text, setting a default on line 7 if it isn't present. In this way, the image
can accept data from a Web page, either in the query string of an image URL or from
form submission. We use imagecreate() on line 8 to acquire an image resource. We
acquire color resources in the usual way and store the path to a TrueType font file in a
variable called $font (lines 9 to 11).

We want to fit the string stored in $text into the available space, but we have no way of
knowing yet whether it will. Within a while statement starting on line 14, we pass the
font path and string to imageTTFbbox() on line 15, storing the resultant array in a variable called $box. The element $box[2] contains the position of the lower-right corner on
the horizontal axis. We take this to be the width of the string and store it in $textwidth
on line 16.

We want to vertically center the text, but only accounting for the area above the text's
baseline. We can use the absolute value of $box[7] to find the height of the text above
the baseline, although we need to adjust this by 2 pixels. We store this value in
$textbodyheight on line 17.

Now that we have a working figure for the text's width, we can test it against the width
of the image (less 10 pixels border). If the text is smaller than the width of the canvas we

are using, then we end the loop on line 19. Otherwise, we reduce the font size on line 20, ready to try again.

Dividing the $height and $width values by 2 (lines 22 and 23), we can find the approximate center point of the image. We write the text to the image on line 24, using the figures we have calculated for the image's center point in conjunction with the text's height and width to calculate the offset.

Finally, we write the image to the browser on line 28. Figure 14.9 shows the output from Listing 14.9.

FIGURE 14.9

Aligning text within a fixed space using imageTTFbbox().

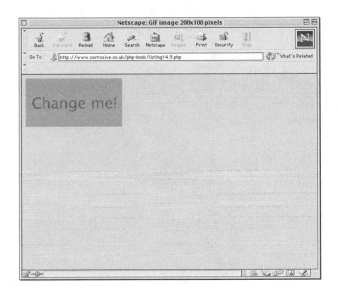

This code can now be called from another page as part of an IMG element. The following fragment writes some simple code that would allow a user to add her own string to be included in the image:

```
1: <?php
2: if ( ! isset( $text ) )
3:     $text = "Dynamic text!";
4: ?>
5: <form action="<? print $PHP_SELF ?>" method="POST">
6: <input type="text" name="text">
7: </form>
8: <p>
9: <img src="listing14.9.php?<? print "text=".urlencode($text) ?>">
```

When we call the script in Listing 14.9 on line 9, we append a query string that includes the text to be added to the image. You can learn more about this technique for passing information from script to script in Hour 19, "Saving State with Cookies and Queries."

14

Bringing It Together

Let's build an example that uses some of the functions that we have looked at in this hour. Suppose that we have been asked to produce a dynamic bar chart that compares a range of labeled numbers. The bar chart must include the relevant label below each bar. Our client must be able to change the number of bars on the chart, the height and width of the image, and the size of the border around the chart. The bar chart will be used for consumer votes, and all that is needed is an "at a glance" representation of the data. A more detailed breakdown will be included in the HTML portion of the containing page.

The easiest way of storing labels and values is in an associative array. After we have this array, we need to calculate the number of bars we will be dealing with and the greatest value in the array:

```
$cells = array ( 'liked'=>200, 'hated'=>400, 'indifferent'=>900 );
$max = max( $cells );
$total = count ( $cells );
```

We must set up some variables to allow the client to customize the image:

```
$totalwidth = 400;
$totalheight = 200;
$xgutter = 20; // left/right margin
$ygutter = 20; // top/bottom margin
$internalgap = 5; // space between cells
$bottomspace = 40; // gap at the bottom (in addition to margin)
$font = "/home/usr/local/jdk1.3.1/jre/lib/fonts/LucidaSansRegular.ttf";
```

The client can change the variables to define the image height and width. The $xgutter and $ygutter variables determine the margin around the chart horizontally and vertically. $internalgap determines the space between the bars. The $bottomspace variable contains the space available to label the bars at the bottom of the screen.

Now that we have these values, we can do some calculations to arrive at some useful variables:

```
$graphCanX = ( $totalwidth - $xgutter*2 );
$graphCanY = ( $totalheight - $ygutter*2 - $bottomspace );
$posX = $xgutter; // starting draw position x - axis
$posY = $totalheight - $ygutter - $bottomspace; // starting draw pos - y - axis
$cellwidth = (int) (( $graphCanX - ( $internalgap * ( $total-1 ) )) / $total) ;
$textsize = (int)($bottomspace);
```

We calculate the graph canvas (the space in which the bars are to be written). On the x–axis, this will be the total width minus twice the size of the margin. On the y–axis, we need also to take account of the $bottomspace variable to leave room for the labels.

$posX stores the point on the x–axis at which we will start drawing the bars, so we set this to the same value as $xgutter, which contains the value for the margin on the $x axis. $posY stores the bottom point of our bars; it is equivalent to the total height of the image less the margin and the space for the labels stored in $bottomheight.

$cellwidth contains the width of each bar. To arrive at this value, we must calculate the total amount of space between bars and take this from the chart width, dividing this result by the total number of bars.

We initially set the size of the text to be the same as the height left free for label text (as stored in $bottomspace).

Before we can create and work with our image, we need to determine the text size. Our problem is that we don't know how long the labels will be, and we want to make sure that each of the labels will fit within the width of the bar above it. We loop through the $cells array to calculate the maximum text size we can use:

```
foreach ( $cells as $key=>$val ) {
    while ( true ) {
        $box = ImageTTFbBox( $textsize, 0, $font, $key );
        $textWidth = $box[2];
        if ( $textWidth < $cellwidth )
            break;
        $textsize--;
    }
}
```

For each of the elements, we begin a loop, acquiring dimension information for the label using imageTTFbbox(). We take the text width to be $box[2] and test it against the $cellwidth variable, which contains the width of a single bar in the chart. We break the loop if the text is smaller than the bar width; otherwise, we decrement $textsize and try again. $textsize continues to shrink until every label in the array fits within the bar width.

Now, at last we can create an image resource and begin to work with it:

```
$image = imagecreate( $totalwidth, $totalheight );
$red = ImageColorAllocate($image, 255, 0, 0);
$blue = ImageColorAllocate($image, 0, 0, 255 );
$black = ImageColorAllocate($image, 0, 0, 0 );
reset ($cells);
foreach ( $cells as $key=>$val ) {
    $cellheight = (int) (($val/$max) * $graphCanY);
    $center = (int)($posX+($cellwidth/2));
    imagefilledrectangle( $image, $posX, ($posY-$cellheight),
        ($posX+$cellwidth), $posY, $blue );
    $box = ImageTTFbBox( $textsize, 0, $font, $key );
    $tw = $box[2];
```

14

```
    ImageTTFText( $image, $textsize, 0, ($center-($tw/2) ),
            ($totalheight-$ygutter), $black, $font, $key );
    $posX += ( $cellwidth + $internalgap);
}
imagegif( $image );
```

We begin by creating an image resource with `imagecreate()` and allocate some colors. Once again, we loop through our `$cells` array. We calculate the height of the bar, storing the result in `$cellheight`. We calculate the center point (on the x–axis) of the bar, which is `$posX` plus half the width of the bar.

We draw the bar, using `imagefilledrectangle()` and the variables `$posX`, `$posY`, `$cellheight`, and `$cellwidth`.

To align our text, we need `imageTTFbbox()` once again, storing its return array in `$box`. We use `$box[2]` as our working width and assign this to a temporary variable, `$tw`. We now have enough information to write the label. We derive our x position from the `$center` variable minus half the width of the text, and our y position from the image's height minus the margin.

We increment `$posX` ready to start working with the next bar.

Finally, we output the image.

You can see the complete script in Listing 14.10 and sample output in Figure 14.10.

FIGURE **14.10**

A dynamic bar chart.

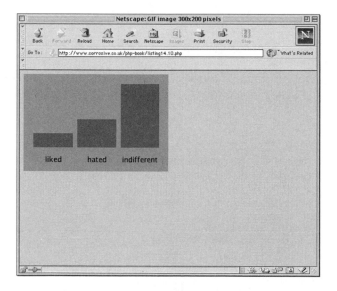

LISTING 14.10 A Dynamic Bar Chart

```php
 1: <?php
 2: header("Content-type: image/gif");
 3: $cells = array ( 'liked'=>200, 'hated'=>400, 'indifferent'=>900 );
 4: $max = max( $cells );
 5: $total = count ( $cells );
 6: $totalwidth = 300;
 7: $totalheight = 200;
 8: $xgutter = 20; // left/right margin
 9: $ygutter = 20; // top/bottom margin
10: $internalgap = 10; // space between cells
11: $bottomspace = 30; // gap at the bottom (in addition to margin)
12: $font = "/home/usr/local/jdk1.3.1/jre/lib/fonts/LucidaSansRegular.ttf";
13: $graphCanX = ( $totalwidth - $xgutter*2 );
14: $graphCanY = ( $totalheight - $ygutter*2 - $bottomspace );// starting draw
➥position x - axis
15: $posX = $xgutter; // starting draw pos - y - axis
16: $posY = $totalheight - $ygutter - $bottomspace;
17: $cellwidth = (int) (( $graphCanX -                ( $internalgap * ( $total-1
➥) )) / $total) ;
18: $textsize = (int)($bottomspace);
19: // adjust font size
20: foreach ( $cells as $key=>$val ) {
21:     while ( true ) {
22:         $box = ImageTTFbBox( $textsize, 0, $font, $key );
23:         $textWidth = abs( $box[2] );
24:         if ( $textWidth < $cellwidth )
25:             break;
26:         $textsize--;
27:     }
28: }
29: $image = imagecreate( $totalwidth, $totalheight );
30: $red = ImageColorAllocate($image, 255, 0, 0);
31: $blue = ImageColorAllocate($image, 0, 0, 255 );
32: $black = ImageColorAllocate($image, 0, 0, 0 );
33: $grey = ImageColorAllocate($image, 100, 100, 100 );
34: foreach ( $cells as $key=>$val ) {
35:     $cellheight = (int) (($val/$max) * $graphCanY);
36:     $center = (int)($posX+($cellwidth/2));
37:     imagefilledrectangle( $image, $posX, ($posY-$cellheight),
➥($posX+$cellwidth), $posY, $blue );
38:     $box = ImageTTFbBox( $textsize, 0, $font, $key );
39:     $tw = $box[2];
40:     ImageTTFText( $image, $textsize, 0, ($center-($tw/2)),
41:             ($totalheight-$ygutter), $black, $font, $key );
42:     $posX += ( $cellwidth + $internalgap);
43: }
44: imagegif( $image );
45: ?>
```

14

Between lines 3 and 18 we declare and assign to the variables that the script will use. The foreach loop between line 20 and line 28 is used to determine the required text size. We finally build the image between lines 29 and 44.

Summary

PHP's support for the GD library enables you to produce dynamic charts and navigation elements with relative ease.

In this hour, you learned how to use `imagecreate()` and `imagegif()` to create and output an image. You learned how to acquire color resources with `imagecolorallocate()` and to use color resources with `imagefill()` to fill areas with color. You learned how to use line and shape functions to create outline and filled shapes. You learned how to use PHP's support for the FreeType library to work with TrueType fonts, and worked through an example that wrote text to an image. Finally, you worked through a bar chart example that brought some of these techniques together into a single script.

Our next hour is timely indeed. We will be looking at dates, and the many useful functions that PHP provides to help work with them.

Q&A

Q Are there any performance issues with regard to dynamic images?

A A dynamically created image will be slower to arrive at the browser than an image that already exists. Depending on the efficiency of your script, the impact is not likely to be noticeable to the user if you use dynamic images sparingly.

Workshop

Quiz

1. What header should you send to the browser before building and outputting a GIF image?

2. What function would you use to acquire an image resource that you can use with other image functions?

3. What function would you use to output your GIF after building it?

4. What function could you use to acquire a color resource?

5. With which function would you draw a line on a dynamic image?

6. What function would you use to fill an area in a dynamic image?

7. What function might you use to draw an arc?

8. How might you draw a rectangle?

9. How would you draw a polygon?

10. What function would you use to write a string to a dynamic image (utilizing the FreeType library)?

Quiz Answers

1. What header should you send to the browser before building and outputting a GIF image?

   To output a GIF image, you should use the `header()` function to send the line `"Content-type: image/gif"` to the browser.

2. What function would you use to acquire an image resource that you can use with other image functions?

   The `imagecreate()` function returns an image resource.

3. What function would you use to output your GIF after building it?

   You can output a GIF with the `imagegif()` function.

4. What function could you use to acquire a color resource?

   You can acquire a color resource with the `imagecolorallocate()` function.

5. With which function would you draw a line on a dynamic image?

   The `imageline()` function will draw a line.

6. What function would you use to fill an area in a dynamic image?

   The `imagefill()` function will fill an area with color.

7. What function might you use to draw an arc?

   You can draw an arc with the `imagearc()` function.

8. How might you draw a rectangle?

   You can draw an outline rectangle with the `imagerectangle()` function. If you want to draw a filled rectangle, you can use `imagefilledrectangle()`.

9. How would you draw a polygon?

   You can draw a polygon with either `imagepolygon()` or `imagefilledpolygon()`.

10. What function would you use to write a string to a dynamic image (utilizing the FreeType library)?

    You can write a string to a dynamic image with the `imageTTFtext()` function.

14

Activities

1. Write a script that creates a "progress bar" such as might be used on a fund-raising site to indicate how much money has been raised in relation to the target.

2. Write a script that writes a headline image based on input from a form or query string. Allow user input to determine the canvas size, background and foreground colors, and the presence and offset of a drop shadow.

HOUR 15

Working with Dates and Times

Dates are so much part of everyday life that it becomes easy to work with them without thinking. The quirks of our calendar can be difficult to work with in programs, though. Fortunately, PHP provides powerful tools for date arithmetic that make manipulating dates easy.

In this chapter, you will learn:

- How to acquire the current date and time
- How to get information about a date
- How to format date information
- How to test dates for validity
- How to set dates
- How to build a simple calendar script
- How to build a class library to generate date pulldowns in HTML forms.

Getting the Date with `time()`

PHP's `time()` function gives you all the information that you need about the current date and time. It requires no arguments but returns an integer. This number is a little hard on the eyes, for us humans, but extremely useful nonetheless.

```
print time();
// sample output: 1127732399
```

The integer returned by `time()` represents the number of seconds elapsed since midnight GMT on January 1, 1970. This moment is known as the UNIX epoch, and the number of seconds that have elapsed since then is referred to as a timestamp. PHP offers excellent tools to convert a timestamp into a form that humans are comfortable with. Even so, isn't a timestamp a needlessly convoluted way of storing a date? In fact, the opposite is true. From just one number, you can extract enormous amounts of information. Even better, a timestamp can make date arithmetic much easier than you might imagine.

Think of a homegrown date system in which you record days of the month, as well as months and years. Now imagine a script that needs to add one day to a given date. If this date happened to be 31 December 1999, rather than add 1 to the date, you would have to write code to set the day of the month to 1, the month to January, and the year to 2000. Using a timestamp, you need only add a day's worth of seconds to your current figure, and you are done. You can convert this new figure into something more friendly at your leisure.

Converting a Timestamp with `getdate()`

Now that you have a timestamp to work with, you must convert it before you present it to the user. `getdate()` optionally accepts a timestamp and returns an associative array containing information about the date. If you omit the timestamp, it works with the current timestamp as returned by `time()`. Table 15.1 lists the elements contained in the array returned by `getdate()`.

TABLE 15.1 The Associative Array Returned by `getdate()`

Key	Description	Example
seconds	Seconds past the minute (0–59)	28
minutes	Minutes past the hour (0–59)	7
hours	Hours of the day (0–23)	12
mday	Day of the month (1–31)	20
wday	Day of the week (0–6)	4

15

TABLE 15.1 continued

Key	Description	Example
mon	Month of the year (1–12)	1
year	Year (4 digits)	2000
yday	Day of year (0–365)	19
weekday	Day of the week (name)	Thursday
month	Month of the year (name)	January
0	Timestamp	948370048

Listing 15.1 uses `getdate()` (line 7) to extract information from a timestamp, using a `foreach` statement to print each element (line 8). You can see a typical output in Figure 15.1. `getdate()` returns the date according to the local time zone.

LISTING 15.1 Acquiring Date Information with `getdate()`

```
 1: <html>
 2: <head>
 3: <title>Listing 15.1 Acquiring date information with getdate()</title>
 4: </head>
 5: <body>
 6: <?php
 7: $date_array = getdate(); // no argument passed so today's date will be used
 8: foreach ( $date_array as $key => $val ) {
 9:     print "$key = $val<br>";
10: }
11: ?>
12: <hr>
13: <?
14: print "Today's date:
➡".$date_array['mday']."/".$date_array['mon']."/".$date_array['year']."<p>";
15: ?>
16: </body>
17: </html>
```

FIGURE **15.1**

Using getdate().

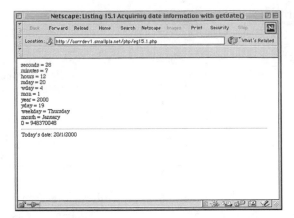

Converting a Timestamp with date()

You can use getdate() when you want to work with the elements that it outputs. Sometimes, though, you only want to display the date as a string. The date() function returns a formatted string representing a date. You can exercise an enormous amount of control over the format that date() returns with a string argument that you must pass to it. In addition to the format string, date() optionally accepts a timestamp. Table 15.2 lists the codes that a format string can contain. Any other data you include in the format string passed to date() will be included in the return value.

TABLE 15.2 Format Codes for Use with date()

Format	Description	Example
a	'am' or 'pm' lowercase	pm
A	'AM' or 'PM' uppercase	PM
d	Day of month (number with leading zeroes)	20
D	Day of week (three letters)	Thu
F	Month name	January
h	Hour (12-hour format—leading zeroes)	12
H	Hour (24-hour format—leading zeroes)	12
g	Hour (12-hour format—no leading zeroes)	12

TABLE 15.2 continued

Format	Description	Example
G	Hour (24-hour format—no leading zeroes)	12
i	Minutes	47
j	Day of the month (no leading zeroes)	20
l	Day of the week (name)	Thursday
L	Leap year ('1' for yes, '0' for no)	1
m	Month of year (number—leading zeroes)	01
M	Month of year (three letters)	Jan
n	Month of year (number—no leading zeroes)	1
s	Seconds of hour	24
r	Full date standardized to RFC 822 (http://www.faqs.org/rfcs/rfc822.html)	Wed, 26 Sep 2001 15:15:14 +0100
U	Timestamp	948372444
y	Year (two digits)	00
Y	Year (four digits)	2000
z	Day of year (0–365)	19
Z	Offset in seconds from GMT	0

Listing 15.2 puts a few format codes to the test.

LISTING 15.2 Formatting a Date with `date()`

```
 1: <html>
 2: <head>
 3: <title>Listing 15.2 Formatting a date with date()</title>
 4: </head>
 5: <body>
 6: <?php
 7: print date("m/d/y G.i:s<br>", time());
 8: // 09/26/01 15.46:30
 9: print "<br>";
10: print "Today is ";
11: print date("j of F Y, \a\\t g.i a", time());
12: // Today is 26 of September 2001, at 3.46 pm
13: ?>
14: </body>
15: </html>
```

In Listing 15.2 we call date() twice, the first time on line 7 to output an abbreviated date format, the second on line 11 for a longer format.

Although the format string looks arcane, it is easy to build. If you want to add a string to the format that contains letters that are format codes, you can escape them by placing a backslash (\) in front of them. For characters that become control characters when escaped, you must escape the backslash that precedes them. "\n" should become "\\n", for example, if you want to include an "n" in the format string. date() returns information according to your local time zone. If you want to format a date in GMT, you should use the gmdate() function, which works in exactly the same way.

Creating Timestamps with `mktime()`

You can already get information about the current time, but you cannot yet work with arbitrary dates. mktime() returns a timestamp that you can then use with date() or getdate(). mktime() accepts up to six integer arguments in the following order:

hour

minute

second

month

day of month

year

Listing 15.3 uses mktime() to get a timestamp that we then use with the date() function.

LISTING 15.3 Creating a Timestamp with `mktime()`

```
 1: <html>
 2: <head>
 3: <title>Listing 15.3 Creating a timestamp with mktime()</title>
 4: </head>
 5: <body>
 6: <?php
 7: // make a timestamp for 1/5/99 at 2.30 am
 8: $ts = mktime( 2, 30, 0, 5, 1, 1999 );
 9: print date("m/d/y G.i:s<br>", $ts);
10: // 05/01/99 2.30:00
11: print "<br>";
12: print "The date is ";
13: print date("j of F Y, \a\\t g.i a", $ts );
```

15

LISTING 15.3   continued

```
14: // The date is 1 of May 1999, at 2.30 am
15: ?>
16: </body>
17: </html>
```

We call `mktime()` on line 8 assigning the returned timestamp to the `$ts` variable. We can then use `date()` on lines 9 and 13 to output formatted versions of the date using `$ts`. You can choose to omit some or all of the arguments to `mktime()`, and the value appropriate to the current time will be used instead. `mktime()` will also adjust for values that go beyond the relevant range, so an hour argument of 25 will translate to 1.00am on the day after that specified in the month, day, and year arguments.

Testing a Date with `checkdate()`

You may need to accept date information from user input. Before you work with this date, or store it in a database, you should check that the date is valid. `checkdate()` accepts three integers: month, day, and year. `checkdate()` returns `true` if the month is between 1 and 12, the day is acceptable for the given month and year (accounting for leap years, and the year is between 0 and 32767. Be careful, though, a date may well be valid but not acceptable to other date functions. For example, the following line returns true:

```
checkdate( 4, 4, 1066 )
```

If you were to attempt to build a date with `mktime()` using these values, you would end up with a timestamp of –1. As a rule of thumb, do not use `mktime()` with years below 1902 and be cautious of using date functions with any date before 1970.

An Example

Let's bring most of these functions together into an example. We are going to build a calendar that can display the dates for any month between 1980 and 2010. The user will be able to select both month and year with pull-down menus, and the dates for that month will be organized according to the days of the week. We will use two global variables `$month` and `$year`, which should be filled by data by the user. We will use these to build a timestamp based on the first day of the month defined. If the input is invalid or absent, we will default to the first day of the current month.

Checking User Input

When the user comes to our page for the first time, he or she will not be submitting any information. We must therefore make sure that our script can handle the fact that the $month and $year variables may not be defined. We could use the isset() function for this. isset() returns false if the variable it has been passed has not been defined. However, we choose instead to use checkdate(). Listing 15.4 shows the fragment of code that checks the $month and $year variables and builds a timestamp based on them.

LISTING 15.4   Checking User Input for the Calendar Script

```
1: <?php
2: if ( ! checkdate( $month, 1, $year ) ) {
3:     $nowArray = getdate();
4:     $month = $nowArray['mon'];
5:     $year = $nowArray['year'];
6: }
7: $start = mktime ( 12, 0, 0, $month,     1, $year );
8: $firstDayArray = getdate($start);
9: ?>
```

Listing 15.4 is a fragment of a larger script so it does not produce any output itself. In our if statement on line 2, we use checkdate() to test the $month and $year variables. If they have not been defined, checkdate() returns false because you cannot make a valid date from undefined month and year arguments. This approach has the added bonus of ensuring that data that has been submitted by the user will make a valid date.

If the date is not valid, we use getdate() on line 3 to create an associative array based on the current time. We then set values for $month and $year ourselves, using the array's mon and year elements (lines 4 and 5).

Now that we are sure that we have valid data in $month and $year, we can use mktime() to create a timestamp for the first day of the month (line 7). We will need information about this timestamp later on, so on line 8 we create a variable called $firstDayArray that will store an associative array returned by getdate() and based on this timestamp.

Building the HTML Form

We need to create an interface by which users can ask to see data for a month and year. For this, we will use SELECT elements. Although we could hard-code these in HTML, we must also ensure that the pull-downs default to the currently chosen month, so we will dynamically create these pull-downs, adding a SELECT attribute to the OPTION element where appropriate. The form is generated in Listing 15.5.

LISTING 15.5   Building the HTML Form for the Calendar Script

```
 1: <?php
 2: if ( ! checkdate( $month, 1, $year ) ) {
 3:     $nowArray = getdate();
 4:     $month = $nowArray['mon'];
 5:     $year = $nowArray['year'];
 6: }
 7: $start = mktime ( 12, 0, 0, $month, 1, $year );
 8: $firstDayArray = getdate($start);
 9: ?>
10: <html>
11: <head>
12: <title><?php print "Calendar: ".$firstDayArray['month']
13:         ." ".$firstDayArray['year'] ?></title>
14: <head>
15: <body>
16: <form method="post">
17: <select name="month">
18: <?php
19: $months = Array("January", "February", "March", "April",
20:                 "May", "June", "July", "August", "September",
21:                 "October", "November", "December");
22: for ( $x=1; $x <= count( $months ); $x++ ) {
23:     print "\t<option value=\"$x\"";
24:     print ($x == $month)?" SELECTED":"";
25:     print ">".$months[$x-1]."\n";
26: }
27: ?>
28: </select>
29: <select name="year">
30: <?php
31: for ( $x=1980; $x<2010; $x++ ) {
32:     print "\t<option";
33:     print ($x == $year)?" SELECTED":"";
34:     print ">$x\n";
35: }
36: ?>
37: </select>
38: <input type="submit" value="Go!">
39: </form>
40: </body>
41: </html>
```

Having created the $start timestamp and the $firstDayArray date array (lines 2 to 8),
we go on to write the HTML for the page. Notice that we use $firstDayArray to add the
month and year to the TITLE element on lines 12 and 13. On line 16 we begin our form,
taking advantage of the fact that leaving the ACTION argument out of a FORM tag will

cause the form to submit to its containing page by default. To create the SELECT element for the month pull-down, we drop back into PHP mode on line 18 to write the individual OPTION tags. First we create an array called $months on line 19 that contains the 12 month names. We then loop through this, creating an OPTION tag for each one (line 23). This would probably be an overcomplicated way of writing a simple SELECT element were it not for the fact that we are testing $x (the counter variable in the for statement) against the $month variable on line 24. If $x and $month are equivalent, we add the string SELECTED to the OPTION tag, ensuring that the correct month will be selected automatically when the page loads. We use a similar technique to write the year pull-down on lines 29 to 37. Finally, back in HTML mode, we create a submit button on line 38.

We should now have a form that can send the month and year parameters to itself, and will default either to the current month and year, or the month and year previously chosen. You can see this in Figure 15.2.

FIGURE **15.2**

The calendar form.

Creating the Calendar Table

We now need to create a table and populate it with dates for the chosen month. We do this in Listing 15.6, which represents the complete calendar script.

LISTING **15.6**   The Complete Calendar Script

```
1: <?php
2: define("ADAY", (60*60*24) );
3: if ( ! checkdate( $month, 1, $year ) ) {
```

15

LISTING 15.6 continued

```php
 4:     $nowArray = getdate();
 5:     $month = $nowArray['mon'];
 6:     $year = $nowArray['year'];
 7: }
 8: $start = mktime ( 12, 0, 0, $month, 1, $year );
 9: $firstDayArray = getdate($start);
10: ?>
11: <html>
12: <head>
13: <title><?php print "Calendar: ".$firstDayArray['month']
14:         ." ".$firstDayArray['year'] ?></title>
15: </head>
16: <body>
17: <form method="post">
18: <select name="month">
19: <?php
20: $months = Array("January", "February", "March", "April",
21:                 "May", "June", "July", "August", "September",
22:                 "October", "November", "December");
23: for ( $x=1; $x <= count( $months ); $x++ ) {
24:     print "\t<option value=\"$x\"";
25:     print ($x == $month)?" SELECTED":"";
26:     print ">".$months[$x-1]."\n";
27: }
28: ?>
29: </select>
30: <select name="year">
31: <?php
32: for ( $x=1980; $x<2010; $x++ ) {
33:     print "\t<option";
34:     print ($x == $year)?" SELECTED":"";
35:     print ">$x\n";
36: }
37: ?>
38: </select>
39: <input type="submit" value="Go!">
40: </form>
41: <p>
42: <?php
43: $days = Array("Sunday", "Monday", "Tuesday", "Wednesday",
44:               "Thursday", "Friday", "Saturday");
45: print "<TABLE BORDER = 1 CELLPADDING=5>\n";
46: foreach ( $days as $day )
47:     print "\t<td><b>$day</b></td>\n";
48: for ( $count=0; $count < (6*7); $count++ ) {
49:     $dayArray = getdate( $start );
50:     if ( (($count) % 7) == 0 ) {
51:         if ( $dayArray['mon'] != $month )
```

LISTING 15.6 continued

```
52:              break;
53:          print "</tr><tr>\n";
54:      }
55:      if ( $count < $firstDayArray['wday'] || $dayArray['mon'] != $month )
56:          print "\t<td><br></td>\n";
57:      else {
58:          print "\t<td>".$dayArray['mday']." ". $dayArray['month']."</td>\n";
59:          $start += ADAY;
60:      }
61: }
62: print "</tr></table>";
63: ?>
64: </body>
65: </html>
```

Because the table will be indexed by days of the week, we loop through an array of day names created on line 43, printing each to its own cell on line 47. All the real magic of the script happens in the final for statement on line 48.

We initialize a variable called $count and ensure that the loop will end after 42 iterations. This is to make sure that we will create enough cells to populate with date information. Within the loop, we transform the $start variable into a date array with getdate(), assigning the result to $dayArray (line 49). Although $start is the first day of the month during the loop's initial execution, we will increment this timestamp by 24 hours for every iteration.

On line 50 we test the $count variable against 7 using the modulus operator. The block of code belonging to this if statement will therefore only be run when $count is either 0 or a multiple of 7. This is our way of knowing whether we should end the loop altogether or start a new row.

After we have established that we are in the first iteration or at the end of a row, we can go on to make another test on line 51. If the mon (month number) element of the $dayArray is no longer equivalent to the $month variable, we must have finished. Remember that $dayArray contains information about the $start timestamp, which is in turn our current place in the month that we are displaying. When $start goes beyond the current month, $dayArray['mon'] will hold a different figure than the $month number provided by user input. Our modulus test demonstrated that we are at the end of a row, and the fact that we are in a new month means that we can leave the loop altogether.

Assuming, however, that we are still in the month that we are displaying, we end the row and start a new one on line 53.

In the next `if` statement on line 55, we determine whether to write date information to a cell. Not every month begins on a Sunday, so it's likely that we will start with an empty cell or two. Few months will finish at the end of one of our rows, so it's also likely that we will need to write a few empty cells before we close the table. We have stored information about the first day of the month in `$firstDayArray`; in particular, we can access the number of the day of the week in `$firstDayArray['wday']`. If `$count` is smaller than this number, then we know that we haven't yet reached the correct cell for writing. By the same token, if the `$month` variable is no longer equal to `$dayArray['mon']`, we know that we have reached the end of the month (but not the end of the row, as we determined in our earlier modulus test). In either case, we write an empty `cell` to the browser on line 56.

In the final `else` clause on line 57, we can do the fun stuff. We have already ascertained that we are within the month that we want to list and that the current day column matches the day number stored in `$firstDayArray['wday']`. Now we must use the `$dayArray` associative array that we established early in the loop to write the day of the month and the month name to a cell.

Finally, on line 59, we need to increment the `$start` variable, which contains our date stamp. We simply add the number of seconds in a day to it (we have defined this value at the top of the script), and we're ready to begin the loop again with a new value in `$start` to be tested. You can see the output from a call to this script in Figure 15.3.

FIGURE 15.3

The calendar script.

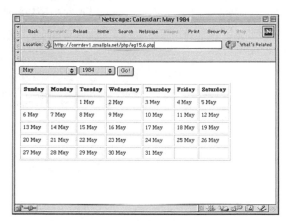

A Calendar Library

Because dates are so ubiquitous in web interfaces and because working with dates is often comparatively non-trivial, now would seem to be a good time to look at a class library to automate some of the work that dates can present. Along the way we will revisit some of the techniques we have already covered.

The simple date_pulldown library was born during the creation of a freelance job listing site. The project necessarily involved the presentation of multiple date pulldowns allowing employers to select both the start and end of contract periods, and for candidates to indicate periods of availability. A date pulldown, in this instance, is three separate select elements, one for day of the month, one for month and another for year.

When a user submits a page, the script will sanity check his input. If there is a problem, then the page will need to be represented with the user's input still in place. This is very easy to accomplish with textboxes but more of a chore with pulldown menus. Pages that display information pulled from a database present a similar problem. Data can be entered straight into the value attributes of text type input elements. Dates, though will need to be split into month, day, and year values, and then the correct option elements selected.

The date_pulldown class aims to make date pulldowns sticky (to remember settings from page to page), and easy to set.

In order to create our class we first need to declare it, and to create a constructor. We can also declare some class properties.

```
class date_pulldown {
   var $name;
   var $timestamp = -1;
   var $months = array("Jan", "Feb", "Mar", "Apr", "May", "Jun",
                       "Jul", "Aug", "Sep", "Oct", "Nov", "Dec");
   var $yearstart = -1;
   var $yearend = -1;

   function date_pulldown( $name ) {
         $this->name = $name;
   }
// ...
```

We declare the $name property. This will be used to the name the HTML select elements. The $timestamp property will hold a Unix timestamp. The $months array property contains the strings we will display in our month pulldown. $yearstart and $yearend both set to −1 pending initialization. They will eventually hold the first and last years of the range that will be presented in the year pulldown.

15

The constructor is very simple. It accepts a string, which we then use to assign to the $name property.

Now that we have the basis of our class we need a set of methods by which the client code can set the date.

```
// ...
   function setDate_global( ) {
           if ( ! $this->setDate_array( $GLOBALS[$this->name] ) )
                   return $this->setDate_timestamp( time() );
           return true;
   }

   function setDate_timestamp( $time ) {
           $this->timestamp = $time;
           return true;
   }

   function setDate_array( $inputdate ) {
           if ( is_array( $inputdate ) &&
                   isset( $inputdate['mon'] ) &&
                   isset( $inputdate['mday'] ) &&
                   isset( $inputdate['year'] ) ) {
                   $this->timestamp = mktime( 11, 59, 59,
                           $inputdate['mon'], $inputdate['mday'],
➥$inputdate['year'] );
                   return true;
           }

           return false;
   }
// ...
```

Of these methods setDate_timestamp() is the simplest. It requires a Unix timestamp and assigns it to the $timestamp property.

setDate_array() expects an associative array with at least three keys 'mon', 'mday', and 'year'. These fields will contain data in the same format as in the array returned by getdate(). This means that setDate_array() will accept a hand-built array like

```
array( 'mday'=> 5, 'mon'=>7, 'year' => 1999 );
```

or the result of a call to getdate()

```
getdate( 931172399 );
```

It is no accident that the pulldowns we will be building later will be constructed to produce an array containing 'mon', 'mday', and 'year' fields. The method uses the mktime() function to construct a timestamp which is then assigned to the $timestamp variable.

The setDate_global() method is called by default. It attempts to find a global variable with the same name as the object's $name property. This is passed to setDate_array(). If a global variable of the right structure is discovered then it is used to create the $timestamp variable. Otherwise the current date is used.

The range for days and months is fixed, but years are a different matter. We create a few methods to allow the client coder to set her own range of years (although we also provide default behavior).

```
// ...
   function setYearStart( $year ) {
           $this->yearstart = $year;
   }

   function setYearEnd( $year ) {
           $this->yearend = $year;
   }

   function getYearStart() {
           if ( $this->yearstart < 0 ) {
                   $nowarray = getdate( time() );
                   $this->yearstart = $nowarray['year']-5;
           }
           return $this->yearstart;
   }

   function getYearEnd() {
           if ( $this->yearend < 0 ) {
                   $nowarray = getdate( time() );
                   $this->yearend = $nowarray['year']+5;
           }
           return $this->yearend;
   }
// ...
```

The setYearStart() and setYearEnd() methods are straightforward. A year is directly assigned to the appropriate property. getYearStart() tests whether or not the $yearstart property has been set. If not, it assigns a $yearstart 5 years before the current year. getYearEnd() performs a similar operation. We're now ready to create the business end of the class:

```
// ...
   function output( ) {
           if ( $this->timestamp < 0 )
                   $this->setDate_global();
           $datearray = getdate( $this->timestamp );
           $out  = $this->day_select( $this->name, $datearray );
           $out .= $this->month_select( $this->name, $datearray );
           $out .= $this->year_select( $this->name, $datearray );
```

```
                return $out;
        }

    function day_select( $fieldname, $datearray ) {
            $out = "<select name=\"$fieldname"."[mday]\">\n";
            for ( $x=1; $x<=31; $x++ )
                    $out .= "<option value=\"$x\"".($datearray['mday']==($x)
                            ?" SELECTED":"").">".sprintf("%02d", $x ) ."\n";
            $out .= "</select>\n";
            return $out;
        }

    function month_select( $fieldname, $datearray ) {
            $out = "<select name=\"$fieldname"."[mon]\">\n";
            for ( $x = 1; $x <= 12; $x++ )
                    $out .= "<option value=\"".($x)."\"".($datearray['mon']==($x)
                            ?" SELECTED":"").">".$this->months[$x-1]."\n";
            $out .= "</select>\n";
            return $out;
        }

    function year_select( $fieldname, $datearray ) {
            $out = "<select name=\"$fieldname"."[year]\">";
            $start = $this->getYearStart();
            $end = $this->getYearEnd();
            for ( $x= $start; $x < $end; $x++ )
                    $out .= "<option value=\"$x\"".($datearray['year']==($x)
                            ?" SELECTED":"").">$x\n";
            $out .= "</select>\n";
            return $out;
        }
}
```

The output() method orchestrates most of this code. It first checks the $timestamp property. Unless the client coder has called one of the setDate methods it will be set to −1 and setDate_global() will be called by default. The timestamp is passed to the getdate() function to construct a date array, and a method is called for each pulldown to be produced.

day_select() simply constructs an HTML select element with an option element for each of the 31 possible days in a month. The object's 'current' date is stored in the $datearray argument variable which is used during the construction of the element to set the selected attribute of the relevant option element. Notice that we use a method called sprintf(). This formats the day number, adding a leading zero to days 1 to 9. You can find out more about the sprintf() function in Hour 17 "Working with Strings." month_select() and year_select() use similar logic to construct the month and year pulldowns.

Why did we break down the output code into four methods, rather than simply create one block of code? When we build a class we have two kinds of user in mind. The client coder who would want to instantiate a date_pulldown object, and the client coder who would want to subclass the date_pulldown class to refine its functionality. For the former we want to provide a simple and clear interface to the class's functionality. The coder can instantiate an object, set its date, and call output(). All complexity is hidden away. For the subclassing coder we want to make it easy to change discrete elements of the class's functionality. By putting all the output code into one method we would force a child class that needed to tweak output to reproduce a lot of code that is perfectly usable. By breaking up this code into discrete methods, we allow for subclasses that can change limited aspects of functionality without disturbing the whole. If a child class needed to represent the year pulldown as two radio buttons, for example, then only the year_select() method would need to be overridden.

In Listing 15.7 we create some code that calls the library class.

LISTING 15.7   Using the date_pulldown Class

```
 1: <html>
 2: <head>
 3: <title>Listing 15.7 Using the date_pulldown Class</title>
 4: </head>
 5: <?php
 6: include("date_pulldown.class.php");
 7: $date1 = new date_pulldown("fromdate");
 8: $date2 = new date_pulldown("todate");
 9: $date3 = new date_pulldown("foundingdate");
10: $date3->setYearStart(1972);
11: if ( empty( $foundingdate ) )
12:     $date3->setDate_array( array( 'mday'=>26, 'mon'=>4, 'year'=>1984 ) );
13: ?>
14: <body>
15:
16: <form>
17: From:<br>
18: <?php print $date1->output( ); ?><p>
19:
20: To:<br>
21: <?php print $date2->output( ); ?><p>
22:
23: Company founded:<br>
24: <?php print $date3->output( ); ?><p>
25:
26: <input type="submit" valu="do it">
27: </form>
28:
29: </body>
30: </html>
```

Notice that we've tucked the class itself away in a library file called `date_pulldown.class.php` which we access using the `include()` statement on line 6. We use the class's default behavior for all of the pulldowns apart from `'foundingdate'`. For this object we override the default year start, setting it to 1972 on line 10. We also define an arbitrary date on line 12 for this pulldown which will be displayed until the form is submitted.

FIGURE 15.4

The pulldowns generated by the date_pulldown *class.*

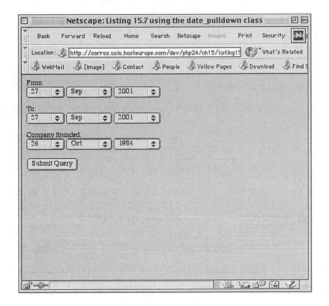

Summary

In this hour, you learned how to use `time()` to get a date stamp for the current date and time. You learned how to use `getdate()` to extract date information from a timestamp and `date()` to convert a timestamp into a formatted string. You learned how to create a timestamp using `mktime()`. You learned how to test a date for validity with `checkdate()`. You worked through an example script, which applies some of the tools you have looked at and built a class library that automates some of the more tedious aspects of working with dates in forms.

In the next hour we will be getting our hands dirty with some of the more advanced issues surrounding data types and arrays.

Q&A

Q Are there any functions for converting between different calendars?

A Yes. PHP provides an entire suite of functions that cover alternative calendars. You can read about these in the official PHP manual at `http://www.php.net/ manual/ref.calendar.php`.

Workshop

Quiz

1. How would you acquire a UNIX timestamp representing the current date and time?
2. What function accepts a timestamp and returns an associative array representing the given date?
3. What function would you use to format date information?
4. How would you acquire a timestamp for an arbitrary date?
5. What function could you use to check the validity of a date?

Quiz Answers

1. How would you acquire a UNIX timestamp representing the current date and time?

   The `time()` function returns the current date in timestamp format.

2. What function accepts a timestamp and returns an associative array representing the given date?

   The `getdate()` function returns an associative array whose elements contain aspects of the given date.

3. What function would you use to format date information?

   The `date()` function is used to format a date.

4. How would you acquire a timestamp for an arbitrary date?

   Given arguments representing the hour, minute, second, month, day of month, and year, the `mktime()` function returns a UNIX timestamp.

5. What function could you use to check the validity of a date?

   You can check a date with the `checkdate()` function.

Activity

1. Create a birthday countdown script. Given form input of month, day, and year, output a message that tells the user how many days, hours, minutes, and seconds until the big day.

HOUR 16

Working with Data

In this hour, we are going to delve a little deeper into data testing and manipulation. We will look again at data types. PHP handles data types for you automatically, but an understanding of how data is handled in your scripts is essential if you are to build robust online applications. We will also return to arrays and discover some of the more advanced features that PHP provides to manipulate and sort these data types.

In this hour, you will learn:

- How to convert data from one type to another
- How PHP automatically converts data for you in expressions
- More ways of testing data types
- Why an understanding of data types can be useful
- How to test whether a variable has been set
- Another method of traversing an array
- How to check that an element exists in an array
- How to transform and filter array values
- How to custom sort arrays

Data Types Revisited

You learned about PHP's data types in some detail in Hour 4, "The Building Blocks." There is a little more ground to cover, however. This section examines a few more functions for checking the data type of a variable and looks at the conditions under which PHP automatically converts data types for you.

A Recap

You already know that PHP variables can contain values that are integers, doubles, strings, booleans, objects, or arrays. And that there are two special types: NULL and resource. You can test the type of any variable with the gettype() function. gettype() requires a value of any type, and returns a string describing the value's data type:

```
$data = 454;
print gettype( $data );
// prints "integer"
```

You can change variables from one type to another, either by casting or with the settype() function. To cast a variable, place the name of a data type in brackets before the variable or value you want to convert. By casting a variable, you do not change the contents of a variable in any way. Instead, a converted copy is returned to you. The following code fragment casts a double to an integer:

```
$data = 4.333;
print ( integer ) $data;
// prints 4
```

The $data variable still contains the double that we assigned to it. We have merely printed the return value of the cast.

To transform the type of a variable, you can use the settype() function. settype() requires the name of a data type and a variable to convert:

```
$data = 4.333;
settype( $data, integer );
print $data;
// prints 4
```

The $data variable now contains an integer. settype() is a rare function in PHP in that it transforms one of the arguments you pass it in your scope as well as its own.

Converting Complex Types

You have already looked in some detail at the process of converting between simple data types (scalars and strings). What happens when you convert between simple data types such as doubles or integers and more complex types such as objects and arrays?

When you cast a simple data type to an array, an array is created, with the original value in the first element:

```
$str = "this is my string";
$arr_str = (array) $str;
print $arr_str[0];
// prints "this is my string"
```

When you cast a scalar or string variable to an object, an object is created with a single property called *scalar*. This contains the original value:

```
$str = "this is my string";
$arr_str = (object) $str;
print $arr_str->scalar;
// prints "this is my string"
```

Things get a little more interesting when you convert between arrays and objects. When you convert an array to an object, a new object is created with a property for each key in the array:

```
$addresses = array ( street => "Williams Street", town => "Stockton" );
$obj_addresses = ( object ) $addresses;
print $obj_addresses->street;
// prints "Williams Street"
```

Conversely, converting an object to an array creates an array with an element for each object property. Methods are discarded.

```
class Point {
    var $x;
    var $y;
    function Point( $x, $y ) {
        $this->x = $x;
        $this->y = $y;
    }
}
$point = new Point( 5, 7 );
$array_point = (array) $point;
print $array_point['x'];
// prints 5
```

Automatic Conversion of Data Types

If you build an expression that has values of two different data types as operands, PHP automatically converts one to the type of the other to arrive at a result. You have probably taken advantage of this already without thinking about it. Variables compiled from form input will always be strings, but you might have used them in a test expression or a calculation as if they were numbers.

16

Suppose that you have asked a user to tell the number of hours they spend online a week, storing the input in a variable called $hours. This initially will be stored as a string.

```
$hours = "15";
if ( $hours == 15 )
    print "As a frequent user you may qualify for a discount";
```

In the test for equivalence, the string "15" is cast to an integer, and the test expression resolves to true.

The rules for automatic conversion are relatively simple. In the context of integers or doubles, strings will be converted according to their contents. If a string begins with an integer, it will be converted to that number. So the following line will give 80:

```
4 * "20mb";
```

If a string does not begin with a number, it will be converted to 0. So this line will give 0:

```
4 * "about 20mb";
```

If a string contains a number followed by a dot, it will be converted into a double. So the following example will give 4.8:

```
4 * "1.2";
```

The autoincrement and autodecrement operators are a special case when applied to strings. Incrementing a string adds 1 to the converted value of the string as you would expect, but only if the string contains nothing but numbers. The new value will itself be a string:

```
$str = "4";
$str++;
print $str;  // prints 5
print gettype( $str ); // prints "string"
```

If you attempt to autoincrement a string that contains letters, the final character alone will be incremented:

```
$str = "hello";
$str++;
print $str;  // prints "hellp"
```

Compare this with another approach to incrementing a string:

```
$str = "hello";
$str += 1;
print $str; // prints 1;
print gettype( $str ); // prints "integer"
```

In the previous example, $str is converted to the integer 0 when we add 1 to it. The result of this operation, 1, is stored back in $str. $str will now hold an integer.

Automatic conversions between integers and doubles are more straightforward. If either operand in an expression is a double, then the other operand will be converted to a double, and the result will be a double:

```
$result = ( 1 + 20.0 );
print gettype ( $result );
// prints "double"
```

It is important to note that when automatic conversions occur for the purposes of evaluating an expression, neither operand in the expression is itself changed. If an operand needs to be converted, it is a transformed copy that will be used as part of the expression.

Testing Data Types

You've already seen that you can test any data type with the gettype() function. This is useful for debugging because it tells you exactly what type any variable is. Often, though, you will only want to check whether a variable contains a specific type. PHP provides a special function corresponding to each data type. These functions accept a variable or value and return a boolean. Table 16.1 lists these functions.

TABLE 16.1 Functions to Test Data Types

Function	Description
is_array()	Returns true if the argument is an array
is_bool()	Returns true if the argument is boolean
is_double()	Returns true if the argument is a double
is_int()	Returns true if the argument is an integer
is_object()	Returns true if the argument is an object
is_string()	Returns true if the argument is a string
is_null()	Returns true if the argument is null
is_resource()	Returns true if the argument is a resource

These functions make testing data types a little easier.

```
if ( gettype( $var ) == "array" )
   print "it's an array";
```

is equivalent to

```
if ( is_array( $var ) )
   print "it's an array";
```

The second way of testing the $var variable is a little more compact and is nicely intuitive.

More Ways of Changing Type

You have already seen two ways of converting data types. You can either cast a value or use the settype() function. In addition to these techniques, PHP provides functions to convert values into integers, doubles, and strings. These functions accept values of any type apart from array or object and return a converted value. Table 16.2 lists these functions.

TABLE 16.2 Functions to Convert Data Types

Function	Description
doubleval()	Accepts a value and returns double equivalent
intval()	Accepts a value and returns integer equivalent
strval()	Accepts a value and returns string equivalent

Why Are Data Types Important?

PHP does not demand that you declare a data type when you create a variable. It implicitly converts types for you when you use variables of different data types in expressions. If PHP makes things so easy, why is it important to be able to keep track of the types of data you are storing?

It is often a good idea to keep track of the data that your variables store to prevent errors. Imagine that you are writing a function that prints the keys and values of an array to the browser. PHP is relaxed about arguments to functions, so you can't demand that the calling code pass you an array when you declare your function.

```
function printArray( $array ) {
    foreach ( $array as $key => $val )
        print "$key: $val<P>";
}
```

The preceding function will work nicely if the function is called with an array argument.

```
printArray( array(4, 4, 55) );
```

If you carelessly pass a scalar, you will get an error, as in the following example:

```
printArray( 4 );
// Warning: Non array argument supplied for foreach() in
// /home/matt/htdocs/php-book/data/test2.php on line 5
```

By testing the data type of the supplied argument, you can make the function more accommodating. You could make the function quietly return if it receives a scalar value:

```
function printArray( $array ) {
    if ( ! is_array( $array ) )
        return false;
    foreach ( $array as $key => $val )
        print "$key: $val<P>";
    return true;
}
```

16

The calling code can now test the return value of the function to ascertain whether it was able to complete its task.

You could even use a cast to convert scalar data into an array:

```
function printArray( $array ) {
    if ( ! is_array( $array ) )
        $array = (array) $array;
    foreach ( $array as $key => $val )
        print "$key: $val<P>";
    return true;
}
```

The printArray() function has become vastly more flexible. It will now output any data type in an array context, even an object.

Checking data types can also be useful when testing the return value of some functions. Some languages, such as Java, always return a predetermined data type from any method. PHP has no such restriction. This flexibility can occasionally lead to ambiguities.

You saw an example of this in Hour 10, "Reading and Writing to Files." The readdir() function returns false when it has reached the end of the directory that you are reading, and a string containing the name of an item in the directory at all other times. Traditionally, you would use a construction similar to

```
$dh = opendir( "mydir" );
while ( $name = readdir( $dh ) )
        print "$name<br>";
closedir( $dh );
```

to read the items in a directory. If a directory is named 0, however, the while statement's test expression will evaluate this string to false, ending the listing. By testing the data type of the return value of readdir(), you can circumvent this problem:

```
$dh = opendir( "mydir" );
while ( is_string( $name = readdir( $dh ) ) )
        print "$name<br>";
closedir( $dh );
```

Variable Variables

PHP provides enormous flexibility when it comes to working with variable names. In fact you can use a string variable to stand in for the name portion of another variable. So, when assigning a value to a variable

```
$user = "bob";
```

is equivalent to

```
$holder="user";
$$holder = "bob";
```

The $holder variable contains the string "user", so you can think of $$holder as a dollar sign followed by the value of $holder. PHP interprets this as $user.

When accessing a dynamic variable, the syntax is exactly the same:

```
$user ="bob";
print $user;
```

is equivalent to

```
$user ="bob";
$holder="user";
print $$holder;
```

If you want to print a dynamic variable within a string, however, you need to give the interpreter some help. The following print statement:

```
$user="bob";
$holder="user";
print "$$holder";
```

does not print "bob" to the browser as you might expect. Instead it prints the strings "$" and "user" together to make "$user". When you place a variable within quotation marks, PHP helpfully inserts its value. In this case, PHP replaces $holder with the string "user". The first dollar sign is left in place. To make it clear to PHP that a variable within a string is part of a dynamic variable, you must wrap it in braces. The print statement in the following fragment:

```
$user="bob";
$holder="user";
print "${$holder}";
```

now prints "bob", which is the value contained in $user.

References to Variables

By default, variables are assigned by value. In other words, if you were to assign $aVariable to $anotherVariable, a *copy* of the value held in $aVariable would be stored in $anotherVariable. Subsequent changes to either one of the variables would have no effect upon the other.

In PHP 4, you can change this behavior, forcing a reference to $aVariable to be assigned to $anotherVariable, rather than a copy of its contents. You can do this by placing an ampersand (&) in front of the $aVariable variable at the point of assignment.

```
$aVariable = 42;
$anotherVariable = &$aVariable;
$aVariable= 325;
print $anotherVariable; // prints 325
```

You can now think of $anotherVariable and $aVariable as aliases to one another. You can disassociate the variables by passing one of them to unset(). Unset will destroy the variable that is passed to it, but any references will be left untouched.

Testing for Absence and Emptiness

Testing the data type of variables can be useful, but you must first be sure that a variable exists and, if it does exist, that a value has been assigned to it. You can do this with the isset() function. isset() requires a variable and returns true if the variable contains a value:

```
$notset;
if ( isset( $notset ) )
    print "\$notset is set";
else
    print "\$notset is not set";
// prints "$notset is not set"
```

A variable that is declared but has not yet been assigned a value will not be recognized as set.

You should be aware of one danger, however. If you assign 0 or an empty string to a variable, it will be recognized as having been set:

```
$notset = "";
if ( isset( $notset ) )
    print "\$notset is set";
else
    print "\$notset is not set";
// prints "$notset is set"
```

16

Variables that have been initialized as a result of form submissions will always be set, even if the user did not add any data to a field. To deal with situations like this, you must test whether a variable is empty. empty() accepts a variable and returns true if the variable is not set, or if it contains data other than 0 or an empty string. It also returns true if the variable contains an empty array:

```
$notset = "";
if ( empty( $notset ) )
    print "\$notset is empty";
else
    print "\$notset contains data";
// prints "$notset is empty"
```

More About Arrays

In Hour 7, "Arrays," we introduced arrays and some of the functions that you can use to work with them. This section introduces some more functions and techniques.

An Alternative Approach to Traversing Arrays

PHP 4 introduced the foreach statement, a powerful tool for reading array elements. We use this in most of the examples in this book. For scripts written in PHP 3, it was necessary to use a different technique to traverse arrays. If you intend to distribute scripts that should be compatible with PHP 3 or are interested in learning from source code that was written before the release of PHP 4, it is essential that you know about this.

When you create an array, PHP maintains an internal pointer that initially points at the first element in the array. You can access this element's key and value with a function called each(). each() requires an array variable and returns a four-element array. Two of these elements will be numerically indexed, and two will be labeled with the names "key" and "value," respectively. After each() has been called, the internal pointer moves on to the next element in the array that you are examining, unless the end of the array has been reached, in which case the function returns false. Let's create an array and try out the each() function:

```
$details = array( school => "Slickly High", course => "Selective Indifference"
);
$element = each( $details );
print "$element[0]<BR>";      // prints "school"
print "$element[1]<P>";         // prints "Slickly High"
print $element['key']."<BR>";    // prints "school"
print $element['value']."<BR>";   // prints "Slickly High"
```

We initialize an array called $details with two elements. We then pass $details to the each() function, storing the return value in a new array called $element. The $element array holds the key and value of the first element of the $details.

Assigning the array returned by each() to an array variable is cumbersome. Fortunately, PHP provides list(), a language construct. list() accepts any number of variables and populates each of them with the corresponding values from an array value:

```
$array = array( 44, 55, 66, 77 );
list( $first, $second ) = $array;
print "$first";          // prints 44
print "<BR>";
print "$second";     // prints 55
```

Notice how we were able to copy the first two elements of the array in the previous example into named variables using list().

We can use list()to assign values to two variables every time each() is called. We can then work with these, just as we would in a foreach statement.

```
$details = array( school => "Slickly High",
                  course => "Selective Indifference" );
while ( list ( $key, $value ) = each( $details ) )
    print "$key: $value<BR>";
```

Although this code will work, a line is still missing. If your array has been traversed before, the internal pointer will still be set beyond the last element. You can set the internal pointer back to the beginning of an array with the reset() function. reset() requires an array variable as its argument.

So, the more familiar construction

```
foreach( $details as $key => $value )
    print "$key: $value<BR>";
```

is equivalent to

```
reset( $details );
while ( list ( $key, $value ) = each( $details ) )
    print "$key: $value<BR>";
```

Checking That a Value Exists in an Array

Prior to PHP 4, if you needed to check whether a value existed in an array, you had to traverse the array until you had either found a match or reached the last element. PHP 4 provides the in_array() function. in_array() requires two arguments, the value for which you are searching and the array you want to search. The function returns true if the value is found with the given array and false otherwise.

```
$details = array( school => "Slickly High",
                  course => "Selective Indifference" );
if ( in_array( "Selective Indifference", $details ) )
    print "This course has been suspending pending investigation<P>\n";
```

in_array() is useful if you want to reassure yourself that a value is present in an array. It does not help you, though, if you want to know *where* to find that value. The array_ search() function is designed to do just that. array_search() requires two arguments, the value for which you are searching and the array you want to search. If your value is found the function will return the key associated with the function, otherwise it will return false.

```
$searchme = array( 33, 44, 77, "22" );
print array_search( 22, $searchme );
// prints 3
```

In the fragment above we searched for '22' in the $searchme array. array_search() will automatically cast when attempting to locate a value, so although the 22 passed to array_search() is an integer and the '22' in $search_me is a string, a match was found. If you want it to be less forgiving than this, you can pass the boolean value true to array_search() as the third argument. The function will then only return a key if the matching value is of the same type as the search value. The function call

```
print array_search( 22, $searchme, true );
```

would now return false. in_array() also accepts an optional third argument that enforces strict matching.

array_search() was introduced in PHP 4.05.

Removing an Element from an Array

You can remove any element from an array with the unset() function. unset() requires a variable or an array element as an argument and will unceremoniously destroy it.

```
unset( $test['address'] );
unset( $numbers[1] );
```

One potential pitfall with unset() is the fact that array indices are not subsequently changed to reflect the new size of the array. So, having removed $numbers[1] in the previous example, the $numbers array might now look something like this:

```
$numbers[0]
$numbers[2]
$numbers[3]
```

You can still loop through this with a foreach statement without problems, however. You could also easily construct a new array with the array_values() function.

```
$numbers = array_values( $numbers );
```

Applying a Function to Every Element in an Array

You can change a scalar variable easily in an expression. Applying a change to every element of an array is a little more difficult. If you want to add a number to the value of every array element, for example, one solution would be to loop through the array updating each element. PHP provides a neater answer, however.

The array_walk() function passes the key and value of every element in an array to a user-defined function. array_walk() requires an array variable, a string representing the name of a function, and an optional additional argument that will be passed to the function you have chosen.

Let's create an example. We have an array of prices acquired from a database, but before working with it we need to add sales tax to each price. First, we should create the function to add the tax:

```
function add_tax( &$val, $key, $tax_pc ) {
    $val += ( ($tax_pc/100) * $val );
}
```

Any function to be used with array_walk() should expect arguments representing a key, a value, and, optionally, a further argument.

If you want to change the value that is passed to your function, you need to append an ampersand to the argument in the function declaration. This ensures that the value will be passed by reference and any changes you make to the value within the function will be reflected in the array. That is why our add_tax() function does not return a value.

Now that we have created the function, we can call it via array_walk():

```
function add_tax( &$val, $key, $tax_pc ) {
    $val += ( ($tax_pc/100) * $val );
}
$prices = array( 10, 17.25, 14.30 );
array_walk( $prices, "add_tax", 10 );
foreach ( $prices as $val )
    print "$val<BR>";
// Output:
// 11
// 18.975
// 15.73
```

We pass the $prices array variable to array_walk() along with the name of the add_tax() function. add_tax() needs to know the current sales tax rate. The optional third argument to array_walk() will be passed to the nominated function, so this is where we set the tax rate.

16

You can also use this technique to call an object method for each element in your array. Instead of passing a function name to the array_walk() you should pass a two element array containing the object and a string representing the method you wish to call. In the fragment below we convert our sales tax code to work with a class.

```
class TaxAdder {
   var $taxrate = 10;
   function add_tax( &$val, $key ) {
       $val += ( ($this->taxrate/100) * $val );
   }
}

$prices = array( 10, 17.25, 14.30 );
$taxer = new TaxAdder();

array_walk( $prices, array( $taxer, "add_tax") );
foreach ( $prices as $val )
    print "$val<BR>";
// Output:
// 11
// 18.975
// 15.73
```

As of PHP 4.0.6 a new tool for applying user defined functions to array elements has become available. array_map() requires the name of a function and at least one array. After passing each element of the array to the callback function array_map() will return a transformed array containing the return values generated—it will have 'mapped' the input array to the return array. If you provide more than one array to array_map() it will traverse all arrays at the same time, passing all values at index 0 to your callback function, then all values at index 1 and so on. Confused? Let's put an example together.

Imagine that we have a list of Web pages and we wish to transform the strings so that they are links.

```
$urls = array( "about.html", "index.html", "contact.html", "service.html" );
function make_link( $a ) {
   return "<a href=\"$a\">a link</a><br>\n";
}
$new_urls = array_map( "make_link", $urls );
foreach ( $new_urls as $val )
   print $val;

// prints:
// <a href="about.html">a link</a><br>
// <a href="index.html">a link</a><br>
// <a href="contact.html">a link</a><br>
// <a href="service.html">a link</a><br>
```

array_map() repeatedly invokes make_link(), passing it each value in the $urls array. It uses the values returned by make_link() to generate a new array.

The great strength of array_map() is its ability to work with multiple arrays at the same time. Imagine that in addition to our $url array we had an array of page names that we wished to incorporate into our link strings.

```
$urls  = array( "about.html", "index.html", "contact.html", "service.html" );
$names = array( "about us",    "home",        "contact us",    "our services" );
function make_link( $a, $b ) {
   return "<a href=\"$a\">$b</a><br>\n";
}
$new_urls = array_map( "make_link", $urls, $names );
foreach ( $new_urls as $val )
   print $val;

// prints:
// <a href="about.html">about us</a><br>
// <a href="index.html">home</a><br>
// <a href="contact.html">contact us</a><br>
// <a href="service.html">our services</a><br>
```

We amend our array_map() function call so that it includes the $names array. We also change the make_link() function so that it accepts two arguments. make_link() is called with values from both the $urls and $names arrays and uses them to construct a single return value, an HTML link. array_map() constructs an array of these return values which is then assigned to $new_urls.

Filtering Arrays with array_filter()

Arrays are very flexible by nature, which is their great strength. There are few restrictions as to the types and range of data that they can store. Sometimes, though we need to extract elements according to an arbitrary constraint. Perhaps we only want the strings in an array, or integers above a certain number. array_filter() is the perfect tool for this. array_filter() requires an array and a reference to a callback function (that is, a function name string or an anonymous function). It will return a filtered array. The callback function you create will be passed each array element in turn and should return a boolean. If the callback function returns true, then the value will be included in the returned array, otherwise it will be discarded. array_filter() will preserve all keys in an associative array. In the fragment below we use array_filter() to create an array whose values are less than 120.

```
function less_than( $a ) {
   return ( $a < 120 );
}
$my_array = array( "a" => 200, "b" => 80, "c" => 90, "d" => 150, "e" => 130,
"f"=> 110 );
```

```
$filtered_array = array_filter( $my_array, less_than );
foreach( $filtered_array as $key=>$val )
  print "$key: $val<br>";
// prints:
// b: 80
// c: 90
// f: 110
```

Notice the way that the less_than() function creates the boolean return value. It combines the return statement with the comparison expression. You might find it more readable to split this into two statements.

```
if ( $a < 120 )
  return true;
return false;
```

Also notice that the array keys are imported into the $filtered_array array as well as the values.

Custom Sorting Arrays

You have already seen how to sort arrays by key or value. You do not always want to sort an array in such a straightforward way, however. You may want to sort it according to the values of an element buried in a multidimensional array, for example, or to use a criterion completely different to the standard alphanumeric comparison.

PHP enables you to define your own comparison functions to sort arrays. To do this for a numerically indexed array, you would call the usort() function, which requires the array you want to sort and the name of the function you want to make the necessary comparisons.

The function you define should accept two arguments, which will hold the array values to be compared. If they are equivalent according to your criterion, the function should return 0; if the first argument should come before the second in the subject array, the function should return –1. If the first argument should come after the second, the function should return 1.

Listing 16.1 uses usort() to sort a multidimensional array.

LISTING 16.1   Using usort() to Sort a Multidimensional Array by One of Its Fields

```
1: <?php
2: $products = array(
3:         array( name=>"HAL 2000",          price=>4500.5  ),
4:         array( name=>"Tricorder",         price=>55.5    ),
```

LISTING 16.1 continued

```
 5:        array( name=>"ORAC AI",          price=>2200.5  ),
 6:        array( name=>"Sonic Screwdriver", price=>22.5    )
 7:        );
 8: function priceCmp( $a, $b ) {
 9:    if ( $a['price'] == $b['price'] )
10:        return 0;
11:    if ( $a['price'] < $b['price'] )
12:        return -1;
13:    return 1;
14: }
15: usort( $products, priceCmp );
16: foreach ( $products as $val )
17:     print $val['name'].": ".$val['price']."<br>\n";
18: ?>
```

We define an array called $products starting on line 2, which we want to sort by the price field of each of its values.

We then create the custom sort function, priceCmp() on line 8. This function accepts two arguments, $a and $b. These arguments will hold two the arrays that make up the second level of the $products array. We compare their price elements, returning 0 if the prices are the same (lines 9 and 10), -1 if the first is less than the second (lines 11 and 12), and 1 otherwise (line 13).

Having defined both function and array, we call the usort() function on line 15, passing it the $products array and the name of our comparison function. usort() calls our function repeatedly, passing it elements from the $products array and switching the order of the elements according to the return value it receives.

Finally, we loop through the array on line 16, to demonstrate our new ordering.

Use usort() for sorting numerically indexed arrays. If you want to apply a similar custom sort to an associative array, use uasort(). uasort() will sort maintaining the association between keys and values. Listing 16.2 sorts an associative array using uasort() (line 15).

LISTING 16.2 Using uasort() to Sort a Multdimensional Associative Array by One of Its Fields

```
1: <?php
2: $products = array(
3:        "HAL 2000" => array( color =>"red",   price=>4500.5  ),
4:        "Tricorder" => array( color =>"blue",  price=>55.5    ),
5:        "ORAC AI" => array( color =>"green", price=>2200.5  ),
```

LISTING 16.2   continued

```
 6:            "Sonic Screwdriver" => array( color =>"red",   price=>22.5    )
 7:            );
 8: function priceCmp( $a, $b ) {
 9:    if ( $a['price'] == $b['price'] )
10:        return 0;
11:    if ( $a['price'] < $b['price'] )
12:        return -1;
13:    return 1;
14: }
15: uasort( $products, priceCmp );
16: foreach ( $products as $key => $val )
17:        print "$key: ".$val['price']."<br>\n";
18: ?>
```

You can custom sort an associative array by its keys using the function uksort(). uksort() is exactly the same in principle as usort() and uasort(), except that uksort() compares the keys of the array.

Listing 16.3 uses uksort() on line 16 to sort an array by the number of characters in each key. Looking ahead to the next hour, we use the function strlen() on lines 10 and 12 to ascertain the length in characters of each key. strlen() requires a single string argument and returns an integer representing the number of characters in the string.

LISTING 16.3   Using uksort() to Sort an Associative Array by the Length of Its Keys

```
 1: <?php
 2: $exes = array(
 3:            'xxxx' => 4,
 4:            'xxx' => 5,
 5:            'xx' => 7,
 6:            'xxxxx' => 2,
 7:            'x' => 8
 8:            );
 9: function priceCmp( $a, $b ) {
10:    if ( strlen( $a ) == strlen( $b ) )
11:        return 0;
12:    if ( strlen( $a ) < strlen( $b ) )
13:        return -1;
14:    return 1;
15: }
16: uksort( $exes, priceCmp );
17: foreach ( $exes as $key => $val )
18:        print "$key: $val<br>\n";
19:
```

LISTING 16.3   continued

```
20: // output:
21: // x: 8
22: // xx: 7
23: // xxx: 5
24: // xxxx: 4
25: // xxxxx: 2
26:
27: ?>
```

16

Summary

In this hour, you got your hands dirty with some of the more advanced aspects of working with arrays and data types. You learned what happens when you cast complex data types to scalars and vice versa. You learned how PHP deals with different data types in an expression, automatically casting one of them for you. You learned about functions, such as is_array(), that test for specific data types, and functions, such as intval(), that convert data to a specific type. You learned about the traditional way of traversing an array in PHP using each() and list(). You learned how to check that a value exists in an array with in_array() and how to remove an element from an array with unset(). You learned how to transform and filter arrays with array_walk(), array_map() and array_filter(). Finally, you learned about the custom sort functions with usort(), uasort(), and uksort().

In the next hour we will begin to explore some of PHP's tools for testing, formatting, and generally manipulating strings.

Q&A

Q **Have we now covered every array function that PHP 4 provides?**

A No, there are even more array functions than we have space to cover in this book! You can see them all listed and described at http://www.php.net/manual/ref.array.php.

Workshop

Quiz

1. What single function could you use to convert any data type to any other data type?

2. Could you achieve the same thing without a function?

3. What will the following code print?

   ```
   print "four" * 200;
   ```

4. How would you determine whether a variable contains an array?

5. Which function is designed to return the integer value of its argument?

6. How would you test whether a variable has been set?

7. How would you test whether a variable contains an empty value, such as 0 or an empty string?

8. What function would you use to delete an array element?

9. What function could you use to custom sort a numerically indexed array?

Quiz Answers

1. What single function could you use to convert any data type to any other data type?

   You can convert data types with the `settype()` function.

2. Could you achieve the same thing without a function?

   You can also change type using a cast—that is, by placing the name of a data type in brackets in front of the value to be converted.

3. What will the following code print?

   ```
   print "four" * 200;
   ```

   Strings that don't begin with numbers will resolve to 0 (zero) in expressions, so

   ```
   print "four" * 200
   ```

   will output `0`.

4. How would you determine whether a variable contains an array?

   To test whether a variable is an array, you could use the `is_array()` function. Alternatively, you could test the return value of `gettype()`.

5. Which function is designed to return the integer value of its argument?

   The `intval()` function returns the integer value of the argument it has passed.

6. How would you test whether a variable has been set?

   The `isset()` function tells you whether a variable has been set.

7. How would you test whether a variable contains an empty value, such as 0 or an empty string?

   The `empty()` function returns `true` if the variable passed to it is unset, or if it contains an empty value.

8. What function would you use to delete an array element?

   You can delete an array element with the `unset()` function.

9. What function could you use to custom sort a numerically indexed array?

   You can custom sort an array using the `usort()` function.

Activities

1. Look back through some of the scripts you have created whilst working with this book. Convert any that use the `foreach` statement so that they are compatible with PHP3.

2. Create an array of mixed data types. Custom sort the array by data type.

16

Hour 17

Working with Strings

The World Wide Web is very much a plain text environment. No matter how rich Web content becomes, HTML lies behind it all. It is no accident, then, that PHP 4 provides many functions with which you can format, investigate, and manipulate strings.

In this hour, you will learn:

- How to format strings
- How to determine the length of a string
- How to find a substring within a string
- How to break a string down into component parts
- How to remove white space from the beginning or end of a string
- How to replace substrings
- How to change the case of a string

Formatting Strings

Until now, we have simply printed any strings that we want to display directly to the browser. PHP provides two functions that allow you first to apply formatting, whether to round doubles to a given number of decimal places, define alignment within a field, or display data according to different number systems. In this section, you will look at a few of the formatting options provided by `printf()` and `sprintf()`.

Working with `printf()`

If you have any experience with C, you will be familiar with the `printf()` function. The PHP version is similar but not identical. `printf()` requires a string argument, known as a format control string. It also accepts additional arguments of different types. The format control string contains instructions as to how to display these additional arguments. The following fragment, for example, uses `printf()` to output an integer as a decimal:

```
printf("This is my number: %d", 55 );
// prints "This is my number: 55"
```

Within the format control string (the first argument), we have included a special code, known as a *conversion specification*.

NEW TERM   A conversion specification begins with a percent (%) symbol and defines how to treat the corresponding argument to `printf()`. You can include as many conversion specifications as you want within the format control string, as long as you send an equivalent number of arguments to `printf()`.

The following fragment outputs two numbers using `printf()`:

```
printf("First number: %d<br>\nSecond number: %d<br>\n", 55, 66 );
// Output:
// First number: 55
// Second number: 66
```

The first conversion specification corresponds to the first of the additional arguments to `printf()`, which is 55. The second conversion specification corresponds to 66. The d following the percent symbol requires that the data be treated as a decimal integer. This part of a conversion specification is a type specifier.

`printf()` and Type Specifiers

You have already come across one type specifier d, which displays data in decimal format. Table 17.1 lists the other type specifiers that are available.

TABLE 17.1 Type Specifiers

Specifier	Description
d	Displays argument as a decimal number
b	Displays an integer as a binary number
c	Displays an integer as ASCII equivalent
f	Displays an integer as a floating-point number (double)
o	Displays an integer as an octal number (base 8)
s	Displays argument as a string
x	Displays an integer as a lowercase hexadecimal number (base 16)
X	Displays an integer as an uppercase hexadecimal number (base 16)

Listing 17.1 uses `printf()` to display a single number according to some of the type specifiers listed in Table 17.1.

Notice that we do not only add conversion specifications to the format control string. Any additional text we include will be printed.

LISTING 17.1 Demonstrating Some Type Specifiers

```
 1: <html>
 2: <head>
 3: <title>Demonstrating some type specifiers</title>
 4: </head>
 5: <body>
 6: <?php
 7: $number = 543;
 8: printf("Decimal: %d<br>", $number );
 9: printf("Binary: %b<br>", $number );
10: printf("Double: %f<br>", $number );
11: printf("Octal: %o<br>", $number );
12: printf("String: %s<br>", $number );
13: printf("Hex (lower): %x<br>", $number );
14: printf("Hex (upper): %X<br>", $number );
15: ?>
16: </body>
17: </html>
```

Figure 17.1 shows the output for Listing 17.1. As you can see, `printf()` is a quick way of converting data from one number system to another and outputting the result.

FIGURE 17.1

*Demonstrating
conversion specifiers.*

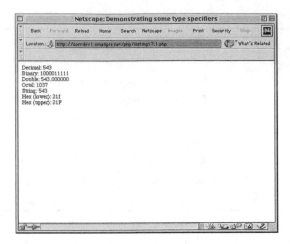

When you specify a color in HTML, you combine three hexadecimal numbers between 00 and FF, representing the values for red, green, and blue. You can use `printf()` to convert three decimal numbers between 0 and 255 to their hexadecimal equivalents:

```
$red = 204;
$green = 204;
$blue = 204;
printf( "#%X%X%X", $red, $green, $blue );
// prints "#CCCCCC"
```

Although you can use the type specifier to convert from decimal to hexadecimal numbers, you can't use it to determine how many characters the output for each argument should occupy. Within an HTML color code, each hexadecimal number should be padded to two characters, which would become a problem if we changed our $red, $green, and $blue variables in the previous fragment to contain 1, for example. We would end up with the output "#111". You can force the output of leading zeroes by using a padding specifier.

Padding Output with the Padding Specifier

You can require that output be padded by leading characters. The padding specifier should directly follow the percent sign that begins a conversion specification. To pad output with leading zeroes, the padding specifier should consist of a zero followed by the number of characters you want the output to take up. If the output occupies fewer characters than this total, the difference will be filled with zeroes:

```
printf( "%04d", 36 );
// prints "0036"
```

To pad output with leading spaces, the padding specifier should consist of a space character followed by the number of characters that the output should occupy:

```
printf( "% 4d", 36 )
// prints "  36"
```

A browser will not display multiple spaces in an HTML document. You can force the display of spaces and newlines by placing <PRE> tags around your output.

```
<pre>
<?php
print "The        spaces        will be visible";
?>
</pre>
```

If you wish to format an entire document as text, you can use the header() function to change the Content-Type header.

```
header("Content-Type: Text/Plain");
```

Remember that your script must not have sent any output to the browser for the header() function to work as desired.

You can specify any character other than a space or a zero in your padding specifier with a single quotation mark followed by the character you want to use:

```
printf ( "%'x4d", 36 );
// prints "xx36"
```

We now have the tools we need to complete our HTML code example. Until now, we could convert three numbers, but we could not pad them with leading zeroes:

```
$red = 1;
$green = 1;
$blue = 1;
printf( "#%02X%02X%02X", $red, $green, $blue );
// prints "#010101"
```

Each variable is output as a hexadecimal number. If the output occupies fewer than two spaces, leading zeroes will be added.

Specifying a Field Width

You can specify the number of spaces within which your output should sit. The field width specifier is an integer that should be placed after the percent sign that begins a conversion specification (assuming that no padding specifier is defined). The following fragment outputs a list of four items, all of which sit within a field of 20 spaces. To make the spaces visible on the browser, we place all our output within a PRE element.

```
print "<pre>";
printf("%20s\n", "Books");
printf("%20s\n", "CDs");
printf("%20s\n", "Games");
printf("%20s\n", "Magazines");
print "</pre>";
```

Figure 17.2 shows the output of this fragment.

FIGURE 17.2

Aligning with field width specifiers.

By default, output is right-aligned within the field you specify. You can make it left-aligned by propending a minus (–) symbol to the field width specifier:

```
printf("%-20s\n", "Left aligned");
```

Note that alignment applies to the decimal portion of any number that you output. In other words, only the portion before the decimal point of a double will sit flush to the end of the field width when right aligned.

Specifying Precision

If you want to output data in floating-point format, you can specify the precision to which you want to round your data. This is particularly useful when dealing with currency. The precision identifier should be placed directly before the type specifier. It consists of a dot followed by the number of decimal places to which you want to round. This specifier only has an effect on data that is output with the f type specifier:

```
printf( "%.2f", 5.333333 );
// prints "5.33"
```

In the C language, it is possible to use a precision specifier with `printf()` to specify padding for decimal output. The precision specifier will have no effect on decimal output in PHP 4. Use the padding specifier to add leading zeroes to integers.

Conversion Specifications: A Recap

Table 17.2 lists the specifiers that can make up a conversion specification in the order that they would be included. Note that it is difficult to use both a padding specifier and a field width specifier. You should choose to use one or the other, but not both.

TABLE 17.2 Components of Conversion Specification

Name	Description	Example
Padding specifier	Determines the number of characters that output should occupy, and the characters to add otherwise	' 4'
Field width specifier	Determines the space within which output should be formatted	'20'
Precision specifier	Determines the number of decimal places to which a double should be rounded	'.4'
Type specifier	Determines the data type that should be output	'd'

Listing 17.2 uses `printf()` to output a list of products and prices.

LISTING 17.2 Using `printf()` to Format a List of Product Prices

```
 1: <html>
 2: <head>
 3: <title>Using printf() to format a list of product prices</title>
 4: </head>
 5: <body>
 6: <?php
 7: $products = Array(    "Green armchair"=>"222.4",
 8:             "Candlestick"=>"4",
 9:             "Coffee table"=>80.6
10:             );
```

LISTING 17.2   continued

```
11: print "<pre>";
12: printf("%-20s%23s\n", "Name", "Price");
13: printf("%'-43s\n", "");
14: foreach ( $products as $key=>$val )
15:     printf( "%-20s%20.2f\n", $key, $val );
16: print("</pre>");
17: ?>
18: </body>
19: </html>
```

We first define an associative array containing product names and prices on line 7. We print a PRE element, so that the browser will recognize our spaces and newlines. Our first printf() call on line 12 defines the following format control string:

```
"%-20s%23s\n"
```

The first conversion specification ("%-20s") uses a field width specifier of 20 characters, with the output left-justified. We use a string type specifier. The second conversion specification ("%23s") sets up a right-aligned field width. This printf() call will output our field headers.

Our second printf() function call on line 13 draws a line of – characters across a field of 43 characters. We achieve this with a padding specifier, which adds padding to an empty string.

The final printf() call on line 15 is part of a foreach statement that loops through our product array. We use two conversion specifications. The first ("%-20s") prints the product name as a string left-justified within a 20-character field. The second conversion specification ("%20.2f") uses a field width specifier to ensure that output will be right-aligned within a 20-character field, and a precision specifier to ensure that the double we output is rounded to two decimal places.

Figure 17.3 shows the output of Listing 17.2.

Argument Swapping

As of PHP 4.0.6 it became possible to use the format control string to change the order in which the provided arguments are incorporated into output.

FIGURE 17.3

Products and prices formatted with printf().

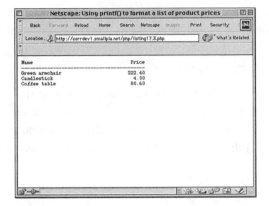

Imagine for example that you are printing dates to the browser. You have the dates in a multidimensional array and you are using printf() to format the output.

```
<?
$dates = array(
            array( 'mon'=> 12, 'mday'=>25, 'year'=>2001 ),
            array( 'mon'=>  5, 'mday'=>23, 'year'=>2000 ),
            array( 'mon'=> 10, 'mday'=>29, 'year'=>2001 )
            );

$format = include( "local_format.php" );
foreach( $dales as $date ) {
    printf( "$format", $date['mon'], $date['mday'], $date['year'] );
}
?>
```

We are getting our format control string from an include file called local_format.php. Assuming that this file contains only:

```
<?php
return "%02d/%02d/%d<br>";
?>
```

Our output will be in the format mm/dd/yyyy.

```
12/25/2001
05/23/2000
10/29/2001
```

Imagine now that we are installing our script for a British site. In the United Kingdom dates are commonly presented with days before months (dd/mm/yyyy). The core code cannot be changed, but configuration files such as `local_format.php` can. Luckily we can now alter the order in which the arguments are presented from within the format control code.

```
return "%2\$02d/%1\$02d/%3\$d<br>";
```

We can insert the argument number we are interested in after the initial percentage character that marks each conversion specification, followed by an escaped dollar ($) character. So in our fragment above we are demanding that the second argument be presented, followed by the first, followed by the third. The result is a list of dates in British format.

```
25/12/2001
23/05/2000
29/10/2001
```

Storing a Formatted String

`printf()` outputs data to the browser, which means that the results are not available to your scripts. You can, however, use the function `sprintf()`, which works in exactly the same way as `printf()` except that it returns a string that you can then store in a variable for later use. The following fragment uses `sprintf()` to round a double to two decimal places, storing the result in $dosh:

```
$dosh = sprintf("%.2f", 2.334454);
print "You have $dosh dollars to spend";
```

A particular use of `sprintf()` is to write formatted data to a file. You can call `sprintf()` and assign its return value to a variable that can then be printed to a file with `fputs()`.

Investigating Strings

You do not always know everything about the data that you are working with. Strings can arrive from many sources, including user input, databases, files, and Web pages. Before you begin to work with data from an external source, you often will need to find out more about it. PHP 4 provides many functions that enable you to acquire information about strings.

A Note About Indexing Strings

We will frequently use the word *index* in relation to strings. You will have come across the word more frequently in the context of arrays. In fact, strings and arrays are not as different as you might imagine. You can think of a string as an array of characters. So you can access individual characters of a string as if they were elements of an array:

```
$test = "scallywag";
print $test[0]; // prints "s"
print $test[2]; // prints "a"
```

It is important to remember, therefore, that when we talk about the position or index of a character within a string, characters, like array elements, are indexed from 0.

Finding the Length of a String with `strlen()`

You can use `strlen()` to determine the length of a string. `strlen()` requires a string and returns an integer representing the number of characters in the variable you have passed it. `strlen()` might typically be used to check the length of user input. The following fragment tests a membership code to ensure that it is four digits long:

```
if ( strlen( $membership ) == 4 )
    print "Thank you!";
else
    print "Your membership number must have 4 digits<P>";
```

The user is thanked for his input only if the global variable `$membership` contains four characters; otherwise, an error message is generated.

Finding a Substring Within a String with `strstr()`

You can use `strstr()` to test whether a string exists embedded within another string. `strstr()` requires two arguments: a source string and the substring you want to find within it. The function returns `false` if the substring is absent. Otherwise, it returns the portion of the source string beginning with the substring. For the following example, imagine that we want to treat membership codes that contain the string AB differently from those that do not:

```
$membership = "pAB7";
if ( strstr( $membership, "AB" ) )
   print "Thank you. Don't forget that your membership expires soon!";
else
   print "Thank you!";
```

Because our test variable `$membership` does contain the string AB, `strstr()` returns the string AB7. This resolves to `true` when tested, so we print a special message. What happens if our user enters "pab7"? `strstr()` is case sensitive, so AB will not be found. The `if` statement's test will fail, and the default message will be printed to the browser. If we want search for either AB or ab within the string, we must use `stristr()`, which works in exactly the same way but is not case sensitive.

17

Finding the Position of a Substring with `strpos()`

`strpos()` tells you both whether a string exists within a larger string and where it is to be found. `strpos()` requires two arguments: the source string and the substring you are seeking. The function also accepts an optional third argument, an integer representing the index from which you want to start searching. If the substring does not exist, `strpos()` returns `false`; otherwise, it returns the index at which the substring begins. The following fragment uses `strpos()` to ensure that a string begins with the string `mz`:

```
$membership = "mz00xyz";
if ( strpos($membership, "mz") === 0 )
   print "hello mz";
```

Notice the trick we had to play to get expected results. `strpos()` finds `mz` in our string, but it finds it at the first element of the string. This means that it will return zero, which will resolve to `false` in our test. To work around this, we use PHP's new equivalence operator `===`, which returns `true` if the left- and right-hand operands are equivalent and of the same type.

Extracting Part of a String with `substr()`

`substr()` returns a portion of a string based on the start index and length of the portion you are looking for. `strstr()` demands two arguments, a source string, and the starting index. It returns all characters from the starting index to the end of the string you are searching. `substr()` optionally accepts a third argument, which should be an integer representing the length of the string you want returned. If this argument is present, `substr()` returns only the number of characters specified from the start index onwards.

```
$test = "scallywag";
print substr($test,6);  // prints "wag"
print substr($test,6,2) // prints "wa"
```

If you pass `substr()` a negative number as its second (starting index) argument, it will count from the end rather than the beginning of the string. The following fragment writes a specific message to people who have submitted an email address ending in `.uk`.

```
$test = "matt@corrosive.co.uk";
if ( $test = substr( $test, -3 ) == ".uk" )
   print "Don't forget our special offers for British customers";
else
   print "Welcome to our shop!";
```

Tokenizing a String with `strtok()`

You can parse a string word by word using `strtok()`. `strtok()` initially requires two arguments, the string to be tokenized and the delimiters by which to split the string. The

delimiter string can include as many characters as you want. strtok() will return the
first token found. After strtok() has been called for the first time, the source string will
be cached. For subsequent calls, you should only pass strtok() the delimiter string. The
function will return the next found token every time it is called, returning false when
the end of the string is reached. strtok() will usually be called repeatedly within a loop.
Listing 17.3 uses strtok() to tokenize a URL, splitting the host and path from the query
string, and further dividing the name/value pairs of the query string. Figure 17.3 shows
the output from Listing 17.3.

LISTING 17.3   Dividing a String into Tokens with strtok()

```
 1: <html>
 2: <head>
 3: <title>Listing 17.3 Dividing a string into
 4:         tokens with strtok()</title>
 5: </head>
 6: <body>
 7: <?php
 8: $test  = "http://www.deja.com/qs.xp?";
 9: $test .= "OP=dnquery.xp&ST=MS&DBS=2&QRY=developer+php";
10: $delims = "?&";
11: $word = strtok( $test, $delims );
12: while ( is_string( $word ) ) {
13:    if ( $word )
14:       print "$word<br>";
15:    $word = strtok( $delims);
16: }
17: ?>
18: </body>
19: </html>
```

strtok() is something of a blunt instrument, and a few tricks are required to work with
it. We first store the delimiters that we want to work with in a variable, $delims on line
10. We call strtok() on line 11, passing it the URL we want to tokenize and the
$delims string. We store the first result in $word. Within the conditional expression of
the while loop on line 12, we test that $word is a string. If it isn't, we know that end of
the string has been reached and no further action is required.

We are testing the return type because a string containing two delimiters in a row would
cause strtok() to return an empty string when it reaches the first of these delimiters. So
a more conventional test such as

```
while ( $word ) {
     $word = strtok( $delims );
}
```

17

would fail if $word is an empty string, even if the end of the source string has not yet been reached.

Having established that $word contains a string, we can go on to work with it. If $word does not contain an empty string, we print it to the browser on line 14. We must then call strtok() again on line 15 to repopulate the $word variable for the next test. Notice that we don't pass the source string to strtok() a second time. If we were to do this, the first word of the source string would be returned once again, and we would find ourselves in an infinite loop.

Manipulating Strings

PHP 4 provides many functions that will transform a string argument, subtly or radically.

Cleaning Up a String with `trim()` and `ltrim()` and `strip_tags()`

When you acquire text from the user or a file, you can't always be sure that you haven't also picked up white space at the beginning and end of your data. trim() shaves any white space characters, including newlines, tabs, and spaces, from both the start and end of a string. It accepts the string to be modified, returning the cleaned-up version.

```
$text = "\t\t\tlots of room to breath         ";
$text = trim( $text );
print $text;
// prints "lots of room to breath";
```

Of course this might be more work than you require. You might want to keep white space at the beginning of a string but remove it from the end. You can use PHP's rtrim() function exactly the same as you would trim(). Only white space at the end of the string argument will be removed, however:

```
$text = "\t\t\tlots of room to breath         ";
$text = rtrim( $text );
print $test;
// prints "            lots of room to breath";
```

PHP provides the ltrim() function to strip white space only from the beginning of a string. Once again, this is called with the string you want to transform and returns a new string, shorn of tabs, newlines, and spaces:

```
$text = "\t\t\tlots of room to breath         ";
$text = ltrim( $text );
print $test;
// prints "lots of room to breath         ";
```

PHP by its nature tends to work with markup text. It is not unusual to have to remove tags from a block in order to present it without formatting. PHP provides the `strip_tags()` function for this purpose. `strip_tags()` accepts two arguments. The first is the text to transform. The second argument is optional and should be a list of HTML tags which `strip_tags()` can leave in place. Tags in the exception list should not be separated by any characters.

```
$string = "I <i>simply</i> will not have it,<br>said Mr Dean<p><b>The end</b>";
print strip_tags( $string, "<br><p>" );
```

In the previous code fragment we create an HTML formatted string. When we call `strip_tags()` we pass it the `$string` variable and a list of exceptions. The result is that the <p> and <br> tags are left in place and all other tags are stripped out.

Replacing a Portion of a String Using `substr_replace()`

`substr_replace()` works similarly to `substr()` except that it allows you replace the portion of a string that you extract. The function requires three arguments: the string you are transforming, the text you want to add to it, and the starting index. It also accepts an optional length argument. `substr_replace()` finds the portion of a string specified by the starting index and length arguments, replacing this portion with the string provided in the replace string argument and returning the entire transformed string.

In the following code fragment, to renew a user's membership code, we must change its second two characters:

```
<?
$membership = "mz99xyz";
$membership = substr_replace( $membership, "00", 2, 2 );
print "New membership number: $membership<p>";
// prints "New membership number: mz00xyz"
?>
```

Replacing Substrings Using `str_replace`

`str_replace()` replaces all instances of a string within another string. It requires three arguments: a search string, the replacement string, and the string on which this transformation is to be effected. The function returns the transformed string. The following example uses `str_replace()` to change all references to 2000 to 2001 within a string:

```
$string  = "Site contents copyright 2000. ";
$string .= "The 2000 Guide to All Things Good in Europe";
print str_replace("2000","2001",$string);
```

17

As of PHP 4.05 `str_replace()` has been enhanced to accept arrays as well as strings for all of its arguments. This allows us to perform multiple search and replace operations on a subject string, and even on more than one subject string.

```php
<?php
$source = array(
        "The package which is at version 4.2 was released in 2000",
    "The year 2000 was an excellent period for PointyThing4.2" );
$search  = array( "4.2", "2000" );
$replace = array( "5.0", "2001" );
$source = str_replace( $search, $replace, $source );
foreach( $source as $str )
   print "$str<br>";

// prints:
// The package which is at version 5.0 was released in 2001
// The year 2001 was an excellent period for PointyThing5.0
?>
```

When `str_replace()` is passed an array of strings for its first and second arguments, it will attempt to switch each search string with its corresponding replace string in the text to be transformed. When the third argument is an array, the `str_replace()` will return an array of strings. The search and replace operation will have been executed upon each string in the array.

Converting Case

PHP provides several functions that allow you to convert the case of a string. When you write user-submitted data to a file or database, you may want to convert it all to upper- or lowercase text first, to make it easy to compare later on. To get an uppercase version of a string, use the function `strtoupper()`. This function requires only the string that you want to convert and returns the converted string:

```php
$membership = "mz00xyz";
$membership = strtoupper( $membership );
print "$membership<P>"; // prints "MZ00XYZ"
```

To convert a string to lowercase characters, use the function `strtolower()`. Once again, this requires the string you want to convert and returns a converted version:

```php
$home_url = "WWW.CORROSIVE.CO.UK";
$home_url = strtolower( $home_url );
if ( ! ( strpos ( $home_url, "http://" ) === 0 ) )
   $home_url = "http://$home_url";
print $home_url; // prints "http://www.corrosive.co.uk"
```

PHP also provides a case function that has a useful cosmetic purpose. `ucwords()` makes the first letter of every word in a string uppercase. In the following fragment, we make the first letter of every word in a user-submitted string uppercase:

```
$full_name = "violet elizabeth bott";
$full_name = ucwords( $full_name );
print $full_name; // prints "Violet Elizabeth Bott"
```

Although this function makes the first letter of each word uppercase, it does not touch any other letters. So if the user had had problems with her shift key in the previous example and submitted VIolEt eLIZaBeTH bOTt, our approach would not have done much to fix the string. We would have ended up with VIolEt ELIZaBeTH BOTt, which isn't much of an improvement. We can deal with this by making the submitted string lowercase with `strtolower()` before invoking `ucwords()`:

```
$full_name = "VIolEt eLIZaBeTH bOTt";
$full_name = ucwords( strtolower($full_name) );
print $full_name; // prints "Violet Elizabeth Bott"
```

Wrapping Text with `wordwrap()` and `nl2br()`

When you present plain text within a Web page you are often faced with the problem that newlines are not displayed, and your text runs together into a featureless blob. `nl2br()` is a convenience method that converts every newline into an HTML break. So

```
$string  = "one line\n";
$string .= "another line\n";
$string .= "a third for luck\n";
print nl2br( $string );
```

will print

```
one line<br />
another line<br />
a third for luck<br />
```

Notice that the <br> tags are output in XHTML compliant form. This was introduced in PHP 4.0.5.

`nl2br()` is great for honoring newlines that are already in the text you are converting. Occasionally though you may wish to add arbitrary linebreaks in order to format a column of text. The `wordwrap()` function is perfect for this. `wordwrap()` requires one argument, the string to be transformed. By default `wordwrap()` will wrap lines every 75 characters, and will use '\n' as its linebreak character. So the code fragment

```
$string  = "Given a long line, wordwrap() is useful as a means of ";
$string .= "breaking it into a column and thereby making it easier to read";
print wordwrap($string);
```

would output

```
Given a long line, wordwrap() is useful as a means of breaking it into a
column and thereby making it easier to read
```

Because the lines are broken with the character '\n', the formatting will not show up in HTML mode, of course. wordwrap() has two more optional arguments; a number representing the maximum number of characters per line, and a string representing the end of line string you would like to use. So applying the function call

```
print wordwrap( $string, 24, "<br>\n" );
```

to our $string variable, our output would be

```
Given a long line,<br>
wordwrap() is useful as<br>
a means of breaking it<br>
into a column and<br>
thereby making it easier<br>
to read
```

wordwrap() won't automatically break at your line limit if a word has more characters than the limit. You can, however, use an optional fourth argument to enforce this. The argument should be a positive integer. So using wordwrap() in conjunction with the fourth argument we can now wrap a string, even where it contains words that extend beyond the limit we are setting. This fragment

```
$string  = "As usual you will find me at http://www.witteringonaboutit.com/";
$string .= "chat/eating_green_cheese/forum.php. Hope to see you there!";
print wordwrap( $string, 24, "<br>\n", 1 );
```

will output

```
As usual you will find<br>
me at<br>
http://www.witteringonab<br>
outit.com/chat/eating_gr<br>
een_cheese/forum.php.<br>
Hope to see you there!
```

Breaking Strings into Arrays with `explode()`

The delightfully named explode() function is similar in some ways to strtok(). explode(), though, will break up a string into an array, which you can then store, sort, or examine as you want. explode() requires two arguments: the delimiter string that you want to use to break up the source string and the source string itself. explode() optionally accepts a third argument which will determine the maximum number of pieces the string can be broken into. The delimiter string can include more than one character, all of which will form a single delimiter (unlike multiple delimiter characters passed to strtok(), each of which will be a delimiter in its own right). The following fragment breaks up a date and stores the result in an array:

```
$start_date = "2000-01-12";
$date_array = explode("-", $start_date);
// $date[0] == "2000"
// $date[1] == "01"
// $date[2] == "12"
```

Summary

Strings are PHP's principal means of communication with the outside world and of storing information for later use. In this hour, you have covered some of the functions that enable you to take control of the strings in your scripts.

You learned how to format strings with printf() and sprint(). You should be able to use these functions both to create strings that transform data and lay it out. You learned about functions that investigate strings. You should be able to discover the length of a string with strlen(), determine the presence of a substring with strpos(), or extract a substring with substr(). You should be able to tokenize a string with strtok().

Finally, you learned about functions that transform strings. You can now remove white space from the beginning or end of a string with trim(), ltrim(), or rtrim(). You can change case with strtoupper(), strtolower(), or ucwords(). You can replace all instances of a string with str_replace().

Believe it or not, you are not finished with strings yet. PHP supports regular expressions that are an even more powerful means of working with strings than the functions already examined. Regular expressions are the subject of the next hour.

Q&A

Q Are there any other string functions that might be useful to me?

A Yes. PHP 4 has about 60 string functions! You can read about them all in the PHP 4 online manual at http://www.php.net/manual/ref.strings.php.

Q In the example that demonstrated printf(), we showed the formatting by wrapping our output in <PRE> tags. Is this the best way of showing formatted plain text on a browser?

A <PRE> tags can be useful if you want to preserve plain text formatting in an HTML context. If you want to output an entire text document to the browser, however, it is

17

neater to tell the browser to format the entire output as plain text. You can do this with the `header()` function:

```
Header("Content-Type: Text/Plain");
```

Workshop

Quiz

1. What conversion specifier would you use with `printf()` to format an integer as a double? Write down the full syntax required to convert the integer 33.

2. How would you pad the conversion you effected in question 1 with zeroes so that the part before the decimal point is four characters long?

3. How would you specify a precision of two decimal places for the floating-point number we have been formatting in the previous questions?

4. What function would you use to determine the length of a string?

5. What function would you use to acquire the starting index of a substring within a string?

6. What function would you use to extract a substring from a string?

7. How might you remove white space from the beginning of a string?

8. How would you convert a string to uppercase characters?

9. How would you break up a delimited string into an array of substrings?

Quiz Answers

1. The conversion specifier `f` is used to format an integer as a double:

   ```
   printf("%f", 33 );
   ```

2. You can pad the output from `printf()` with the padding specifier—that is, a space or a zero followed by a number representing the number of characters you want to pad by.

   ```
   printf("%04f", 33 );
   ```

3. The precision specifier consists of dot (.) followed by a number representing the precision you want to apply. It should be placed before the conversion specifier:

   ```
   printf("%04.2f", 33 );
   ```

4. The `strlen()` function returns the length of a string.

5. The `strstr()` function returns the starting index of a substring.

6. The `substr()` function extracts and returns a substring.

7. The `ltrim()` function removes white space from the start of a string.

8. The `strtoupper()` function converts a string to uppercase characters.

9. The `explode()` function will split up a string into an array.

Activities

1. Create a feedback form that accepts a user's full name and an email address. Use case conversion functions to capitalize the first letter of each name the user submits and print the result back to the browser. Check that the user's email address contains the @ symbol and print a warning otherwise.

2. Create an array of doubles and integers. Loop through the array converting each element to a floating-point number with a precision of 2. Right-align the output within a field of 20 characters.

17

HOUR 18

Working with Regular Expressions

Regular expressions are a powerful way of examining and modifying text. They enable you to search for patterns within a string, extracting matches flexibly and precisely. Be warned that because they are more powerful, they are also slower than the more basic string function examined in Hour 17, "Working with Strings." You should use string functions, therefore, if you don't need the extra power afforded by the use of a regular expression function.

PHP supports two flavors of regular expression. It has a set of functions that emulate regular expressions as employed in Perl, and a set of function that support the more limited POSIX regular expressions. You will examine both.

In this hour, you will learn:

- How to match patterns in strings using regular expressions
- The basics of regular expression syntax

- How to replace text in strings using regular expressions
- How to work with powerful Perl compatible regular expressions to match and replace patterns in text

POSIX Regular Expression Functions

POSIX regular expression functions make it possible for you to match and replace complex patterns in strings. They are commonly known simply as regular expression functions, but we refer to them as POSIX regular expression functions to distinguish them from the similar but more powerful Perl compatible regular expressions, and because they follow the POSIX definition for extended regular expressions.

A regular expression is a combination of symbols that match a pattern in text. Learning how to use regular expressions, therefore, is much more than learning the arguments and return types of PHP's regular expression functions. We will begin with the functions and use them to introduce regular expression syntax.

Using `ereg()` to Match Patterns in Strings

`ereg()` requires a string representing a pattern, a string representing the text to be searched, and an array variable into which the results of the search will be placed. `ereg()` returns an integer representing the number of characters matched if the pattern was discovered in the source string, or `false` otherwise. Let's search the string "Aardvark advocacy" for the letters "aa."

```
print ereg("aa","aardvark advocacy",$array);
print "<br>$array[0]<br>";
// output:
// 2
// aa
```

The letters "aa" exist in "aardvark," so `ereg()` returns 2, which is the number of letters it matched. The first element of the `$array` variable is also filled with the matched string, which we print to the browser. This might seem strange given that we already know the pattern we are looking for is "aa". We are not, however, limited to looking for predefined characters. We can use a single dot (.) to match any character:

```
print ereg("d.","aardvark advocacy",$array);
print "<br>$array[0]<br>";
// output:
// 2
// dv
```

d. matches "d" followed by any character. We don't know in advance what the second character will be, so the value in `$array[0]` becomes useful.

Using Quantifiers to Match a Character More Than Once

When you search for a character in a string, you can use a quantifier to determine the number of times this character should repeat for a match to be made. The pattern a+, for example, will match at least one "a" followed by "a" zero or more times. Let's put this to the test:

```
if ( ereg("a+","aaaa", $array) )
   print $array[0];
// prints "aaaa";
```

Notice that this regular expression greedily matches as many characters as it can. Table 18.1 lists the quantifiers you can use to test for a recurring character.

TABLE 18.1 Quantifiers for Matching a Recurring Character

Symbol	Description	Example
*	Zero or more instance	a*
+	One or more instances	a+
?	Zero or one instance	a?
{n}	n instances	a{3}
{n,}	At least n instances	a{3,}
{,n}	Up to n instances	a{,2}
{n1,n2}	At least n1 instances, no more than n2 instances	a{1,2}

The numbers between braces in Table 18.1 are called *bounds*. Bounds let you pinpoint exactly the number of times a character should repeat to be matched.

NEW TERM *Bounds* define the number of times a character or range of characters should be matched in a regular expression. You should place your upper and lower bounds between braces after the character you wish to match. For example,

a{4,5}

will match no fewer than 4 and no more than 5 instances of the character a.

Let's create an example. A club has allocated membership codes to its members. A valid code can be between one and four instances of the letter "y" followed by any number of alphanumeric characters, followed by the number 99. We have been requested by the club to parse a backlog, pulling out the membership codes where possible.

```
$test = "the code is yyXGDH99 — have you received my sub?";
if ( ereg( "y{1,4}.*99 ", $test, $array ) )
   print "Found membership: $array[0]";
// prints "Found membership: yyXGDH99 "
```

In the previous code fragment, the membership code begins with two y characters, followed by four uppercase letters, followed by 99. y{1,4} matches the two y characters, and the four uppercase letters are matched by .*, which will match any number of characters of any type.

So that would seem to do the job. In fact, we have a long way to go yet. To ensure that the matched pattern ends at 99, we have required a space as the last character. This is returned when we match. Worse than this, if the string we were testing was

```
"my code is yyXGDH99 did you get my 1999 sub?"
```

the previous regular expression would match

```
"y code is yyXGDH99 did you get my 1999 "
```

So what went wrong? The regular expression matched the y in my, and then matched any number of characters until it reached 99 followed by a space. Regular expressions are greedy; in other words, they match as many characters as they can. For this reason, we match all characters until the 99 of 1999 is reached, rather than the final 99 in our membership code. We might go some way towards fixing this if only we could make sure that the characters that we match between y and 99 are truly alphanumeric and contain no spaces. In fact, we can do this easily with a character class.

Matching Ranges of Characters with Character Classes

Until now we have either matched specified characters or used . to match any character. Character classes enable you to match any one of a group of characters. To define a character class, you surround the characters you want to match in square brackets. [ab] will match "a" or "b." After you have defined a character class, you can treat it as if it were a character. So [ab]+ will match "aaa," "bbb," or "ababab."

You can also match ranges of characters with a character class: [a-z] will match any lowercase letter, [A-Z] will match any uppercase letter, and [0-9] will match any number. You can combine ranges and individual characters into one character class, so [a-z5] will match any lowercase letter or the number "5".

You can also negate a character class by including a caret (^) character after the opening square bracket: [^A-Z] will match anything apart from an uppercase character.

Let's return to the example from the previous section. We need to match "y" between one and four times, any alphanumeric character any number of times, and the characters "99."

```
$test = "my code is yyXGDH99 did you get my 1999 sub?";
if ( ereg( "y{1,4}[a-zA-Z0-9]*99 ", $test, $array ) )
    print "Found membership: $array[0]";
// prints "Found membership: yyXGDH99 "
```

We're getting closer. The character class that we have added will no longer match spaces, so the membership code is now returned. If we add a comma after the membership code in our test string, however, the regular expression fails again:

```
$test = "my code is yyXGDH99, did you get my 1999 sub?";
if ( ereg( "y{1,4}[a-zA-Z0-9]*99 ", $test, $array ) )
    print "Found membership: $array[0]";
// regular expression fails
```

This is because we have demanded a space at the end of the pattern to ensure that we are at the end of the membership code. So if a text includes a membership code in parentheses, or before a hyphen or comma, the match will fail. We can amend our regular expression, so that we match anything other than an alphanumeric character, which will get us some way towards a solution:

```
$test = "my code is yyXGDH99, did you get my 1999 sub?";
if ( ereg( "y{1,4}[a-zA-Z0-9]*99[^a-zA-Z0-9]", $test, $array ) )
    print "Found membership: $array[0]";
// prints "Found membership: yyXGDH99,"
```

We're closer still, but there are still two problems. First, we have included the comma in our returned match, and second, the match will fail if the membership code is at the end of the string we are testing because it requires a character to exist after the membership code. We need, in other words, to find a reliable way of testing for a word boundary. We will return to this problem.

Working with Atoms

NEW TERM An *atom* is a pattern enclosed in parentheses (often referred to as a *subpattern*). After you have defined an atom, you can treat it as if it were itself a character or character class. In other words, you can match the same pattern as many times as you want using the syntax described in Table 18.1.

In the next fragment, we define a pattern, enclose it in parentheses, and require that the atom should match twice for the regular expression to succeed:

18

```
$test = "abbaxabbaxabbax";
if ( ereg( "([ab]+x){2}", $test, $array ) )
    print "$array[0]";
// prints "abbaxabbax"
```

`[ab]+x` will match "abbax", but `([ab]+x){2}` will match "abbaxabbax".

The first element of the array variable that is passed to `ereg()` will contain the complete matched string. Subsequent elements will contain each individual atom matched. This means that you can access the component parts of a matched pattern (up to a maximum of 10 subpatterns) as well as the entire match.

In the following code fragment, we match an IP address and access not only the entire address, but also each of its component parts:

```
$test = "158.152.55.35";
if ( ereg( "([0-9]+)\.([0-9]+)\.([0-9]+)\.([0-9]+)", $test, $array ) ) {
    foreach ( $array as $val )
        print "$val<BR>";
}
// Output:
// 158.152.1.58
// 158
// 152
// 1
// 58
```

Notice that we have used a backslash (\) to escape the dots in the regular expression. By doing this, we signal that we want to strip . of its special meaning and treat it as a specific character. You must do the same for any character that has a function in a regular expression if you want to refer to it.

Branches

You can combine patterns with the pipe (|) character to create branches in your regular expressions. A regular expression with two branches will match either the first pattern or the second. This adds yet another layer of flexibility to regular expression syntax. In the next code fragment, we match either .com or .co.uk in a string:

```
$test = "www.adomain.com";
if ( ereg( "\.com|\.co\.uk", $test, $array ) )
    print "it is a $array[0] domain<BR>";
// prints "it is .com domain"
```

Anchoring a Regular Expression

Not only can you determine the pattern you want to find in a string, you also can decide where in the string you want to find it. To test whether a pattern is at the beginning of a string, prepend a caret (^) symbol to your regular expression. ^a will match "apple", but not "banana".

To test that a pattern is at the end of a string, append a dollar ($) symbol to the end of your regular expression. a$ will match "flea" but not "dear".

The Membership Code Example Revisited

We now have the tools to complete our membership code examples. Remember that we are parsing emails to extract membership codes that consist of between one and four instances of the letter "y" followed by any number of any alphanumeric characters followed by "99." Our current problem is to determine when a matched pattern is on a word boundary. We can't use a space because a word can be bounded by punctuation. We can't require that a nonalphanumeric character bound the match because our pattern could begin or end a string.

Now that we can create branches and anchor patterns, we can require that the membership code be followed either by a nonalphanumeric character or the end of the string. We can use the same logic to determine a word boundary at the beginning of the code. We can also use parentheses to recover the membership code shorn of any punctuation or spaces as follows:

```
$test = "my code is yyXGDH99, did you get my 1999 sub?";
if ( ereg( "(^|[^a-zA-Z0-9])(y{1,4}[a-zA-Z0-9]*99)([^a-zA-Z0-9]|$)", $test,
$array ) )
    print "Found membership: $array[2]";
// prints "Found membership: yyXGDH99"
```

As you can see, regular expressions are daunting at first glance. After you break them down into smaller chunks, however, they usually reveal their secrets quite easily. We have ensured that our matched pattern is on a word boundary (as we define it for these purposes). This means that it must either be preceded by a nonalphanumeric character or the beginning of the string. It must be also be followed by a nonalphanumeric character or the end of the string. We don't want to record any preceding or following characters, so we wrap the pattern we want to extract in parentheses. We can then be sure to access it in the second element of the $array array.

> ereg() is case sensitive. If you don't want to match case, you can use eregi(), which is not case sensitive but is the same as ereg() in all other respects.

Using ereg_replace() to Replace Patterns in Strings

Until now we have searched for patterns in a string, leaving the search string untouched. ereg_replace() enables you to find a pattern in a string and replace it with a new substring. ereg_replace() requires three strings: a regular expression, the text with which to replace a found pattern, and the text to modify. ereg_replace() returns a string, including the modification if a match was found or an unchanged copy of the original source string otherwise. In the following fragment, we search for the name of a club official, replacing it with name of her successor:

```
$test = "Our Secretary, Sarah Williams is pleased to welcome you.";
print ereg_replace("Sarah Williams", "Rev. P.W. Goodchild", $test);
// prints "Our Secretary, Rev. P.W. Goodchild is pleased to welcome you."
```

Note that although ereg() will only match the first pattern it finds, ereg_replace() will find and replace every instance of a pattern.

Using Back References with ereg_replace()

Back references make it possible for you to use part of a matched pattern in the replacement string. To use this feature, you should use parentheses to wrap any elements of your regular expression that you might want to use. The text matched by these subpatterns will be available to the replacement string if you refer to them with two backslashes and the number of the atom (\\1, for example). Atoms are numbered in order, outer to inner, left to right starting at \\1. \\0 stores the entire match.

The following fragment converts dates in dd/mm/yy format to mm/dd/yy format:

```
$test = "25/12/2000";
print ereg_replace("([0-9]+)/([0-9]+)/([0-9]+)", "\\2/\\1/\\3", $test);
// prints "12/25/2000"
```

ereg_replace() is case sensitive. If you don't want to match case, you can use eregi_replace(), which is not case sensitive but is identical to ereg_replace() in all other respects.

Using split() to Break Up Strings

In Hour 17, "Working with Strings," you saw that you could split a string of tokens into an array using explode(). This is powerful but limits you to a single set of characters that can be used as a delimiter. PHP's split() function enables you to use the power of regular expressions to define a flexible delimiter. split() requires a string representing a pattern to use as a delimiter and a source string. It also accepts an optional third argument representing a limit to the number of elements you want returned. split() returns an array.

The following fragment uses a regular expression with two branches to split a string on either a comma followed by a space or the word and surrounded by two spaces:

```
$text = "apples, oranges, peaches and grapefruit";
$fruitarray = split( ", | and ", $text );
foreach ( $fruitarray as $item )
    print "$item<BR>";
// output:
// apples
// oranges
// peaches
// grapefruit
```

split() is case sensitive. If you would like to match independently of case, you can use spliti(). spliti() works in exactly the same way as split(), except that case will be ignored when the regular expression is interpreted.

Perl Compatible Regular Expressions (PCREs)

If you are migrating from Perl to PHP, you are likely to find the POSIX regular expression functions somewhat cumbersome. The good news is that PHP 4 supports Perl compatible regular expressions. PCREs are even more powerful than the syntax that you have already examined. We will explore the differences in this section.

Matching Patterns with `preg_match()`

`preg_match()` accepts three arguments: a regular expression, a source string, and an array variable, which will store matches. `preg_match()` returns `true` if a match is found and `false` otherwise. The difference between this function and `ereg_match()` lies in the regular expression argument. Perl compatible regular expressions should be enclosed by delimiters. Conventionally, these delimiters are forward slashes, although you can use any character that isn't alphanumeric (apart from the backslash character). The following fragment uses `preg_match()` to match the character p followed by any character, followed by the character t:

```
$text = "pepperpot";
if ( preg_match( "/p.t/", $text, $array ) )
   print $array[0];
// prints "pot"
```

PCREs and Greediness

By default, regular expressions will attempt to match as many characters as possible. So,

```
"/p.*t/"
```

18

will find the first "p" in a string and match as many characters as possible until the last possible "t" character is reached. So, this regular expression matches the entire test string in the following fragment:

```
$text = "pot post pat patent";
if ( preg_match( "/p.*t/", $text, $array ) )
    print $array[0];
// prints "pot post pat patent"
```

By placing a question mark (?) after any quantifier, you can force a Perl compatible regular expression to be more frugal. So, whereas

```
"p.*t"
```

means "p followed by as many characters as possible followed by t,"

```
"p.*?t"
```

means "p followed by as few characters as possible followed by t."

The following fragment uses this technique to match the smallest number of characters starting with "p" and ending with "t":

```
$text = "pot post pat patent";
if ( preg_match( "/p.*?t/", $text, $array ) )
    print $array[0];
// prints "pot"
```

PCREs and Backslashed Characters

You can escape certain characters with Perl compatible regular expressions, just as you can within strings. \t, for example represents a tab character, and \n represents a new-line. PCREs also define some escape characters that will match entire character types. Table 18.2 lists these backslash characters.

TABLE 18.2   Escape Characters that Match Character Types

Character	Matches
\d	Any number
\D	Anything other than a number
\s	Any kind of whitespace
\S	Anything other than whitespace
\w	Alphanumeric characters (including the underscore character)
\W	Anything other than an alphanumeric character or an underscore

These escape characters can vastly simplify your regular expressions. Without them, you would be forced to use a character class to match ranges of characters. Compare the `ereg()` and `preg_match()` syntax for matching word characters:

```
ereg( "p[a-zA-Z0-9_]+t", $text, $array );
preg_match( "/p\w+t/, $text, $array );
```

PCREs also support a number of escape characters that act as anchors. *Anchors* match positions within a string, without matching any characters. These are listed in Table 18.3.

TABLE 18.3 Escape Characters That Act as Anchors

Character	Matches
\A	Beginning of string
\b	Word boundary
\B	Not a word boundary
\Z	End of string (matches before final newline or at end of string)
\z	End of string (matches only at very end of string)

Remember the problems we had matching word boundaries in our membership code example? PCREs make this job much easier. Compare the `ereg()` and `preg_match()` syntax for matching word characters and boundaries:

```
ereg( "(^|[^a-zA-Z0-9_])(p[a-zA-Z0-9_]+t)([^a-zA-Z0-9_]|$)", $text, $array );
preg_match( "\bp\w+t\b", $text, $array );
```

The `preg_match()` call in the previous fragment will match the character "p" but only if it is at a word boundary, followed by any number of word characters, followed by "t," but only if it is at a word boundary. The word boundary escape character does not actually match a character; it merely confirms that a boundary exists for a match to take place. For the `ereg_match()` call, you must construct a pattern for a nonword character and match either that or a string boundary.

You can also escape characters to turn off their meanings. To match a "." character, for example, you should add a backslash to it.

Finding Matches Globally with `preg_match_all()`

One of the problems with POSIX regular expressions is that it is difficult to match every instance of a pattern within a string. So, using `ereg()` to search for words beginning with "p" and ending with "s," we will match only the first found pattern. Let's try it out:

```
$text = "I sell pots, plants, pistachios, pianos and parrots";
if ( ereg( "(^|[^a-zA-Z0-9_])(p[a-zA-Z0-9_]+s)([^a-zA-Z0-9_]|$)",
           $text, $array ) ) {
```

```
    for ( $x=0; is_string( $array[$x] ); $x++ )
        print "\$array[$x]: $array[$x]<br>\n";
}
// output:
// $array[0]: pots,
// $array[1]:
// $array[2]: pots
// $array[3]: ,
```

As we would expect, the first match, "pots", is stored in the third element of the `$array` array. The first element contains the complete match, the second contains a space, and the fourth contains a comma. To get at every pattern match in our test string, we would have to use `ereg_replace()` in a loop to remove each match from the string before testing again.

We can use `preg_match_all()` to access every match in the test string in one call. `preg_match_all()` accepts a regular expression, a source string, and an array variable, and will return `true` if a match is found. The array variable is populated with a multidimensional array, the first element of which will contain every match to the complete pattern defined in the regular expression.

Listing 18.1 tests a string using `preg_match_all()`, using two `for` statements to output the multidimensional array of results.

LISTING 18.1   Using `preg_match_all()` to Match a Pattern Globally

```
 1: <html>
 2: <head>
 3: <title>Using preg_match_all() to match a pattern globally</title>
 4: </head>
 5: <body>
 6: <?php
 7: $text = "I sell pots, plants, pistachios, pianos and parrots";
 8: if ( preg_match_all( "/\bp\w+s\b/", $text, $array ) ) {
 9:     for ( $x=0; $x< count( $array ); $x++ ) {
10:         for ( $y=0; $y< count( $array[$x] ); $y++ )
11:             print "\$array[$x][$y]: ".$array[$x][$y]."<BR>\n";
12:         }
13: }
14: // Output:
15: // $array[0][0]: pots
16: // $array[0][1]: plants
17: // $array[0][2]: pistachios
18: // $array[0][3]: pianos
19: // $array[0][4]: parrots
20: ?>
21: </body>
22: </html>
```

The first and only element of the $array variable that we passed to preg_match_all() on line 8 has been populated with an array of strings. This array contains every word in the test string that begins with "p" and ends with "s".

preg_match_all() populates a multidimensional array to store matches to subpatterns. The first element of the array argument passed to preg_match_all() will contain every match of the complete regular expression. Each additional element will contain the matches that correspond to each atom (subpattern in parentheses). So with the following call to preg_match_all()

```
$text = "01-05-99, 01-10-99, 01-03-00";
preg_match_all( "/(\d+)-(\d+)-(\d+)/", $text, $array );
```

$array[0] will store an array of complete matches:

```
$array[0][0]: 01-05-99
$array[0][1]: 01-10-99
$array[0][2]: 01-03-00
```

$array[1] will store an array of matches that corresponds to the first subpattern:

```
$array[1][0]: 01
$array[1][1]: 01
$array[1][2]: 01
```

$array[2] will store an array of matches that corresponds to the second subpattern:

```
$array[2][0]: 05
$array[2][1]: 10
$array[2][2]: 03
```

and so on.

Using preg_replace() to Replace Patterns

preg_replace() behaves in the same way as ereg_replace(), except that you have access to the additional functionality of Perl compatible regular expressions. preg_replace() requires a regular expression, a replacement string, and a source string. If a match is found, it returns a transformed string; otherwise, it returns a copy of the source string. preg_replace() also optionally accepts a fourth argument; an integer representing the maximum number of replacement that should be made. The following fragment transforms dates in a string from dd/mm/yy to mm/dd/yy format:

```
$t = "25/12/99, 14/5/00";
$t = preg_replace( "|\b(\d+)/(\d+)/(\d+)\b|", "$2/$1/$3",  $t );
print "$t<br>";
// prints "12/25/99, 5/14/00"
```

Notice that we have used a pipe (|) symbol as a delimiter. This is to save us from having to escape the forward slashes in the pattern we want to match. `preg_replace()` supports back references in the same way as `ereg_replace()`.

Notice also that we have used a different syntax for back references. Although the syntax you have already encountered will work (two backslashes followed by the back reference number), the preferred syntax for Perl compatible regular expressions is now a dollar character followed by the back reference number.

Instead of a source string, you can pass an array of strings to `preg_replace()`, and it will transform each string in turn. In this case, the return value will be an array of transformed strings.

You can also pass arrays of regular expressions and replacement strings to `preg_replace()`. Each regular expression will be applied to the source string, and the corresponding replacement string will be applied. The following fragment transforms date formats as before, but also changes copyright information in the source string:

```
$text = "25/12/99, 14/5/00. Copyright 1999";
$regs = array( "|\b(\d+)/(\d+)/(\d+)\b|",  "/([Cc]opyright) 1999/" );
$reps = array( "$2/$1/$3",                 "$1 2000" );
$text = preg_replace( $regs, $reps,  $text );
print "$text<br>";
// prints "12/25/99, 5/14/00. Copyright 2000"
```

We create two arrays. The first, `$regs`, contains two regular expressions, and the second, `$reps`, contains replacement strings. The first element of the `$reps` array corresponds to the first element of the `$reps` array, and so on.

If the array of replacement strings contains fewer elements than the array of regular expressions, patterns matched by those regular expressions without corresponding replacement strings will be replaced with an empty string.

If you pass `preg_replace()` an array of regular expressions but only a string as replacement, the same replacement string will be applied to each pattern in the array of regular expressions.

Modifiers

Perl compatible regular expressions allow you to modify the way that a pattern is applied through the use of pattern modifiers.

NEW TERM   A *pattern modifier* is a letter that should be placed after the final delimiter in your Perl compatible regular expression. It will refine the behavior of your regular expression.

Table 18.4 lists the PCRE pattern modifiers

TABLE 18.4   Perl Compatible Regular Expression Modifiers

Pattern	Description
/i	Case insensitive.
/e	Treats replacement string in preg_replace() as PHP code.
/m	$ and ^ anchors match at new lines as well as the beginning and end of the string.
/s	Matches new lines (new lines are not normally not matched by .).
/x	White space outside character classes is not matched to aid readability. To match white space, use \s, \t, or \ .
/A	Matches pattern only at start of string (this modifier is not found in Perl).
/E	Matches pattern only at end of string (this modifier is not found in Perl).
/U	Makes the regular expression ungreedy—minimum number of allowable matches found (this modifier is not found in Perl).

Where they do not contradict one another, you can combine pattern modifiers. You might want to use the x modifier to make your regular expression easier to read, for example, and also the i modifier to make it match patterns regardless of case. / b \S* t /ix will match "bat" and "BAT" but not "B A T", for example. Unescaped spaces in a regular expression modified by x are there for aesthetic reasons only and will not match any patterns in the source string.

The m modifier can be useful if you want to match an anchored pattern on multiple lines of text. The anchor patterns ^ and $ match the beginning and ends of an entire string by default. The following fragment uses the m modifier to change the behavior of $:

```
$text = "name: matt\noccupation: coder\neyes: blue\n";
preg_match_all( "/^\w+:\s+(.*)$/m", $text, $array );
foreach ( $array[1] as $val )
    print "$val<br>";
// output:
// matt
// coder
// blue
```

We create a regular expression that will match any word characters followed by a colon and any number of space characters. We then match any number of characters followed by the end of string ($) anchor. Because we have used the m pattern modifier, $ matches the end of every line rather than the end of the string.

The s modifier is useful when you want use . to match characters across multiple lines. The following fragment attempts to access the first and last words of a string:

```
$text = "start with this line\nand you will reach\na conclusion in the end\n";
preg_match( "/^(\w+).*?(\w+)$/", $text, $array );
print "$array[1] $array[2]<br>";
```

18

This code will print nothing. Although the regular expression will find word characters at the beginning of the string, the . will not match the newline characters embedded in the text. The s modifier will change this:

```
$text = "start with this line\nand you will reach\na conclusion in the end\n";
preg_match( "/^(\w+).*?(\w+)$/s", $text, $array );
print "$array[1] $array[2]<br>";
// prints "start end"
```

The e modifier can be particularly powerful. It allows you to treat the replacement string in preg_replace() as if it were PHP. You can pass back references to functions as arguments, for example, or process lists of numbers. In the following example we use the e modifier to pass matched numbers in dates to a function that returns the same date in a new format.

```
<?php
function convDate( $month, $day, $year ) {
        $year = ($year < 70 )?$year+2000:$year;
    $time = ( mktime( 0,0,0,$month,$day,$year) );
    return date("l d F Y", $time);
}

$dates = "3/18/99<br>\n7/22/00";
$dates = preg_replace(  "/([0-9]+)\/([0-9]+)\/([0-9]+)/e",
            "convDate($1,$2,$3)", $dates);
print $dates;

// prints:
// Thursday 18 March 1999
// Saturday 22 July 2000
?>
```

We match any set of three numbers separated by slashes, using parentheses to capture the matched numbers. Because we are using the e modifier, we can call the user-defined function convDate() from the replacement string argument, passing the three back references to the function. convDate() simply takes the numerical input and produces a more verbose date which replaces the original. Because in our example we are matching numbers, we do not need to enclose the back references in quotes. If we were matching strings, quotes would be necessary around each string back reference.

Using `preg_replace_callback()` to Replace Patterns

preg_replace_callback() allows you to assign a callback function which will be called for every full match your regular expression finds. preg_replace_callback() requires a regular expression, a reference to a callback function, and the string to be analyzed. Like preg_replace() it also optionally accepts a limit argument.

The callback function should be designed to accept a single array argument. This will contain the full match at index '0' and each submatch in subsequent positions in the array. Whatever the callback function returns will be incorporated into the string returned by preg_replace_callback().

We can use preg_replace_callback() to rewrite our date replacement example.

```
function convDate( $matches ) {
    $year = ($year < 70 )?$matches[3]+2000:$matches[3];
    $time = ( mktime( 0,0,0,$matches[1],$matches[2],$matches[3]) );
    return date("l d F Y", $time);
}

$dates = "3/18/99<br>\n7/22/00";
$dates = preg_replace_callback(  "/([0-9]+)\/([0-9]+)\/([0-9]+)/",
            "convDate", $dates);
print $dates;

// prints:
// Thursday 18 March 1999
// Saturday 22 July 2000
```

In this example the convDate() function is called twice, once for each time the regular expression matches. The day, month and year figures are then easy to extract from the array that is passed to convDate() and stored in the $matches argument variable.

Summary

Regular expressions are a huge subject, and we've really only scraped the surface of their power in this hour. Nevertheless, you should now be able to use regular expression functions to find and replace complex patterns in text.

You should be able to use the ereg() regular expression function to find patterns in strings and the ereg_replace() function to replace all instances of a pattern in a string. You should be able to find ranges of characters using character classes, multiple patterns using quantifiers, and alternative patterns using branches. You should be able to extract subpatterns and refer to them with back references. With the aid of Perl compatible regular expressions, you should be able to use escape characters to anchor patterns or to match character types. You should be able to use modifiers to change the way in which PCREs work.

In the next hour we will examine some core techniques for creating environments that can retain information across multiple requests.

Q&A

Q **Perl compatible regular expressions seem very powerful. Is there anywhere I can find out more about them?**

A The relevant section in the PHP manual at http://www.php.net will offer some information about regular expression syntax. You can also find some useful information at http://www.perl.com—in particular, an introduction to Perl regular expressions at http://www.perl.com/pub/doc/manual/html/pod/perlre.html and an article by Tom Christiansen at http://www.perl.com/pub/doc/manual/html/pod/perlfaq6.html. For a challenging but comprehensive guide to regular expressions you should acquire *Mastering Regular Expressions* by Jeffrey Friedl (O'Reilly).

Workshop

Quiz

1. Using POSIX regular expression functions, what function would you use to match a pattern in a string?

2. What regular expression syntax would you use to match the letter "b" at least once but not more than six times?

3. How would you specify a character range between "d" and "f"?

4. How would you negate the character range you defined in question 3?

5. What syntax would you use to match either any number or the word "tree"?

6. What POSIX regular expression function would you use to replace a matched pattern?

7. The regular expression

   `.*bc`

   will match greedily—that is, it will match "abc000000bc" rather than "abc". Using Perl compatible regular expressions, how would you make the preceding regular expression match only the first instance of a pattern it finds?

8. Using PCREs, what backslash character will match white space?

9. What PCRE function could you use to match every instance of a pattern in a string?

10. Which modifier would you use in a PCRE function to match a pattern independently of case?

Quiz Answers

1. The `ereg()` function can be used to find a pattern in a string.

2. You can use braces containing the minimum and maximum instances (the bounds) of a character to match:

   `b{1,6}`

3. You can specify a character range using square brackets:

   `[d-f]`

4. You can negate a character range with the caret symbol:

   `[^d-f]`

5. You can match alternative branches with the pipe (|) character:

   `[0-9]|tree`

6. The `ereg_replace()` function can be used to replace a matched pattern with a given alternative.

7. By adding a question mark to a quantifier, you can force the match to be non-greedy when using PCREs:

   `/.*?bc/`

8. `\s` will match white space in a PCRE.

9. The `preg_match_all()` function will match every instance of a pattern in a string.

10. The `/i` modifier will make a PCRE function match independently of case.

Activity

1. Use regular expressions to extract email addresses from a file. Add them to an array and output the result to the browser. Refine your regular expression across a number of files.

18

Hour 19

Saving State with Cookies and Query Strings

HTTP is a stateless protocol. This means that every page a user downloads from your server represents a separate connection. On the other hand, Web sites are perceived by users and publishers alike as environments, as spaces within which a single page is part of a wider whole. It's not surprising, therefore, that strategies to pass information from page to page are as old as the Web itself.

In this hour, we will examine two methods of storing information on one page that can then be accessed on subsequent pages. In this hour, you will learn:

- What cookies are and how they work
- How to read a cookie
- How to set a cookie

- How to use cookies to store site usage information in a database
- About query strings
- How to build a function to turn an associative array into a query string

Cookies

Netscape originated the "magic cookie" back in the days of Netscape 1. The origin of the name is the subject of some debate, though it seems reasonable to assume that the fortune cookie may have played a role in the thinking behind it. Since then, the standard has been embraced by other browser producers.

NEW TERM   A *cookie* is a small amount of data stored by the user's browser in compliance with a request from a server or script. A host can request that up to 20 cookies be stored by a user's browser. Each cookie consists of a name, value, and expiry date, as well as host and path information. An individual cookie is limited to 4KB.

After a cookie is set, only the originating host can read the data, ensuring that the user's privacy is respected. Furthermore, the user can configure his browser to notify him of all cookies set, or even to refuse all cookie requests. For this reason, cookies should be used in moderation and should not be relied on as an essential element of an environment design without first warning the user.

Having said that, cookies can be an excellent way of saving small amounts of information about a user from page to page or even from visit to visit.

The Anatomy of a Cookie

Cookies are usually set in an HTTP header (although JavaScript can also set a cookie directly on a browser). A PHP script that sets a cookie might send headers that look something like this:

```
HTTP/1.1 200 OK
Date: Tue, 02 Oct 2001 13:39:58 GMT
Server: Apache/1.3.12 Cobalt (Unix) PHP/4.0.6 mod_perl/1.24
X-Powered-By: PHP/4.0.6
Set-Cookie: vegetable=artichoke; expires=Tue,
[ic:ccc]02-Oct-01 14:39:58 GMT; path=/; domain=corrosive.co.uk
Connection: close
Content-Type: text/html
```

As you can see, the Set-Cookie header contains a name value pair, a GMT date, a path, and a domain. The name and value will be URL encoded. The expires field is an instruction to the browser to "forget" the cookie after the given time and date. The path field defines the position on a Web site below which the cookie should be sent back to the server. The domain field determines the Internet domains to which the cookie should be sent. The domain cannot be different from the domain from which the cookie was sent, but it can nonetheless specify a degree of flexibility. In the preceding example, the browser will send the cookie to the server corrosive.co.uk and the server www.corrosive.co.uk. You can read more about HTTP headers in Hour 13, "Beyond the Box."

If the browser is configured to store cookies, it will then keep this information until the expiry date. If the user points the browser at any page that matches the path and domain of the cookie, it will resend the cookie to the server. The browser's headers might look something like this:

```
GET / HTTP/1.0
Connection: Keep-Alive
User-Agent: Mozilla/4.73 (Macintosh; U; PPC)
Host: www.corrosive.co.uk
Accept: image/gif, image/x-xbitmap, image/jpeg, image/pjpeg, image/png, */*
Accept-Encoding: gzip
Accept-Language: en,pdf
Accept-Charset: iso-8859-1,*,utf-8
Cookie: vegetable=artichoke
```

A PHP script will then have access to the cookie in the environmental variable HTTP-COOKIE (which holds all cookie names and values), in the global variable $vegetable, or in the global array variable HTTP_COOKIE_VARS["vegetable"]:

```
print "$HTTP_COOKIE<BR>";                    // prints "vegetable=artichoke"
print getenv("HTTP_COOKIE")."<BR>";          // prints "vegetable=artichoke"
print "$vegetable<BR>";                      // prints "artichoke"
print $HTTP_COOKIE_VARS['vegetable']."<BR>"; // prints "artichoke"
```

Setting a Cookie with PHP

You can set a cookie in a PHP script in two ways. You can use the header() function to set the Set-Cookie header. You encountered the header() function in Hour 9, "Working with Forms." header() requires a string that will then be included in the header section of the server response. Because headers are sent automatically for you, header() must be called before any output at all is sent to the browser.

```
header ("Set-Cookie: vegetable=artichoke; expires=Tue,
[ic:ccc]02-Oct-01 14:39:58 GMT; path=/; domain=corrosive.co.uk ");
```

Although not difficult, this method of setting a cookie would require you to build a function to construct the header string. Formatting the date as in this example and URL encoding the name/value pair would not be a particularly arduous task. It would, however, be an exercise in wheel reinvention because PHP provides a function that does just that.

setcookie() does what the name suggests—it outputs a Set-Cookie header. For this reason, it should be called before any other content is sent to the browser. The function accepts the cookie name, cookie value, expiry date in Unix epoch format, path, domain, and integer that should be set to 1 if the cookie is only to be sent over a secure connection. All arguments to this function are optional apart from the first (cookie name) parameter.

Listing 19.1 uses setcookie() to set a cookie.

LISTING 19.1   Setting and Printing a Cookie Value

```
 1: <?php
 2: setcookie( "vegetable", "artichoke", time()+3600, "/",
 3:             "corrosive.co.uk", 0 );
 4: ?>
 5: <html>
 6: <head>
 7: <title>Listing 19.1 Setting and printing a cookie value</title>
 8: </head>
 9: <body>
10: <?php
11: if ( isset( $vegetable ) )
12:     print "<p>Hello again, your chosen vegetable is $vegetable</p>";
13: else
14:     print "<p>Hello you. This may be your first visit</p>";
15: ?>
16: </body>
17: </html>
```

Even though we set the cookie (line 2) when the script is run for the first time, the $vegetable variable will not be created at this point. A cookie is only read when the browser sends it to the server. This will not happen until the user revisits a page in your domain. We set the cookie name to "vegetable" on line 2 and the cookie value to "artichoke". We use the time() function to get the current time stamp and add 3600 to it (there are 3600 seconds in an hour). This total represents our expiry date. We define a path of "/", which means that a cookie should be sent for any page within our server environment. We set the domain argument to "corrosive.co.uk", which means that a cookie will be sent to any server in that group (www.corrosive.co.uk as well as dev. corrosive.co.uk, for example). If you want the cookie returned only to the server hosting your script you can use the $SERVER_NAME environmental variable instead of hard coding the server name. The added advantage of this is that your code will work as expected even if you move it to a new server. Finally, we pass 0 to setcookie() signaling that cookies can be sent in an insecure environment.

Although you can omit all but the first argument, it is a good idea to include all the arguments with the exception of the domain and secure. This is because the path argument is required by some browsers for cookies to be used as they should be. Also without the path argument, the cookie will only be sent to documents in the current directory or its subdirectories.

Passing setcookie() an empty string ("") for string arguments or 0 for integer fields will cause these arguments to be skipped.

Deleting a Cookie

Officially, to delete a cookie you should call setcookie() with the name argument only:

```
setcookie( "vegetable" );
```

This does not always work well, however, and should not be relied on. It is safest to set the cookie with a date that has already expired:

```
setcookie( "vegetable", "", time()-60, "/", "corrosive.co.uk", 0);
```

You should also ensure that you pass setcookie() the same path, domain, and secure parameters as you did when originally setting the cookie.

Creating Session Cookies

To create a cookie that only lasts as long as the user is running his or her browser, pass setcookie() an expiry argument of 0. While the user's browser continues to run, cookies will be returned to the server. The browser will not remember the cookie, however, after it has been quit and restarted.

This can be useful for scripts that validate a user with a cookie, allowing continued access to personal information on multiple pages after a password has been submitted. You will not want the browser to have continued access to these pages after it has been restarted because you can't be sure that it has not been booted by a new user.

```
setcookie( "session_id", "55435", 0 );
```

An Example—Tracking Site Usage

Imagine that we have been given a brief by a site publisher to use cookies and MySQL to gather statistics about visitors to the site. The client wants to get figures for the number of individual visitors to the site, average number of hits per visit for each visitor, and average time spent on the site for each user.

19

Our first duty will be to explain the limitations of cookies to the client. First, not all users will have cookies enabled on their browsers. If not passed a cookie by a browser, a cookie script is likely to assume that this is the user's first visit. The figures are therefore likely to be skewed by browsers that won't or can't support cookies. Furthermore, you cannot be sure that the same user will use the same browser all the time, or that a single browser won't be shared by multiple users.

Having done this, we can move on to fulfilling the brief. In fact, we can produce a working example in fewer than 90 lines of code!

We need to create a database table with the fields listed in Table 19.1.

TABLE 19.1 Database Fields

Name	Type	Description
id	integer	An autoincremented field that produces and stores a unique ID for each visitor
first_visit	integer	A time stamp representing the moment of the first page request made by a visitor
last_visit	integer	A time stamp representing the moment of the most recent page request made by a visitor
num_visits	integer	The number of distinct sessions attributed to the visitor
total_duration	integer	The estimated total time spent on the site (in seconds)
total_clicks	integer	The total number of requests made by the visitor

To create the MySQL table called track_visit, we need to use a CREATE statement:

```
create table track_visit (
            id INT NOT NULL AUTO_INCREMENT,
            PRIMARY KEY( id ),
            first_visit INT,
            last_visit INT,
            num_visits INT,
            total_duration INT,
            total_clicks INT
            );
```

Now that we have a table to work with, we need to write the code that will open a database connection and check for the existence of a cookie. If the cookie does not exist, we need to create a new row in our table, setting up the initial values for the fields we will maintain. We create this code in Listing 19.2.

LISTING 19.2 A Script to Add New User Information to a MySQL Database

```php
 1: <?php
 2: $link = connect( "localhost", "", "", "test" );
 3:
 4: if ( ! isset( $visit_id ) ) {
 5:     newuser( );
 6:     print "Welcome, first time user!";
 7: } else {
 8:     print "Welcome back $visit_id<P>";
 9: }
10:
11: function newuser( ) {
12:     $visit_data = array (
13:                     'first_visit' => time(),
14:                     'last_visit' => time(),
15:                     'num_visits' => 1,
16:                     'total_duration' => 0,
17:                     'total_clicks' -> 1
18:                     );
19:
20:     insert_visit( $visit_data );
21:     setcookie( "visit_id", $visit_data['id'],
22:                 time()+(60*60*24*365*10), "/" );
23:     return $visit_data;
24: }
25:
26: function connect( $host, $user, $pass, $db ) {
27:     $link = mysql_connect( $host, $user, $pass ) or
28:         die("Connection error");
29:     mysql_select_db( $db, $link ) or die ( mysql_error() );
30:     return $link;
31: }
32:
33: function insert_visit( &$visit_data ) {
34:     global $link;
35:     $query  = "INSERT INTO track_visit ( ";
36:     $query .= implode( ", ", array_keys( $visit_data ) );
37:     $query .= " ) VALUES( ";
38:     $query .= implode(", ", array_values( $visit_data ) );
39:     $query .= " );";
40:     $result = mysql_query( $query, $link );
41:     $visit_data['id'] = mysql_insert_id();
42: }
43: ?>
```

19

We connect to the MySQL server via a convenience function called connect(), declared on line 26. This connects to the server on line 27 and selects the database that contains our table on line 29 (you can read more about working with MySQL in Hour 12,

"Database Integration—MySQL"). connect() returns a MySQL resource value which is stored in a global variable called $link. This will be accessed by all functions that work with the database. On line 4 we test for the presence of the variable $visit_id, which is the name of the cookie that identifies an individual user. If this variable does not exist, then we assume that we are dealing with a new user, calling a function that we have called newuser().

newuser() is declared on line 11. It requires no arguments and will return an array of the values that we will add to our table. Within the function, we create an array called $visit_data on line 12. We set the first_visit and last_visit elements to the current time in seconds. Because this is the first visit, we set the num_visits and total_clicks elements to 1. No time has elapsed in this visit, so we set total_duration to 0.

On line 20 we call a function called insert_visit() (declared on line 33) that accepts the $visit_data array and uses its elements to create a new row in our table, setting each field to the value of the element of the same name. Notice that we use the built-in implode() function on line 36 to construct our SQL statement. Because the id field autoincrements, this does not need to be inserted. We can subsequently access the value set for id using the mysql_insert_id() function on line 41. Now that we have an ID for our new visitor, we add this to our $visit_data array, which then accurately reflects the visitor's row in the MySQL table. The $visit_data array was passed to insert_visit() by reference, so the array we manipulate here is also referenced from the variable of the same name in the calling newuser() function.

Finally in the newuser() function, we use setcookie() on line 21 to set a visit_id cookie and return the $visit_data array to the calling code on line 23.

The next time our visitor hits this script, the $visit_id variable will have been populated with the value of the visit_id cookie. Because this variable is set, the user will be welcomed and no action will be taken.

In fact, we will need to update information in the track_visit table if we detect the return of a known visitor. We will need to test whether the current request is part of an ongoing visit or represents the beginning of a new visit. We will do this with a global variable that will define a time in seconds. If the time of the last request added to this interval is greater than the current time, then we will assume that the current request is part of a session in progress. Otherwise, we are welcoming back an old friend.

Listing 19.3 adds new functions to the code created in Listing 19.2.

LISTING 19.3 A Script to Track Users Using Cookies and a MySQL Database

```php
 1: <?php
 2: $slength = 300;
 3: $link = connect( "localhost", "", "", "test" );
 4: $user_stats;
 5: if ( ! isset( $visit_id ) ) {
 6:     $user_stats = newuser( );
 7:     print "Welcome, first time user!";
 8: } else {
 9:     print "Welcome back $visit_id<P>";
10:     $user_stats = olduser( $visit_id );
11: }
12:
13: function newuser( ) {
14:     $visit_data = array (
15:                 'first_visit' => time(),
16:                 'last_visit' => time(),
17:                 'num_visits' => 1,
18:                 'total_duration' => 0,
19:                 'total_clicks' => 1
20:                 );
21:
22:     insert_visit( $visit_data );
23:     setcookie( "visit_id", $visit_data['id'],
24:             time()+(60*60*24*365*10), "/" );
25:     return $visit_data;
26: }
27:
28: function olduser( $visit_id ) {
29:     global $slength;
30:     $now = time();
31:     $visit_data = get_visit( $visit_id );
32:     if ( ! $visit_data )
33:         return newuser( );
34:     $visit_data['total_clicks']++;
35:     if ( ( $visit_data['last_visit'] + $slength ) > $now )
36:         $visit_data['total_duration'] +=
37:                     ( $now - $visit_data['last_visit'] );
38:     else
39:         $visit_data['num_visits']++;
40:
41:     $visit_data['last_visit'] = $now;
42:     update_visit( $visit_data );
43:     return $visit_data;
44: }
45:
46: function connect( $host, $user, $pass, $db ) {
47:     $link = mysql_connect( $host, $user, $pass ) or
48:         die("Connection error");
```

19

LISTING **19.3**   continued

```
49:      mysql_select_db( $db, $link ) or die ( mysql_error() );
50:      return $link;
51: }
52:
53: function get_visit( $visit_id ) {
54:      global $link;
55:      $query = "SELECT * FROM track_visit WHERE id=$visit_id";
56:      $result = mysql_query( $query, $link );
57:
58:      if ( ! mysql_num_rows( $result ) )
59:          return false;
60:      return mysql_fetch_assoc( $result, $link );
61: }
62:
63: function update_visit( &$visit_data ) {
64:      global $link;
65:      $update_pairs = array();
66:      foreach( $visit_data  as $field=>$val )
67:
68:                array_push( $update_pairs, "$field=$val" );
69:      $query  = "UPDATE track_visit SET ";
70:      $query .= implode( ", ", $update_pairs );
71:      $query .= " WHERE id=".$visit_data['id'];
72:      mysql_query( $query, $link );
73: }
74:
75: function insert_visit( &$visit_data ) {
76:      global $link;
77:      $query  = "INSERT INTO track_visit ( ";
78:      $query .= implode( ", ", array_keys( $visit_data ) );
79:      $query .= " ) VALUES( ";
80:      $query .= implode(", ", array_values( $visit_data ) );
81:      $query .= " );";
82:      $result = mysql_query( $query, $link );
83:      $visit_data['id'] = mysql_insert_id();
84: }
85:
86: ?>
```

We added a new global variable to the script called $slength on line 2. This defines the interval after which we assume that a new visit is taking place. If the $visit_id variable is found, then we know that the cookie was in place. We call the olduser() function on line 10, passing it the $visit_id variable.

Within the olduser() function, we first acquire visit data by calling the get_visit() function on line 31. get_visit() is declared on line 53. It requires the visit ID which it stores in an argument variable called $visit_id. This is used to extract the relevant row from the track_visit table using mysql_query() on line 56. Assuming that we have located the row in our table that matches the visit_id cookie, we use mysql_fetch_assoc() on line 60 to populate an array variable ($visit_data) with the row's field names and values. This is returned. The olduser() function should now have a populated $visit_data array. If not, then we give up, and call newuser() (line 33) which will add a row to the database.

On line 35 we test to see whether the value of the $visit_data['last_visit'] element added to the interval stored in $slength is greater than the current time. If so, it means that less than $slength seconds have elapsed since the last hit, and we can assume that this request is part of a current session. We therefore add the time elapsed since the last hit to the $visit_data['total_duration'] element on line 36.

If the request represents a new visit, we increment $visit_data['num_visits'] on line 39.

Finally, we pass $visit_data to update_visit() on line 42. update_visit() is declared on line 63 and it constructs an SQL UPDATE statement by looping through the altered values in the array. The statement is passed to mysql_query() on line 72 to update the user's row in the track_visit table. olduser() returns the altered $visit_data array to the calling code.

Now that we've created the code, we should create a quick function to demonstrate it in action. The outputStats() function simply calculates the current user's averages and prints the result to the browser. In reality, you would probably want to create some analysis screens for your client, which would collate overall information. Listing 19.4 creates the outputStats() function. The code from previous examples is incorporated into this script using an include() statement.

LISTING 19.4   A Script to Output Usage Statistics Gathered in Listing 19.3

```
 1: <?php
 2: include("listing19.3.php");
 3: outputStats();
 4: function outputStats() {
 5:     global $user_stats;
 6:     $clicks = sprintf( "%.2f",
 7:             ($user_stats['total_clicks']/$user_stats['num_visits']) );
 8:     $duration =  sprintf( "%.2f",
 9:             ($user_stats['total_duration']/$user_stats['num_visits']) );
10:     print "<p>Hello! Your id is ".$user_stats['id']."</p>\n\n";
11:     print "<p>You have visited
12:             ".$user_stats['num_visits']." time(s)</p>\n\n";
```

LISTING **19.4**   continued

```
13:      print "<p>Av clicks per visit: $clicks</p>\n\n";
14:      print "<p>Av duration of visit: $duration seconds</p>\n\n";
15: }
16: ?>
```

Figure 19.1 shows the output from Listing 19.4. We use an include() statement on line 2 to call the tracking code we have written. We will be including a similar line on every page of our client's site. The outputStats() function called on line 3 and declared on line 4 works with the global $user_stats array variable. This was returned by either newuser() or olduser() and contains the same information as our user's row in the track_visit table.

On line 6, to calculate the user's average number of clicks, we divide the $user_ stats ['total_clicks'] element by the number of visits we have detected. Similarly on line 8, we divide the $user_stats['total_duration'] element by the same figure. We use sprint() to round the results to two decimal places. All that remains is to write a report to the browser.

FIGURE **19.1**

Reporting usage statistics.

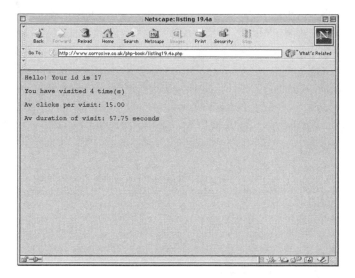

We could, of course, extend this example to track user preference on a site, as well as to log browser types and IP addresses. Imagine a site that analyzes a user's movements and emphasizes content according to the links he chooses.

Working with the Query String

The great drawback of the cookie is its dependence on the client. Not only are you at the mercy of the user, who may choose not to allow cookies, you must also rely on the browser's implementation of the standard. Some browsers have documented bugs concerning the way that they deal with cookies. If you only want to save state for a single session, you might decide to use a more traditional approach.

When you submit a form using the GET method, its fields and values are URL encoded and appended to the URL to which the form is sent. They then become available to the server and to your scripts. Assuming a form with two fields, user_id and name, the query string should end up looking something like the following:

```
http://www.corrosive.co.uk/test5.php?name=344343&user_id=matt+zandstra
```

Each name and value is separated by an equals (=) sign, and each name/value pair is separated by an ampersand (&). PHP decodes this string and makes each of the pairs available in the $HTTP_GET_VARS associative array variable. If the register_globals php.ini directive is set, PHP also creates a global variable for each name, populating it with the corresponding value. So, to access the user_id GET variable, you could use either of the following variables:

```
$HTTP_GET_VARS['user_id'];
$user_id;
```

You are not limited, however, to using forms to send query strings. You can build your own relatively easily and in so doing pass substantial amounts of information from page to page.

19

Creating a Query String

To create a query string, you need to be able to URL encode the keys and values you want to include. Assume that we want to pass a URL to another page as part of a query string. The forward slashes and the colon in a full URL would create ambiguity for a parser. We must therefore convert the URL into hexadecimal characters. We can do this using PHP's urlencode() function. urlencode() accepts a string and returns an encoded copy:

```
print urlencode("http://www.corrosive.co.uk");
// prints http%3A%2F%2Fwww.corrosive.co.uk
```

Now that you can URL encode text, you can build your own query string. The following fragment builds a query string from two variables:

```
<?php
$interest = "arts";
```

```
$homepage = "http://www.corrosive.co.uk";
$query = "homepage=".urlencode( $homepage );
$query .= "&interest=".urlencode( $interest );
?>
<A HREF="newpage.php?<?print $query ?>">Go</A>
```

The URL in the link will reach the browser including an encoded query string:

```
newpage.php?homepage=http%3A%2F%2Fwww.corrosive.co.uk&interest=arts
```

The homepage and interest parameters will become available within newpage.php as global variables.

This approach is clumsy, however. Because we have hard-coded variable names into the query string, we cannot reuse the code easily. To pass information effectively from page to page, we need to make it easy to embed names and values into a link and generate a query string automatically. This is especially important if we are to maintain the benefit of PHP that it is easy for a non-programmer to work around.

Listing 19.5 creates a function called qlink() that accepts an associative array and returns a query string.

LISTING 19.5   A Function to Build Query Strings

```
 1: <html>
 2: <head>
 3: <title>Listing 19.5 A function to build query strings</title>
 4: </head>
 5: <body>
 6: <?php
 7: function qlink( $q ) {
 8:     if ( ! $q )
 9:     return $GLOBALS['QUERY_STRING'];
10:     $ret = "";
11:     foreach( $q as $key => $val ) {
12:         if ( strlen( $ret ) ) $ret .= "&";
13:         $ret .= urlencode( $key ) . "=" . urlencode( $val );
14:     }
15:     return $ret;
16: }
17: $q = array (
18:          'name' => "Arthur Harold Smith",
19:          'interest' => "Cinema (mainly art house)",
20:          'homepage' => "http://www.corrosive.co.uk/harold/"
21:          );
22: print qlink( $q );
23: // prints name=Arthur+Harold+Smith&interest=Cinema+%28mainly+art+house
24: //        %29&homepage=http%3A%2F%2Fwww.corrosive.co.uk%2Fharold%2F
25: ?>
```

LISTING 19.5 continued

```
26: <p>
27: <a href="anotherpage.php?<? print qlink($q) ?>">Go!</a>
28: </p>
29: </body>
30: </html>
```

Defined on line 7, qlink() expects an associative array, which it stores in the parameter variable $q. If $q is not set, we simply return the current script's query string as stored for us in $QUERY_STRING on line 9. In this way, qlink() can be used simply to pass on unchanged GET request data.

Assuming that $q has been set, we initialize a variable called $ret on line 10, assigning an empty string to it. This will contain our query string.

A foreach statement is used on line 11 to iterate through the $q array, placing each key in $key and each value in $val.

Key/value pairs are separated from one another by an ampersand (&) character, so if we are not on our first journey through the loop, we print this character on line 12. We know that the length of the string in $ret will be 0 for the first iteration, so we can use this fact to avoid prepending & to the string.

On line 13 we use urlencode() to encode both the $key and $val variables and append them, separated by an equals (=) character to our $ret variable.

Finally, we return the encoded $query string.

Using this function, we can pass information between pages with the minimum of PHP code within HTML elements.

Summary

In this hour, we have looked at the two ways of passing information between requests. You can use these to create multiscreen applications and sophisticated environments that respond to user preferences.

You learned how to use the setcookie() function to set cookies on the user's browser. Developing this, you saw how a database could be used in conjunction with cookies to store information about a user between sessions. You learned about query strings and how to encode them, and developed a function to automate their creation.

PHP 4 is nothing if not versatile, and in the next hour we will be looking at some built-in functions for automating many of the tasks that we have examined in this chapter.

19

Q&A

Q **Are there any serious security or privacy issues raised by cookies?**

A A server can only access a cookie set from its own domain. Although a cookie can be stored on the user's hard drive, there is no other access to the user's file system. It is possible, however, to set a cookie in response to a request for an image. So if many sites include images served from a third-party ad server or counter script, the third party may be able to track a user across multiple domains.

Q **The query string looks ugly in the browser window. Would it be true to say that cookies are the neatest way of saving state?**

A Unfortunately, it isn't that simple. At best, cookies are a transparent way of saving state. Some users, however, set their browsers to warn them every time a cookie is set. These users are likely to find a site that saves state information frequently somewhat frustrating.

Workshop

Quiz

1. What function is designed to allow you to set a cookie on a visitor's browser?
2. How would you delete a cookie?
3. What function could you use to escape a string for inclusion in a query string?
4. Which built-in variable contains the raw query string?
5. The name/value pairs submitted as part of a query string will become available as global variables. They will also be included in a built-in associative array. What is its name?

Quiz Answers

1. The `setcookie()` function allows you to set a cookie (although you could also output a `Set-Cookie` header using the `header()` function).
2. You can delete a cookie by calling `setcookie()` with a date that has already passed.
3. The `urlencode()` function translates a string so that it can be included in a query string.
4. The entire query string is made available to you in the `$QUERY_STRING` variable.
5. The `$HTTP_GET_VARS` variable will contain the name/value pairs submitted as part of a query string.

Activities

1. Create a user preference form in which a user can choose a page color and enter a name. Use a cookie to ensure that the user is greeted by name on subsequent pages and that the page is set to the color of her choice.

2. Amend the scripts you created in Activity 1 so that the information is stored in a query string rather than a cookie.

19

Hour **20**

Saving State with Session Functions

In the previous hour, we looked at saving state from page to page, using a cookie or a query string. Once again, PHP 4 is one step ahead of us. With the release of PHP 4, functions for managing user sessions were built into the language. These use techniques similar to those explored in the previous hour, but build them into the language, making saving state as easy as calling a function.

In this hour, you will learn:

- What session variables are and how they work
- How to start or resume a session
- How to register variables with a session
- How to destroy a session
- How to unset session variables

What Are Session Functions?

Session functions implement a concept that you have already seen. That is the provision to users of a unique identifier, which can then be used from access to access to acquire information linked to that ID. The difference is that most of the work is already done for you. When a user accesses a session-enabled page, she will either be allocated a new identifier or reassociated with one that has already been established for her in a previous access. Any variables that have been associated with the session will become available to your code. If the php.ini `register_globals` directive is set, session data will become available in global namespace. Otherwise, you will be able to access them through the built-in `$HTTP_SESSION_VARS` associative array.

Both the techniques for transmitting information from access to access that you looked at in the previous hour are automatically supported by PHP 4's session functions. Cookies are used by default, but you can ensure success for all clients by encoding the session ID into all links in your session-enabled pages.

Session state is usually stored in a temporary file, though you can implement database storage using a function called `session_set_save_handler()`. `session_set_save_handler()` is beyond the scope of this book but you can get more information at `http://www.php.net/manual/en/function.session-set-save-handler.php`.

Starting a Session with `session_start()`

You need to explicitly start or resume a session unless you have changed your `php.ini` configuration file. By default, sessions do not start automatically. In `php.ini`, you will find a line containing the following:

```
session.auto_start = 0
```

By changing the value of `session.auto_start` to 1, you ensure that a session is initiated for every PHP document. If you don't change this setting, you need to call the `session_start()` function.

After a session has been started, you instantly have access to the user's session ID via the `session_id()` function. `session_id()` allows you to either set or get a session ID. Listing 20.1 starts a session and prints the session ID to the browser.

LISTING 20.1 Starting or Resuming a Session

```
1: <?php
2: session_start();
3: ?>
```

LISTING 20.1 continued

```
 4: <html>
 5: <head>
 6: <title>Listing 20.1 Starting or resuming a session</title>
 7: </head>
 8: <body>
 9: <?php
10: print "<p>Welcome, your session ID is ".session_id()."</p>\n\n";
11: ?>
12: </body>
13: </html>
```

When this script is run for the first time from a browser, a session ID is generated by the session_start() function call on line 2. If the page is later reloaded or revisited, then the same session ID is allocated to the user. This presupposes, of course, that the user has cookies enabled on his or her browser. If you examine headers output by the script in Listing 20.1, you can see the cookie being set:

```
HTTP/1.1 200 OK
Date: Mon, 01 Oct 2001 14:10:40 GMT
Server: Apache/1.3.12 Cobalt (Unix) PHP/4.0.6 mod_perl/1.24
X-Powered-By: PHP/4.0.6
Set-Cookie: PHPSESSID=98aac0bafaa7915f3cbcfe691aca65dc; path=/
Expires: Thu, 19 Nov 1981 08:52:00 GMT
Cache-Control: no-store, no-cache, must-revalidate, post-check=0, pre-check=0
Pragma: no-cache
Connection: close
Content-Type: text/html
```

Because start_session() attempts to set a cookie when initiating a session for the first time, it is important to call it before you output anything else at all to the browser. Notice that no expiry date is set in the cookie that PHP sets for the session. This means that the session only remains current as long as the browser is active. When the user reboots his or her browser, the cookie will not be stored. You can change this behavior by altering the session.cookie_lifetime setting in your php.ini file. This defaults to 0, but you can set an expiry period in seconds. This causes an expiry date to be set for any session cookies sent to the browser.

20

Working with Session Variables

Accessing a unique identifier on each of your PHP documents is only the start of PHP's session functionality. You can register any number of global variables with the session and then access them on any session-enabled page.

To register a variable with a current session, you must use the session_register() function. session_register() requires a string representing one or more variable names and returns true if the registration is successful. The syntax of the argument you must pass to this function is unusual in that you must pass only the name of the variable and not the variable itself.

Listing 20.2 registers two variables with a session (lines 10 and 11).

LISTING 20.2   Registering Variables with a Session

```
 1: <?php
 2: session_start();
 3: ?>
 4: <html>
 5: <head>
 6: <title>Listing 20.2 Registering variables with a session</title>
 7: </head>
 8: <body>
 9: <?php
10: session_register( "product1" );
11: session_register( "product2" );
12: $product1 = "Sonic Screwdriver";
13: $product2 = "HAL 2000";
14: print "The products have been registered";
15: ?>
16: </body>
17: </html>
```

The magic in Listing 20.2 will not become apparent until the user moves to a new page. Listing 20.3 creates a separate PHP script that accesses the variables registered in Listing 20.2 (line 11).

LISTING 20.3   Accessing Registered Variables

```
 1: <?php
 2: session_start();
 3: ?>
 4: <html>
 5: <head>
 6: <title>Listing 20.3 Accessing registered variables</title>
 7: </head>
 8: <body>
 9: <?php
10: print "Your chosen products are:\n\n";
```

LISTING 20.3   continued

```
11: print "<ul><li>$product1\n<li>$product2\n</ul>\n";
12: ?>
13: </body>
14: </html>
```

Figure 20.1 shows the output from Listing 20.3. As you can see, we have access to the $product1 and $product2 variables in an entirely new page.

FIGURE 20.1

Accessing registered variables.

So how does the magic work? Behind the scenes, PHP 4 is writing to a temporary file. You can find out where this is being written on your system with the session_save_path() function. session_save_path() optionally accepts a path to a directory and then writes all session files to this. If you pass it no arguments, it returns a string representing the current directory to which session files are saved. On my system,

```
print session_save_path();
```

prints /tmp. A glance at my /tmp directory reveals a number of files with names like the following:

```
sess_2638864e9216fee10fcb8a61db382909
sess_76cae8ac1231b11afa2c69935c11dd95
sess_bb50771a769c605ab77424d59c784ea0
```

20

Opening the file that matches the session ID I was allocated when I first ran Listing 20.1,
I can see how the registered variables have been stored:

```
product1|s:17:"Sonic Screwdriver";product2|s:8:"HAL 2000";
```

When `session_register()` is called, PHP writes the variable name and value to a file.
This can be read, and the variables resurrected, later.

When you register a variable using `session_register()`, you can still change its value
at any time during the execution of your script, and the altered value will be reflected in
the session file.

The example in Listing 20.2 demonstrates the process of registering variables with a session. It is not very flexible, however. Ideally, you should be able to register a varying
number of values. You might want to let users pick products from a list, for example.
Luckily, you can pass the name of an array variable to `session_register()`, and it will
store and encode this data for you.

Listing 20.4 creates a form that allows a user to choose multiple products. You should
then be able to use session variables to create a rudimentary shopping cart.

LISTING 20.4   Registering an Array Variable with a Session

```php
 1: <?php
 2: session_start();
 3: ?>
 4: <html>
 5: <head>
 6: <title>Listing 20.4 Registering an array variable with a session</title>
 7: </head>
 8: <body>
 9: <h1>Product Choice Page</h1>
10: <?php
11: if ( isset( $form_products ) ) {
12:     if ( empty( $products ) )
13:         $products=$form_products;
14:     else
15:     $products = array_unique(
16:                     array_merge( $products, $form_products ) );
17:     session_register( "products" );
18:     print "<p>Your products have been registered!</p>";
19: }
20: ?><p>
21: <form method="POST">
22: <select name="form_products[]" multiple size=3>
23: <option> Sonic Screwdriver
24: <option> Hal 2000
25: <option> Tardis
```

LISTING 20.4 continued

```
26: <option> ORAC
27: <option> Transporter bracelet
28: </select>
29: </p><p>
30: <input type="submit" value="choose">
31: </form>
32: </p>
33: <a href="listing20.5.php">A content page</a>
34: </body>
35: </html>
```

We start or resume a session with session_start() on line 2. This should give us access to any previously set session variables. We begin an HTML form on line 21 and, on line 22, create a SELECT element named form_products[], which contains OPTION elements for a number of products. Remember that HTML form elements that allow multiple selections should have square brackets appended to the value of their NAME arguments. This makes the user's choices available in an array.

Within the block of PHP code beginning on line 10, we test for the presence of the $form_products array (line 11). If the variable is present, we can assume that the form has been submitted. We test for an array called $products on line 12. If it is non-existent or empty, then we declare it on line 13 and assign the $form_products array to it. If the array exists, it will have been populated on a previous visit to this script. We merge it with the $form_products array, extract the unique elements and assign the result back to the $products variable (lines 15 and 16). We then register $products using session_register() on line 17. We do not directly register $form_products because this will then conflict with the POST variable of the same name if the form is resubmitted. At the bottom of this page (line 33), there is a link to another, which we will use to demonstrate our access to the products the user has chosen. We create this new script in Listing 20.5.

LISTING 20.5 Accessing Session Variables

20

```
 1: <?php
 2: session_start();
 3: ?>
 4: <html>
 5: <head>
 6: <title>Listing 20.5 Accessing session variables</title>
 7: </head>
 8: <body>
 9: <h1>A Content Page</h1>
10: <?php
```

LISTING 20.5   continued

```
11: if ( isset( $products ) ) {
12:     print "<b>Your cart:</b><ol>\n";
13:     foreach ( $products as $p )
14:         print "<li>$p";
15:     print "</ol>";
16: }
17: ?>
18: <a href="listing20.4.php">Back to product choice page</a>
19: </body>
20: </html>
```

Once again, we use session_start() to resume the session (line 2). We test for the presence of the $products variable on line 11. If it exists, we loop through it on line 13, printing each of the user's chosen items to the browser.

For a real shopping cart program, of course, you would keep product details in a database and test user input, rather than blindly storing and presenting it, but Listings 20.4 and 20.5 demonstrate the ease with which you can use session functions to access array variables set in other pages.

Destroying Sessions and Unsetting Variables

You can use session_destroy() to end a session, erasing all session variables. session_destroy() requires no arguments. You should have an established session for this function to work as expected. The following code fragment resumes a session and abruptly destroys it:

```
session_start();
session_destroy();
```

When you move on to other pages that work with a session, the session you have destroyed will not be available to them, forcing them to initiate new sessions of their own. Any variables that have been registered will have been lost.

However, session_destroy() does not instantly destroy registered variables. These will remain accessible to the script in which session_destroy() is called (until it is reloaded). The following code fragment resumes or initiates a session and registers a variable called $test, which we set to 5. Destroying the session does not destroy the registered variable.

```
session_start();
session_register( "test" );
$test = 5;
```

```
session_destroy();
print $test; // prints 5
```

To remove all registered variables from a session, you need to use the session_unset() function. This destroys all variables associated with a session, both in the session file and within your script. session_unset() is a blunt instrument; use it carefully.

```
session_start();
session_register( "test" );
$test = 5;
session_unset();
session_destroy();
print $test; // prints nothing. The $test variable is no more
```

Before destroying the session, we call session_unset(), which entirely removes the $test variable from memory and wipes any other registered session variables.

Passing Session IDs in the Query String

So far you have relied on a cookie to save the session ID between script requests. On its own, this is not the most reliable way of saving state because you cannot be sure that the browser will accept cookies. You can build in a failsafe, however, by passing the session ID from script to script embedded in a query string. PHP makes a name/value pair available in a constant called SID if a cookie value for a session ID cannot be found. You can add this string to any HTML links in session-enabled pages:

```
<a href="anotherpage.html?<?php print SID; ?>">Another page</a>
```

will reach the browser as

```
<a href="anotherpage.html?PHPSESSID=08ecedf79fe34561fa82591401a01da1">Another
page</a>
```

The session ID passed in this way will automatically be recognized in the target page when session_start() is called, and you will have access to session variables in the usual way.

If PHP 4 was compiled with the --enable-trans-sid option set, you will find that this query string is automatically added to every link in your pages. This option is disabled by default, however, so explicitly adding the SID constant to links will make your scripts more portable.

20

Encoding and Decoding Session Variables

You have already seen the way in which PHP encodes and saves (serializes) session variables when you peeked into a session file. You can in fact gain access to the encoded string at any time with `session_encode()`. This can be useful in debugging your session-enabled environments. You can use `session_encode()` to reveal the state of all session variables:

```
session_start();
print session_encode()."<br>";
// sample output: products|a:2:{i:0;s:8:"Hal 2000";i:1;s:6:"Tardis";}
```

From the sample output in the previous fragment, you can see the session variables that are stored. You can use this information to check that variables are being registered and updated as you expect. `session_encode()` is also useful if you need to freeze-dry session variables for storage in a database or file.

After having extracted an encoded string, you can decode it and resurrect its values using `session_decode()`. The following code fragment demonstrates this process:

```
session_start();
session_unset(); // there should now be no session variables
session_decode( "products|a:2:{i:0;s:8:\"Hal 2000\";i:1;s:6:\"Tardis\";}" );
foreach ( $products as $p ) {
    print "$p<br>\n";
}
// Output:
// Hal 2000
// Tardis
```

We start a session as usual. To ensure that we are working with a blank canvas, we use `session_unset()` to clear all session variables. We then pass an encoded string to `session_decode()`. Rather than returning values, `session_decode()` populates our name space with the unserialized variables. We confirm this by looping through the newly resurrected `$products` array.

Checking That a Session Variable Is Registered

As you have seen, you can test for the presence of a registered variable in a session-enabled script using `isset()`. You can, however, explicitly test that a variable has been registered with a session using the `session_is_registered()` function. This accepts a string representing a variable name and returns `true` if the variable has been registered.

```
if ( session_is_registered ( "products" ) )
    print "'products' is registered!";
```

This would be useful if you need to be sure of the source of a variable. You might want to make sure that the variable you are testing is available to you as a session variable as opposed to data passed to you as part of a GET request.

Working with the $HTTP_SESSION_VARS Array

If your register_globals php.ini directive is set to off or 0 you will not be able to work directly with session variables. Instead, you will have to set and access session variables via the $HTTP_SESSION_VARS array. For larger projects, this can be advisable because it removes the danger of a session variable clashing with a global variable set within the script. So, to set a session variable called test to 5 you should call session_register() as normal, but you should assign via $HTTP_SESSION_VARS.

```
session_start();
session_register( "test" );
$HTTP_SESSION_VARS['test'] = 5;
```

To access the session variable in a subsequent script, you should also use the $HTTP_SESSION_VARS array.

```
session_start();
print "test is.. ";
print $HTTP_SESSION_VARS['test'];
```

Summary

In this hour and the previous hour, you looked at different ways of saving state in a stateless protocol. All methods use some combination of cookies and query strings, sometimes combined with the use of files or databases. These approaches all have their benefits and problems.

A cookie is not intrinsically reliable and cannot store much information. On the other hand, it can persist over a long period of time.

Approaches that write information to a file or database involve some cost to speed that might become a problem on a popular site. Nonetheless, a simple ID can unlock large amounts of data stored on disk.

A query string is unlikely to persist as a cookie will. It looks ugly in the location window. Even so, it can pass relatively large amounts of information from request to request. The choice you make depends on the circumstances of your project.

In this hour, you learned how to initiate or resume a session with session_start(). Once in a session, you can register variables with it using session_register(), check

20

that a variable is registered with `session_is_registered()`, and unset all registered variables with `session_unset()`. You should be able to destroy a session with `session_destroy()`.

To ensure that as many users as possible get the benefit of your session-enabled environment, you can now use the `SID` constant to pass a session ID to the server as part of a query string.

In the next hour we will look at ways that you can use PHP to access other tools on your server.

Q&A

Q Are there any pitfalls with session functions I should be aware of?

A The session functions are generally reliable. However, remember that cookies cannot be read across multiple domains, so if your project uses more than one domain name on the same server (perhaps as part of an e-commerce environment), you might need to consider disabling cookies for sessions by setting the

`session.use_cookies`

directive to `0` in the `php.ini` file.

Workshop

Quiz

1. Which function would you use to start or resume a session?
2. Which function contains the current session's ID?
3. How can you associate a variable with a session?
4. How would you end a session and erase all traces of it for future visits?
5. How would you destroy session variables both within the current script and the session?
6. What does the `SID` constant return?
7. How would you test whether a variable called `$test` is registered with a session?

Quiz Answers

1. You can start a session with the `session_start()` function.
2. You can access the session's ID with the `session_id()` function.

3. The `session_register()` function associates the given variable with the current session.

4. The `session_destroy()` function removes all traces of a session for future requests.

5. The `session_unset()` function removes session variables from the current script as well as the session.

6. If cookies are not available, the `SID` constant contains a name/value pair that can be incorporated in a query string. This will pass the session ID from script request to script request.

7. You can use the `session_is_registered()` function to check that a variable is associated with the current session.

```
is_registered("test")
```

Activities

1. In the previous hour's "Activities" section, you created a script that uses a cookie or query string to save user preferences from page to page. Each page in the environment should display a user-defined background color and greet the user by name. Recreate this using PHP 4's session functions.

2. Create a script that uses session functions to remember which pages in your environment the user has visited. Provide the user with a list of links on each page to make it easy for her to retrace her steps.

20

Hour **21**

Working with the Server Environment

In previous hours, we have looked at techniques for communicating with remote machines and for gaining input from the user. In this hour, we look outward again, this time at some techniques for running external programs on our own machine. The examples in this hour are designed for the Linux operating system, but most of the principles hold true for Windows.

In this hour, you will learn:

- How to pipe data to and from external applications
- Other ways of sending shell commands and displaying the results on the browser
- The security implications of interprocess communication from a PHP script

Opening Pipes to and from Processes with popen()

Just as you open a file for writing or reading with fopen(), you can open a pipe to a process with popen(). popen() requires the path to a command and a string representing a mode (read or write). It returns a file pointer that can be used similarly to the file pointer returned by fopen(). You can pass popen() one of two mode flags: "w" to write to the process and "r" to read from it. You cannot both read and write to a process in the same connection.

When you have finished working with the file handle returned by popen(), you must close the connection by calling pclose(), which requires a valid file handler.

Reading from popen() is useful when you want to parse the output from a process on a line-by-line basis. Listing 21.1 opens a connection to the GNU version of the who command and parses its output, adding a mailto link to each username.

LISTING 21.1   Using popen() to Read the Output of the UNIX who Command

```
 1: <html>
 2: <head>
 3: <title>Listing 21.1 Using popen() to read the
 4:        output of the Unix who command</title>
 5: </head>
 6: <body>
 7: <h2>Administrators currently logged on to the server</h1>
 8: <?php
 9: $ph = popen( "who", "r" )
10:        or die( "Couldn't open connection to 'who' command" );
11: $host="corrosive.co.uk";
12: while ( ! feof( $ph ) ) {
13:     $line = fgets( $ph, 1024 );
14:     if ( strlen( $line ) <= 1 )
15:        continue;
16:     $line = ereg_replace(    "^([a-zA-Z0-9_\-]+).*",
17:               "<a href=\"mailto:\\1@$host\">\\1</a><BR>\n",
18:               $line );
19:     print "$line";
20: }
21: pclose( $ph );
22: ?>
23: </table>
24: </body>
25: </html>
```

We acquire a file pointer from popen() on line 9 and then use a while statement on line 12 to read each line of output from the process. If the output is a single character, we skip the rest of the current iteration (lines 14 and 15). Otherwise, we use ereg_replace() on line 16 to add an HTML link to the string before printing the line on line 19. Finally, we close the connection with pclose() on line 21. Figure 21.1 shows sample output from Listing 21.1.

FIGURE 21.1

Reading the output of the UNIX who *command.*

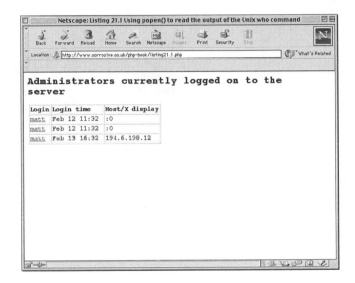

You can also use a connection established with popen() to write to a process. This is useful for commands that accept data from standard input in addition to command-line arguments. Listing 21.2 opens a connection to the column application using popen().

LISTING 21.2   Using popen() to Pass Data to the column Application

```
1: <html>
2: <head>
3: <title>Listing 21.2 Using popen() to pass
4:        data to the column command</title>
5: </head>
6: <body>
7: <?php
8: $products = array(
9:         array( "HAL 2000", 2, "red" ),
10:         array( "Tricorder",  3, "blue" ),
11:         array( "ORAC AI", 1, "pink"  ),
12:         array( "Sonic Screwdriver", 1, "orange"   )
13:         );
```

21

LISTING 21.2   continued

```
14: $ph = popen( "column -tc 3 -s / > purchases/user3.txt", "w" )
15:     or die( "Couldn't open connection to 'column' command" );
16: foreach ( $products as $prod )
17:     fputs( $ph, join('/', $prod)."\n");
18: pclose( $ph );
19: ?>
20: </table>
21: </body>
22: </html>
```

The purpose of the script in Listing 21.2 is to take the elements of a multidimensional array (defined on line 8) and output them to a file as an ASCII table. We open a connection to the `column` command on line 14, adding some command-line arguments. `-t` requires that the output should be formatted as a table, `-c 3` determines the number of columns we require, and `-s /` sets the "/" character as the field delimiter. We ensure that the results will be written to a file called `user3.txt`. Note that the `purchases` directory must exist on your system and that your script must be able to write to it.

Notice that we are doing more than one thing with this command. We are calling the `column` command and writing its output to file. In fact, we are issuing commands to a noninteractive shell. This means that in addition to piping content to a process, we can initiate other processes as well. We could even have the output of the `column` command mailed on to someone:

```
popen( "column -tc 3 -s / | mail matt@corrosive.co.uk", "w" )
```

This level of flexibility can open our system to a grave threat if we ever pass user input to a PHP function that issues shell commands. We will look at precautions you can take later in the hour.

Having acquired a pipe resource, we loop through the `$product` array on line 16. Each value is itself an array, which we convert to a string using the `join()` function on line 17. Rather than joining on a space character, we join on the delimiter we established as part of our command-line arguments. Using the "/" character to join the array is necessary because the spaces in the product array would otherwise confuse the `column` command. Having joined the array, we pass the resultant string and a newline character to the `fputs()` function.

Finally, we close the connection. Taking a peek into the `user3.txt` file, we should see the table neatly formatted:

```
HAL 2000        2  red
Tricorder       3  blue
```

```
ORAC AI            1  pink
Sonic Screwdriver  1  orange
```

We could have made the code more portable by formatting the text using the sprintf() function, but the approach you take is a matter of choice.

Running Commands with exec()

exec() is one of many functions that enable you to pass commands to the shell. The function requires a string representing the path to the command that you want to run. It also optionally accepts an array variable that will be populated with the command's output, and a scalar variable that will be populated with the command's return value.

To get a listing for the current working directory, for example, you might pass exec() the command "ls -al .". We do this in Listing 21.3 (line 7), printing the result to the browser.

LISTING 21.3   Using exec() to Produce a Directory Listing

```
 1: <html>
 2: <head>
 3: <title>Listing 21.3 Using exec() to produce a directory listing</title>
 4: </head>
 5: <body>
 6: <?php
 7: exec( "ls -al .", $output, $return );
 8: print "<p>Returned: $return</p>";
 9: foreach ( $output as $file )
10:     print "$file<br>";
11: ?>
12: </table>
13: </body>
14: </html>
```

Figure 21.2 shows the output from Listing 21.3.

Notice that the ls command returns 0 on success. If it were unable to find or read the directory passed to it, it would have returned 1.

Once again, we have reinvented the wheel to a certain extent with this example. We could have used the opendir() and readdir() functions to acquire a directory listing. There will be times, however, when a command on your system can achieve an effect that would take a long time to reproduce using PHP's functionality. You might have created a shell or Perl script that performs a complex task. If speed of development is an important factor in your project, you might decide that it is worth calling the external

21

script instead of porting it to PHP, at least in the short term. Remember, however, that calling an external process will always add an overhead to your script in terms of both time and memory usage.

FIGURE 21.2

Using exec() *to produce a directory listing.*

Running External Commands with system() or the Backtick Operator

The system() function is similar to the exec() function in that it launches an external application. It requires the path to a command and, optionally, a variable, which will be populated with the command's return value. system() prints the output of the shell command directly to the browser. The following code fragment prints the manual page for the man command itself:

```php
<?php
print "<pre>";
system(  "man man | col -b", $return );
print "</pre>";
?>
```

We print PRE tags to the browser to maintain the formatting of the page. We use system() to call man, piping the result through another application called col, which reformats the text for viewing as ASCII. We capture the return value of our shell command in the $return variable. system() returns its output.

You can achieve a similar result by using the backtick operator. This involves surrounding a shell command in backtick (`) characters. The enclosed command will be executed, and any output returned. You can print the output or store it in a variable.

We can re-create the previous example using backticks:

```
print "<pre>";
print `man man | col -b`;
print "</pre>";
```

Note that we have to explicitly print the return value from the backtick operator.

Plugging Security Holes with `escapeshellcmd()`

Before looking at escapeshellcmd(), let's examine the danger it guards against. We want to allow users to type in the names of manual pages and view output online. Now that we can output one manual page, it is a trivial matter to output any available page. Do not install the code in Listing 21.4; we are deliberately leaving a major security gap unplugged.

LISTING 21.4   Calling the man Command

```
 1: <html>
 2: <head>
 3: <title>Listing 21.4 Calling the man command.
 4:       This script is not secure</title>
 5: </head>
 6: <body>
 7: <form>
 8: <input type="text" value="<?php print  $manpage; ?>" name="manpage">
 9: </form>
10: <pre>
11: <?php
12: if ( isset($manpage) )
13:     system(  "man $manpage | col -b" );
14: ?>
15: </pre>
16: </table>
17: </body>
18: </html>
```

21

We extend our previous examples a little by adding a text field on line 8 and including the value from the form submission to the shell command we pass to the system()

function on line 13. We are being trusting, however. On a UNIX system, a malicious user would be able to add his own commands to the manpage field, thus gaining limited access to the server. Figure 21.3 shows a simple hack that could be applied to this script.

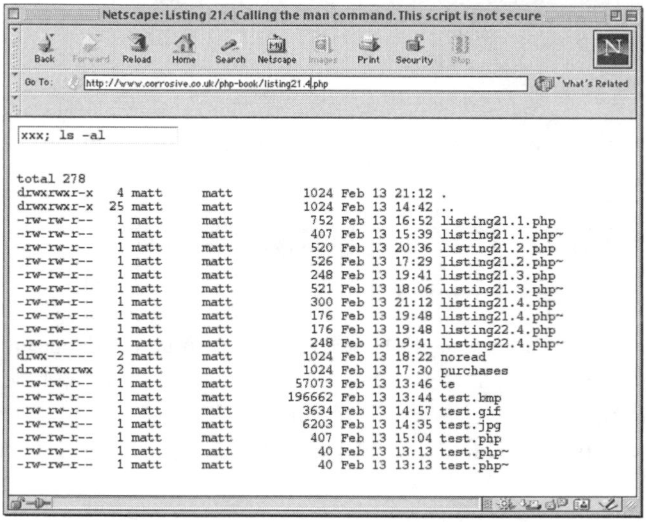

FIGURE 21.3

Calling the man *command.*

The malicious user has submitted the value xxx; ls -al via the form. We have stored this value in the $manpage variable. After we combine this text with the shell command string we pass to system(), we end up with the following string:

```
"man xxx; ls -al | col -b"
```

This instructs the shell to fetch the manual page for xxx, which doesn't exist. It then performs a full directory listing, running the output through the col command. If you think that this is as bad as it gets, think again. An unfriendly visitor can list any readable directory on your system. He or she can even read your /etc/passwd file by adding the following line to the form field:

```
xxx; cat /etc/passwd
```

Fortunately, our encrypted passwords are stored in a file called /etc/shadow, which can only be read by the root user, but this still represents a grave breach in security. We clearly cannot allow this to happen. The safest way of protecting against this is never to pass user input directly to a shell. You can make yourself a little safer, though, by using the escapeshellcmd() function to add backslashes to any metacharacters that the user might submit. escapeshellcmd() requires a string and returns a converted copy. We can now amend our code, making our script a little safer, as shown in Listing 21.5.

LISTING 21.5   Escaping User Input with the `escapeshellcmd()` Function

```
 1: <html>
 2: <head>
 3: <title>Listing 21.5 Escaping user input with
 4:        the escapeshellcmd() function</title>
 5: </head>
 6: <body>
 7: <form>
 8: <input type="text" value="<?php print  $manpage; ?>" name="manpage">
 9: </form>
10: <pre>
11: <?php
12: if ( isset($manpage) ) {
13:     $manpage = escapeshellcmd( $manpage );
14:     system(  "man $manpage | col -b" );
15: }
16: ?>
17: </pre>
18: </table>
19: </body>
20: </html>
```

The only addition to this example is the use of escapeshellcmd() on line 13. If the user attempts to enter "xxx; cat /etc/passwd " now, it will be amended to "xxx\; cat /etc/passwd ", preventing a new command from being issued. In fact, she will be presented with the manual page for the cat command rather than our password file!

Although you can improve security by using escapeshellcmd(), avoid passing user-submitted content to the shell. We could make our script even safer by compiling a list of all valid manual pages on our system and testing user input against this before calling system(). We do something similar in the next section.

Running External Applications with passthru()

passthru() is similar to system() except that any output from the shell command you send will not be buffered. This makes it suitable for running commands that produce binary as opposed to text data. passthru() accepts a shell command and an optional variable. The variable will be filled with the return value of the command.

Let's construct an example. We want to create a script that outputs images as thumbnails and that can be called from HTML or PHP pages. We are going to let external applications do all the work so that our script will be simple. Listing 21.6 shows the code that locates the image and outputs the data to the browser.

21

LISTING 21.6   Using passthru() to Output Binary Data

```
1: <?php
2: if ( isset($image) && file_exists( $image ) ) {
3:     header( "Content-type: image/gif" );
4:     passthru( "giftopnm $image | pnmscale -xscale .5 -yscale .5 | ppmtogif"
);
5: } else
6:     print "The image $image could not be found";
7: ?>
```

Notice that we have not used escapeshellcmd(). Instead, we have tested the user input against our file system on line 2 using the file_exists() function. We will not pass the $image variable to the shell if the image requested does not exist. For additional security we could also limit the extension we will accept and the directory that can be accessed.

In the call to passthru() on line 4, we issue a command that calls three applications. Note that for this script to work on your system, you must have these applications installed, and they must be available in your path. First, we call giftopnm, passing it the $image variable. This reads a GIF image and outputs data in portable anymap format. This output is piped to pnmscale, which scales the image to 50 percent of its original size. The output from pnmscale is in turn piped to ppmtogif, which converts the data to GIF format. This data is finally output to the browser.

We can now call this script from any Web page.

```
<img src="listing21.6.php?image=<?php print urlencode("/path/to/image.gif") ?>">
```

Calling an External CGI Script with the virtual() Function

If you are converting a site from plain HTML to PHP-enabled pages, you may have noticed that your server-side includes no longer work. If you are running PHP as an Apache module, you can use the virtual() function to call CGI scripts, such as Perl or C Web counters, and include their output in your pages. Any CGI script you write must output HTTP headers.

Let's write a simple Perl CGI script. If you don't know Perl, don't worry about this. It simply outputs an HTTP header and all the environmental variables available to it:

```
#!/usr/bin/perl -w
print "Content-type: text/html\n\n";
foreach ( keys %ENV ){
    print "$_: $ENV{$_}<br>\n";
}
```

Assuming that this script is saved in an executable file called test.pl in a cgi-bin directory, you can now call it with the virtual() function, including its output in your PHP document:

```php
<?php
virtual("/cgi-matt/test.pl");
?>
```

Summary

In this hour, you learned how to communicate with the shell and through it with external applications. PHP is a powerful language, but it sometimes will be faster to call on an application than it will be to create similar functionality yourself.

You learned how to pipe data to and from a command using the popen() function. This approach is useful for applications that accept data on standard input and when you want to parse data as it is sent to you by an application.

You learned how to use exec(), system(), and the backtick operator to pass commands to the shell and to acquire user input. You learned about the dangers of passing user input to the shell and examined the escapeshellcmd() function, which will afford you some protection from malicious input. You learned how to use the passthru() function to accept binary data resulting from a shell command. Finally, you learned how to emulate server-side includes with the virtual() function.

In the next hour we will examine PHP's support for XML. In addition to the stable PHP parser functions we will explore some functions which were so new at the time of writing that they were still under development!

Q&A

Q You've mentioned security a lot in this hour. Where can I go to get more information about security on the Web?

A Probably the most authoritative introduction to Web security is the Frequently Asked Questions document by Lincoln Stein (author of the famous Perl module, CGI.pm). You can find this at http://www.w3.org/Security/Faq/.

Q When should I consider calling an external process rather than re-creating its functionality in a script?

A The issues you should consider when weighing this are portability, speed of development, and efficiency.

21

If you build functionality into your script instead of relying on an external process, your script should run easily on different platforms or on systems that don't include the third-party application you would be calling. For simple tasks (such as obtaining a directory listing, for example), it is likely to be more efficient to handle the problem within your code, saving you the overhead of spawning a second process every time your script is called.

On the other hand, some tasks may be difficult to achieve in PHP or slow to complete (grepping a large file, for example). In these cases, it may be advisable to use a tool specifically designed for the job.

Workshop

Quiz

1. Which function would you use to open a pipe to a process?

2. How would you read data from a process after you have opened a connection?

3. How can you write data to a process after you have opened a connection to it?

4. Will the exec() function print the output of a shell command directly to the browser?

5. What does the system() function do with the output from an external command it executes?

6. What does the backtick operator return?

7. How can you escape user input to make it a little safer before passing it to a shell command?

8. How might you execute an external CGI script from within your script?

Quiz Answers

1. You open a connection to a process with the function popen().

2. You can read from a process that you have opened with popen() as you would from a file. In other words, you can use functions such as feof() and fgets().

3. You can write to a process as you could with a file, usually with the fputs() function.

4. The exec() function accepts an array variable, which it fills with the output of the shell command it makes. Output is not sent directly to the browser.

5. The system() function prints the output of the external command directly to the browser.

6. The backtick operator returns the output of the external command that it calls. This can be stored, parsed, or printed.

7. You can escape user input to make it safer using the escapeshellcmd() function. The safest way to execute shell commands, though, is to refrain from passing user input at all.

8. The virtual() function will call an external CGI script.

Activities

1. Create a script that uses the UNIX ps command to output the currently running processes to the browser. Given that knowledge is power, it might not be good idea to make this script available to your users!

2. Check the ps man page for command-line arguments for the ps command. Add a form to your script to allow users to choose from a range of command-line arguments to ps so that they can change the information output. Do not send *any* user input directly to the command line.

21

HOUR **22**

PHP 4 and XML

It would have been hard to miss the buzz created by XML in recent years.
XML is fast becoming a tremendously important tool for sharing data
between applications and for separating logic from presentation in larger
projects. Since the first release of this book, PHP has continued to improve
its support for XML. With PHP and Zend increasingly at the heart of larger
e-business applications, reliable support for XML is essential. For the Web
programmer, too, an understanding of XML is no longer an optional extra.

In this hour, you will learn:

- Some basics about XML
- How to parse XML documents with the XML Parser functions
- How to create XML documents with the DOM functions
- How traverse an XML data structure
- How to use an XSL document to transform XML

What Is XML?

XML stands for Extensible Markup Language, and its very flexibility makes it notoriously hard to define. It is beyond the scope of this book to provide a complete introduction to XML, but we can cover some of the basics. If you would like to read more about XML, please read *Sams Teach Yourself XML in 24 Hours* (ISBN 0-672-32213-7). For a formal definition see `http://www.w3.org/XML/`.

XML is a markup language that enables you to define your own markup languages. In fact, it is more a set of rules than a language in itself. These rules determine the ways in which you can define tags and elements (similar to HTML elements). As long as you obey the rules you have complete freedom to create languages that fulfill a whole range of functions. Because the rules are strict, XML interpreters can easily read XML documents, and make their contents available to scripts that can then act on the instructions they contain.

An XML document will usually start with an XML declaration:

```
<?xml version="1.0"?>
```

It may also refer to a DTD (Document Type Declaration). DTDs are beyond the scope of this book, but they define which elements a document can contain, and in what order.

```
<!DOCTYPE <rootel> SYSTEM "http://www.corrosive.co.uk/sample.dtd">
```

The rest of an XML document is made up primarily of tags that combine to form elements and attributes. XML elements look very like HTML elements. An XML element is made up of starting and ending tags which can surround text or other elements.

A starting tag consists of a lesser than sign ('<') followed by an element name, followed by a greater than sign ('>'). Open tags can also contain attributes that consist of an attribute name and a quoted attribute value separated by an equals sign. The fragment below illustrates an open tag containing an attribute.

```
<newsitem type="world">
```

Both attribute and element names must begin with a letter or an underscore followed by any combination of letters and numbers. No element name can begin with the letters "xml".

A closing tag consists of a lesser than sign ('<'), a forward slash ('/') followed by an element name, followed by a greater than sign ('>').

```
</newsitem>
```

As you can see, XML elements look pretty familiar. One variation you may not be used to however, is the empty element. These are compressed into a single tag, so,

```
<nothinghere></nothinghere>
```

would become

```
<nothinghere />
```

Listing 22.1 pulls all this together into a sample XML document. This is a shortened version of the XML document that we will be working throughout the chapter.

LISTING 22.1 An XML Document

```
 1: <?xml version="1.0"?>
 2: <banana-news>
 3:      <newsitem type="world">
 4:           <headline>Banana sales reach all time high</headline>
 5:           <image>/res/high.gif</image>
 6:           <byline>William Curvey</byline>
 7:           <article>Research published today by the World Banana
 8:                    Tribunal suggests that we have never had it so
 9:                    good banana-wise...</article>
10:      </newsitem>
11:
12:      <newsitem type="home">
13:           <headline>Domestic banana use beggars belief</headline>
14:           <image>/res/use.gif</image>
15:           <byline>Charles Split</byline>
16:           <article>Bananas are for more than eating it seems. Local
17:                    Innovation Centers have been showcasing some
18:                    exciting banana related technologies...</article>
19:      </newsitem>
20: </banana-news>
```

Although Listing 22.1 looks a little like an HTML document, you can see that it contains entirely made-up element names. That is the point of XML. It hands the control and the responsibility over to the developer. An XML interpreter will validate syntax, and will make it easy for us to access the elements, but it is up to us to write code to act on the information received.

In our example we have illustrated a structure for news items. The entire document is enclosed by a single element, <banana-news> (from line 2 to line 20). This is called the root element. A document must have a single root element that encloses all other elements in a document. Every subsequent element must completely enclose any children it might have. Any elements that overlap

```
<A><B></A></B>
```

will generate an error in any compliant XML parser.

Am XML document is often represented as a tree of data. Listing 22.1 is drawn out in this way in Figure 22.1. <banana-news> is at the root, branching out to two sibling <newsitem> elements. The <newsitem> elements further divide, leading to the deepest elements.

FIGURE 22.1

An XML document represented as a tree.

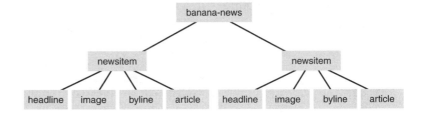

So what is XML for? Well the short answer is that it is up to us. But in practical terms, XML documents tend to fulfill a range of purposes.

1. To structure data logically for sharing (as in Listing 22.1).
2. To format data (as in HTML).
3. To send instructions to an interpreter.

In this chapter we will be concentrating on the first use. Our banana news structure is designed to provide structures that make it easy for ourselves and our partners to work with news items.

XML Parser Functions

In this section we will examine the most stable of PHP's XML tools. The parser functions enable us to access XML documents quickly and with minimal programming.

The functions Jim Clarke's Expat library (XML Parser Toolkit), which is available from http://www.jclark.com/xml/expat.html. If you are running Apache 1.3.7 or later, you will already have Expat bundled with your server, and you may find that the XML functions are available to you without explicit compile options. Otherwise you should install Expat and add

```
—with-xml
```

to your configure options. See Hour 2 "Installing PHP" for more information about configuring and installing PHP.

The parser model is 'event-based'. As components of the XML document are reached, user-created callback functions will be called.

Acquiring a Parser Resource

In order to begin parsing a document you will need a parser resource. You can acquire one of these with the `xml_parser_create()` function. `xml_parser_create()` does not require any arguments and will return a parser resource if all goes well, or `false` otherwise. The function optionally accepts a string containing one of three character encodings "ISO-8859-1" which is the default, "US-ASCII" and "UTF-8". We will stick to the default:

```
$parser = xml_parser_create();
```

When you have finished working with the parser resource, you may wish to free up the memory that it is using to reduce your script's overhead. `xml_parser_free()` requires a valid parser resource and returns a Boolean, `true` if the operation was successful, and `false` otherwise.

```
xml_parser_free( $parser )
```

Setting XML Handlers

There are seven XML events that can be associated with a handler, of these we will cover the two that you are most likely to use frequently. That is, the start and end of an element, and character data.

To associate a function with element events, you should use the `xml_set_element_handler()` function. This requires three arguments; a valid parser resource, the name of handler for start elements and the name of a handler for end elements.

You should build the functions in question, designing the start element handler to accept three arguments. The first will be a parser resource, the second a string containing the element's name, and the third an associative array of attributes. The end element handler should be designed to accept two arguments; the parser resource, and the name of the element. Unless you have specified otherwise, all element and attribute names will have been converted to uppercase characters.

```
// ...
xml_set_element_handler( $parser, "start_handler", "end_handler" );
// ...
function start_handler( $parser, $el_name, $attribs ) {
    print "$el_name: <br><ul>";
    foreach( $attribs as $at_name=>$at_val )
        print "<li>$at_name=>\"$at_val\"";
    print "</ul>";
}
function set_end_handler( $parser, $el_name ) {
    print "END: $el_name><br>";
}
```

The previous fragment illustrates two very simple element handlers. The start element handler prints out the element name and an unordered list of attribute names and values. This will be called for the beginning of every element encountered in an XML document. The end handler merely prints out the element name once again.

Now that we know where elements begin and end, it would be nice to access any text that they might contain. We can do this by setting up a character handler with the `xml_set_character_data_handler()` function. `xml_set_character_data_handler()` requires a valid parser resource and the name of a handler function. The handler function should be designed to accept a parser resource and the found string.

```
xml_set_character_data_handler( $parser, "char_data" );
function char_data( $parser, $data ) {
    print "<i>$data</i><br>";
}
```

You can read about the other XML events that are supported by PHP and Expat at the appropriate PHP manual page <http://www.php.net/manual/en/ref.xml.php>. You can also see the complete list in Table 22.1.

TABLE 22.1 The XML Handler Functions

Function	Trigger event
xml_set_character_data_handler()	Character data
xml_set_default_handler()	Events not covered by specific handlers
xml_set_element_handler()	Element start and end
xml_set_external_entity_ref_handler()	External entities
xml_set_notation_decl_handler()	Notation Declaration
xml_set_processing_instruction_handler()	Processing instructions
xml_set_unparsed_entity_decl_handler()	Unparsed Entity (NDATA)

xml_parser_set_option()

I mentioned that element names are passed to handlers as upper case strings by default. This is not advisable since element names should be case sensitive. You can turn off this feature using the `xml_parser_set_option()` function. This function requires a parser resource, an integer which determines which option is to be set, and the value for the option itself. To turn off the feature that renders element names upper case ('case folding') you can use the built-in constant, `XML_OPTION_CASE_FOLDING`, passing 0 to the function.

```
xml_parser_set_option( $parser, XML_OPTION_CASE_FOLDING, 0 );
```

You can also change the target character encoding using this function. To do this you should call `xml_parser_set_option()` with a `$parser` resource, the constant XML_OPTION_TARGET_ENCODING, and a string value set to one of "ISO-8859-1", "US-ASCII" or "UTF-8". This will make the parser convert character encoding before passing data to your handlers. By default the target encoding is the same as that set for the source encoding (ISO-8859-1 by default, or whatever you set with the `xml_parser_create()` function).

There are two additional constants designed to work with `xml_parser_set_option()`. They are `XML_OPTION_SKIP_WHITE` and `XML_OPTION_SKIP_TAGSTART`.

Parsing the Document

So far we've merely been setting the correct conditions for a parse. To actually begin the parse process we need a function called `xml_parse()`. `xml_parse()` requires a valid parser resource and a string containing the XML to be parsed. You can call `xml_parse()` repeatedly, and it will treat additional data as part of the same document. If you wish to inform the parser that it should treat any subsequent call to `xml_parse()` as the start of a new document, you should pass it a positive integer as an optional third argument.

```
$xml_data="<?xml version="1.0"?><banana-news><test /></banana-news>";
xml_parse( $parser, $xml_data, 1 );
```

`xml_parse()` returns a Boolean; `true` if the parse was successful, and `false` if an error was encountered.

Reporting Errors

When parsing an XML document, you should make allowances for the possibility of errors in the document. If an error is encountered the parser will stop working with your document, but it will not output a message to the browser. It is up to you to generate an informative error message, including the nature of the error and line number at which it occurred.

Expat will only report errors in well-formedness. That is errors in XML syntax. It is not capable of validating an XML document against a DTD.

You can detect whether or not an error has occurred by testing the return value of `xml_parse()`. If a failure has occurred the parser will store an error number, which you can access with the `xml_get_error_code()` function. `xml_get_error_code()` requires a valid parser resource.

```
$code = xml_get_error_code( $parser );
```

The code will be an integer that should match an error constant provided for you by PHP, such as XML_ERROR_TAG_MISMATCH. Rather than work your way through all the relevant constants to produce an error message, you can simply pass the code to another function, `xml_error_string()`. `xml_error_string()` requires only an XML error code, and produces a clear error report.

```
$str = xml_error_string( $code );
```

Now all you need is to find the line number at which the error occurred. This you can do with the `xml_get_current_line_number()`. `xml_get_current_line_number()` requires a parser resource and will return the current line number. Because the parser stops at any error it finds, the current line number will be the line number at which the error is to be found.

```
line = xml_get_current_line_number( $parser );
```

We can now create a function to report on errors:

```
function format_error( $p ) {
        $code = xml_get_error_code( $p );
        $str = xml_error_string( $code );
        $line = xml_get_current_line_number ( $p );
        return "XML ERROR ($code): $str at line $line";
}
```

You can see all the previous fragments brought together in Listing 22.2.

LISTING 22.2   Parsing an XML Document

```
1: <?php
2:
3: $parser = xml_parser_create();
4: xml_parser_set_option( $parser, XML_OPTION_CASE_FOLDING, 0 );
5:
6: xml_set_element_handler( $parser, "start_handler", "end_handler" );
7: xml_set_character_data_handler( $parser, "char_data" );
8: xml_parser_set_option( $parser, XML_OPTION_CASE_FOLDING, 0 );
9: $xml_str = implode('', file( "listing22.1.xml", 0 ));
```

LISTING **22.2**   continued

```
10:
11: xml_parse( $parser, $xml_str )
12:     or die( format_error( $parser ) );
13:
14: function start_handler( $parser, $el_name, $attribs ) {
15:     print "START: $el_name: <br>";
16:     foreach( $attribs as $at_name=>$at_val )
17:         print "    $at_name=>\"$at_val\"<br>";
18: }
19:
20: function end_handler( $parser, $el_name ) {
21:     print "END: $el_name<br>";
22: }
23:
24: function char_data( $parser, $data ) {
25:     print "        char data:<i>$data</i><br>";
26: }
27:
28: function format_error( $p ) {
29:     $code = xml_get_error_code( $p );
30:     $str = xml_error_string( $code );
31:     $line = xml_get_current_line_number ( $p );
32:     return "XML ERROR ($code): $str at line $line";
33: }
34:
35: ?>
```

We create a parser on line 3 and establish our handlers (lines 6 to 8). We also declare the handler functions themselves, start_handler() on line 14, end_handler() on line 20, and char_data() on line 24. Listing 2.2 simply dumps all the data it encounters to the browser. This illustrates the parser code in action, but it is not very useful. In the next section we will discuss a small script that outputs something more sensible.

An Example

We are running a banana related news site. Our partner provides us with a news feed, consisting of an XML document. We would like to extract only the headlines and article authors for display on our site.

We already have all the tools we need to achieve this. The only new feature we will be introducing is a technique. You can see the code in Listing 22.3:

LISTING 22.3   An Example: Parsing an XML Document

```php
 1: <?php
 2: $open_stack = array();
 3: $parser = xml_parser_create();
 4: xml_set_element_handler( $parser, "start_handler", "end_handler" );
 5: xml_set_character_data_handler( $parser, "character_handler");
 6: xml_parser_set_option( $parser, XML_OPTION_CASE_FOLDING, 0 );
 7: xml_parse( $parser, implode('', file( "listing22.1.xml" )) ) or die(
➥format_error( $parser ) );
 8: xml_parser_free( $parser );
 9:
10: function start_handler( $p, $name, $atts ) {
11:         global $open_stack;
12:         $open_stack[] = array($name, "");
13: }
14:
15: function character_handler( $p, $txt ) {
16:     global $open_stack;
17:     $cur_index = count($open_stack)-1;
18:     $open_stack[$cur_index][1] .= $txt;
19: }
20:
21: function end_handler( $p, $name ) {
22:         global $open_stack;
23:         $el = array_pop( $open_stack );
24:     if ( $name == "headline")
25:         print "<b>$el[1]</b><br>";
26:     if ( $name == "byline") {
27:         print "<i>$el[1]</i><p>";
28:     }
29: }
30:
31: function format_error( $p ) {
32:     $code = xml_get_error_code( $p );
33:     $str = xml_error_string( $code );
34:     $line = xml_get_current_line_number ( $p );
35:     return "XML ERROR ($code): $str at line $line";
36: }
37:
38: ?>
```

We begin by establishing a global array variable, $open_stack on line 2. We will be treating this as a way of determining the current enclosing element at any time. The parser is initialized and the handlers are set as we have already seen (lines 3 to 6). When an element is encountered start_handler() (declared on line 10) is called. We create a two element array consisting of the element name and an empty string and add it to the end of the $open_stack() array on line 12. As character data is encountered the character_handler() function is called. We can access the most recently opened XML element by looking at the last array element in $open_stack. We add the character data to the second element of the array representing the currently open XML element (line 18). When the end of an element is encountered, the end_handler() function (declared on line 21) is called. We first remove the last element of the $open_stack array on line 23. The array which is returned to us should contain two elements, firstly the name of the XML element that has just been closed and secondly any character data that was contained by that element. If the element in question is one we wish to print, we can go ahead, adding any formatting we wish.

You can see the output from Listing 22.3 (using a more substantial XML document) in Figure 22.2.

FIGURE 22.2
XML input parsed and formatted for output.

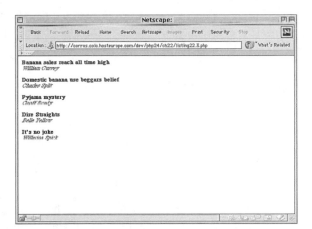

An Introduction to the DOM XML Functions

The XML Parser functions are event based, that is, the document is read from top to bottom and your handlers are triggered as and when the relevant features are encountered. The DOM (Document Object Model) approach is tree-based. The entire XML document is read, and rendered as a tree of objects. This means that you can traverse the tree at your leisure, manipulating its nodes should you wish to. You can also construct your own document trees that can then be output to XML text.

DOM support for PHP is still under development, so code samples in this section are not guaranteed to work with future releases of PHP 4. You should check the manual at `<http://www.php.net/manual/en/ref.domxml.php>` for any changes.

In order to use the functions you will need to have installed the Gnome XML Library, libxml. You will need version 2.2.7 or higher. You can find libxml at `<http://www.xmlsoft.org/>`. You will also need to compile DOM support into PHP. To do this add

```
--with-dom=/path/to/libxml/distrib
```

to your configure script command line options (see hour 2 "Installing PHP 4" for more information about installation issues). Unless you have libxml installed somewhere exotic, you will probably strike paydirt with

```
--with-dom=/usr
```

The first thing you need if you are going to work with the DOM functions is a `DomDocument` object. The `DomDocument` object is container for all elements, which are themselves represented by objects.

Acquiring a `DomDocument` Object

To create a `DomDocument` object you can use the `new_xmldoc()` function. This requires a string containing the XML that will be parsed. You can manipulate this data as you want, so you should use this function if you want to construct a tree from scratch. You should at least pass it the XML declaration.

```
$doc = new_xmldoc('<?xml version="1.0"?>');
```

You can then go ahead and begin to add elements. In fact you can get away with passing `new_xmldoc()` the version number alone ("1.0") and it will construct the XML declaration for you.

```
$doc = new_xmldoc('1.0');
```

If you would like to parse data from a file you can use the `xmldocfile()` function. This accepts the name of a file and will return a `DomDocument` object.

```
$doc = xmldocfile("listing22.1.xml");
```

The Root Element

Just as the DOM model provides an analog for an XML document, it provides an object to represent an element. The `DomElement` and `DomDocument` objects derive from a common parent class (`DomNode`) and are therefore similar in structure.

Every XML document must have a singe root element. Similarly, a `DomDocument` object has a root `DomElement` object. You can either create or access this object. To set a root `DomElement` you should call the `add_root()` method. `add_root()` requires the name of the element you wish to create. `add_root()` will construct a root `DomElement` object, add it to the data tree and return it to you.

```
$root = $doc->add_root("banana-news");
```

To access an existing root `DomElement` object you just need to call the `root()` method.

Adding New `DomElement` Objects to the Tree

Once you have access to a `DomElement` (initially via the `DomDocument` `root()` or `add_root()` functions) you can add more using the `DomElement` object's `new_child()` method. `new_child()` requires a string representing the element's name, and a string representing its textual contents, if any. If an element does not contain text, you should nonetheless pass an empty string to the `new_child()` method.

```
$item = $root->new_child("newsitem", "");
$item->new_child( "headline", "The Banana Story" );
```

The `new_child()` method will return a new `DomElement` object which can be used to add further children if necessary.

We now have enough information to be able to use the DOM functions to create the XML document in Listing 22.1. We use data from an associative array (declared on line 2), but it could just as easily have been pulled from a database. You can see the code in Listing 22.4.

LISTING 22.4 Constructing an XML Document with the DOM Functions

```
 1: <?php
 2: $news = array(
 3:     array(  "headline" => "Banana sales",
 4:         "image" => "/res/high.gif",
 5:         "byline" => "William Curvey",
 6:         "article" => "Research published today by...",
 7:         "type" => "world"
 8:         ),
 9:     array(  "headline" => "Domestic banana use beggars belief",
10:         "image" => "/res/use.gif",
11:         "byline" => "Charles Split",
12:         "article" => "Bananas are for more than eating...",
13:         "type" => "world"
14:         )
15: );
16:
```

LISTING 22.4   continued

```
17: $doc = new_xmldoc("1.0");
18:
19: $root = $doc->add_root("banana-news");
20: foreach( $news as $newselement ) {
21:     $item = $root->new_child("newsitem", "");
22:     $item->set_attribute("type", $newselement['type'] );
23:     $item->new_child( "headline", $newselement['headline'] ) ;
24:     $item->new_child( "image", $newselement['image'] ) ;
25:     $item->new_child( "byline", $newselement['byline'] ) ;
26:     $item->new_child( "article", $newselement['article'] ) ;
27: }
28: print $doc->dumpmem( );
29: ?>
```

The only new feature of Listing 22.4 is a call to method of the DomDocument object. dumpmem(), called on line 28 will output the entire tree to an XML string. The output of Listing 22.4, therefore, is exactly the same as the text of Listing 22.1, with only one key difference. dumpmem() does not prettify its output with linebreaks or indentations.

Getting Information from DomElement Objects

Usually the first thing you will want to know about an DomElement is its name. This will be stored in the $tagname property.

```
print "Iam a ".$el->tagname." element";
```

Once you know the name of an element, you will want to know if it has any attributes. Attributes are stored in DomAttribute objects. You can acquire an array of DomAttribute objects associated with an element by calling the attributes() method.

```
$atts = $el->attributes();
```

In order to access the name and value of each DomElement object you can use the conveniently named name() and value() methods.

```
$atts = $el->attributes();
if ( ! empyt( $atts ) ) {
    foreach( $atts as $att ) {
        print $att->name().": ".$att->value()."<br>";
    }
}
```

In order to navigate an XML tree you must take advantage of the methods that DOM objects provide about their place in the structure.

Given a `DomElement` object you can discover whether or not it has child elements with the `has_child_nodes()` method. This method returns a Boolean.

```
if ( $el->has_child_nodes() )
    print "I am blessed with progeny";
```

If the element has children you can access the first child with `first_child()`. If the element does not have children `$el->first_child()` will return `false`.

```
if ( $el->has_child_nodes() )
    $child = $el->first_child();
```

We can climb the tree vertically, but what about horizontally? Elements know about their siblings as well. You can access an element's next sibling with the `next_sibling()` method and its previous sibling with the `previous_sibling()` method. Both these methods will return `false` if there is no sibling to be found.

```
$child = $el->first_child();
do {
    print $child->tagname."<br>";
} while( $child = $child->next_sibling() );
```

A parent, of course, can access all of its children. The `children()` method will return an array of element objects. If the element is childless it will `false`.

```
$kids = $el->children();
foreach( $kids as $child ) {
    print $child->tagname."<br>";
}
```

Children also know about their parents. The `parent()` method will return an element's parent element.

Examining Text Nodes

Armed with the methods we have covered we can now swing about an XML tree pretty well. But we haven't got right down to the most important features of the tree. An element is not the only kind of node that we want to deal with. Among its children we will find text nodes, comment nodes, and others beyond the scope of this book.

Our main concern is the text node. We use these to acquire document content. The first thing we need to be able to do is to distinguish between `DomElement` objects and `DomText` elements. The `DomElement` and `DomText` classes share a common parent class: `DomNode`. All `DomNode` objects have a `$type` property that contains an identifying integer. These integers can be tested using built-in constants. For `DomElement` and `DomText` objects you would use XML_ELEMENT_NODE and XML_TEXT_NODE respectively.

```
if ( $child->type == XML_ELEMENT_NODE ) {
    // work with the element
} elseif ( $child->type == XML_TEXT_NODE ) {
    // work with the text node
}
```

Once you have located a text node you still need to access its contents. You can do this with the node_value() method.

```
if ( $child->type == XML_TEXT_NODE ) {
    print $child->node_value();
}
```

Traversing a Tree: Two Approaches

We now have enough information to work our way through a tree, but how do we go about it? In this section we will lay down two approaches to this task.

The first approach is designed to do the work of acquiring each node in turn, and return it to the calling code. Listing 22.5 demonstrates:

LISTING 22.5   Traversing a Tree of XML Nodes

```
 1: <?
 2:
 3: $doc = xmldocfile("listing22.1.xml");
 4: $root = $doc->root();
 5: $pointer = $root;
 6:
 7: do {
 8:     print $pointer->tagname()."<br>";
 9: } while ( $pointer = next_element( $pointer ) );
10:
11: function next_element( $pointer ) {
12:     while ( $pointer = next_node( $pointer ) ) {
13:         if ( $pointer->type == XML_ELEMENT_NODE )
14:             return $pointer;
15:     }
16:     return false;
17: }
18:
19: function next_node( $pointer ) {
20:     if ( $pointer->has_child_nodes() )
21:         return( $pointer->first_child() );
22:     if ( $next = $pointer->next_sibling() )
23:         return $next;
24:     while( $pointer = $pointer->parent() ) {
25:         if ( $next=$pointer->next_sibling() ) {
26:             return $next;
```

LISTING 22.5   continued

```
27:           }
28:      }
29: }
30: ?>
```

As you can see, the real work is done by the next_node() function on line 19. This accepts a node object and tests it to see if it has any children. If so, it returns the first one on line 21. If the node has no children, the function then looks for a sibling, returning it on line 23 if it is found. If the node has no children or siblings we then climb back up the tree in a while loop starting on line 24, looking for siblings as we go. As soon as we find a sibling object on our climb, we return it on line 26. By repeatedly calling next_node() we will eventually traverse the entire tree.

The next approach traverses the tree in the same way. It differs from the previous example in that the calling code does not repeatedly request the next node. Instead the traversing function calls itself recursively until the tree has been completely explored. You can see this in action in Listing 22.6

LISTING 22.6   Traversing a Tree of XML Nodes

```
1: <?php
2: $doc = xmldocfile( "listing22.1.xml" );
3: $root = $doc->root();
4: traverse( $root );
5:
6: function traverse( $node, $level=0 ){
7:     handle_node( $node, $level );
8:     if ( $node->has_child_nodes() ) {
9:         $children - $node->children();
10:        foreach( $children as $kid ) {
11:            traverse( $kid, $level+1 );
12:        }
13:    }
14: }
15:
16: function handle_node( $node, $level ) {
17:     for ( $x=0; $x<$level; $x++ )
18:         print "  ";
19:     if ( $node->type == XML_ELEMENT_NODE ) {
20:         print $node->tagname()."<br>";
21:     }
22: }
23: ?>
```

The `traverse()` function on line 6 does all the work. Passed a node object it looks for children. If children are present it then works through them using a `foreach` loop on line 10, calling itself recursively with each child node in turn. Every time `traverse()` is called it will call `handle_node()` (declared on line 16) where application specific code can work with the node.

XSL: A Brief Discussion

XSL stands for Extensible Stylesheet Language. It is a templating system for XML documents, and with it you can process an XML document for output. With the same XML source, you might apply different XSL documents to format for the Web, PDAs, interactive television, and mobile phone.

Unfortunately the details of XSL are beyond the scope of this book, but we can briefly examine PHP's support for it.

PHP and XSL

As with its support for DOM, PHP's support for XSL is still in the early stages. The XSLT (the 'T' stands for 'Transformations') functions are under development, and both names and behaviors are subject to change. Before using XSL in projects you should visit the PHP manual (`<http://www.php.net/manual/en/ref.xslt.php>`) to check the current stability of support for the technology.

In order to run the XSLT functions you will need to install the Sablotron XSLT processor (`<http://www.gingerall.com/>`), and to compile PHP with XSL support. You should include the argument

`--with-sablot=/path/to/sablotron/libs`

when you run the configure script. For an standard install

`--with-sablot=/usr`

will probably work for you.

An XSL Document

In Listing 22.7 we will apply a very simple XSL document to the XML we created in listing 22.1. It will output a table for each article, adding formatting and changing the order of two of the siblings.

LISTING 22.7   An XSL Document

```
1: <?xml version="1.0"?>
2: <xsl:stylesheet
3: version="1.0"
4: xmlns:xsl="http://www.w3.org/1999/XSL/Transform">
5:     <xsl:template match="banana-news">
6:         <xsl:for-each select="newsitem">
7:             <p>
8:             <table>
9:              <tr><td>
10:                 <i><xsl:value-of select="byline" /></i>
11:                 <xsl:text> writes</xsl:text>
12:             </td></tr>
13:             <tr><td> <b><xsl:value-of select="headline" /></b> </td></tr>
14:             </table>
15:             </p>
16:         </xsl:for-each>
17:     </xsl:template>
18: </xsl:stylesheet>
```

Without getting in too deep with XSL, the purpose of this document should be relatively clear with a close look. First of all take a look at the first line. An XSL document is also an XML document! The root element

```
<xsl:stylesheet
version="1.0"
xmlns:xsl="http://www.w3.org/1999/XSL/Transform">
```

should always take this form. It establishes the XSL namespace, and version number.

The `<xsl:template>` element on line 5 establishes the zone we wish to transform—in this case the whole XML document. With `<xsl:for-each>` on line 6 we can apply the same formatting to every `<newsitem>` element. Having established this we can go ahead and begin formatting. The HTML you see in Listing 22.7 is subject to the same rules as any XML document, which means we must be careful to close our `<P>` elements. The `<xsl:value-of>` tags (lines 10 and 13) will be substituted by the value of the elements stipulated in their select attribute (`<byline>` and `<headline>`). Notice that we have switched the positions of byline and headline elements we are matching. XSL gives you control over the structure of data in output as well as its format.

Applying XSL to XML with PHP

Now that we have an XSL document we can use it to transform our XML. In fact in order to do this we only need to encounter a very few functions. Listing 22.8 introduces them.

LISTING 22.8   Using XSL to Transform an XML Document

```
 1: <?php
 2: $xsl_string = join( "", file("listing22.7.xsl") );
 3: $xml_string = join( "", file("listing22.1.xml") );
 4:
 5: if ( xslt_process($xsl_string, $xml_string, $result) )
 6:     print $result;
 7: else
 8:     die( format_xslt_error() );
 9:
10: function format_xslt_error() {
11:     $ret = "XSLT ERROR (".xslt_errno()."): ".xslt_error();
12:     return $ret;
13: }
14: ?>
```

We acquire both the XML and XSL data from files and store them in variables on lines 2 and 3. We then invoke a function called xslt_process() on line 5. xslt_process() requires three strings, the XSL, the XML to be transformed, and a variable in which the results will be stored (third argument is passed by reference). The function returns true if all goes well and false otherwise.

If the function fails in a way that does not throw a fatal error, you can format an error message with the xslt_errno() and xslt_error() functions (line 11). These functions optionally accept an XSLT parser resource. xslt_process() does away with the need to generate a parser resource, so it is lucky that both xslt_error() and xslt_errno() can be called with no arguments. Without a resource xslt_error() will return a string describing the last XSLT error produced during the lifetime of the script. xslt_errno() will return an integer which is the error's reference number.

Summary

XML is a large topic, worthy of a book in its own right, as the bookstore shelves testify. It would be impossible to cover all its intricacies in a single chapter. However, you should already be able to see some of the possibilities that XML offers the programmer.

In this hour you learned how to how to parse XML documents using the Expat based XML Parser functions. You explored the developmental DOM Functions, and learned how to use them to build an XML document. You learned two simple techniques for traversing a DOM structure. Finally, you examined an XSL template and learned how to use it with the XSLT functions to transform an XML document.

In the next hour we will examine Smarty, a PHP template engine designed to improve the organization of large projects.

Q&A

Q Discussion about XML seems to be everywhere at the moment. Is it all hype?

A People do love a bandwagon, but XML remains an excellent way of sharing data and of making larger projects more durable and extensible. The fact that you can define standards using DTDs also means that it is possible to build lightweight interpreters that do not need to waste time on error checking. If you have ever tried to download a browser from the Web, you will know how enormous they have become. One of the reasons that XHTML, the XML version of HTML is so important is the likely rise of lightweight browsers in cell phones, PDAs, and other devices that simply will not have the processing power available to handle HTML unless it conforms to a standard. You can read more about XHTML at http://www.w3.org/TR/xhtml1/.

Q You warned that DOM and XSLT functions were under development. Should I bother with them?

A First of all, check the PHP site at http://www.php.net for your version of PHP. These functions may be fully supported by the time you read this. For now, if you are intent upon writing code for a production environment, you should stick to the XML parser functions which are very stable. Nonetheless, for the purposes of longer term development and learning, now is the time to be working on those DOM and XSLT skills. Don't forget, by the way, that if you want to create a tree of objects similar to the DOM objects, you can handroll your own version relatively easily with the parser functions and user defined objects.

Workshop

Quiz

1. How would you acquire a parser resource?
2. What arguments will the XML parser pass to an element start handler?
3. How would you turn off the feature that converts all element names to uppercase characters?
4. How would you get current line number while an XML document is being parsed?
5. What function would you use to get a DomDocument object using an existing XML file?

6. Given an DomElement object, how would you add a child element to your tree?

7. What function might you use to apply XSL to an XML document?

Quiz Answers

1. You can get a parser resource with the xml_parser_create() function.

   `$parser = xml_parser_create();`

2. The user-defined element start handler function will automatically be passed a $parser resource, the name of the element which is starting, and an array of attributes.

3. You can use the xml_parser_set_option() function to disable case folding.

   `xml_parser_set_option( $parser, XML_OPTION_CASE_FOLDING, 0 );`

4. The xml_get_current_line_number() function will return the current line number.

5. The xmldocfile() function will return a DomDocument object.

   `$doc = xmldocfile("my_doc.xml");`

6. The new_child() method will add a new element to a tree:

   `$child = $el->new_child("elname", "element text goes here");`

7. The xslt_process() function will accept an XSL string, an XML string and an empty string variable. The string variable will hold the transformation.

   `xslt_process($xsl_string, $xml_string, $result );`

Activities

1. Create a script that uses the daily XML newsfeed provided at http:// slashdot. org/slashdot.xml, and outputs an HTML version. Create another script to output a neatly formatted text version.

2. Using the XML Parser functions and object-oriented techniques create your own tree of DOM-like element objects. Write code to traverse the tree.

PART IV
Extending PHP

Hour

HOUR 23

Smarty: A Template Engine

Throughout this book we have covered many core PHP features. In this hour we are going to look at a library written in PHP. The Smarty template engine is a powerful way of organizing larger projects, and demonstrates the ways in which library code can substantially extend the language.

In this hour, you will learn:

- How to install the Smarty engine
- How to pass script variables to Smarty templates
- How to give Smarty templates the power to make decisions about what to display
- How to loop in Smarty templates
- How to modify variables in Smarty templates

What Is Smarty?

Smarty is a template engine. That is, it is a system that helps you to separate the presentation of your output from the logic of your application. This is increasingly important for large projects, in which the design and build teams are often distinct from the engineering group.

Use of a template system, whether hand-rolled or third party can contribute greatly to a project's flexibility. When code logic is deeply embedded in design elements, projects quickly become hard to manage, and debug. When they are separated, programmers are free to concentrate on building elegant and extensible code, while HTML builders can concentrate on building effective user interfaces without choking on lots of embedded PHP.

Smarty was developed by Monte Ohrt and Andrei Zmievski to solve this problem. It is very rich in features, so rich in fact, that this chapter can only really start to deal with the things that it can do. Itself entirely written in PHP, it overcomes the largest drawback to many template engines.

Template engines replace specially flagged keywords embedded within template files with the values generated by a script. In order to do this, the template file must be parsed by the engine. For larger documents the process of parsing the template file and substituting keywords for the values generated by a script can be slow and resource intensive. Smarty handles this problem by compiling templates into PHP code.

Acquiring and Installing Smarty

Smarty can be downloaded from `http://www.phpinsider.com/php/code/Smarty/download/`. At the time of writing the latest version was 1.4.5.

To install you should first unpack the Smarty distribution.

```
tar -xvzf Smarty-1.4.5.tar.gz
```

Looking inside you should see the PHP files that make up Smarty:

```
Config_File.class.php
Smarty.addons.php
Smarty.class.php
Smarty_Compiler.class.php
```

You should move these to a library directory available to your scripts. I created one called `smartylib` in my Web directory. In order for Smarty to work correctly, you will need to ensure that PHP can find the directory that contains these files when your projects are run.

You can do this by setting the php.ini directive include_path.

```
include_path = ".:/usr/local/lib/php:/home/corrdev/htdocs/smartylib"
```

Notice that you can include multiple directories in the directive value. Each path should be separated by a colon (a semi-colon for windows). If you do not have access to the php.ini file, remember that you might be able to use an .htaccess file with Apache to set directives.

```
php_value include_path  ".:/usr/local/lib/php:/home/corrdev/htdocs/smartylib"
```

Alternatively you can set php.ini directives within your code with the ini_set() function.

```
ini_set("include_path".:/usr/local/lib/php:/home/corrdev/htdocs/smartylib");
```

Smarty also requires PEAR code. PEAR stands for the PHP Extension and Application Repository, and the required code is used to provide functionality for library code. All you need to worry about is that the directory containing the PEAR.php class is included in your include path. On Linux this will be

```
/usr/local/lib/php
```

and on Windows it will be

```
\php\pear
```

You should now have installed the library side of Smarty. This leaves us with the project side. We still need to set up directories to hold our templates. Go to the directory that will hold your projects. You will need to create three directories, configs, templates, and templates_c. You will be creating your templates in the templates directory. Compiled templates will be automatically written to templates_c consequently you should make sure that the server will have the rights to write to the templates c directory. On Unix systems you can do this by changing the owner of the directory to the user that the server runs under (usually nobody).

```
chown nobody:nobody templates_c
```

If you are running Apache you can check the user that httpd runs as in the httpd.conf file. Look for the User and Group directives. If you do not have the privileges to change the owner of template_c you can make the directory world writeable, which will work but is not encouraged.

```
chown 777 templates_c
```

Although we will not be covering Smarty's caching facility in this hour, in order to use it yourself you should also create a directory called cache with the same permissions as templates_c.

23

You should have now installed Smarty. If the code fragments in this chapter generate errors, you may need to work your way back through this section. The Smarty distribution also contains clear installation instructions.

A First Script

First of all let's create a template document. By convention we will be saving all templates with the extension .tpl. We will save all templates into the templates directory. Listing 23.1 shows our first template file.

LISTING 23.1   Listing22.1.tpl—A First Template

```
 1: <html>
 2: <head>
 3: <title>{$page_title}</title>
 4: </head>
 5: <body>
 6: <h3>{$page_title}</h3>
 7: <p>
 8: <b>{$page_subhead}</b>
 9: </p>
10: {$page_text}
11: </body>
12: </html>
```

Listing 23.1 should look oddly familiar, a mix of HTML and variables. On close inspection, though, some differences should present themselves. There are no PHP start and end tags, and the variables are all enclosed by braces. The braces are the way that Smarty signals where substitutions or executable code reside. Smarty can be configured to work with other delimiting characters, but we will work with the default throughout this hour.

In order to use the template we need to create a PHP script that uses Smarty. Let's dive straight in and examine it in detail afterwards. Listing 22.2 shows our script.

LISTING 23.2   Listing22.2.php—A First Smarty Script

```
1: <?php
2: require_once("Smarty.class.php");
3:
4: $page_vals = array(
5:         "page_title" => "Listings 23.1 and 23.2",
6:         "page_subhead"=>"Separating script logic from formatting",
7:         "page_text" => "The look and feel of this data is handled by
➥listing23.1.tpl"
```

LISTING 23.2 continued

```
 8:          );
 9:
10: $templ = new Smarty();
11: $templ->assign( $page_vals );
12: $templ->display("listing23.1.tpl");
13:
14: ?>
```

23

The very first thing that we do is to use `require_once()` on line 2 to include `Smarty.class.php`. If this call generates an error you will need to go back and check your include path, and ensure that the directory that includes `Smarty.class.php` is correctly specified in the `include_path` directive.

We set up an associative array to include all of our page variables on line 4. Notice that the keys match the variable names in Listing 23.1. We create a `Smarty` object and store it in a variable called `$templ` on line 10. The `assign()` method (invoked on line 11) accepts either a single associative array as in our example, or a variable name and a value. Once we have associated our data with the `Smarty` object we can go ahead and output the page on line 12. At its simplest the `display()` method accepts a path to the template file you wish to use. Notice that we do not have to refer to the `templates` directory. Smarty requires paths that begin from the template directory.

You can see the output from Listing 23.1 and Listing 23.2 in Figure 23.1.

FIGURE 23.1

The output from Listing 23.1 and Listing 23.2.

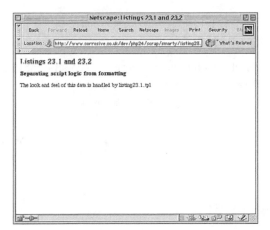

The first time that Listing 23.2 is run, Smarty will read `listing23.1.tpl` and make any necessary substitutions. It will not, though, directly insert values. Instead it will generate a compiled version of the template containing PHP code to request the values. This means that for subsequent calls to Listing 23.2 there will not be the overhead of parsing `listing23.1.tpl`. You do not normally need to worry about what `template_c` contains, but let's have a look at the compiled version of Listing 23.1. You can see it in Listing 23.3.

LISTING 23.3   The Compiled Version of Listing 23.1

```
 1: <?php /* Smarty version 1.4.5, created on 2001-10-12 16:21:01
 2:            compiled from listing23.1.tpl */ ?>
 3: <html>
 4: <head>
 5: <title><?php echo $this->_tpl_vars['page_title']; ?>
 6: </title>
 7: </head>
 8: <h3><?php echo $this->_tpl_vars['page_title']; ?>
 9: </h3>
10: <p>
11: <b><?php echo $this->_tpl_vars['page_subhead']; ?>
12: </b>
13: </p>
14: <?php echo $this->_tpl_vars['page_text']; ?>
15:
16: </html>
```

Template Variables

Because it is such a useful technique, we have jumped straight in and demonstrated the way in which associative arrays are assigned to Smarty, but we can also assign individual scalars. In Listing 23.4 we rewrite our PHP script to work with individual variables.

LISTING 23.4   Passing Individual Variables to the `assign()` Method

```
1: <?php
2: require_once("Smarty.class.php");
3:
4: $templ = new Smarty();
5: $templ->assign( "page_title", "Listings 23.1 and 23.4");
6: $templ->assign( "page_subhead", "Separating script logic from formatting");
```

LISTING 23.4   continued

```
 7: $templ->assign( "page_text", "The look and feel of this data is handled by
➥listing23.1.tpl");
 8: $templ->display("listing23.1.tpl");
 9:
10: ?>
```

23

The output for Listing 23.4 would be almost exactly the same as that for Listing 23.2. Instead of passing a single associative array to the `assign()` method, we have invoked it three times, each time with two arguments, the name of the template variable, and its value.

There is another way of passing an associative array to the `assign()` method.

```
$templ->assign( "page_vals", $page_vals );
```

In the previous code fragment we passed $page_vals to `assign()` as we did in Listing 22.2, but this time it was passed as the second argument. For the first argument we passed a template variable name. This means that the template file will now be able to access individual elements of the $page_vals array using this syntax:

```
($page_vals.page_title}
($page_vals.page_subhead}
($page_vals.page_text}
```

We can even pass an object to the `assign()` method.

```
class page_vals {
   var $page_title = "Passing an object to assign()";
   var $page_subhead = "Separating script logic from formatting";
   var $page_text = "Objects use the '->' notation in templates";
}
$templ->assign( $page_vals, new page_vals() );
```

The template can then refer to the object's properties using the arrow ('->') characters.

```
($page_vals->page_title}
($page_vals->page_subhead}
($page_vals->page_text}
```

As well as passing variables from your script to a template, you can access some of PHP's built in arrays using the special {$smarty} variable. Table 23.1 lists these variables, and in Listing 23.5 we write a template to show the feature in action.

TABLE 23.1   Smart Equivalents for Built-In PHP Variables

PHP Array	Smarty Name	Syntax Example
$ENV	env	{$smarty.env.LANGUAGE}
$SERVER	server	{$smarty.server.REMOTE_ADDR}
$HTTP_GET_VARS	get	{$smarty.get.username}
$HTTP_POST_VARS	post	{$smarty.post.username}
$HTTP_SESSION_VARS	session	{$smarty.session.firstname}
$HTTP_COOKIE_VARS	cookie	{$smarty.cookie.last_visit}

LISTING 23.5   Using the Special {$smarty} Variable

```
 1: <html>
 2: <head>
 3: <title>Listing 23.5 using the special {$smarty} variable</title>
 4: </head>
 5: <body>
 6: Hello user at <b>{$smarty.server.REMOTE_ADDR}</b><br>
 7: You submitted this value: <b>{$smarty.get.name}</b><br>
 8: I am set up to handle <b>{$smarty.env.LANGUAGE}</b><br>
 9: <body>
10: </html>
```

The {$smarty} variable is similar to a multidimensional associative array. The only unfamiliar aspect to this is that you must access individual elements using a dot rather than square brackets.

Built-In Template Functions

Even though you will want to keep most of your script logic in the PHP side of your application, you will occasionally need your templates to make decisions based on your script's output. For this reason, Smarty provides functions for a whole range of purposes. We will deal with some of them in this section.

Functions are separated from static content in the same way as variables. That is, their names (and arguments) are surrounded by braces ('{' and '}').

{if}, {elseif}, and {else}

Believe it or not, Smarty templates support the kind of control structures you would expect to see in a fully fledged scripting language.

The {if} function behaves in a similar way to its PHP cousin. The condition to be tested is also placed between the braces.

```
{if $user == "admin" }
        <p>Message of the Day: {$motd}</p>
{/if}
```

The block to be executed if the condition is fulfilled should be enclosed between the {if} function call and a closing {/if}. This is the logic that Smarty uses to define a block of output.

In the code fragment above we test the value of the {$user} variable. If it evaluates to "admin" we then output a message. Smarty is fussy about the syntax of the {if} function. You should always leave a space between each operand and the operator.

You can also use the {elseif} and {else} functions when using {if}.

```
{if $user == "admin" }
        <p>Message of the Day: {$motd}</p>
{elseif $user == "super" }
        <p>System Status: {$sys_status}</p>
{else}
        <p>Hope you enjoy our site!</p>
{/if}
```

Even if the syntax looks a little different, the logic of the previous fragment should look very familiar indeed.

Looping with the {section} Function

Looping is a common requirement for template engines. Given a variable number of rows pulled from a database, the template creator needs a flexible way of presenting the information. In Listing 23.6 we simulate a result array that could have been taken from a database pass it to assign().

LISTING 23.6 An Array of Names for Passing to a Template

```
 1: <?php
 2: require_once("Smarty.class.php");
 3:
 4: $search = array(
 5:                 "Douglas Adams",
 6:                 "Neal Stephenson",
 7:                 "Dan Simmons",
 8:                 "Peter F. Hamilton"
 9:                 );
10:
```

23

LISTING 23.6   continued

```
11: $templ = new Smarty();
12: $templ->assign( "search", $search );
13: $templ->display("listing23.7.tpl");
14: ?>
```

Given the array defined on line 4 a template can use the {section} function to loop through it. In Listing 23.7 we show the function in practice.

LISTING 23.7   Looping with the {section} Function

```
 1: <html>
 2: <head>
 3: <title>Listing 23.7 Looping with the section Function</title>
 4: </head>
 5: <body>
 6:
 7: <h3>Author Search Results</h3>
 8: {section name=search_row loop=$search}
 9:     {$search[search_row]}<br>
10: {/section}
11:
12: </body>
13: </html>
```

Like all loop constructs {section} needs a way of limiting the number of iterations to perform. This is provided by the loop argument. In Listing 23.6 we made the $search array available to the template. In the {section} function call on line 8 Smarty is merely helpfully counting the number of elements in $search. In fact

```
{section name=search_row loop=$search}
```

and

```
{section name=search_row loop=4}
```

are equivalent. While the loop argument determines the limit to loop iterations, the name argument provides a way of accessing element indices in an array. So, in the first loop iteration

```
$search[search_row]
```

is equivalent to

```
$search[0]
```

and so on. You can provide any one word string for the name argument. Within the loop this name can be used as a variable to access the relevant index for any array that the template has access to. You are not limited, in other words to using it to access the array counted by the loop argument.

You can also use the {section} function to access associative array fields in a multidimensional array. If we were to extend our authors example in Listing 23.6 to include book titles

```
$search = array(
            array( 'name'=>"Douglas Adams",
                   'book'=>"So Long and Thanks for all the Fish" ),
            array( 'name'=>"Neal Stephenson",
                   'book'=>"Cryptonomicon" ),
            array( 'name'=>"Dan Simmons",
                   'book'=>"Endymion" ),
            array( 'name'=>"Peter F Hamilton",
                   'book'=>"The Neutronium Alchemist" ),
            );
```

we could access each of the associative array elements using the now familiar dot notation.

```
{section name=search_row loop=$search}
        {$search[search_row].name} .. {$search[search_row].book}<br>
{/section}
```

But what if $search array were empty? Is there any way that the template writer can handle a default case? The {sectionelse} function is called into play when the {section} function's loop argument evaluates to zero.

```
{section name=search_row loop=$search}
        {$search[search_row].name} .. {$search[search_row].book}<br>
{sectionelse}
        No authors found. Try another search
{/section}
```

{section} functions provide you with a number of special variables which tell you about the state of the loop. These have a specific format:

```
{%loopname.variable%}
```

Among the most useful of the section variables is iteration, which will hold the number of the iteration indexed from 1. This makes it perfect for counting rows.

```
{section name=search_row loop=$search}
        {%search_row.iteration%}. {$search[search_row].name} ..
{$search[search_row].book}<br>
{sectionelse}
```

The `index` variable is similar to the `iteration` section variable. It returns the current index number of the loop, and so counts from zero. The difference becomes more pronounced if two additional arguments to `{section}` are used. `start` sets the beginning index for the loop and `step` sets the increment by which the index number should rise. If these are set, the `index` section variable will reflect the `start` and `step` numbers while `iteration` will count up sequentially from 1 regardless.

Also useful are the `first` and `last` section variables. These contain `true` in the first and final iterations of the loop respectively. That makes it easy to top and tail an output.

```
{section name=search_row loop=$search}
        {if %search_row.first%}
                <hr>
        {/if}
        {%search_row.iteration%}. {$search[search_row].name} ..
{$search[search_row].book}<br>
        {if %search_row.last%}
                <hr>
        {/if}
{sectionelse}
        No authors found. Try another search
{/section}
```

It would also nice to be able to tell the user how many hits her query accessed. The `total` section variable holds the total number of iterations for the loop, no matter at which iteration it is accessed.

```
{section name=search_row loop=$search}
        {if %search_row.first%}
                {%search_row.total%} found
                <hr>
        {/if}
        {%search_row.iteration%}. {$search[search_row].name} ..
{$search[search_row].book}<br>
        {if %search_row.last%}
                <hr>
                {%search_row.total%} found
        {/if}
{sectionelse}
        No authors found. Try another search
{/section}
```

So, we have now looked at a number of features that allow you to included quite sophisticated decision making and flow control within your templates. It is a good idea for your presentation layer to work flexibly with the information available to it—it saves application logic from concerning itself with presentation issues. On the other hand, you should be wary of letting application logic creep into your templates. As a rule of thumb, your templates should have little knowledge of any processes outside of the graceful presentation of data.

Combining Templates with the {include} Function

You will not always want to be limited to a single template when you call the Smarty object's display() method. Some page components (primary navigation, for example) are so ubiquitous that will naturally live in a separate template that can be included in any template required.

You can choose to include other templates from within a template file using the {include} function. {include} has a name argument that should be the path to the template file to be included (once again paths are relative to the 'templates' directory). You can also include arbitrarily named arguments that will become available to the called template. Because {include} requires a file argument, you cannot pass a variable named 'file' to the included template. Apart from this the name of any variables you pass are up to you.

If we were to add the following code to our template example

```
{include file="brand_top.tpl" section="author search"}
```

then the brand_top.tpl template would be inserted. It would also have access to a {$section} variable.

```
<h1>books unlimited</h1>
<ul>
<h4>{$section}</h4>
</ul>
```

Modifying Template Variables

Smarty has taken us a long way towards separating application logic from presentation, but we are still missing one essential element. Data frequently needs modification before it is fit to be presented to the public. Tags may need to be stripped out, newlines converted into <br> tags, letters may need to be capitalized. Smarty has tools for just this kind of filtration.

In order to apply a variable modifier to a template variable you must use the pipe ('|') symbol.

```
{$variable|modifier}
```

You can chain modifiers together.

```
{$variable|firstmodifier|secondmodifier}
```

and they will operate on the $variable from left to right.

If a modifier requires arguments, each one should be provided after a separating colon character.

```
{$variable|modifier:"an_arg":"another_arg"}
```

Modifier arguments can be strings, numbers, or variables.

capitalize and lower

The `capitalize` variable modifier makes the first letter of every word in a string variable uppercase.

```
{$author|capitalize}
```

The `lower` function will render every character in a string variable lowercase.

```
{$author|lower}
```

Of course, they can be usefully chained. Making a string lowercase first and then capitalizing each first letter will deal with strings in all caps.

```
{$author|lower|capitalize}
```

regex_replace

Occasionally you will need more power than that afforded by the built-in modifiers. `regex_replace` allows you to apply a Perl compatible regular expression to a variable. `regex_replace` requires two arguments, the match pattern and the replacement string. In the fragment below we use a regular expression to switch an author's last name with his first name and initials.

```
{$author|regex_replace:"/^(.*)\s(.*)$/":'$2, $1'}
```

string_format

`string_format` uses `sprintf()` to format a variable. It requires a single argument, the format control string. If for example we wanted to display currency we could pass the following argument to `string_format`.

```
That will be
{$price|regex_replace:"%.2f"}
dollars please.
```

You can brush up your `sprintf()` skills in Hour 17, "Working with Strings."

default

default is an extremely useful variable modifier. It enables you to degrade your page gracefully if an expected variable is not forthcoming. It requires a single argument, the variable to output if the expected variable is not available to Smarty.

```
{$author|default:"anonymous"}
```

A Recap: Our Example in Full

23

Although we have not got time or space to cover the whole of Smarty which is an extremely rich library, we have covered a lot of ground. In this section we will bring the code fragments of the last few sections together, and add a bit of flesh to our book site example.

In Listing 23.8 you can see the PHP code once again. Not much has changed.

LISTING 23.8   PHP Code Invoking Smarty Template Code

```
 1: <?php
 2: require_once("Smarty.class.php");
 3:
 4: $search = array(
 5:                  array( 'name'=>"Douglas Adams",
 6:                  'book'=>"So Long and Thanks for all the Fish" ),
 7:                  array( 'name'=>"NEAL STEPHENSON",
 8:                          'book'=>"CRYPTONOMICON" ),
 9:                  array( 'name'=>"dan simmons",
10:                          'book'=>"endymion" ),
11:                  array( 'name'=>"Peter F Hamilton",
12:                          'book'=>"The Neutronium Alchemist" ),
13:                  array( 'name'=>"",
14:                          'book'=>"Prime Colors" ),
15:                  );
16: $templ = new Smarty();
17: $templ->assign( "section", "book search" );
18: $templ->assign( "search", $search );
19: $templ->display("listing23.9.tpl");
20: ?>
```

The most interesting thing to note is how compact the code remains. The prime purpose of this code is compile data. It then hands it on to the templates to format. Imagine how the code would look if the output was included in Listing 23.8. We have made a few minor changes. First, we have introduced a new book, with no author (line 13), and messed around with the case of some books and authors. Second, we have added a new call to assign(), that passes the section name to the template (line 17).

In Listing 23.9 you can see the main template.

LISTING 23.9   The Main Template

```
 1: {include file="listing23.10.tpl" section=$section}
 2:
 3: {section name=search_row loop=$search}
 4:     {if %search_row.first%}
 5:         {%search_row.total%} found
 6:         <hr>
 7:     {/if}
 8:     {%search_row.iteration%}.
 9:
➡{$search[search_row].name|lower|capitalize|regex_replace:"/^(.*)\s(.*)$/":'$2,
➡$1'|default:"anonymous"}
10:     ..
11:     {$search[search_row].book|lower|capitalize} <br>
12:     {if %search_row.last%}
13:         <hr>
14:         {%search_row.total%} found
15:     {/if}
16: {sectionelse}
17:     No authors found. Try another search
18: {/section}
19:
20: </body>
21: </html>
```

The presentation of the document's header is handed on to another file using the {include} function on line 1. The {$section} variable is passed to it as a parameter.

That means that most of the work done by this template is in the {section} function on line 3. For the first iteration (tested line 4) we write out a string confirming the number of matches in the loop. We use the total section variable for this on line 5.

We use the iteration section variable on line 8 to count out each row. In outputting the author (line 9) and book (line 11) we use variable modifiers to format the text. lower and capitalize are chained to handle the inconsistent use of case that our data displayed. The authors' first and last names are swapped using regex_replace, and a default value of 'anonymous' is put in place for those cases where we are not passed an author name.

For the final iteration (tested on line 12), we restate the number of rows we have dealt with. If by some chance we had found no data in the $search array the {sectionelse} block on line 16 would have been executed and a simple string output.

Listing 23.10 shows the included header file. The only points to note here are the fact that it has access to the {$section} variable, and that it uses the default variable modifier to ensure that something sensible is output should the caller fail to provide a parameter (lines 3 and 9).

LISTING 23.10   The Header Template

```
 1: <html>
 2: <head>
 3: <title>books unlimited: {$section|default:"The Book Source"}</title>
 4: </head>
 5: <body>
 6: <h1>books unlimited</h1>
 7:
 8: <ul>
 9: <h4>{$section|default:"The Book Source"}</h4>
10: </ul>
```

You can see the results of our template work in Figure 23.2. Of course, we haven't let the design team lose on the templates yet!

FIGURE 23.2

The templates in operation.

Summary

If you intend to work on larger projects with PHP, you would be well advised to think very carefully about using a template engine. Your code will be much easier to maintain and extend if you can drive a wedge between the application logic and the output layer. If you do decide to work with a template engine, you should consider Smarty. It is fast because it compiles the templates you write into PHP, it is feature rich, and it is easy to extend.

In this hour you learned about Smarty. You saw how to install it and get a basic template up and running. You learned about template variables and how to pass them from your PHP code to the template. You learned about template functions and how to use them to control output. Finally you learned how to modify template variables.

Having experienced the power of a library written in PHP, we will have a go at creating our own in the next hour.

Q&A

Q **Has this chapter covered all I need to know about Smarty?**

A No. Smarty is a very flexible package, and we've only had time to address some of its functionality. You should now have enough information to get up and running, but if you are going to use Smarty intensively you should read the documentation at `http://www.phpinsider.com/php/code/Smarty/docs/`. There you will be able to find out about many more functions. You'll also be able to learn about writing your own functions and variable modifiers for Smarty.

Workshop

Quiz

1. What document should we `require()` in order to run Smarty?

2. What Smarty method would you use to register a variable with Smarty?

3. Which directory does PHP need to be able to write to in order for Smarty to work?

4. How would I access the PHP variable `$SERVER["SERVER_NAME"]` from a Smarty template?

5. What is wrong with the following fragment?
```
{if $user=="admin" }
        <p>Message of the Day: {$motd}</p>
{/if}
```

6. How do we discover the number of iterations a {section} named "thisloop" loop went through?

7. What Smarty variable modifier outputs a string in lowercase letters?

Quiz Answers

1. The `Smarty.class.php` document contains the core Smarty code.

2. The `assign()` method is used to pass values to Smarty.

3. The `includes_c` directory is written to by the Smarty engine.

4. The {$smarty} variable gives you access to the PHP $SERVER array.

   `{$smarty.server.SERVER_NAME}`

5. There should always be a space between operands and operators in the {if} function.

   ```
   {if $user == "admin" }
           <p>Message of the Day: {$motd}</p>
   {/if}
   ```

6. The section variable `total` contains the total number of iterations of a loop

   `{%thisloop.total%}`

7. The `lower` variable modifier transforms a string, outputting a lowercase version.

   `{$myvar|lower}`

Activities

1. Acquire and install Smarty.

2. Look back through your sample scripts and projects and choose a few to rewrite using Smarty. Consider the ways in which your program logic can be cleaned up now it is separated from presentation.

23

HOUR **24**

An Example: Page.inc.php

In this hour we will create a set of reusable code libraries which may come in handy in the future. Along the way, we will be using language constructs and techniques that we have covered in previous hours.

In this hour, you will create code to

- Automate session handling
- Make user feedback easy
- Test whether a form has been submitted
- Implement a password protected environment
- Implement access control within a protected environment

The Framework Class

Our project will be initially defined by a framework class called Page. This will determine the procedure for almost every script request in an environment. We will also include some convenient functionality. It is important to bear in mind that Page is not really designed to be directly instantiated. It is designed to be subclassed to provide project specific functionality.

The Framework

Every script that uses a Page object will have three stages: initialization, execution, and clean up. Initialization will take place inside a method called init(). Everything required for script start up will live here. The Page object will do a fair amount of work in this method, but more work will probably be done by any subclass. The execution phase will take place in the main() method. Typically, this is where the meat of a script will live; form input will be processed here, feedback prepared and so on. The Page class defines this method, but leaves it to subclasses to override. Clean up takes place in the clean_up() method. This is where database connections should be closed and any other loose ends tied up. Once again Page does not itself do anything with this method.

In Listing 24.1 we lay down the skeleton of the class.

LISTING 24.1   The Skeleton of the Page Class

```
 1: <?
 2: class Page {
 3:
 4:         function Page( ) {
 5:                 session_start();
 6:                 global $page_class_sess;
 7:                 if ( ! session_is_registered( "page_class_sess" ) ) {
 8:                         $page_class_sess = array();
 9:                         session_register( "page_class_sess" );
10:                 }
11:         }
12:
13:     function init() { }
14:
15:     function main() { }
16:
17:     function clean_up() { }
18: }
19: ?>
```

The only thing the our Page class will do at this stage is to start a session (line 5). We will cover the session code in more detail in another section. Now we have the skeleton, we can begin to put a bit of flesh on the bones.

Acquiring POST and GET Parameters

PHP provides a perfectly good interface for working with GET and POST variables in the $HTTP_POST_VARS and $HTTP_GET_VARS arrays. However, we are going to store request parameters as an object property. We can add some simple code to the init() method to make this happen.

```
$this->rdata = array_merge( $GLOBALS['HTTP_GET_VARS'],
              $GLOBALS['HTTP_POST_VARS'] );
```

In early versions of PHP 4 the $HTTP_*_VARS arrays would not be present if there were no elements to populate them. Now the arrays are always there, whether populated or not. That means that we don't have to provide any clever testing. We simply merge the two arrays and assign to a property: $rdata. We chose the order so that POST variables will overwrite GET variables.

Getting the Message Across

One essential element of many scripts is the need to feedback to the user. Messages such as "Welcome!" and "OOPS! You forgot to fill in the phone field" are ubiquitous. The Page class provides an interface for generating such messages, and even a mini-template for message output. Messages can also be passed from script to script, so our class will extract it from the $rdata property. Time to add some more code to our init() method.

```
if ( ! empty( $this->rdata['page_obj_msg'] )) {
       $this->message = $this->rdata['page_obj_msg'];
       unset( $this->rdata['page_obj_msg'] );
}
```

We test for a request parameter called "page_obj_msg". If it is present we assign its value to a new property called $message. We then tidy up our $rdata array by removing the "page_obj_msg" element.

We will also want client code to be able to set the $message property, so we will need a new method.

```
function setMessage( $str ) {
       $this->message = $str;
}
```

Client coders will also want to retrieve the message:

```
function getMessage( ) {
     return stripslashes( $this->message );
}
```

Finally, we want to make it easy for programmers to present a feedback message to their users. They could of course simply wrap a call to getMessage() in some formatting.

When using this code we found, however, that we often only wanted to present the message formatting (tables, bold tags, etc) when there was a message present. If there was no message we wanted no output at all. Once again the client coder could handle this himself by adding an `if` statement to the HTML. For convenience, however, we provide a template-like solution. The `outputMessage()` method accepts a template string. If any message is present it will be placed in the template, replacing the string "%msg%".

```
function outputMessage( $template_str = "" ) {
    if ( ! empty( $template_str ) )
        $out = str_replace( "%msg%", $this->message, $template_str );
    else
        $out = $this->message;
    print $out;
}
```

Now that our class actually does a thing or two, we should subclass it to see it in action.

A Subclass for Testing

In Listing 24.2 we create a class called my_page that subclasses Page.

LISTING 24.2   Subclassing the Page Class

```
 1: <?php
 2: include_once("lib/Page.inc.php");
 3:
 4: class my_page extends Page {
 5:     function my_page() {
 6:         Page::Page();
 7:     }
 8:
 9:     function main() {
10:         $this->setMessage("Hello, welcome to Page");
11:     }
12: }
13:
14: $p = new my_page();
15: $p->init();
16: $p->main();
17: $p->clean_up();
18: ?>
19: <html>
20: <head>
21: <title>Testing the Page class</title>
22: </head>
23: <body>
24:
25: <?php
```

LISTING 24.2   continued

```
26: $p->outputMessage('
27:     <table cellpadding="5">
28:     <tr><td bgcolor="gray">%msg%</td></tr>
29:     </table>');
30: ?>
31:
32: </body>
33: </html>
```

Notice that in subclassing Page, we only bother to override the constructor and the main() method. Because main() does not do anything in Page there is no need to call the overridden method, although we would always do this with the init() method as we do with the constructor. All we do in main() is to call setMessage() with a test string (line 10). Outside of the class we instantiate a new my_page object on line 14. We call init(), main() and clean_up() on lines 15 to 17. Within the body of the HTML we call outputMessage() with a template string (line 26). The string will be displayed because a message is present. Without the message, the template string would never be output.

Session Support

The Page class's constructor may have given you the clue that we intend to support sessions. We are building a tool to underpin online environments, so session support is essential.

We started the session in the constructor and associated a global variable called $page_class_sess with it using session_register(). All session variables that the object will deal with will be stored in this array. This is to keep object session data neatly separate from any sessions variables set outside of the class. You can see the code which sets up the session in Listing 24.1.

We can now create some wrapper methods to make it easy to set and acquire session data.

```
function forget_session() {
        global $page_class_sess;
        $page_class_sess = array();
}

function set_session_var( $name, $val ) {
        global $page_class_sess;
        $page_class_sess[$name] = $val;
}
```

```
function get_session_var( $name ) {
        global $page_class_sess;
        return $page_class_sess[$name];
}
```

Has the Form Been Submitted?

If you often use the same script to present and process a form, it is essential to test whether or not the form has been submitted. Because this is such a common procedure Page provides a couple of convenience functions to help with this.

```
function fflag( $val ) {
        return "<input type=\"hidden\" name=\"fflag\"
value=\"$val\">\n";
}

function checkfflag( $val ) {
        return ( isset( $this->rdata['fflag'] ) &&
                $this->rdata['fflag'] == $val );
}
```

The `fflag()` function accepts a string value and returns a hidden field with 'fflag' as the name and the provided string as the value. The `checkfflag()` method also accepts a value. It checks to see whether or not the request parameters contain an element called 'fflag' with the given value.

In Listing 24.3, we extend our `my_page` class to use these functions to test whether or not a form has been submitted.

LISTING 24.3 Testing Form Submission

```
 1: <?php
 2: include_once("lib/Page.inc.php");
 3:
 4: class my_page extends Page {
 5:     function my_page() {
 6:         Page::Page();
 7:     }
 8:
 9:     function main() {
10:         if ( $this->checkfflag("subbed") )
11:             $this->setMessage("FORM SUBMITTED");
12:         else
13:             $this->setMessage("Hello, welcome to Page");
14:
15:     }
16: }
17:
```

LISTING 24.3 continued

```
18: $p = new my_page();
19: $p->init();
20: $p->main();
21: $p->clean_up();
22: ?>
23: <html>
24: <head>
25: <title>Testing the Page class</title>
26: </head>
27: <body>
28:
29: <?php
30: $p->outputMessage('
31:     <table cellpadding="5">
32:     <tr><td bgcolor="gray">%msg%</td></tr>
33:     </table>');
34: ?>
35: <form>
36: <?php print $p->fflag("subbed") ?>
37: Type into this box and hit return<br>
38: <input type="text" name="input">
39: </body>
40: </html>
```

We add a call to fflag() to the form in Listing 24.3 (line 36). This outputs a hidden field. In the main() method we can test for the presence of the fflag parameter with a call to the checkfflag() method (line 10). If the form has been submitted we alter the feedback message.

Moving On

Page redirection is such a common procedure in PHP coding that the Page class simply must support it. The code for this is, of course, very simple. We complicate it a little, though, by adding support for the $message property.

```
function redirect( $page, $msg="" ) {
        if ( ! empty( $msg ) )
                $this->message = $msg;
        $this->clean_up();
        if ( ! strstr( $page, "?" ))
                header("Location: $page?page_obj_msg=".urlencode($this-
➥>message));
        else
                header("Location: $page&page_obj_msg=".urlencode($this-
➥>message));
        exit;
    }
```

The redirect method requires a URL which is stored in the $page argument variable. It optionally accepts a $msg argument variable. If the $msg variable is not empty, we assign it the $message property. Before redirecting the browser, we first call clean_up() to ensure that all loose ends have been tied. We are then ready to move on. We check for a question mark in the $page variable. If one exists we can assume that a query string already exists in the URL, and so we use an ampersand to add our $message property to the end. If no question mark is found, we use a question mark ourselves.

That completes our basic framework for a PHP Web environment. Although it has some functionality, part of the intention is to make it easy to subclass for specific purposes. In the next section we will explore one such purpose.

You can see the complete Page class in Listing 24.4.

LISTING 24.4   The Page Class

```
 1: <?
 2: class Page {
 3:     var $rdata;
 4:     var $message;
 5:
 6:     function Page( ) {
 7:         session_start();
 8:         global $page_class_sess;
 9:         if ( ! session_is_registered( "page_class_sess" ) ) {
10:             $page_class_sess = array();
11:             session_register( "page_class_sess" );
12:         }
13:     }
14:
15:     function init() {
16:         $this->set_session_var("lastclick", time());
17:         $this->rdata = array_merge( $GLOBALS['HTTP_GET_VARS'],
➥$GLOBALS['HTTP_POST_VARS'] );
18:         if ( ! empty( $this->rdata['page_obj_msg'] )) {
19:             $this->message = $this->rdata['page_obj_msg'];
20:             unset( $this->rdata['page_obj_msg'] );
21:         }
22:     }
23:
24:     function main() { }
25:
26:     function clean_up() { }
27:
28:     function forget_session() {
29:         global $page_class_sess;
30:         $page_class_sess = array();
```

LISTING 24.4 continued

```
31:     }
32:
33:     function set_session_var( $name, $val ) {
34:         global $page_class_sess;
35:         $page_class_sess[$name] = $val;
36:     }
37:
38:     function get_session_var( $name ) {
39:         global $page_class_sess;
40:         return $page_class_sess[$name];
41:     }
42:
43:
44:     function fflag( $val ) {
45:         return "<input type=\"hidden\" name=\"fflag\" value=\"$val\">\n";
46:     }
47:
48:     function checkfflag( $val ) {
49:         return ( isset( $this->rdata['fflag'] ) && $this->rdata['fflag'] ==
➥$val );
50:     }
51:
52:     function redirect( $page, $msg="" ) {
53:         if ( ! empty( $msg ) )
54:             $this->message = $msg;
55:         $this->clean_up();
56:         if ( ! strstr( $page, "?" ))
57:             header("Location: $page?page_obj_msg=".urlencode($this-
➥>message));
58:         else
59:             header("Location: $page&page_obj_msg=".urlencode($this-
➥>message));
60:     }
61:
62:     function setMessage( $str ) {
63:         $this->message = $str;
64:     }
65:
66:     function getMessage( ) {
67:         return stripslashes( $this->message );
68:     }
69:
70:     function outputMessage( $template_str = "" ) {
71:         if ( ! empty( $template_str ) )
72:             $out = str_replace( "%msg%", $this->message, $template_str );
73:         else
74:             $out = $this->message;
75:         print $out;
```

LISTING 24.4   continued

```
76:      }
77: }
78: ?>
```

Extending the Page Class

The Page class is designed to be extended. In this section we are going to add some of the functionality needed to create a password protected environment. In particular, we will be using the Page class's session functionality to test a username and password against values in a DBA database. We are also going to implement a flexible access control system. The client coder will be able to define page and user types. Only certain user types will then be allowed to visit certain page types.

This kind of access control is common in multi-user environments, where different users are given access only to site areas relevant to their job types. On a content management system, for example, a publication editor is likely to have different access to a freelance writer.

The system we are going to build will itself be designed for subclassing. We will call the class Access.

The access class subclasses Page. Its own constructor accepts and stores a path to a DBA database.

```
function Access( $user_file ) {
        $this->user_file = $user_file;
        Page::Page();
}
```

The Access class has inherited all of the functionality of the Page object. It's now time to extend it.

Defining Flexible Site Areas

Because the Access class is designed to work flexibly with different kinds of site, we are not going to hardcode information about site areas. Instead, we are going to create a method that enables a client coder to define a set of site areas. We will store each label and a number that we generate in an array property called $access_types.

```
function addAccessType( $label ) {
        if ( ! empty( $this->access_types[$label] ) )
                return false;
        $this->access_types[$label] = $this->type_pointer;
```

```
        $this->type_pointer <<= 1;
        return true;
    }
```

So in adding an access type, the user will provide a label. We store the current number available for assignment to access types in a property called $type_pointer. After assignment we left shift $type_pointer. That means, in effect that the number will be multiplied by two. In binary terms it means that for each consecutive access type the number will progress like this.

```
00001
00010
00100
01000
10000
```

This will result in a flexible system, but it is worth noting that there are only a limited number of bits in an integer and we will be limited to a maximum of 31 access types. This should be ample for most purposes, especially when you consider that different users will have access to different combinations of access type.

Having allowed the client coder define the access types for our environment, we need to give him or her the ability to access the numbers we have generated.

```
function getAccessType( $label ) {
    if ( empty( $this->access_types[$label] ) )
        return false;
    return $this->access_types[$label];
}
```

The getAccessType() method requires a string representing the label of the type in question. If the key is in the $access_types array property, then the number will be returned.

The addAccessType() and getAccessType() methods apply across an environment. We also need a way of telling the library which of the available access types the current script belongs to. For this we use the setPageType() method.

```
function setPageType( $label ) {
    if ( empty( $this->access_types[$label] ) )
        return false;

    $this->page_type = $this->access_types[$label];
    return true;
}
```

24

This method accepts a label, and, if it exists in the $access_types array property, sets the $page_type property to the relevant number.

So we are now at the stage at which an implementing class could define a set of access types using addAccessType() in its init() method. Individual scripts could then set their own access type using the setPageType() method.

Adding and Acquiring User Data

Now we can set access types for a site, we need to get and set information about site users so that we can match up one with the other.

For this example we have decided to use a simple DBA database. In the database we will store a username (which must be unique), a password, and a user type. The user type will be a number that we will be comparing with individual pages' access types. Methods that access and set user data could easily be overridden by a subclass to speak with another database.

The add_user() method is used to create a new user.

```
function add_user( $user, $pass, $type ) {
        $res = dba_open( $this->user_file, "c", "gdbm" ) or die("no user
db");
        if ( dba_fetch( $user, $res ) ) {
                dba_close( $res );
                return false;
        }
        $add_array = array( 'pass'=>$pass, 'type'=>$type );
        dba_replace( $user, serialize( $add_array ), $res );
        dba_close( $res );
    }
```

The method requires strings for username, password and user type. It uses the database path that was provided to the constructor to open the database. If a user of the same name does not already exist, then the user is added. The username is used as the key for this database. Other data is serialized and added as the value.

Acquiring user data is just as simple. The get_user_data() method handles this.

```
function get_user_data( $user ) {
        $res = dba_open( $this->user_file, "c", "gdbm" ) or die("no user
➡db");
        $user_data = dba_fetch( $user, $res );
        dba_close( $res );
        if ( ! $user_data )
                return false;
        return unserialize( $user_data );
    }
```

`get_user_data()` connects to the database, uses the provided key to attempt to extract a row, and, if successful, returns the unserialized data.

Enforcing Access Control

Now that we can define users and access types we need to build the engine that tests them both.

The `access_control()` method is the heart of this class:

```
function access_control() {
        if ( $this->page_type == 0 )
                return true;
        $user = $this->get_session_var( "user" );
        $pass = $this->get_session_var( "pass" );
        if ( empty( $user ) || empty( $pass ) )
                $this->bump("Not enough user data");
        $user_array = $this->get_user_data( $user );
        if ( ! $user_array )
                $this->bump("Unknown user");
        if ( $pass != $user_array['pass'] )
                $this->bump("Incorrect password");
        if ( ! $this->codeAllowed( $user_array['type'] ) )
                $this->bump("Access to this resource forbidden");
        return true;
}
```

If the $page_type property has not been given a value, then we assume that the page is designed to be wide open, and simply return true.

We acquire user and password information from the session data. If either of these are missing, our user is history. We call a method called bump() which sends the user away with an error message. If we have information now stored in the $user and $pass variables we use get_user_data() with the $user variable to try to extract information from the database. If nothing is returned by get_user_data() we know that the user does not exist, and once again our visitor is expelled. Next, we test the password returned from the database against the password stored in $pass. If they do not match, the user is rejected. Finally we test our zone based access control. We call a method called codeAllowed() with the now validated user's type number.

```
function codeAllowed( $num ) {
        return ( $this->page_type & $num );
}
```

By using the 'binary and' ('&') we are comparing the bits in $page_type and the provided $num argument variable. Each bit of each number is compared against its opposite number. If both bits are set, then the corresponding bit in the return value will be set. So our codeAllowed() method returns a positive number only if there is overlap between the $num argument and the $page_type property.

If our user's type number does not match the page type, then zero will be returned and once again bump() would be called.

```
function bump( $msg ) {
        $this->redirect($this->login_page, $msg );
        exit;
}
```

As you can see bump() merely calls the redirect() method in the parent Page class. The $login_page property is set by default to "login.php" but this can be changed.

The Access Class in Full

We now have the complete library. Listing 24.5 shows the whole of Access.

LISTING 24.5   The Access Class

```
 1: <?php
 2: include_once("Page.inc.php");
 3:
 4: class Access extends Page {
 5:     var $access_types = array();
 6:     var $type_pointer = 1;
 7:     var $login_page = "login.php";
 8:     var $page_type = 0;
 9:
10:     function Access( $user_file ) {
11:         $this->user_file = $user_file;
12:         Page::Page();
13:     }
14:
15:     function addAccessType( $label ) {
16:         if ( ! empty( $this->access_types[$label] ) )
17:             return false;
18:         $this->access_types[$label] = $this->type_pointer;
19:         $this->type_pointer <<= 1;
20:         return true;
21:     }
22:
23:     function setPageType( $label ) {
24:         if ( empty( $this->access_types[$label] ) )
25:             return false;
26:
27:         $this->page_type = $this->access_types[$label];
28:         return true;
29:     }
```

LISTING 24.5 continued

```
30:
31:     function getAccessType( $label ) {
32:         if ( empty( $this->access_types[$label] ) )
33:             return false;
34:         return $this->access_types[$label];
35:     }
36:
37:     function codeAllowed( $num ) {
38:         return ( $this->page_type & $num );
39:     }
40:
41:     function set_login_page( $login ) {
42:         $this->login_page = $login;
43:     }
44:
45:     function bump( $msg ) {
46:         $this->redirect($this->login_page, $msg );
47:         exit;
48:     }
49:
50:         function init() {
51:                 Page::init();
52:         }
53:
54:     function access_control() {
55:         if ( $this->page_type == 0 )
56:             return true;
57:         $user = $this->get_session_var( "user" );
58:         $pass = $this->get_session_var( "pass" );
59:         if ( empty( $user ) || empty( $pass ) )
60:             $this->bump("Not enough user data");
61:         $user_array = $this->get_user_data( $user );
62:         if ( ! $user_array )
63:             $this->bump("Unknown user");
64:         if ( $pass != $user_array['pass'] )
65:             $this->bump("Incorrect password");
66:         if ( ! $this->codeAllowed( $user_array['type'] ) )
67:             $this->bump("Access to this resource forbidden");
68:         return true;
69:     }
70:
71:     function remove_user( $user ) {
72:         $res = dba_open( $this->user_file, "c", "gdbm" ) or die("no user
➥db");
73:         $val = dba_delete( $user, $res );
74:         db_close( $res );
75:     }
76:
```

24

LISTING 24.5   continued

```
77:    function add_user( $user, $pass, $type ) {
78:        $res = dba_open( $this->user_file, "c", "gdbm" ) or die("no user
➥db");
79:        if ( dba_fetch( $user, $res ) ) {
80:            dba_close( $res );
81:            return false;
82:        }
83:        $add_array = array( 'pass'=>$pass, 'type'=>$type );
84:        dba_replace( $user, serialize( $add_array ), $res );
85:        dba_close( $res );
86:    }
87:
88:    function get_user_data( $user ) {
89:        $res = dba_open( $this->user_file, "c", "gdbm" ) or die("no user
➥db");
90:        $user_data = dba_fetch( $user, $res );
91:        dba_close( $res );
92:        if ( ! $user_data )
93:            return false;
94:        return unserialize( $user_data );
95:    }
96: }
```

Now that we have a code library we are still really sitting on potential functionality. We have to write some more code to implement what we have.

A Project Class

If our user types and page types are to marry up sensibly they should be defined in a central location. In Listing 24.6 we are going to create a simple class that will act as the template for a number of pages in a project. It will be directly instantiated by some scripts. In others it may itself be subclassed. We will call the class ProjectBase.

LISTING 24.6   The ProjectBase Class

```
1: <?php
2: include_once("Access.inc.php");
3:
4: class ProjectBase extends Access {
5:        var $db_file = "users/user_dir";
6:        var $freelance_user;
7:        var $admin_user;
8:        var $super_super;
9:
10:       function ProjectBase( ) {
```

LISTING 24.6   continued

```
11:                        Access::Access( $this->db_file );
12:            }
13:
14:            function init() {
15:                    Access::init();
16:                    $this->addAccessType( "freelance" );
17:                    $this->addAccessType( "admin" );
18:                    $this->addAccessType( "superuser" );
19:                    $this->freelance_user  = ( $this-
➥>getAccessType("freelance"));
20:                    $this->admin_user    = ( $this->getAccessType("freelance") |
21:                                        $this->getAccessType("admin"));
22:                    $this->super_user    = ( $this->getAccessType("freelance") |
23:                                        $this->getAccessType("admin") |
24:                                        $this->getAccessType("superuser"));
25:            }
26: }
27: ?>
```

ProjectBase offers very little original in itself. All it does is to subclass Access and to define some user types and access types. Our project will have three access types, 'feelance', 'admin', and 'superuser' (lines 16, 17, and 18). It will have three corresponding user types, which will be stored in ProjectBase properties (lines 19 to 22). The $freelance_user type will only be allowed to visit pages of type 'freelance'. The $admin_user type will only be able to access pages of either 'freelance' or 'admin' types. The $super_user type will have 'access all areas' privileges. We set up these rights by using the 'binary or' operator. This combines the bits of its operators, so if 'freelance' is binary 1 and 'admin' is binary 10 then 'freelance' or'ed with 'admin' is binary 11.

Creating Some Sample Users

In order to test our system we must create some sample users with different access rights. In Listing 24.7 we do just that.

LISTING 24.7   Adding Users to the System

```
1: <?php
2: include("ProjectBase.inc.php");
3:
4: $p = new ProjectBase( );
5: $p->init();
6: $p->add_user( "matt", "pass", $p->super_user );
```

LISTING 24.7   continued

```
 7: $p->add_user( "bob",  "pass", $p->admin_user );
 8: $p->add_user( "mary", "pass", $p->freelance_user );
 9: ?>
10: done
```

As you can see, now we're at the implementation stage, the really hard work is being largely done elsewhere. We create three users with very easy to remember passwords and different access rights. If we were to properly implement our code, of course we would need to create a full user control center available to allow super users to add and remove users. For now, though, our sample data will have to do.

A Simple Login Screen

Now that we have our environment established, and some users in our database, we can provide a login interface. The code in Listing 24.8 presents password form and then processes the input.

LISTING 24.8   A Login Screen

```
 1: <?php
 2: include("ProjectBase.inc.php");
 3:
 4: class MyPage extends ProjectBase {
 5:     function MyPage() {
 6:         ProjectBase::ProjectBase();
 7:     }
 8:     function main() {
 9:         if ( $this->checkfflag("subbed") ) {
10:             $user = $this->rdata['user'];
11:             $pass = $this->rdata['pass'];
12:             $user_array = $this->get_user_data( $user, $pass);
13:             if ( ! $user_array )
14:                 $this->setMessage("unknown user");
15:             elseif ( $pass != $user_array['pass'] )
16:                 $this->setMessage("Incorrect password");
17:             else {
18:                 $this->set_session_var("user", $user );
19:                 $this->set_session_var("pass", $pass );
20:                 $this->setMessage("Welcome to the system");
21:                 $this->redirect( "welcome.php" );
22:             }
23:         }
24:     }
25: }
26:
```

LISTING 24.8   continued

```
27: $p = new MyPage( );
28: $p->init();
29: $p->main();
30: $p->clean_up();
31: ?>
32: <html>
33: <head>
34: <title>login</title>
35: </head>
36: <body>
37:
38: <?php
39: $p->outputMessage('
40:     <table cellpadding="5">
41:     <tr><td bgcolor="gray">%msg%</td></tr>
42:     </table>');
43: ?>
44:
45: <form>
46:
47: <?php print $p->fflag("subbed") ?>
48: user<br>
49: <input type="text" name="user"><br>
50: pass<br>
51: <input type="password" name="pass"><br>
52: <input type="submit" value="go">
53:
54: </form>
55: </body>
56: </html>
```

Notice that we use fflag() (line 47) and checkfflag() (line 9) to test for form submission. We also use the outputMessage() method (called on line 39) to format feedback. The core of the code, though, lives in the main() method. If the form has been submitted we call get_user_data() on line 12 to find out if the user exists. If not, we use setMessage() to inform the user (line 14).

Assuming the username exists, we test the password on line 15. If the password matches then we can prepare the user for the protected environment. This means using set_ session_var() to set the 'user' and 'pass' session variables (lines 18 and 19). These will be used throughout the protected area for validation.

Protected Pages

On all protected pages the controlling object will have non-zero $page_type properties set (using setPageType()). The access_control() method will always be called. The most minimal protected page would look something like

```php
<?php
include("ProjectBase.inc.php");
$p = new ProjectBase( );
$p->init();
$p->setPageType("freelance");
$p->access_control();
$p->main();
$p->clean_up();
?>
<html>
<head>
<title>freelance</title>
</head>
<body>
<?php
$p->outputMessage('
        <table cellpadding="5">
        <tr><td bgcolor="gray">%msg%</td></tr>
        </table>');
?>
This is a frelance page<p>

<a href="welcome.php">freelance only</a><br>
<a href="admin_only.php">admin only</a><br>
<a href="super_only.php">super only</a>
</body>
</html>
```

In order to determine which user type can access which page you would only need to change the setPageType() argument.

What Needs Doing?

A coder's work is never done, and neither these libraries nor the code that uses them are complete. If you intend to work with the code presented in this chapter, you should give thought to some issues before deploying it.

Don't forget that by default the session functions write files to a publicly available directory. You should consider writing your session data to a more secure place.

We do not implement any system for ending sessions, and apologetically expelling a user when a long period has elapsed between requests. This is a feature that you should consider.

We store passwords in plain text. If security is a major consideration, you might want to consider using the `crypt()` function to protect passwords in the database.

An additional layer of security could be provided by recording an IP address when the user first logs on and checking it on every subsequent hit in the session. This should provide a further safeguard against session hijacking.

Summary

In this hour we have built a reasonably rich code library. In doing so we have revisited many of the techniques that we have covered throughout the book. In particular we have worked with classes and objects; sessions; and the DBA functions.

You have also learned some techniques for user authentication, and for access control.

I very much hope that you have enjoyed reading this book as much as I have enjoyed writing it.

Q&A

Q Well, that's it. What next?

A Now it's over to you. This book contains enough information for you to build your own sophisticated scripts and environments. Armed with this and with the wealth of information available online, there should be no stopping you! If this book has been a good starting point for you, you might want to consider some books that take up where we must leave off. In particular you might like to take a look at *The PHP Developer's Cookbook* by Sterling Hughes and *PHP and MySQL Web Development* by Luke Welling and Laura Thomson.

Workshop

Quiz

1. What function do you use to combine two arrays?
2. Which built-in array variable holds GET request parameters?
3. How do we test whether a variable has been set?
4. Which function do you use to register a variable with a session?
5. Which function would we use to acquire an element from a DBA database?

24

Quiz Answers

1. The `array_merge()` function will merge two arrays.
2. You can access GET request parameters using the $HTTP_GET_VARS array,
3. The `isset()` function will tell us whether a variable has been set.
4. The `session_register()` function will register a variable with a function.
5. The `dba_fetch()` function is used to acquire a named element from a DBA database.

Activities

1. Review the code presented in this hour. Are there any techniques or issues that might have relevance for your own projects?
2. Implement a 'session timed out' feature in the Access class. Add a layer of security to the Access class that checks the user's IP address for each page request in a session.
3. Flip back through the book and through your notes if you have been making them. If you have followed the book as a course, remember that you should revisit your notes a few times to get the full benefit from the work you have done.

GLOSSARY

anonymous function   Function that is created 'on the fly' during script execution and stored in a variable or passed to other functions.

Argument   A value passed to a function. Arguments are included within the parentheses of a function call. User-defined functions include comma-separated argument names within the parentheses of the function definition. These arguments then become available to the function as local variables.

array   A list variable. That is, a variable that contains multiple elements indexed by numbers or strings. It enables you to store, order, and access many values under one name. An *array* is a data type.

associative array   An array indexed by strings.

Atom   With reference to regular expressions an *atom* is a pattern enclosed in parentheses (often referred to as a *subpattern*). After you have defined an atom, you can treat it as if it were itself a character or character class.

Boolean   A data type. Booleans can contain one of the special values true or false.

Bounds   The number of times a character or range of characters should be matched in a regular expression.

break statement   Consists of the keyword break. It forces the immediate end of a for or while loop iteration. No further iterations of the loop will take place.

Cast   The process by which one data type is converted to another.

Class   A collection of special functions called methods and special variables called properties. You can declare a class with the class keyword. Classes are the templates from which objects are created.

color resource   A special value of the data type 'resource'. It is returned by the imagecolorallocate() function and is passed to other image manipulation functions which can then work with the specified color.

Comment   Text in a script that is ignored by the interpreter. Comments can be used to make code more readable, or to annotate a script.

Constant   A value that is set with the define() function and does not change throughout the execution of a script. A constant is global in scope and can only be a number or string.

continue statement   Consists of the keyword continue. It forces the immediate end of the current for or while loop iteration. Execution begins again from the test expression (in for loops the modification expression will be executed first) and the next loop iteration is begun if the expression resolves to true.

conversion specification   Contained within a format control string, a conversion specification begins with a percent (%) symbol and defines how to treat the corresponding argument to printf() or sprintf(). You can include as many conversion specifications as you want within the format control string, as long as you send an equivalent number of arguments to printf().

Cookie   A small amount of data stored by the user's browser in compliance with a request from a server or script.

data type   Different types of data take up different amounts of memory and behave in different ways when operated upon. A data type is the named means by which these different kinds of data are distinguished. PHP has eight data types: integer, double, string, Boolean, object, array, resource, and NULL.

DBA   Database abstraction layer. These functions are designed to provide a common interface to a range of file-based database systems.

DBA resource   A special value of the data type 'resource'. It is returned by the dba_open() function and is passed to other DBA functions which can then work with the opened database.

DBM   Database manager. DBM and DBM-like systems allow you to store and manipulate name/value pairs on your system.

DOM (Document Object Model)   A means of accessing an XML document that involves the traversal of a tree of nodes organized as parents, children, and siblings.

Double   A data type. Also known as a float, a floating-point number or a real number a double is defined by The Free On-line Dictionary of Computing as 'A number representation consisting of a mantissa [the part after the decimal point], ... an exponent, ... and an (assumed) radix (or "base")'. For the purposes of this book you can think of a double as a number that can contain a fraction of a whole number, that is a number with a decimal point.

DTD (Document Type Definition)   A set of rules that lay down which XML elements may be used in which order for an XML document. A validating XML parser will read a DTD and enforce the rules it describes.

else statement   Can only be used in the context of an if statement. The else statement consists of the keyword else and a statement (or series of statements). These statements will only be executed if the test expression of the associated if statement evaluates to false.

entity body   The substance of a document returned by a server to a client. An entity body may also be sent by a client to a server as part of a POST request.

Escape   The practice of removing special significance from characters within strings or regular expressions by preceding them with a backslash character (\).

Expression   Any combination of functions, values, and operators that resolve to a value. As a rule of thumb, if you can use it as if it were a value, it is an expression.

field width specifier   Contained within a conversion specification, a field width specifier determines the space within which output should be formatted.

file resource   A special value of the data type 'resource'. It is returned by the fopen() function and is passed to other file functions which can then work with the opened file.

Float   A data type. It is a synonym for *double*.

for statement   A loop that can initialize a counter variable (initialization expression), test a counter variable (test expression), and modify a counter variable (modification expression) on a single line. As long as the test expression evaluates to true the loop statement will continue to be executed.

format control string   The first argument to `printf()` or `sprintf()`. It contains conversion specifications that determine the way in which additional arguments to these functions will be formatted.

function   A block of code that is not immediately executed but can be called by your scripts when needed. Functions can be built-in or user-defined. They can require information to be passed to them and usually return a value.

GET request   A request made to a server by a client in which additional information can be sent appended to the URL.

global statement   Consists of the keyword `global` followed by a variable or variables. It causes the associated variables to be accessed in global rather than local scope.

header section   Part of an HTTP request or response (it follows the request line or response line). It consists of name/value pairs on separate lines. Names are separated from values by colons.

.htaccess file   A document read by the Apache server that can contain certain server directives. The server administrator can control which available directives (if any) are allowed to be set in an .htaccess file on a directory by directory basis. If allowed, directives will affect the current directory and those below it. .htaccess files can contain PHP directives prefixed by `php_flag` or `php_value`. The .htaccess file can also be used to set an `AddType` directive that can change the extension associated by the server with PHP documents.

HTTP (*hypertext transfer protocol*)   A set of rules that define the process by which a client sends a request and a server returns a response.

if statement   Consists of a test expression and a statement or series of statements. The statement will only be executed if the test expression evaluates to `true`.

image resource   A special value of the data type 'resource'. It is returned by the `imagecreate()` function and is passed to other image manipulation functions which can then work with the dynamic image.

inheritance   A term used in the context of object oriented programming. It is used to describe the process by which one class is set up to include the member variables and methods of another. This is achieved by using the `extends` keyword when the child class is declared.

integer   A data type. Integers include all whole negative and positive numbers and 0 (zero).

iteration   A single execution of a statement (or series of statements) associated with a loop. A loop that executes five times has five iterations.

link resource   A special value of the data type 'resource'. It is returned by the `mysql_connect()` function and is passed to other MySQL functions which can then work with the opened database.

multidimensional array   An array that contains another array as one of its elements.

NULL   A special data type. It consists of the value NULL. It represents an uninitialized variable, that is a variable that holds no value.

object   Existing in memory rather than as code, an *object* is an instance of a class. That is, an object is the working embodiment of the functionality laid down in a class. An object is instantiated with the new statement in conjunction with the name of the class of which it is to be a member. When an object is instantiated, you can access all its properties and all its methods. An object is a data type.

operand   A value used in conjunction with an operator. There are usually two operands to one operator.

Operator   A symbol or series of symbols that, when used in conjunction with values, performs an action and usually produces a new value.

padding specifier   Contained within a conversion specification, a padding specifier determines the number of characters that output should occupy, and the characters to add otherwise.

pattern modifier   A letter placed after the final delimiter in Perl compatible regular expressions to refine their behavior.

POST request   A request made to a server by a client in which additional information can be sent within the request entity body.

precision specifier   Contained within a conversion specification, a precision specifier determines the number of decimal places to which a double should be rounded.

predefined variables   Variables that are automatically given values and made available to the script by the PHP engine. These are global in scope and include server variables like $HTTP_REFERER.

query string   A set of name/value pairs which are appended to a URL as part of a GET request. Names are separated from values by equals signs, and pairs are separated from each other by ampersand (&) characters. The query string is separated from the rest of the URL by a question mark (?). Both names and values are encoded so that characters with significance to the server are not present.

Reference   The means by which multiple variables can point to the same value. By default arguments are passed, and assignments are made by value in PHP. This means that copies of values are passed around. By assigning or passing by reference, the new variable created points to the same value as that pointed to by the original variable. A change made to the new variable will be seen if you access the original variable.

regular expression   A powerful way of examining and modifying text.

request headers   Key value pairs sent to the server by a client providing information about the client itself and the nature of the request.

request line   The first line of a client request to a server. It consists of a request method, typically GET, HEAD, or POST; the address of the document to required; and the HTTP version to be used (HTTP/1.0 or HTTP/1.1).

resource   A special data type. Resources represent 'handles' used to work with external entities (databases and files are good examples of this).

response headers   Key value pairs sent to the client in response to a request. They provide information about the server environment and the data that is being served.

result identifier   See result resource.

result resource   A special value of the data type 'resource'. It is returned by the mysql_query() function and is passed to other MySQL functions which can then work with the results of an SQL query.

server variables   Predefined variables that PHP makes available for you in conjunction with your server. Which variables are made available are server dependent, but they are likely to include common variables such as $HTTP_USER_AGENT and $REMOTE_ADDR.

SQL (Structured Query Language)   A standardized syntax by which different types of database can be queried.

statement   Represents an instruction to the interpreter. Broadly, it is to PHP what a sentence is to written or spoken English. A sentence should end with a period; a statement should usually end with a semicolon. Exceptions to this include statements that enclose other statements, and statements that end a block of code. In most cases, however, failure to end a statement with a semicolon will confuse the interpreter and result in an error.

static statement   Consists of the keyword static followed by a variable declaration and assignment. It is used within the context of a function. Any changes to the associated variable are remembered between function calls.

status line The first server response to a client request. The status line consists of the HTTP version that the server is using (HTTP/1.0 or HTTP/1.1), a response code, and a text message that clarifies the meaning of the response code.

String A data type. It is a series of characters.

Subclass A class that inherits member variables and methods from another ('parent') class.

ternary operator Returns a value derived from one of two expressions separated by a colon. Which expression is used to generate the value returned depends on the result of an initial test expression which precedes the return expressions and is separated from them by a question mark (?).

timestamp The number of seconds that have elapsed since midnight GMT on January 1, 1970. This number is used in date arithmetic.

type specifier Contained within a conversion specification, a type specifier determines the data type that should be output.

variable A holder for a type of data. It can hold numbers, strings of characters, objects, arrays, or booleans. The contents of a variable can be changed at any time.

while statement A loop that consists of a test expression and a statement (or series of statements). The statements will be repeatedly executed as long as the test expression evaluates to true.

XML (Extensible Markup Language) A set of rules for defining and parsing markup languages. Such languages are often constructed to structure data for sharing, to format data for display, or to send instructions to an interpreter.

XSLT (Extensible Stylesheet Language Transformations) A template system for XML documents that makes it easy to convert from XML to other formats like HTML or WML.

INDEX

Y–Z